WINDOWS NT
IN A NUTSHELL

*A Desktop Quick Reference
for System Administrators*

WINDOWS NT
IN A NUTSHELL

*A Desktop Quick Reference
for System Administrators*

by Eric Pearce

Graphic interface mapping
by Chris Reilley and Beverly Murray Scherf

O'REILLY™

Cambridge · *Köln* · *Paris* · *Sebastopol* · *Tokyo*

Windows NT in a Nutshell

by Eric Pearce

Copyright © 1997 O'Reilly & Associates, Inc. All rights reserved.
Printed in the United States of America.

Published by O'Reilly & Associates, Inc., 101 Morris Street, Sebastopol, CA 95472.

Editor: Robert Denn

Production Editor: Nancy Wolfe Kotary

Printing History:

June 1997:   First Edition.

This book is printed on acid-free paper with 85% recycled content, 15% post-consumer waste. O'Reilly & Associates is committed to using paper with the highest recycled content available consistent with high quality.

ISBN: 1-56592-251-4   [3/98]

Table of Contents

Preface

If you have ever installed Windows NT, created a user, added a printer, or shared a directory, this book is for you. You may not think of yourself as an administrator, but you are if you have done something other than run Word and Pinball. Administrative tasks include creating accounts and groups, sharing files and printers, making backups, and installing software.

This book is intended to be used as a quick reference. The first place you should look for something is the index. The book is designed so you can jump around, choosing between different GUI menus and commands. The book assumes that for the most part, you know what you are doing, but have not memorized where a menu option lives or what options a command takes. It does not document the obvious. It also skips games and applications that the administrator of an NT machine is unlikely to use to solve problems.

Contents

This book is organized in the same order as that in which you are likely to learn about NT. Everybody starts out using the GUI tools, but eventually learns that some things are easier or possible only from the command line.

Chapter 1, *Using Windows NT*
   An introduction to some features of Windows NT.

Chapter 2, *The Control Panel*
   You will be visiting the control panel to install new software or hardware and tweak system settings on the local computer.

Chapter 3, *Administrative Tools*
   You will spend most of your administrative time with these tools, managing services that affect multiple computers on the network.

Chapter 4, *Accessories*

Describes a subset of the accessories that are useful for NT administration.

Chapter 5, *RAS and DUN*

A Remote Access Service (RAS) and Dial-Up Networking (DUN) reference. Includes tutorials on debugging RAS sessions and writing DUN scripts.

Chapter 6, *Using the Command Line*

How to bypass the GUI.

Chapter 7, *Uncommon Sense*

Some specific examples of how to apply techniques to manage and configure NT.

Appendix A, *NetBIOS*

Reference for NetBIOS information, including Node Types and Name Types.

Appendix B, *TCP/IP*

Reference for TCP/IP information, including IP addressing, address classes, subneting, and TCP/IP-specific file formats.

Appendix C, *Server vs. Workstation*

A comparison of available NT services, protocols, and administrative tools for each version of NT.

Appendix D, *NT Resources*

Where to look for more information on NT, including books, magazines, web sites, and newsgroups.

Glossary

NT and networking terms are defined here. For example, what is a MAC address?

Task Index

A cross reference of tasks, GUI tools, and commands.

Index

In some ways, the most important feature of the book. Start here to find what you are looking for.

Font Conventions Used in This Book

The following typographical conventions are used in this book:

Constant width

is used to indicate command-line computer output and code examples.

Italic

is used to introduce new terms, and to indicate variables, command-line commands, and user-specified file and directory names. It is also used for comments within examples.

Bold

is used to indicate program names, user input in examples, and button names and menu items.

Chapter Conventions

The chapters have a specific format for the type of information being presented. This is either a GUI map, tutorial, or command description.

GUI Chapters

Chapters 2, 3, and 4 describe the NT Graphical User Interface (GUI). Each accessory, control panel, and administrative tool is described in the following format:

Requires
> The requirements sections lists the version of NT (Server or Workstation), and optional software components and hardware that are required to use this GUI tool or control panel.

Command-line equivalents
> If there are commands that can do all or part of what a GUI tool does, they are listed here.

Summary
> The summary provides a short description of the GUI tool, including the possible uses, how it fits into the overall administration of NT, and any special caveats or tricks to using it. If you want a quick overview of the NT tools for administration, read the summary section for each tool.

GUI map
> The GUI maps explode the GUI menu structure, showing every menu option. Usually you are trying to find some option buried four levels deep within a menu. The map allows you to find what you are looking for first, and then work backwards up the menu tree until you find familiar territory.

> For example:

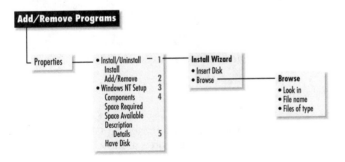

Callouts
> The callouts describe any menu item that is confusing, obtuse, depends on optional software, or requires further explanation. The syntax of the callout is as follows:

> 1   **end-node** [menu-path]
>   callout description

The callout number corresponds with the number in the GUI map. The end-node is the last menu item in the sequence of menus. The menu-path is the sequence of menus that must be traversed to reach the end node.

For example:

1   **Install/Uninstall**
    Install or uninstall programs that are not part of the Windows NT operating system distribution. In most cases, you will use the installer/deinstaller that came with the optional software instead of this tool.

2   **Add/Remove** [Install/Uninstall]
    Remove programs or add components of incompletely installed programs. In most cases, you will be able to remove software only with the **Add/Remove** button.

Tutorials

Chapters 5 and 7 describe areas of NT that are neglected in other books or are poorly understood. The tutorial format tries to show how you can use the tools, by giving real-life problems and example solutions.

Commands

Chapter 6 presents each command available on the NT command line as a separate topic and groups them by function. The topic format has the following fields:

Command name and synopsis
    The command name as typed on command line and a short description of the main uses of the command.

Options
    Options that modify behavior and specify files.

Examples
    Examples of command and option use.

Notes
    Any caveats or special knowledge required to use the command.

See also
    Related commands.

GUI equivalents
    If the functionality of the command is also present in GUI tool(s), the name of the GUI tool and the specific menu selections are listed.

Requires
    Lists NT version (Workstation or Server), optional software component, or hardware required by the command.

Request for Comments

We invite you to help us improve this book. If you have an idea that could make this a more useful quick reference, or if you find a bug in an example or an error in the text, let us know by writing to us at the following address:

O'Reilly & Associates, Inc.
101 Morris Street
Sebastopol, CA 95472
1-800-998-9938 (in the U.S. or Canada)
1-707-829-0515 (international/local)
1-707-829-0104 (FAX)

You can also send us messages electronically. To be put on the mailing list or request a catalog, send email to:

nuts@oreilly.com

To ask technical questions or comment on a book, send email to:

bookquestions@oreilly.com

Acknowledgments

I would like to thank my editor, Robert Denn, and his boss, Frank Willison, for getting Robert and me together for this project. And special thanks go to Chris Reilley and Beverly Murray Scherf. Chris designed the unique presentation of the graphical user interface and implemented all the GUI maps. Beverly painstakingly created the hierarchies for Chris to map and ensured that they were accurate (no easy task, given that menus and options come and go depending on whether you're running Workstation or Server). She contributed to the overall design of the book and guaranteed the consistency of the writing style throughout as well.

A number of people reviewed drafts of the book for technical accuracy and completeness. I am indebted to Russ Cooper and Robert Bruce Thompson who answered questions along the way, to Steve Clark, for help with printing, and to Jon Forrest, Derrel R. Blain, Mary Jane Caswell, Larry Chapman, Pat Dutkiewicz, Jonathan Manheim, Dustin Mollo, Sean Daily, and Lynda Scherf for reading the book and providing comments.

Thanks to the production staff at O'Reilly who got this book out speedily. Thanks to Sheryl Avruch, who kept everyone sane; Nancy Wolfe Kotary, project manager and production editor; Edie Freedman, who designed the cover; Nancy Priest, who designed the inside layout; Nicole Gipson Arigo, Jane Ellin, and Mary Anne Weeks Mayo, for quality control; Seth Maslin, for writing the index; Ellie Fountain Maden and Madeleine Newell, for production support; and Lenny Muellner, for his extensive tools support.

CHAPTER 1

Using Windows NT

Many of the features in Windows NT are new to PC users and administrators. These include multiprotocol networking, multiple users, multitasking, file system security, and Internet services. Windows NT does a good job of making it easier for the typical person to accomplish a complicated task such as running a web server or setting up a router or a remote access server. Other operating systems (such as UNIX and Novell NetWare) have a high learning curve that keep you from getting into trouble until you make a large investment in time and training. NT lowers these requirements, but also allows setup of large and complex networking environments without requiring that you really know what you're doing.

The Start Menu

As with Windows 95, the Windows NT GUI menu system is rooted at the **Start** menu.

The **Start-Run** menu can be used to run commands or access computers and shares by specifying UNC (Universal Naming Convention) pathnames. For example, you can type *regedt32* to start the Registry editor or type *\\NTSERVER1\SHARED* to use the *SHARED* directory on the remote computer *NTSERVER1*. The scrolled list contains a history of previous commands.

The **Start-Help** menu starts up Windows NT Help for general help. Using the **Help** menu within an application or tool brings up help for that application (with some notable exceptions). Some help files are external to the NT help system and have to be viewed individually.

The **Start-Settings** menu allows configuration of the local computer, such as control panels, printers, and the desktop taskbar. Control panels are described in Chapter 2, *The Control Panel*.

The **Start-Programs** menu contains most of the programs and tools that can be started from the GUI, including **Accessories**, covered in Chapter 4, *Accessories*, and **Administrative Tools**, covered in Chapter 3, *Administrative Tools*.

Workstation vs. Server

There has been some discussion in the press about Workstation and Server being the same thing except for a few Registry settings. Even if this were the case, the differences in the available software provide plenty of product differentiation. For example, the ability to act as a domain controller and manage other computers sets Server apart from Workstation. There are also more subtle differences, such as the RAID features that are supported only on Server. This book covers both versions and indicates if a feature depends on a specific version. For a complete list of optional services, protocols, and administrative tools available for each version of NT, see Appendix C, *Server vs. Workstation.*

Security

One of the most powerful features of NT is security. It allows you to restrict access to files, printers, and network resources based on users and groups. One of NT's biggest failures is that it doesn't make its security features readily comprehensible. Unless you are willing to take the time to figure out how it works, you will be tempted to "just make everything readable," effectively bypassing security and rendering it ineffective.

Note that you have to use the NT file system (NTFS) as your file system format in order to take advantage of NT file and directory security. You may be tempted to use FAT for backwards-compatibility, but realize that you are giving up the ability to control access based on users and groups.

One of the confusing aspects of file and directory security is that you have to visit more than one dialog box to configure security for a share. The first dialog (security) controls security for a user logged on locally at the NT console. The second dialog (sharing) controls security for users accessing the directory as a share (over the network). The permissions that the remote user receives are the more restrictive of the two permissions settings. For example, a directory could have the Full Control permission for Everyone on the local computer, but if the share permission is set to Read, the remote user has only Read. If the directory has Read permission for the local users and Full Control for the share, the resulting permission for the remote user is Read. See Figure 1-1.

You will see the same behavior when NT Server is acting as a gateway for NetWare using **Gateway Services for NetWare** (GSNW) or providing Macintosh file sharing using **Services for Macintosh** (SFM). The resulting permissions for users accessing a NetWare or Macintosh volume are the more restrictive of the NetWare or Macintosh file and directory permissions and NT share permissions. Note: the same share could be made available to three different clients (Microsoft Networking, NetWare, and Macintosh) and have a different permissions set for each.

The Registry

The Registry is the database for all system information. It replaces the *AUTOEXEC.BAT, CONFIG.SYS,* and *WIN.INI* files familiar to Windows users. For the most part, you will no longer be able to edit system configuration files with text editors. You will have to use Registry editors (or write programs or scripts) to change system parameters directly. Nearly all of the GUI administration tools serve as front ends to the Registry and store all their data in it.

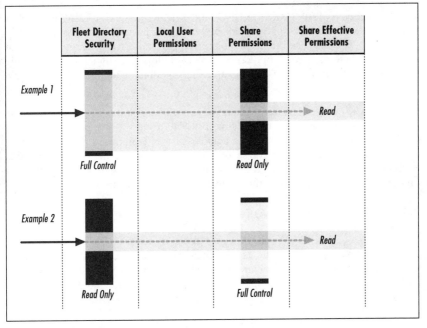

Fleet Directory Security	Local User Permissions	Share Permissions	Share Effective Permissions

Example 1

Full Control .... Read Only .... → Read

Example 2

Read Only .... Full Control .... → Read

Figure 1-1: NT file and directory permissions vs. share permissions

Microsoft gives conflicting advice about the Registry. They frequently state that editing the Registry is the only way to fix a problem and at the same time give dire warnings about the dangers of editing it. In practice, you will probably change the Registry frequently without ruining your system in the process.

One really powerful feature of Registry editors is the ability to read in Registry settings from datafiles. This makes updating the Registry as easy as double-clicking on a file, but can have negative effects if you double-click on the wrong file.

Managing Remote NT systems

It is important to think of the GUI tools in the right context. Control panels usually control only the local computer. Most of the administrative tools can manage the local computer and remote computers. The remote control functionality varies with each command. There is no general, system-wide remote control facility. Microsoft has made several attempts at limited remote management. These include the Nexus tools for NT management and a web front end to NT. Both can be obtained for free from the Microsoft ftp site (*ftp.microsoft.com*).

Multiprotocol Networking

One of the really neat features of NT is its support of multiple protocols. This enables it to communicate with almost any computer system in wide use today. The downside of this feature is that networking is complex. Most people are not fluent in more than one network operating system or protocol. A good example of this complexity is the ability to have protocol-specific computer names. For example, the same computer could be known as as NTSERVER1 under NetBEUI,

NTSRV1 under TCP/IP, ACCOUNTING under IPX/SPX, and NTMACSRV under AppleTalk. When you have a network problem, you have to know issues specific to the protocol being used. For example, if you get an error message saying that the network interface was shut down due to a duplicate IP address, this only means that TCP/IP was shut down, and the computer could still be reachable through three other protocols!

NT has lots of network-related terminology, such as *domains, scope, workgroup,* and so on, that may take a while to sink in. NT terms also overlap with UNIX and the Internet, which will undoubtedly confuse people coming from those environments—is a *domain* name an NT security domain or an Internet domain name? Is a *name server* a NetBIOS name server or a DNS server? When talking about a problem, make sure you know the context of the terms you are using.

Multiuser Network OS

The concept of multiple user accounts is still new to lots of PC users. PC users are used to thinking of desktop PCs as their personal islands. They may not be aware that people can get to their machine even when they are not physically logged in and sitting at their desks. They may be surprised when people complain that they could not reach their web server or disk shares because they turned their PC off when they left the office.

One of the most important features of NT is the ability to create a "generic" workstation. Any user with an account can log on and get their personal settings, screen savers, file systems, and printers regardless of what machine they are using. This is a new concept to someone coming from a Windows 3.x background, where PCs are highly personalized devices.

PC users are also used to rebooting their computer any time something seems wrong. This could be extremely disruptive to remote users. If an NT server is acting as your gateway to the Internet, web server, mail server, and file server, it is worth trying to find out what is happening before rebooting or power-cycling.

The GUI vs. Command Line

I am a firm believer in the command line. The promise of GUIs being easier to use always seems to break down when you start doing something really complicated. The more experienced you are, the more likely you are to use the command line for administration and troubleshooting. When something is going wrong, it is useful to know the command-line equivalent of a GUI function, as they tend to give more useful error messages and do something other than hang.

Scripting

If you have to perform a task multiple times, you should look into scripting languages, such as Perl (see *www.activeware.com*). Tasks such as mass account creation can be automated by running scripts that generate hundreds or thousands of accounts at a time. Scripting languages also come in handy for manipulating data files. If you can get a GUI tool to produce a data file, you can process it with a script and read data back into the GUI tool. This technique can be used for event logs, Registry settings, DNS data files, user and group accounts, etc.

CHAPTER 2

The Control Panel

The control panel adds, deletes, and configures software and hardware on the local computer. It configures the network and allows permanent connections to be created with Novell NetWare servers and Macintosh clients.

Some of the control panel functionality is also available within **Server Manager**, which can configure remote computers in addition to the local computer. For the most part, networking software and hardware has to be added using the control panel, but once added it can be administered from **Server Manager**.

Most of the control panels exist only within the **Control Panel** menu, but some have multiple menu entries. For example, the **Printers** control panel is also available from **Start-Settings-Printers** and **My Computer**.

Add/Remove Programs

Requires
> NT Workstation or Server

Summary
> The **Add/Remove Programs** control panel installs, modifies, or removes programs or their components from your system. It displays space requirements for the optional software components. In practice, this control panel is not always used, since the **Network** control panel is used to install optional components of the NT distribution, and third-party software usually comes with its own installer.

1   **Install/Uninstall** [Properties]

Install or uninstall programs that are not part of the Windows NT operating system distribution. In most cases, you will be using the installer/deinstaller that came with the optional software in place of this tool.

2   **Add/Remove** [Properties-Install/Uninstall]

Remove programs or add components of incompletely installed programs. In most cases, you will be able to remove software only with the **Add/Remove** button.

3   **Windows NT Setup** [Properties]

Add or remove components of the Windows NT operating system distribution.

4   **Components** [Properties-Windows NT Setup]

Add or remove components from the software categories. Lists disk space required for the component, file description, and details of the component. The checkbox indicates the installation status of each component:

- Every component added (checked white checkbox)

- Partially installed components (checked gray checkbox)

- No components installed (blank checkbox)

5   **Details** [Properties-Windows NT Setup-Description]

Displays installation status of individual components within a software category.

Console

Requires

NT Workstation or Server

Summary

The **Console** control panel configures default settings for DOS command-line sessions.

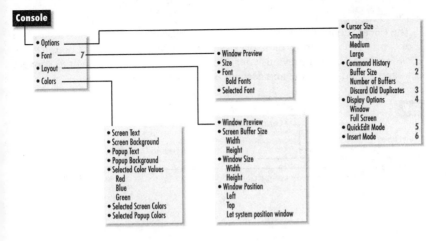

Console
- Options
- Font — 7
- Layout
- Colors

- Cursor Size
  - Small
  - Medium
  - Large
- Command History   1
  - Buffer Size   2
  - Number of Buffers
  - Discard Old Duplicates 3
- Display Options   4
  - Window
  - Full Screen
- QuickEdit Mode   5
- Insert Mode   6

- Window Preview
- Size
- Font
  - Bold Fonts
- Selected Font

- Screen Text
- Screen Background
- Popup Text
- Popup Background
- Selected Color Values
  - Red
  - Blue
  - Green
- Selected Screen Colors
- Selected Popup Colors

- Window Preview
- Screen Buffer Size
  - Width
  - Height
- Window Size
  - Width
  - Height
- Window Position
  - Left
  - Top
  - Let system position window

Control Panel

1 Command History [Options]
Configure the number of commands to be kept in the command history. This is the familiar **DOSKEY** feature, which allows previous commands to be edited or re-executed by scrolling up and down the command history.

2 Buffer Size [Options-Command History]
Number of commands kept in history (from 1 to 999, default is 50).

3 Discard Old Duplicates [Options-Command History]
Remove duplicate commands from command history. For example, if you typed the *dir* command 20 times, the command history would retain only one instance.

4 Display Options [Options]
Specify whether the command-line session appears in a window or full screen. Hit ALT-ENTER to toggle between full-screen mode and window mode.

5 Quick Edit Mode [Options]
Use a mouse to cut and paste rather than using **Edit**. To copy, select text with left mouse button and then right-click to paste the selection.

6 Insert Mode [Options]
Inserts new text instead of overwriting existing text.

7 Font
Font selections appear in window view only, not full screen.

CSNW

Requires
NT Workstation
Client Services for NetWare (CSNW) service

Summary

The **Client Service for NetWare** control panel allows the computer to access file and print services from the Novell NetWare server. The **CSNW** Control Panel assumes you have a previously installed and working Novell server to connect to and a valid username and account on the Novell server.

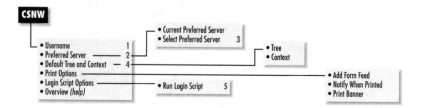

1 **Username**

Shows name of currently logged-on user. If the Windows NT password for this username is different from the password on the NetWare server, you will get a second login prompt while attaching to the NetWare server.

2 **Preferred Server**

Displays current preferred server for non-NDS (**NetWare Directory Services**) environments (such as Netware 3.x).

3 **Select Preferred Server** [Preferred Server]

The scroll list contains a list of NetWare servers discovered on the network. If the list is empty, there may be a communications problem between the local computer and the NetWare server.

Check the Frame Type settings for the IPX Protocol in the **Network** control panel to see if they match those being used by the NetWare server; this should be visible from the *net view /network:nw* command. The *ipxroute* command is useful for learning the frame types in use on the network.

4 **Default Tree and Context**

Defines NDS name and position of your login username for NDS environments (NetWare 4.x).

5 **Run Login Script** [Login Script Options]

Run login script when logging in to NetWare server.

Devices

Requires

NT Workstation or Server

Summary

The **Devices** control panel shows the current status of device drivers, and allows you to stop and start them and to modify their startup behavior. Its primary use is customizing hardware profiles and disabling installed hardware. A device driver must be loaded and running in order for a higher level service or program to use it. If you are creating a hardware profile, use the **Devices** control panel to control how or if a device driver is started for the profile. If you

---

have hardware installed that you want to make unavailable, disabling the device driver for that hardware prevents the system from using it.

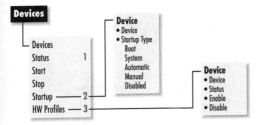

1 Status

If the Status field is blank, the device driver is not loaded.

2 Startup

There are five startup types:

Boot
> Start upon system boot before other device drivers

System
> Start upon system boot after Boot device drivers

Automatic
> Start upon system boot after System device drivers

Manual
> Start only when requested by system or user

Disabled
> Start only when requested by system, unavailable to users

3 HW Profiles

Enable or disable devices for a specific hardware profile. Changes will take effect only after the next reboot.

Dial-Up Monitor

Requires
> NT Workstation or Server
> Remote Access Server (RAS)

Summary
> The **Dial-Up Monitor** control panel can be used to display various statistics about a Dial-Up Networking RAS session. It is normally used to monitor a PPP or SLIP session running over an analog phone line or ISDN line, but it can also monitor a PPTP session. **Dial-Up Monitor** may be useful when debugging errors that occur after a RAS session is successfully started, such as line errors or errors caused by insufficient system resources.

Dial-Up Monitor

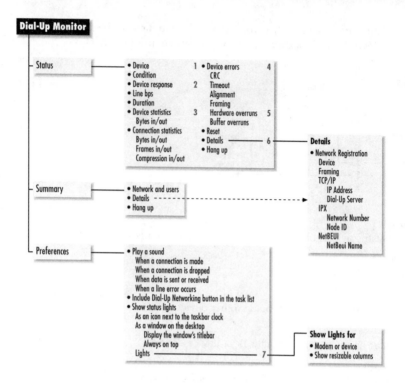

1 **Device** [Status]

The communications device or PPTP virtual device being monitored.

2 **Device response** [Status]

If the device (modem) generated a **CONNECT** message when it connected to the remote device, it is displayed here. The **CONNECT** message can contain the baud rate, the bps rate, and various error control and compression messages.

3 **Device statistics** [Status]

If you have several devices on your computer and you want to prove that traffic is using a specific device, try generating traffic and watching the **Bytes In** and **Bytes Out** counters.

4 **Device errors** [Status]

Nonzero counters could indicate a noisy phone line or a hardware problem.

5 **Hardware overruns** [Status-Device errors]

If nonzero, your serial port may be too slow for the device and speed it is being used at.

6 **Details** [Status]

Display various network protocol information for the RAS connection. If the information is obtained dynamically from the remote server, this window can be used to confirm that the client side has obtained the right values. For example, the IP address is displayed for the client side of the connection.

If you do not want to see flashing lights for each packet transmitted over the RAS session, the lights can be enabled or disabled for each device. For example, if you are running a PPTP session over a dedicated network connection, the status lights are fairly meaningless and can be disabled.

Display

Requires

NT Workstation or Server

Summary

The **Display** control panel can customize your display with personal preferences for background, screensavers, fonts, colors, and icons. You can also install and remove display adapter drivers and configure display hardware settings such as color depth, desktop size, font size, and refresh rates.

If you are adding new hardware, the **Resources** tab of the **Windows NT Diagnostics** tool is a good place to look for system-wide resource settings. Carefully choose the new settings to avoid conflicts with existing hardware.

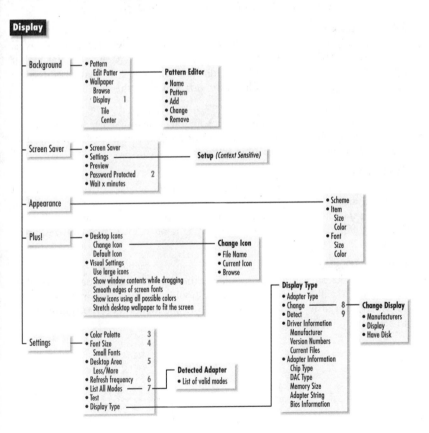

1 **Display** [Background-Wallpaper]

If you choose a bitmap as wallpaper, the bitmap can be repeated multiple times to cover the entire display (**Tiled**) or displayed once on the center of the display (**Center**).

2 **Password Protected** [Screen Saver]

Requiring a password can increase security of the NT computer by locking the console if you happen to leave yourself logged on or leave sensitive information on the screen.

3 **Color Palette** [Settings]

The number of colors is controlled by how many bits are used to describe color information (the color depth). The more colors you use, the better images will look, but there will also be a performance penalty.

4 **Font Size** [Settings]

If you choose a large size for the **Desktop Area**, you may wish to use the **Large Fonts** selection to increase the size of text. Unlike the other settings, changing font size requires rebooting before the new fonts take effect.

5 **Desktop Area** [Settings]

The slider bar changes the display size in pixels in increments supported by the installed display adapter. Unlike previous versions of Windows NT, no reboot is required to change display settings or refresh frequency.

6 **Refresh frequency** [Settings]

The refresh frequency (or refresh rate) determines how often the display is refreshed, which affects the amount of display flicker. Generally, the higher the refresh frequency, the better the display will look. You may also need to adjust the frequency to allow filming or videotaping of the display.

7 **List All Modes** [Settings]

All the color depth (palette), screen resolution (desktop area), and refresh frequencies supported by the display adapter are listed as a single option, making it easy to choose a compatible setting.

8 **Change** [Settings-Display Type]

If you are installing a new display adapter, either select a driver from the list or install a new driver from disk. You might use this window if you installed NT using the default VGA settings and now wish to take advantage of better features offered by the video adapter. Changing display type will require a reboot.

9 **Detect** [Settings-Display Type]

The **Detect** button will try to auto-detect the type of display adapter installed. Sometimes it will be incorrect, so you should check the reported type carefully. You can also check the **Display** tab of the **Windows NT Diagnostics** tool to see what it reports.

FPNW

Requires

NT Server
File and Print Services for NetWare (FPNW) service

Summary

The **File and Print Services for NetWare** (FPNW) control panel administers shares for the FPNW service. FPNW is not part of the base NT distribution and has to be purchased separately. FPNW enables an NT Server to emulate a NetWare server. NetWare clients can log in and access file and print services. The **FPNW** control panel allows you to view only existing shares and disconnect users. **File Manager** or **Server Manager** must be used to create the shares and set permissions.

The **FPNW** control panel can also be run from within **Server Manager** by using the **FPNW-Properties** menu.

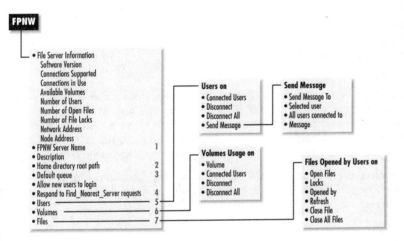

1 FPNW Server Name

Set the NT server name that is to be advertised to NetWare clients. The default is the computer name with _FPNW appended. The computer is known to Microsoft Networking clients by its computer name and to NetWare clients by its FPNW server name.

2 Home directory root path

Share for NetWare clients to attach to for their home directories.

3 Default queue

Select default print queue for NetWare clients. NetWare printers are created with the **Add Printer** wizard in the **Printers** control panel. NetWare print servers and queues are created with the **FPNW-Print Servers** menu of **Server Manager**.

4 Respond to Find_Nearest_Server requests

Enabling this option makes the NT server respond to NetWare client broadcasts. When a NetWare client boots, it can either broadcast for a NetWare server to attach to or look for a specific server. This could cause NetWare clients to attach to the wrong server if you are not careful, as the first server to respond is used.

5 Users

List connected NetWare users, disconnect users, or send messages to connected users.

6 Volumes

List shared volumes, showing connected users. You can also send messages to connected users.

7 Files

List or close individual files opened by connected users.

GSNW

Requires

> NT Server
> Gateway Services for NetWare (GSNW) service

Summary

> The **Gateway Services for NetWare** (GSNW) control panel allows NT Server to connect to an existing Novell NetWare server and access NetWare file and print services. It offers the same functionality as **Client Services for NetWare** (CSNW) available under NT Workstation, but it also adds the ability to redistribute the NetWare file and print services to Microsoft Networking clients.
>
> An interesting feature of GSNW is that the gateway function counts as only one logon on the NetWare server, but allows any number of Microsoft clients to connect to it.

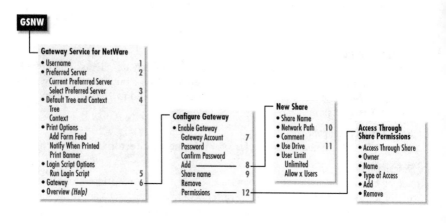

1   **Username**
    Show name of user(s) currently logged on. If the Windows NT password for this username is different from the password on the NetWare server, you will get a second login prompt while attaching to the NetWare server.

2   **Preferred Server**
    Display current preferred server for non-NDS (NetWare Directory Services) environments (such as NetWare 3.x).

3   **Select Preferred Server** [Preferred Server]
    The scroll list contains a list of NetWare servers discovered on the network. If the list is empty, there may be a communications problem between the local computer and the NetWare server.

    Check the Frame Type settings for the IPX Protocol in the **Network** control panel to see if they match those being used by the NetWare server, which should be visible from the *net view /network:nw* command. The *ipxroute* command is useful for learning the frame types in use on the network.

4   **Default Tree and Context**
    Define NDS name and position of your login username for NDS environments (NetWare 4.x).

5   **Run Login Script** [Login Script Options]
    Run login script when logging in to NetWare server.

6   **Gateway**
    When you enable the gateway, you are making whatever NetWare resources the computer is currently connected to available to other Microsoft clients on the network. The NetWare file and print resources appear to be normal Microsoft Networking shares and printers, and the clients do not need any special software in order to use them.

7   **Gateway Account** [Gateway-Enable Gateway]
    The user account that logs in to the NetWare server when attaching to file and print resources. The gateway user must be a member of the NTGATEWAY group on all NetWare servers that this server will gateway. The permissions on the gateway user and NTGATEWAY group determine the rights of clients connecting to the gateway shares.

8   **Add** [Gateway-Enable Gateway]
    Add each NetWare volume that you want to share to the Microsoft Network.

9   **Share name** [Gateway-Enable Gateway]
    Add a new share for Microsoft clients. If MS-DOS workstations will access this share, keep the name to eight characters or less.

10 **Network Path** [Gateway-Enable Gateway-Add]
    The network path (UNC name) of the NetWare server and volume to redistribute to Microsoft clients.

11 **Use Drive** [Gateway-Enable Gateway-Add]
    Map a drive letter to the share. This may be more convenient for some clients.

12 **Permissions** [Gateway-Enable Gateway]
    The permissions of the share are the union of the NT share permissions and the permissions of the gateway user and NTGATEWAY group on the NetWare

server. For example, you can leave the share open to anyone using the NT share permissions, but the permissions of the gateway user and NTGATEWAY group determine who can do what. On the other hand, if the gateway user and NTGATEWAY group are open, clients may be constricted by the NT share permissions. The client's rights are determined by the more restrictive of the existing NT or NetWare permissions.

Internet

Requires

NT Workstation or Server
TCP/IP protocol

Summary

The **Internet** control panel configures the Internet Explorer web browser. Note that if you have installed a newer version of Microsoft Internet Explorer (MSIE) since you have installed NT, the control panel contents may be much more complex. Newer versions of Explorer will invoke the **Internet** control panel from **View-Options**.

1 Use Proxy Server

Connect to a proxy instead of connecting directly to remote sites. This may be useful for performance or security reasons. If you are using a caching web server to improve performance, you can force the computer to connect to the cache server instead of directly connecting to hosts on the Internet. It can also be used to force outgoing **FTP** and **HTTP** connections to go through a firewall or proxy server.

2 Proxy Server [Settings]

TCP/IP hostname and port number of proxy server.

3 Bypass Proxy on [Settings]

A list of exceptions that should be connected to directly, bypassing the proxy server. The exception list takes the form of hostnames, domains, or port numbers. Each entry is separated by a comma. The following example allows direct connections to any host within the *ora.com* and *songline.com* domains, and port 80 on any other host:

```
ora.com,songline.com,:80
```

A list of exceptions might include any hosts within a company firewall or others known to be safe.

Licensing

Requires

NT Workstation or Server

Summary

The **Licensing** control panel manages licenses for clients that connect to an NT computer. In addition to the purchase price of the NT distribution, Microsoft charges for the ability of clients (other Windows computers) to connect to a computer running Windows NT.

Control Panel

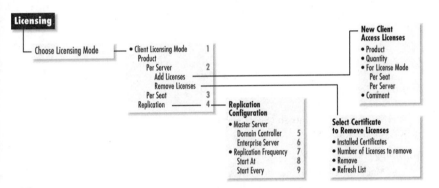

1   **Client Licensing Mode** [Choose Licensing Mode]
The licensing mode is either per seat or per server for each server product installed. If you are unsure of what mode to use, choose **Per Server**. You are allowed only one opportunity to change the licensing mode.

2   **Per Server** [Choose Licensing Mode-Client Licensing Mode-Product]
Enter the number of concurrent Client Access License connections you have purchased for your server. You can set the number of concurrent connections to zero if you do not need basic network services. Using this mode limits client connections to a specific server, regardless of how many clients or other servers there are on the network.

3   **Per Seat** [Choose Licensing Mode-Client Licensing Mode-Product]
Allow individual users to access all servers. Using this mode limits the total number of clients that can accessed on any server at one time.

4   **Replication** [Choose Licensing Mode-Client Licensing Mode]
If the local computer is not the primary domain controller (PDC), you may wish to coordinate licensing with the PDC or an *Enterprise Server*, which is a computer managing licenses for an entire organization. The license information is replicated to the remote computer at specified intervals.

5   **Domain Controller** [Choose Licensing Mode-Client Licensing Mode-Replication-Master Server]
Select this if the computer is a server or backup DC in the main domain, but not the primary domain controller. Also use this if it is a standalone server or a PDC that you do not want to replicate to other computers.

6 **Enterprise Server** [Choose Licensing Mode-Client Licensing Mode-Replication-Master Server]

Select this if the computer is a standalone server and part of a larger enterprise, and you wish to replicate it to an enterprise server.

7 **Replication Frequency** [Choose Licensing Mode-Client Licensing Mode-Replication]

You can manually specify when and how often license information is replicated to other servers.

8 **Start At** [Choose Licensing Mode-Client Licensing Mode-Replication-Replication Frequency]

Specify the time for licensing information to be replicated to a master server. It is up to you to stagger the replication times if you have multiple computers replicating to a single server.

9 **Start Every** [Choose Licensing Mode-Client Licensing Mode-Replication-Replication Frequency]

Specify the frequency of replications for licensing information.

MacFile

Requires

NT Server
Services for the Macintosh (SFM) service
NTFS Partition

Summary

The **MacFile** control panel administers Macintosh volumes being offered by **Services for the Macintosh (SFM)**. It can disconnect Macintosh users, send them messages, and control several file-sharing security parameters. The control panel can display which Macintosh user is attached to a volume, which volumes are being shared, and which files on each volume are in use. **File Manager** or **Server Manager** must be used to create the volumes and set permissions.

The MacFile control panel can also be run from within **Server Manager** by using the **MacFile-Properties** menu.

Note that NT creates a new directory called **Microsoft UAM Volume** when SFM is installed, but you are free to share any disk or subdirectory as a Macintosh volume (as long as it is an NTFS partition).

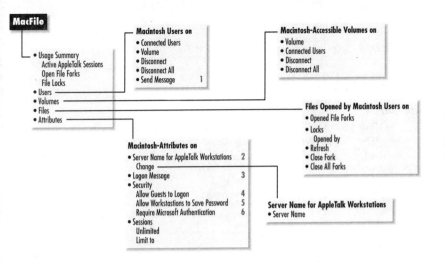

1   **Send Message** [Users]

You can send a message that will pop up on all currently connected Macintosh clients. This can be used to warn clients about upcoming downtime or other events.

2   **Server Name for AppleTalk Workstations** [Attributes]

Set the name that will show up in Macintosh client chooser for Apple file sharing.

3   **Logon Message** [Attributes]

You can have up to four lines of a logon message appear when the Macintosh clients connect to a share. This can be used to provide instructions or other helpful information.

4   **Allow Guests to Logon** [Attributes-Security]

Allow Macintosh users to connect to the volume even if they do not have an account on the NT server.

5   **Allow Workstations to Save Password** [Attributes-Security]

Allow Macintosh clients to reconnect without being prompted for their passwords. Normally, the client would be prompted for a password each time regardless of how often it connects. This may be desirable for volumes that are frequently used (such as those containing fonts), but it also decreases system-wide security.

6   **Require Microsoft Authentication** [Attributes-Security]

Force the Macintosh client to encrypt the password before sending it over the network, which improves security.

Modems

Requires

NT Workstation or Server

Summary

The **Modems** control panel adds, configures, or removes modems from the system. The **Install New Modem** wizard appears if no modem is currently installed. In most cases, all the modem settings are automatically configured when your modem is installed.

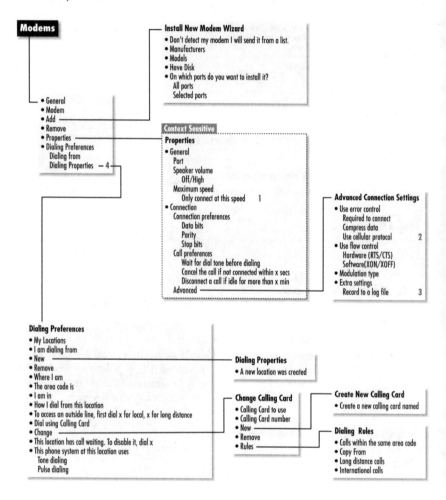

1 **Only connect at this speed** [Properties-General-Maximum speed]

Do not allow the modem to connect at a lower baud rate than the specified speed. In other words, if only a poor connection is available, don't use it.

2 **Use cellular protocol** [Properties-Connection-Advanced-Use error control]

Modems that support cellular protocols such as MNP10, ECP, or ZyCELL usually require a special set of commands to configure them for a cellular connection.

3 **Record to a log file** [Properties-Connection-Advanced-Extra settings]

If you are having problems dialing the modem, recording the interaction in a log file will enable you to debug the process. The log file is created in the root directory of the Windows NT installation and is named *ModemLog_* followed by the name and model of the modem. For example, a US Robotics Courier creates a file called *ModemLog_Courier V.Everything.txt*. The log file, as shown in the following text, contains the settings used by the modem and the commands sent to and the replies received from the modem by the local computer.

```
03-09-1997 17:16:42.948 - Dialing.
03-09-1997 17:16:42.948 - Send: ATDT#############<cr>
03-09-1997 17:17:00.473 - Recv: <cr><lf>CONNECT 33600/ARQ/V34/LAPM/V42BIS<cr><lf>
03-09-1997 17:17:00.473 - Interpreted response: Connect
03-09-1997 17:17:00.473 - Connection established at 33600bps.
03-09-1997 17:17:00.473 - Error-control on.
03-09-1997 17:17:00.473 - Data compression on.
03-09-1997 17:19:25.862 - Hanging up the modem.
```

4 **Dialing Properties** [Dialing Preferences]

This window can be used to set up *locations* with different dialing configurations. For example, if you have a laptop that you use at both work and home, you can create a location named **Work** that dials a 9 before the phone number and a location named **Home** that disables call waiting.

Multimedia

Requires

NT Workstation or Server

Summary

The **Multimedia** control panel adds, configures, and deletes multimedia devices such as sound and video cards and CD-ROM drives.

If you are adding new hardware, the **Resources** tab of the **Windows NT Diagnostics** tool is a good place to look for system-wide resource settings. Carefully choose the new settings to avoid conflicts with existing hardware.

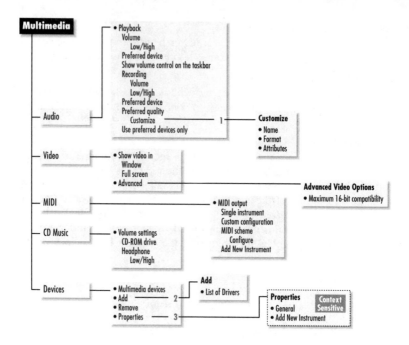

1 Customize [Audio-Record-Preferred quality]

Change quality of recording using different sampling rates and encoding methods.

2 Add [Devices]

Add new multimedia hardware device or driver. Select the type of driver for the hardware you are adding, and then any resource information such as IRQ, I/O Port, and DMA channel.

3 Properties [Devices]

View or change settings for selected device. If a device is not working, check here to see the status of the device.

Network

Requires

NT Workstation or Server

Summary

The **Network** control panel installs, configures, and removes NT services, network protocols, and network adapters. It is a catchall for installing any optional software and hardware that uses the network in some manner. The sheer number of options available in the **Network** control panel may seem overwhelming.

It be may helpful to think of the **Network** control panel as an installation and configuration tool that runs specific installers for each service, protocol, or adapter being added. If you separate the general functionality of the control panel to install, configure, and remove services, protocols, and adapters from the configuration tasks specific to each service, protocol, and adapter, it may make it easier to understand. For example, when you are configuring the TCP/IP protocol, you are leaving the **Network** control panel and entering the **TCP/IP** control panel.

There are a number of optional services, protocols, and adapters that can be installed from the NT installation media. In addition, there are separately purchased Microsoft products and third-party products that are installed via the control panel. However, it is beyond the scope of this book to document every option.

If you are adding new hardware, the **Resources** tab of the **Windows NT Diagnostics** tool is a good place to look for system-wide resource settings. Carefully choose the new settings to avoid conflicts with existing hardware.

General Network Control Panel Description

You can pretty much count on having to reboot your computer to effect any changes you make in this control panel.

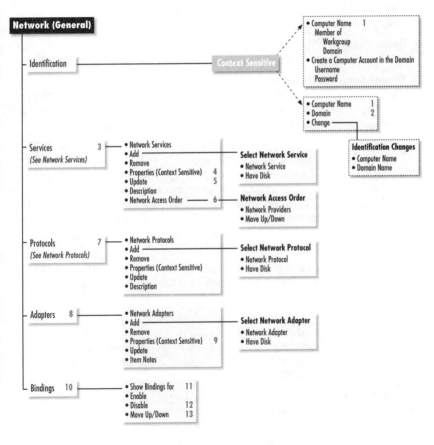

1 Computer Name [Identification]

The computer name is used to identify the computer for Microsoft Networking functions. Note that the computer could be known by different names under each network protocol.

2 Domain [Identification]

The NT domain name identifies a group of computers sharing a common security policy and account database. The combination of domain name and computer name uniquely identify the computer on the network. The NT domain name has nothing to do with the DNS domain name.

3 Services

Install, configure, and delete services. (See the section entitled *Services* later in this chapter for a complete list of services.) Installing a service adds some network functionality to the local computer. The service may include an NT service that will be started at boot time, a network protocol to communicate with other network devices, an administrative tool, and help files. For example, installing the **Services for Macintosh** service adds the **File Server for Macintosh** and **Print Server for Macintosh** NT services, the AppleTalk protocol, **MacFile** control panel, and **MacFile** menu options in **Server Manager** and **File Manager**.

4 Properties [Services]

Reconfigure an existing service.

5 Update [Services]

Update an existing service.

6 Network Access Order [Services]

Change the type of networking (typically Microsoft Networking or Netware Compatible Network) the computer tries to use first. In most cases, you will want the most commonly used type of networking to be tried first.

7 Protocols

Install, configure, and delete network protocols. (See the section entitled *Protocols* later in this chapter for a complete list.) Adding a network protocol enables the local computer to communicate with another network device speaking the same protocol. Some protocols are automatically added as part of services and others must be manually added. For example, the DLC protocol must be added before the **Remoteboot** service.

8 Adapters

Install, configure, or remove network adapters. Each brand and model of adapter card has different options, making it impossible to list all the possible options.

9 Properties [Adapters]

Configure existing adapter. Common options are hardware resources such as IRQ, Memory Range, and I/O port, and network media-specific settings such as speed (10Mb/s, 100Mb/s or Auto-Sense) or media types (10BaseT/UTP, AUI/10Base5, or BNC/10Base2).

10 Bindings

Bindings are the relationships between services, protocols, and adapters. When a service is bound to a protocol, it can communicate over the network via that protocol. When a protocol is bound to an adapter, the adapter can use the protocol. Removing a binding prevents communication. The order of binding is also significant, as a service that has several protocols bound to it tries to use the protocols in the order in which they are bound. In practice, you should have to alter bindings only when performance tuning, or when working around bugs and unusual networking situations.

11 **Show Bindings for** [Bindings]
Select the criteria for the display. Double-clicking on a selection brings up the bindings for an individual service, protocol, or adapter.

12 **Disable** [Bindings]
When you disable a binding, you remove the ability to communicate. This may be desirable in some situations. For example, if you are configuring an NT computer as a firewall, removing a binding from a protocol prevents someone from using the protocol to communicate with the firewall.

For performance reasons, you can disable a protocol for an adapter if the adapter is never going to use the protocol.

13 **Move Up/Down** [Bindings]
You can also reorder bindings to improve performance. For example, if you know an adapter or service is using one protocol more frequently than others, moving the protocol to the top of the list could improve performance.

Services

All of the listed services can be installed from the Windows NT Server or Workstation CD-ROM using the **Add** button. Services that are available only on Server or Workstation are noted. Configurable services will either present a configuration window when initially installed or enable the **Properties** button when selected after installation. For example, if you need to configure a RAS port after RAS is installed, use the **Properties** button with **Remote Access Service** selected.

Refer to the following figure for an illustration of these services.

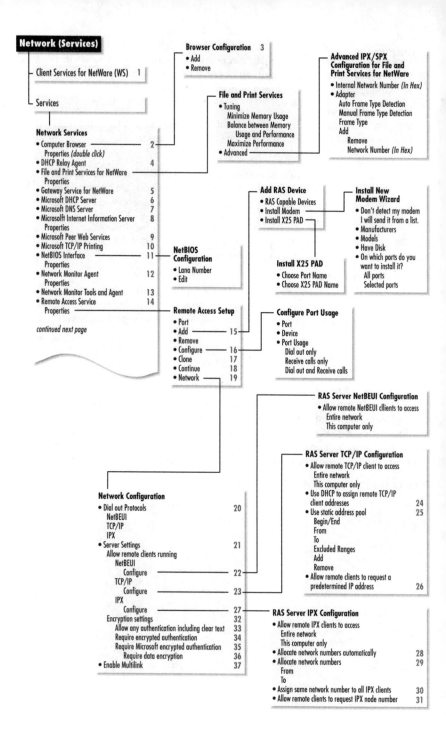

Network (Services)

Client Services for NetWare (WS)   1

Services

Network Services
- Computer Browser   2
  Properties *(double click)*
- DHCP Relay Agent   4
- File and Print Services for NetWare
  Properties
- Gateway Service for NetWare   5
- Microsoft DHCP Server   6
- Microsoft DNS Server   7
- Microsolft Internet Information Server   8
  Properties
- Microsoft Peer Web Services   9
- Microsoft TCP/IP Printing   10
- NetBIOS Interface   11
  Properties
- Network Monitor Agent   12
  Properties
- Network Monitor Tools and Agent   13
- Remote Access Service   14
  Properties

continued next page

Browser Configuration   3
- Add
- Remove

File and Print Services
- Tuning
  Minimize Memory Usage
  Balance between Memory
    Usage and Performance
  Maximize Performance
- Advanced

**Advanced IPX/SPX
Configuration for File and
Print Services for NetWare**
- Internal Network Number *(In Hex)*
- Adapter
  Auto Frame Type Detection
  Manual Frame Type Detection
  Frame Type
  Add
    Remove
    Network Number *(In Hex)*

Add RAS Device
- RAS Capable Devices
- Install Modem
- Install X25 PAD

**Install New
Modem Wizard**
- Don't detect my modem
  I will send it from a list.
- Manufacturers
- Models
- Have Disk
- On which ports do you
  want to install it?
  All ports
  Selected ports

**NetBIOS
Configuration**
- Lana Number
- Edit

Install X25 PAD
- Choose Port Name
- Choose X25 PAD Name

Remote Access Setup
- Port
- Add   15
- Remove
- Configure   16
- Clone   17
- Continue   18
- Network   19

Configure Port Usage
- Port
- Device
- Port Usage
  Dial out only
  Receive calls only
  Dial out and Receive calls

RAS Server NetBEUI Configuration
- Allow remote NetBEUI cllients to access
  Entire network
  This computer only

RAS Server TCP/IP Configuration
- Allow remote TCP/IP client to access
  Entire network
  This computer only
- Use DHCP to assign remote TCP/IP
  client addresses   24
- Use static address pool   25
  Begin/End
  From
  To
  Excluded Ranges
  Add
  Remove
- Allow remote clients to request a
  predetermined IP address   26

Network Configuration
- Dial out Protocols   20
  NetBEUI
  TCP/IP
  IPX
- Server Settings   21
  Allow remote clients running
    NetBEUI
      Configure   22
    TCP/IP
      Configure   23
    IPX
      Configure   27
  Encryption settings   32
    Allow any authentication including clear text   33
    Require encrypted authentication   34
    Require Microsoft encrypted authentication   35
      Require data encryption   36
- Enable Multilink   37

RAS Server IPX Configuration
- Allow remote IPX clients to access
  Entire network
  This computer only
- Allocate network numbers automatically   28
- Allocate network numbers   29
  From
  To
- Assign same network number to all IPX clients   30
- Allow remote clients to request IPX node number 31

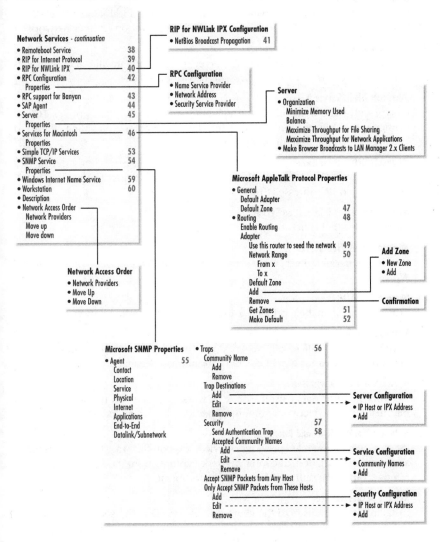

Network Services - *continuation*
- Remoteboot Service   38
- RIP for Internet Protocol   39
- RIP for NWLink IPX   40
- RPC Configuration   42
    Properties
- RPC support for Banyan   43
- SAP Agent   44
- Server   45
    Properties
- Services for Macintosh   46
    Properties
- Simple TCP/IP Services   53
- SNMP Service   54
    Properties
- Windows Internet Name Service   59
- Workstation   60
- Description
- Network Access Order
    Network Providers
    Move up
    Move down

RIP for NWLink IPX Configuration
- NetBios Broadcast Propagation   41

RPC Configuration
- Name Service Provider
- Network Address
- Security Service Provider

Server
- Organization
    Minimize Memory Used
    Balance
    Maximize Throughput for File Sharing
    Maximize Throughput for Network Applications
- Make Browser Broadcasts to LAN Manager 2.x Clients

Microsoft AppleTalk Protocol Properties
- General
    Default Adapter
    Default Zone   47
- Routing   48
    Enable Routing
    Adapter
    Use this router to seed the network   49
    Network Range   50
      From x
      To x
    Default Zone
    Add
    Remove
    Get Zones   51
    Make Default   52

Add Zone
- New Zone
- Add

Confirmation

Network Access Order
- Network Providers
- Move Up
- Move Down

Microsoft SNMP Properties
- Agent   55
    Contact
    Location
    Service
    Physical
    Internet
    Applications
    End-to-End
    Datalink/Subnetwork

- Traps   56
    Community Name
      Add
      Remove
    Trap Destinations
      Add
      Edit
      Remove
    Security   57
      Send Authentication Trap   58
      Accepted Community Names
       Add
       Edit
       Remove
      Accept SNMP Packets from Any Host
      Only Accept SNMP Packets from These Hosts
       Add
       Edit
       Remove

Server Configuration
- IP Host or IPX Address
- Add

Service Configuration
- Community Names
- Add

Security Configuration
- IP Host or IPX Address
- Add

Control Panel

---

1 Client Service for NetWare

(Workstation only) CSNW allows an NT Workstation to use NetWare file and print services.

2 Computer Browser [Services]

The Browser maintains a list of computers on the network.

3 Browser Configuration [Services-Computer Browser]

If the computer is a server participating in multidomain browsing, add all the domains here.

4   **DHCP Relay Agent** [Services]
    (Server only) If a DHCP server is unavailable on the local subnet, the DHCP Relay Agent can relay DHCP requests to a DHCP server on another network.

5   **Gateway Service for NetWare** [Services]
    (Server only) GSNW allows an NT server to use NetWare file and print services and redistribute them to Microsoft networking clients.

6   **Microsoft DHCP Server** [Services]
    (Server only) The **Dynamic Host Configuration Protocol** server supplies TCP/IP configuration information to TCP/IP client computers, enabling them to become self-configuring upon bootup.

7   **Microsoft DNS Server** [Services]
    (Server only) The **Domain Name System** server maps hostnames to IP addresses and IP addresses to hostnames.

8   **Microsoft Internet Information Server** [Services]
    (Server only) IIS is Microsoft's web server.

9   **Microsoft Peer Web Server** [Services]
    (Workstation only) **Peer Web** services is a cut-down version of IIS for NT Workstation.

10 **Microsoft TCP/IP Printing** [Services]
    TCP/IP Printing enables printing using the UNIX LPD protocol over TCP/IP.

11 **NetBIOS Interface** [Services]
    NetBIOS enables Microsoft Networking. The LANA number enumerates the network interfaces for NetBIOS and is not normally changed.

12 **Network Monitor Agent** [Services]
    Network Monitor Agent listens on a network interface and transmits captured information to the **Network Monitor** application on a remote computer.

13 **Network Monitor Tools and Agent** [Services]
    (Server only) Same as previous service, except that the **Network Monitor** application is installed, allowing network captures from the local computer or remote computers running **Network Monitor Agent**.

14 **Remote Access Service** [Services]
    Installing RAS installs both the client side of RAS (Dial-Up Networking) and the server side (the RAS service). Dial-Up Networking enables the NT computer to call out to other computers or to the Internet. The RAS service enables an NT computer to become a communications server for remote RAS clients. This window can add and change the network settings for ports used by RAS.

15 **Add** [Services-Remote Access Service-Properties]
    Add a RAS port. This includes physical ports such as COM ports and virtual ports used by PPTP.

16 **Configure** [Services-Remote Access Service-Properties]
    Configure use of port (dial-out, dial-in, or both). This setting also affects the contents of **Remote Access Service-Network**.

17 **Clone** [Services-Remote Access Service-Properties]
    Copy the configuration of an existing port to a new one.

18 **Continue** [Services-Remote Access Service-Properties]
Exit RAS setup.

19 **Network** [Services-Remote Access Service-Properties]
Configure the network settings of the selected port. The available settings depend on the **Configure** button. If a port is enabled for dial-out, the **Dial-out Protocols** menu is enabled. If the port is enabled for dial-in, the **Server Settings** menu is enabled.

20 **Dial-out Protocols** [Services-Remote Access Service-Properties-Network]
Select which protocols are allowed to run over outgoing connections using this port. In most cases, you will not need NetBEUI, as TCP/IP can take its place. If you have a NetWare application that runs over the RAS connection, you may need IPX.

21 **Server Settings** [Services-Remote Access Service-Properties-Network]
Select which protocols are allowed to run over incoming connections using this port and whatever authentication protocols are used.

22 **Configure** [Services-Remote Access Service-Properties-Network-Server Settings-Allow remote clients running-NetBEUI]
Allow dial-in clients to see entire network or restrict them to just the local computer.

23 **Configure** [Services-Remote Access Service-Properties-Network-Server Settings-Allow remote clients running-TCP/IP]
Allow dial-in clients to see entire network or restrict them to just the local computer. Also determine how a TCP/IP client obtains an IP address.

24 **Use DHCP to assign remote TCP/IP addresses** [Services-Remote Access Service-Properties-Network-Server Settings-Allow remote clients running-TCP/IP-Configure]
Use a DHCP server to supply TCP/IP information to dial-in clients.

25 **Use static address pool** [Services-Remote Access Service-Properties-Network-Server Settings-Allow remote clients running-TCP/IP-Configure]
Hand out addresses from a pool. This address pool is private to the RAS server and care should be taken so that the address does not conflict with existing DHCP address pools.

26 **Allow remote clients to request predetermined IP address** [Services-Remote Access Service-Properties-Network-Server Settings-Allow remote clients running-TCP/IP-Configure]
If the client already has an IP address, use it instead.

27 **Configure** [Services-Remote Access Service-Properties-Network-Server Settings-Allow remote clients running-IPX]
Allow dial-in clients to see entire network or restrict them to just the local computer. Also determine how a IPX client obtains a network and node number. The server can give each client its own network number, which will make each remote client appear to be on its own physical network, or it can make all remote clients share the same network, which still allows you to identify them as RAS clients, but reduces routing and RAS traffic.

28 **Allocate network numbers automatically** [Services-Remote Access Service-Properties-Network-Server Settings-Allow remote clients running-IPX-Configure]
Let the server allocate network numbers.

29 **Allocate network numbers** [Services-Remote Access Service-Properties-Network-Server Settings-Allow remote clients running-IPX-Configure]
Allocate network numbers from a specified range.

30 **Assign same network number to all IPX clients** [Services-Remote Access Service-Properties-Network-Server Settings-Allow remote clients running-IPX-Configure]

Give all clients the same network number, reducing the size of routing table and network traffic.

31 **Allow clients to request IPX node number** [Services-Remote Access Service-Properties-Network-Server Settings-Allow remote clients running-IPX-Configure]

Allow remote client to set its own node number, possibly letting it impersonate another computer.

32 **Encryption Settings** [Services-Remote Access Service-Properties-Network-Server Settings]

Set the accepted authentication protocols for dial-in clients.

33 **Allow any authentication including clear text** [Services-Remote Access Service-Properties-Network-Server Settings-Encryption Settings]

Allow any of the following PPP authentication protocols: PAP, SPAP, CHAP, or MS-CHAP. See Chapter 5, *RAS and DUN*, for details.

34 **Require encrypted authentication** [Services-Remote Access Service-Properties-Network-Server Settings-Encryption Settings]

Require an authentication protocol that uses encrypted passwords such as SPAP, CHAP, or MS-CHAP.

35 **Require Microsoft encrypted authentication** [Services-Remote Access Service-Properties-Network-Server Settings-Encryption Settings]

Require MS-CHAP.

36 **Require data encryption** [Services-Remote Access Service-Properties-Network-Server Settings-Encryption Settings-Require Microsoft encrypted authentication]

Use Microsoft encryption for the data being sent over the RAS session.

37 **Enable Multilink** [Services-Remote Access Service-Properties-Network]

Multiple RAS sessions can be combined in parallel to provide higher bandwidth. Both ends of the PPP connection have to support this option for it to work.

38 **Remoteboot Service** [Services]

The **Remoteboot** service allows diskless Windows or DOS workstations to boot by downloading files from an NT Server.

When the **Remoteboot** service is first installed, it prompts for a directory to be used for storing remote boot files and asks if you want to use existing LAN Manager boot information. The DLC protocol must be installed before **Remoteboot**.

39 **RIP for Internet Protocol** [Services]

Routing Information Protocol for IP. This is the most common routing protocol used within small to medium TCP/IP networks. It is not powerful enough for use on the Internet itself.

40 **RIP for NWLink IPX** [Services]

RIP (see previous entry) for IPX.

41 **NetBIOS Broadcast Propagation** [Services-RIP for NWLink IPX]

The IPX protocol uses broadcasts to find network resources. Enabling propagation makes it possible for servers to find each other even if separated by a router. As IPX is a very chatty protocol, this can have a serious performance penalty when used over a WAN link.

42 RPC Configuration [Services]

Remote Procedure Call (RPC) services for NT. RPC allows distributed computing, with different parts of an application distributed on multiple networked computers.

43 RPC support for Banyan [Services]

Remote Procedure Call support for Banyan VINES.

44 SAP Agent [Services]

The Service Advertising Protocol broadcasts the presence of network resources (file and print) on the LAN.

45 Server [Services]

The server side of Microsoft Networking. You can customize the behavior of the **Server** service based on performance criteria.

46 Services for Macintosh [Services]

(Server only) Adds the AppleTalk protocol and file and printer sharing for Macintosh clients. NT Server can act as router for AppleTalk and seed the network with AppleTalk zones.

47 Default Zone [Services-Services for Macintosh-General]

Selecting a default zone makes the NT server show up in this zone if it is offering file and print services via AppleTalk. The NT server shows up in the Macintosh client's chooser.

48 Routing [Services-Services for Macintosh]

If routing is enabled, AppleTalk traffic flows from one network interface to the other. AppleTalk is very chatty and will generate lots of traffic between interfaces.

49 Use this router to seed the network [Services-Services for Macintosh-Routing-Adapter]

The seed router defines the zone name and network number for a physical network. AppleTalk devices remember the zone, so new zones should not be created without care and planning.

50 Network Range [Services-Services for Macintosh-Routing-Adapter]

AppleTalk network numbers group computers on physical LANs. There can be multiple networks on the same LAN, but networks cannot span multiple LANs. To enter a single network number for a LAN, use the same number in the **From** and **To** fields.

51 Get Zones [Services-Services for Macintosh-Routing-Adapter]

Refresh the list of zones.

52 Make Default [Services-Services for Macintosh-Routing-Adapter]

Make the NT server appear in this zone.

53 Simple TCP/IP Services [Services]

The Simple TCP/IP services add the ability to respond to echo, discard, daytime, quote of the day, and chargen requests. These services can be used to debug TCP/IP networking, but they will not be interesting to most people.

54 SNMP Service [Services]

The **Simple Network Management Protocol** (SNMP) is intended to facilitate remote monitoring and management of large and complex networks. Any network device can be queried for statistics or can generate messages (traps) if some event occurs. Typically, you need a network management console (such as HP OpenView) to gather all the SNMP information and process it. The contents and types of SNMP messages are described in a Management Information Base (MIB). Computers and network devices that participate in SNMP can be grouped in *communities*, providing a method to structure network management based on geographical position, management responsibility, or some other criteria.

55 **Agent** [Services-SNMP Service-Properties]

The **Agent** is a service running on the computer which either responds to SNMP queries or sends traps to the management console when something occurs.

56 **Traps** [Services-SNMP Service-Properties]

A trap is a condition that causes the computer to send a message to the management console.

57 **Security** [Services-SNMP Service-Properties-Traps]

Since SNMP messages could give away information about your network, make sure that the computer is sending SNMP packets to the right community and receiving SNMP packets from legitimate sources.

58 **Send Authentication Trap** [Services-SNMP Service-Properties-Traps-Security]

The management console can be notified if there are authentication failures (possibly indicating a break-in attempt).

59 **Windows Internet Name Service** [Services]

(Server only) The WINS service maps computer names to IP addresses.

60 **Workstation** [Services]

The **Workstation** service adds the client side of Microsoft Networking.

Protocols

All of the following protocols can be installed on Windows NT Workstation and Server from the CD-ROM distribution.

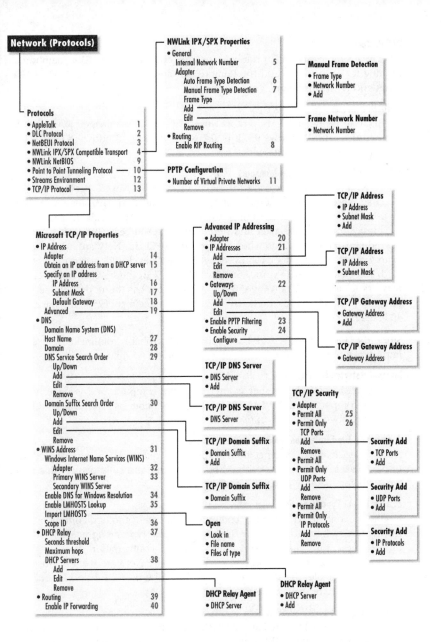

Network (Protocols)

Protocols
- AppleTalk — 1
- DLC Protocol — 2
- NetBEUI Protocol — 3
- NWLink IPX/SPX Compatible Transport — 4
- NWLink NetBIOS — 9
- Point to Point Tunneling Protocol — 10
- Streams Environment — 12
- TCP/IP Protocol — 13

NWLink IPX/SPX Properties
- General
  Internal Network Number — 5
  Adapter
    Auto Frame Type Detection — 6
    Manual Frame Type Detection — 7
    Frame Type
    Add
    Edit
    Remove
- Routing
  Enable RIP Routing — 8

Manual Frame Detection
- Frame Type
- Network Number
- Add

Frame Network Number
- Network Number

PPTP Configuration
- Number of Virtual Private Networks — 11

Microsoft TCP/IP Properties
- IP Address
  Adapter — 14
  Obtain an IP address from a DHCP server — 15
  Specify an IP address
    IP Address — 16
    Subnet Mask — 17
    Default Gateway — 18
  Advanced — 19
- DNS
  Domain Name System (DNS)
  Host Name — 27
  Domain — 28
  DNS Service Search Order — 29
  Up/Down
  Add
  Edit
  Remove
  Domain Suffix Search Order — 30
  Up/Down
  Add
  Edit
  Remove
- WINS Address — 31
  Windows Internet Name Services (WINS)
  Adapter — 32
  Primary WINS Server — 33
  Secondary WINS Server
  Enable DNS for Windows Resolution — 34
  Enable LMHOSTS Lookup — 35
  Import LMHOSTS
  Scope ID — 36
- DHCP Relay — 37
  Seconds threshold
  Maximum hops
  DHCP Servers — 38
  Add
  Edit
  Remove
- Routing — 39
  Enable IP Forwarding — 40

Advanced IP Addressing
- Adapter — 20
- IP Addresses — 21
  Add
  Edit
  Remove
- Gateways — 22
  Up/Down
  Add
  Edit
- Enable PPTP Filtering — 23
- Enable Security — 24
  Configure

TCP/IP Address
- IP Address
- Subnet Mask
- Add

TCP/IP Address
- IP Address
- Subnet Mask

TCP/IP Gateway Address
- Gateway Address
- Add

TCP/IP Gateway Address
- Gateway Address

TCP/IP DNS Server
- DNS Server
- Add

TCP/IP DNS Server
- DNS Server

TCP/IP Domain Suffix
- Domain Suffix
- Add

TCP/IP Domain Suffix
- Domain Suffix

Open
- Look in
- File name
- Files of type

TCP/IP Security
- Adapter
- Permit All — 25
- Permit Only — 26
  TCP Ports
  Add
  Remove
- Permit All
- Permit Only
  UDP Ports
  Add
  Remove
- Permit All
- Permit Only
  IP Protocols
  Add
  Remove

Security Add
- TCP Ports
- Add

Security Add
- UDP Ports
- Add

Security Add
- IP Protocols
- Add

DHCP Relay Agent
- DHCP Server

DHCP Relay Agent
- DHCP Server
- Add

1 **AppleTalk**

AppleTalk is the native protocol of the Apple Macintosh. Windows NT Workstation and Server can both print to AppleTalk printers, and NT Server can share files to Macintosh clients. For some strange reason, the AppleTalk protocol does not appear in the **Protocols** list when it is installed on NT Server.

2   DLC Protocol

DLC is a simple network protocol used for connectivity to IBM mainframes, printing to HP printers, and the **Remoteboot** service for booting diskless Windows and DOS computers.

3   NetBEUI Protocol

NetBEUI is the default LAN protocol used by MS LAN Manager, Windows for Workgroups, and Windows 95. It is also supported by Windows NT. TCP/IP is preferable in most situations.

4   NWLink IPX/SPX Compatible Transport

The IPX/SPX protocol is used to communicate with Novell NetWare servers. Because there is a huge number of NetWare installations, IPX may already be in use on your LAN. It is similar to NetBEUI and AppleTalk in that it uses broadcasts to configure itself and find network resources. This makes for very few administration options when compared to TCP/IP. NetWare addresses are simply a network number followed by the MAC-level address of the network card: for example, 40.00AA00A584EF. This NetWare address is interpreted as network 40 and node 00AA00A584EF. A broadcast has the node field set to all ones, which is represented by FF in hexadecimal (255 in base 10), 40.FFFFFFFFFFFF.

Since the Internet is TCP/IP-based, IPX will probably diminish in use and importance over time, but it will still be around for a while.

5   Internal Network Number [NWLink IPX/SPX Compatible Transport-General]

The Internal Network Number is internal to the computer and is never visible to other computers on the LAN. It can be any number as long as it is different from any network number in use on the LAN.

6   Auto Frame Type Detection [NWLink IPX/SPX Compatible Transport-General]

Novell has changed Ethernet frame types over different versions of NetWare. In most cases, the computer should be able to automatically detect what frame type is being used by other IPX computers.

7   Manual Frame Type Detection [NWLink IPX/SPX Compatible Transport-General]

If you are unable to establish communication with another computer using IPX, you may have to manually specify the frame type being used. If you are unsure, you can check the NetWare server configuration files (such as *autoexec.ncf*) or run the *config* command on the NetWare server console. If this is not possible, the *ipxroute* command may be useful for finding out what frame types are in use on the network.

8   Enable RIP Routing [NWLink IPX/SPX Compatible Transport-Routing]

If you have the **RIP for NwLink IPX/SPX compatible transport** service installed, the computer can route IPX traffic using the IPX RIP routing protocol. TCP/IP also has a routing protocol called RIP, but they are not the same.

9   NWLink NetBIOS

NWLink NetBIOS is a NetWare-specific version of NetBIOS that is supported by both NetWare and Windows NT.

10   Point to Point Tunneling Protocol

PPTP is used to create encrypted tunnels between RAS clients and servers called **Virtual Private Networks** (VPN). It is part of RAS and is configured with

Dial-Up Networking in the **Accessories** menu and **Remote Access Admin** in the **Administrative Tools** menu.

11 **Number of Virtual Private Networks** [Point to Point Tunneling Protocol]
The number of VPNs is the maximum number of simultaneous PPTP sessions. For DUN clients, you probably need only one VPN. For RAS servers, you will need as many VPNs as the number of clients that could be dialed-in at one time.

12 **Streams Environment**
The Streams Environment makes it easier to port applications that use STREAMS networking from UNIX to NT.

13 **TCP/IP Protocol**
The TCP/IP protocol suite is the native protocol of the UNIX and the Internet. When compared to other protocols, it is better suited for complex networks of LANs and WANs.

As the TCP/IP protocol is not very good at autoconfiguration, several pieces of information must be manually entered before TCP/IP can be used. DHCP can provide most of the basic configuration, but anything advanced has to be entered manually.

14 **Adapter** [TCP/IP Protocol-IP Address]
Each adapter needs a unique IP address.

15 **Obtain an IP address from a DHCP server** [TCP/IP Protocol-IP Address]
If there is a DHCP server on the network, this may make manual configuration unnecessary.

16 **IP Address** [TCP/IP Protocol-IP Address-Specify an IP address]
Specify an IP address for the selected adapter.

17 **Subnet Mask** [TCP/IP Protocol-IP Address-Specify an IP address]
The subnet mask tells TCP/IP what part of the IP address is the network number and what part is the host number.

18 **Default Gateway** [TCP/IP Protocol-IP Address-Specify an IP address]
Any packet to networks that do not have a known route is sent to the default gateway.

19 **Advanced** [TCP/IP Protocol-IP Address]
The advanced menu lets you create multiple IP addresses and default gateways for a single adapter and configures security options.

20 **Adapter** [TCP/IP Protocol-IP Address-Advanced]
All of the following settings apply to the selected adapter.

21 **IP Addresses** [TCP/IP Protocol-IP Address-Advanced]
A single adapter can have multiple IP addresses on the same network. This is called *multihoming*, and is widely used on web servers to track which hostname was used to contact the web server.

22 **Gateways** [TCP/IP Protocol-IP Address-Advanced]
It is possible to have multiple gateways on the same network. As they are tried in the order they are listed, you can use the up/down arrows to re-order them.

23 **Enable PPTP Filtering** [TCP/IP Protocol-IP Address-Advanced]

PPTP filtering prevents any use of the network interface other than PPTP. This may be helpful when securing an interface against the Internet. Be aware that this has the effect of preventing any other protocol from using the interface.

24 **Enable Security** [TCP/IP Protocol-IP Address-Advanced]

The security settings enable a simple packet filtering feature so that you can select which protocols and port numbers are allowed to use the selected interface.

25 **Permit All** [TCP/IP Protocol-IP Address-Advanced-Enable Security-Configure]

All TCP, UDP, or IP packets are allowed.

26 **Permit Only** [TCP/IP Protocol-IP Address-Advanced-Enable Security-Configure]

Allow only certain port or protocol numbers through the network interface. You can examine the *SERVICES* file for UDP and TCP port numbers and the *PROTOCOLS* file for IP protocol numbers. Both files are in *<winnt root>\SYS-TEM32\DRIVERS\ETC.* Unfortunately, you cannot use aliases for ports and protocols. For example, you have to type in *25* instead of *SMTP*. There also does not seem to be a way to enter a range of ports, which would be important for many common TCP and UDP services. For example, FTP uses TCP port 21 when it establishes a control connection, but it chooses a random port number (above 1023) for the data connection.

27 **Host Name** [TCP/IP Protocol-DNS]

The TCP/IP hostname can be either the same as or completely different from the NetBIOS computer name.

28 **Domain** [TCP/IP Protocol-DNS]

The DNS domain name of the organization to which this computer belongs. This has nothing to do with Windows NT domains.

29 **DNS Service Search Order** [TCP/IP Protocol-DNS]

Up to three different DNS servers can be specified in order to provide some redundancy in DNS lookups. If the first DNS server is unreachable, the second is tried, and so on. If all three DNS servers are unreachable, the lookup fails.

30 **Domain Suffix Search Order** [TCP/IP Protocol-DNS]

A list of domain names that should be appended to a hostname when looking up the name. If you have multiple domains within a single organization, this can make it easier for people to type hostnames without specifying the domain name, but there will be a slight delay for each unsuccessful lookup.

31 **WINS Address** [TCP/IP Protocol]

Configure the computer to contact a WINS server for computer name lookups (as opposed to broadcasting a request).

32 **Adapter** [TCP/IP Protocol-WINS Address-Windows Internet Name Services (WINS)]

WINS server information must be separately configured for each adapter.

33 **Primary WINS Server** [TCP/IP Protocol-WINS Address-Windows Internet Name Services (WINS)]

If the computer is a WINS server, put its own IP address as the primary.

34 **Enable DNS for Windows Resolution** [TCP/IP Protocol-WINS Address]

Consult DNS when looking up NetBIOS computer names. This will be most useful if the NetBIOS computer names are the same as the TCP/IP hostnames.

35 **Enable LMHOSTS Lookup** [TCP/IP Protocol-WINS Address]

Look for computer names in the LMHOSTS file (found in *<winnt root>\SYS-TEM32\DRIVERS\ETC*).

36 **Scope ID** [TCP/IP Protocol-WINS Address]

A *scope* is a little-used method of grouping computers on the network. If a scope ID is entered, only computers with the same ID can see each other on the network. The scope ID has nothing to do with a DHCP Scope.

37 **DHCP Relay** [TCP/IP Protocol]

If a DHCP server is not available on the local subnet, the computer can relay DHCP broadcasts to a DHCP server on a separate network. Normally, a router would prevent the remote DHCP server from receiving the DHCP broadcasts.

38 **DHCP Servers** [TCP/IP Protocol-DHCP Relay]

The IP addresses of the remote DHCP servers to relay DHCP requests.

39 **Routing** [TCP/IP Protocol]

NT 4.0 comes with support for the TCP/IP RIP protocol, which is the most common routing protocol used in small to medium networks.

40 **Enable IP Forwarding** [TCP/IP Protocol-Routing]

IP forwarding is the process of sending network traffic received on one network interface to another interface. Normally, the computer would process only traffic specifically addressed to itself.

Network Monitor Agent

Requires

NT Workstation or Server
Network Monitor Agent service

Summary

The **Network Monitor Agent** acts as a proxy for the **Network Monitor** tool. It allows someone running **Network Monitor** on another computer on the network to connect to the local computer's network interface, capture network traffic, and send the capture back to the remote computer. The agent can work with either the **Network Monitor** application included with NT 4.0 Server or the one included with **System Management Server** (SMS). It is very useful, as it allows a central monitoring station to connect to computers distributed over various remote networks and to gather data and statistics. This functionality is similar to SNMP RMON devices.

Note that **Network Monitor Agent** is set to manual startup by default and must be started before a remote computer can connect to it. This is desirable, as it lessens the chance that you would allow someone to connect unintentionally.

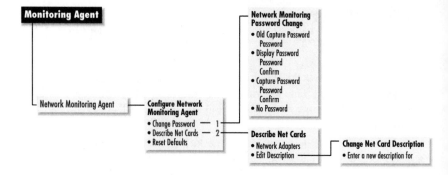

1   **Change Password** [Network Monitoring Agent]

Set a password for the remote **Network Monitor** application that is going to connect to the local agent. There are two levels of access:

- *Display* allows viewing of previously captured data.

- *Capture* allows capture of current network traffic by the remote application.

2   **Describe Net Cards** [Network Monitoring Agent]

Allows you to add a comment to the network interface description that will be displayed to the remote **Network Monitor** application. While running the **Network Monitor**, this description appears in the **Capture-Networks** window when you make a connection to machine running the **Network Monitor Agent**.

ODBC

Requires

NT Workstation or Server

Summary

The **ODBC** (Open Database Connectivity) control panel adds, configures, or removes data sources for ODBC-compliant databases. The ODBC control panel associates an ODBC driver with a data source name (DSN), allowing an application to interact with a database on the local computer or a remote computer on the network. A DSN can be either a user DSN, which is tied to a specific user, or a system DSN, which can be used by any user on the computer. The control panel has a rather confusing layout, but the options for setting up a user DSN are identical to those for the system DSN.

In some cases, ODBC drivers will be installed as part of the database installation process, meaning that you will not have to visit the control panel. You may still find it useful for creating a DSN to access a remote database server over the network.

When you hit the **Add** or **Setup** buttons you leave the generic control panel menu and enter information specific to the selected ODBC driver.

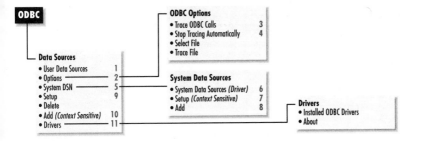

1   User Data Sources

The initial display lists all installed user DSNs, with drivers. If you are working on system DSNs, use the **System DSN** button.

2   Options

Set debugging options for ODBC calls.

3   Trace ODBC Calls [Options]

Record all ODBC calls in a file.

4   Stop Tracing Automatically [Options]

Stop tracing when an application terminates ODBC. The tracing must be manually enabled before it starts again. This is useful when you want to trace a single session at a time.

5   System DSN

Modify system DSN for local computer data sources.

6   System Data Sources [System DSN]

List of installed system DSNs and drivers.

7   Setup [System DSN]

Configure an existing system DSN. The fields are specific to the selected driver.

8   Add [System DSN]

Add a new system DSN. The fields are the same as in **Setup**.

9   Setup

Configure an existing user DSN. The fields are specific to the selected driver.

10   Add

Add a user DSN. The fields are the same as in **Setup**.

11   Drivers

Lists installed ODBC drivers.

PC Card (PCMCIA)

Requires

NT Workstation or Server
PC Card Slot

Summary

The **PC Card** control panel installs, configures, and removes PC Card devices. The primary use of the control panel is to install modems and Ethernet cards on laptop computers.

In practice, the PC Card will probably come with an installer from the card manufacturer and the function of the control panel will be to check if the card is working properly.

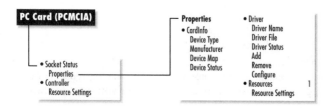

1   **Resources** [Socket Status-Properties]

Displays the IRQ and I/O range used by the selected PC Card device. As NT 4.0 lacks true plug-and-play functionality, this control panel is helpful in confirming that there are no IRQ conflicts.

Ports

Requires

NT Workstation or Server

Summary

The **Ports** control panel specifies communication settings for serial ports. As NT may not automatically detect a new port, you may have to manually add and configure the ports before they can be used by hardware such as printers, mice, or modems, and applications such as RAS or HyperTerminal.

If you are adding new hardware, the **Resources** tab of the **Windows NT Diagnostics** tool is a good place to look for system-wide resource settings. Carefully choose the new settings to avoid conflicts with existing hardware.

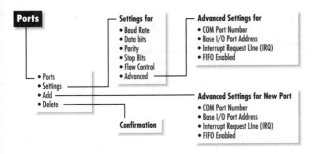

Printers

Requires

NT Workstation or Server

Summary

The **Printers** control panel adds, configures, and deletes local and network printers. It controls how printers are shared on the network and share permissions. Both local and network print queues can be monitored from the control panel.

The **Add Printer** wizard adds the ability to print to a printer via a local port or network port and to accept print jobs from other computers via the network. New printers are added with the **Add Printer** wizard. Existing printers can be modified by selecting the printer icon and **File-Properties** (or right-clicking on the printer icon).

Note: the **Printers** control panel is actually a shortcut to **Start-Settings-Printers**. Refer to the following figure for an illustration of the menu structure.

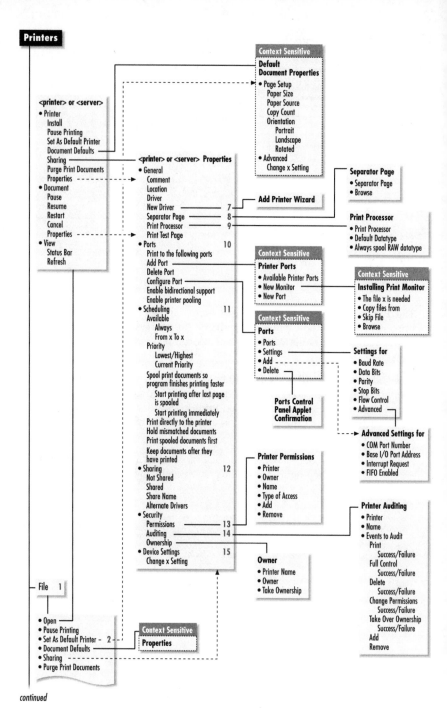

Printers

<printer> or <server>
- Printer
  Install
  Pause Printing
  Set As Default Printer
  Document Defaults
  Sharing
  Purge Print Documents
  Properties
- Document
  Pause
  Resume
  Restart
  Cancel
  Properties
- View
  Status Bar
  Refresh

Context Sensitive
Default Document Properties
- Page Setup
  Paper Size
  Paper Source
  Copy Count
  Orientation
  Portrait
  Landscape
  Rotated
- Advanced
  Change x Setting

<printer> or <server> Properties
- General
  Comment
  Location
  Driver
  New Driver ———— 7
  Separator Page ———— 8
  Print Processor ———— 9
  Print Test Page
- Ports   10
  Print to the following ports
  Add Port
  Delete Port
  Configure Port
  Enable bidirectional support
  Enable printer pooling
- Scheduling   11
  Available
  Always
  From x To x
  Priority
  Lowest/Highest
  Current Priority
  Spool print documents so
  program finishes printing faster
  Start printing after last page
  is spooled
  Start printing immediately
  Print directly to the printer
  Hold mismatched documents
  Print spooled documents first
  Keep documents after they
  have printed
- Sharing   12
  Not Shared
  Shared
  Share Name
  Alternate Drivers
- Security
  Permissions ———— 13
  Auditing ———— 14
  Ownership
- Device Settings   15
  Change x Setting

Add Printer Wizard

Separator Page
- Separator Page
- Browse

Print Processor
- Print Processor
- Default Datatype
- Always spool RAW datatype

Context Sensitive
Printer Ports
- Available Printer Ports
- New Monitor
- New Port

Context Sensitive
Installing Print Monitor
- The file x is needed
- Copy files from
- Skip File
- Browse

Context Sensitive
Ports
- Ports
- Settings
- Add
- Delete

Ports Control Panel Applet Confirmation

Settings for
- Baud Rate
- Data Bits
- Parity
- Stop Bits
- Flow Control
- Advanced

Advanced Settings for
- COM Port Number
- Base I/O Port Address
- Interrupt Request
- FIFO Enabled

Printer Permissions
- Printer
- Owner
- Name
- Type of Access
- Add
- Remove

Printer Auditing
- Printer
- Name
- Events to Audit
  Print
  Success/Failure
  Full Control
  Success/Failure
  Delete
  Success/Failure
  Change Permissions
  Success/Failure
  Take Over Ownership
  Success/Failure
  Add
  Remove

Owner
- Printer Name
- Owner
- Take Ownership

File   1
- Open
- Pause Printing
- Set As Default Printer - 2
- Document Defaults
- Sharing
- Purge Print Documents

Context Sensitive
Properties

continued

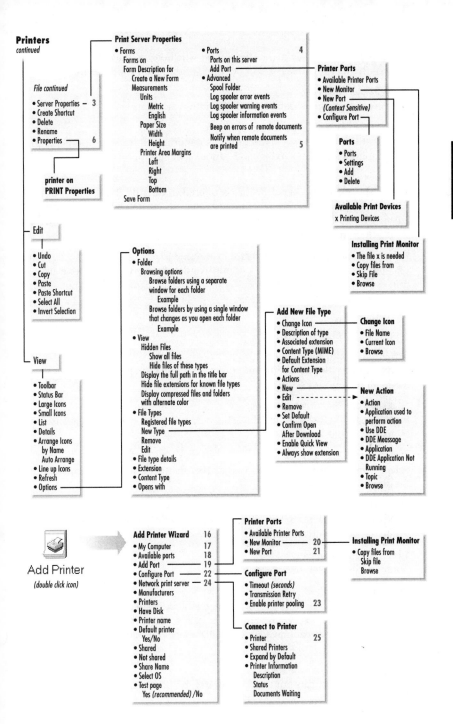

Printers
continued

Print Server Properties

• Forms
  Forms on
  Form Description for
    Create a New Form
    Measurements
      Units
        Metric
        English
      Paper Size
        Width
        Height
      Printer Area Margins
        Left
        Right
        Top
        Bottom
  Save Form

• Ports   4
  Ports on this server
  Add Port
• Advanced
  Spool Folder
  Log spooler error events
  Log spooler warning events
  Log spooler information events
  Beep on errors of remote documents
  Notify when remote documents
  are printed   5

File continued

• Server Properties — 3
• Create Shortcut
• Delete
• Rename
• Properties ——— 6

**printer on
PRINT Properties**

Printer Ports
• Available Printer Ports
• New Monitor
• New Port
  (Context Sensitive)
• Configure Port

Ports
• Ports
• Settings
• Add
• Delete

Available Print Devices
x Printing Devices

Edit
• Undo
• Cut
• Copy
• Paste
• Paste Shortcut
• Select All
• Invert Selection

Installing Print Monitor
• The file x is needed
• Copy files from
• Skip File
• Browse

Options
• Folder
  Browsing options
    Browse folders using a separate
    window for each folder
      Example
    Browse folders by using a single window
    that changes as you open each folder
      Example
• View
  Hidden Files
    Show all files
    Hide files of these types
  Display the full path in the title bar
  Hide file extensions for known file types
  Display compressed files and folders
  with alternate color
• File Types
  Registered file types
  New Type
  Remove
  Edit
• File type details
• Extension
• Content Type
• Opens with

View
• Toolbar
• Status Bar
• Large Icons
• Small Icons
• List
• Details
• Arrange Icons
  by Name
  Auto Arrange
• Line up Icons
• Refresh
• Options

Add New File Type
• Change Icon
• Description of type
• Associated extension
• Content Type (MIME)
• Default Extension
  for Content Type
• Actions
• New
• Edit
• Remove
• Set Default
• Confirm Open
  After Download
• Enable Quick View
• Always show extension

Change Icon
• File Name
• Current Icon
• Browse

New Action
• Action
• Application used to
  perform action
• Use DDE
• DDE Meassage
• Application
• DDE Application Not
  Running
• Topic
• Browse

Add Printer
(double click icon)

Add Printer Wizard   16
• My Computer   17
• Available ports   18
• Add Port ——— 19
• Configure Port ——— 22
• Network print server — 24
• Manufacturers
• Printers
• Have Disk
• Printer name
• Default printer
  Yes/No
• Shared
• Not shared
• Share Name
• Select OS
• Test page
  Yes *(recommended)* /No

Printer Ports
• Available Printer Ports
• New Monitor ——— 20
• New Port   21

Configure Port
• Timeout *(seconds)*
• Transmission Retry
• Enable printer pooling   23

Connect to Printer
• Printer   25
• Shared Printers
• Expand by Default
• Printer Information
  Description
  Status
  Documents Waiting

Installing Print Monitor
• Copy files from
  Skip file
  Browse

1 **File**

The contents of the **File** menu depend on whether you have a printer selected. Most of the menu items can also be found within the **Properties** menu.

2 **Set As Default Printer** [File]

Set selected printer as default for all Windows applications.

3 **Server Properties** [File]

The Properties window controls various paper and form sizes, ports for printing, monitors for print serving, and various logging options.

4 **Ports** [File-Server Properties]

This is the same port window that is offered in the **Add Printer** wizard. If you have a large number of printers to add, you can create all the needed ports in advance of adding the printers. To add the individual printers, all you need to do is select from the list of existing ports.

5 **Notify when remote documents are printed** [File-Server Properties-Advanced]

Enabled by default; produces a popup window every time someone uses the print server running on the local computer. This can be very annoying and should be turned off in most cases.

6 **Properties** [File]

Configure existing printer.

7 **New Driver** [File-Open-Printer-Properties-General]

Change printer driver. Use this if you are changing the printer type but wish to retain all the current settings.

8 **Separator Page** [File-Open-Printer-Properties-General]

Insert a page between print jobs. This may be useful when a printer is shared by many people.

9 **Print Processor** [File-Open-Printer-Properties-General]

Select how the print job is processed. This will depend on the capabilities of the printer.

10 **Ports** [File-Open-Printer-Properties]

Configure printing ports for selected printer. See **My Computer-Available Ports** inside the **Add Printer** wizard.

11 **Scheduling** [File-Open-Printer-Properties]

Configure how print jobs are prioritized.

12 **Sharing** [File-Open-Printer-Properties]

Share the printer on the network for all enabled protocols. For example, if you have AppleTalk and TCP/IP Printing installed, the printer will be shared on AppleTalk and be made available to LPD clients, in addition to Microsoft Networking clients.

13 **Permissions** [File-Open-Printer-Properties-Security]

Select which users can print and/or control the printer queue.

14 **Auditing** [File-Open-Printer-Properties-Security]

Audit printer-related events to the Event Viewer log for the selected users. You can use this information to determine who uses the printers and how often.

15 **Device Settings** [File-Open-Printer-Properties]

Configure settings specific to printer type and model.

16 **Add Printer**

The **Add Printer** wizard is one of the few wizards that you will use all the time.

17 **My Computer** [Add Printer]

Use this option if the printer is directly connected to the local computer via a parallel or serial port, or if the local computer is going to send jobs directly to a networked printer. If another computer is acting as a print server for the printer you want to use, you should probably connect to it instead of the printer. Use **Network Print Server** for this situation.

18 **Available ports** [Add Printer-My Computer]

A port could be either a physical port such as parallel (LPT) or serial (COM) port, or a network port. A network port uses a network protocol, such as Net-BEUI, AppleTalk, TCP/IP, or DLC to send print jobs from the local computer to the remote printer. The Available Ports window is rather small and you may have to resize the description field in order to see the full name of network ports.

19 **Add Port** [Add Printer-My Computer]

When you add a port, you are adding another possible destination for print jobs. The configuration options depend on the type of port being added. If you are using a network port, you need the correct protocol installed in order to communicate with the network printer. The list of available printer ports is determined by what optional services and protocols you have installed previously using the **Network** control panel. For example, if you want to print to an Apple LaserWriter that supports only AppleTalk, you will have to install the AppleTalk protocol. In this case, you have to install **Services for the Macintosh** using the **Services-Add** button in the **Network** control panel.

20 **New Monitor** [Add Printer-My Computer-Add Port]

A monitor listens on the network for print jobs being sent via a certain protocol. This gives the computer the ability to act as a print server for other computers that speak this protocol. In practice, the ability to act as print server for a specific protocol is usually added with the **Network** control panel.

21 **New Port** [Add Printer-My Computer-Add Port]

When you select a specific printer port type, a protocol-specific menu appears. For example, an AppleTalk port requires that you choose an AppleTalk printer within an AppleTalk Zone. An LPR port requires the TCP/IP hostname or IP address of the remote printer and the remote printer name.

22 **Configure Port** [Add Printer-My Computer]

Some of port types have configuration options that can be set here. For COM ports, this invokes the **Ports** control panel.

23 Enable printer pooling [Add Printer-My Computer-Configure Port]

If you have two identical printers, you can set up a single print queue to print to them. This way, you distribute the print load and add some transparent redundancy to printing.

24 Network print server [Add Printer]

If the printer you want to use is being offered by another computer acting as print server, connect to it using this option. If you want to connect directly to a printer, use the **My Computer** option.

25 Printer [Add Printer-My Computer-Network Print Server]

Either type in the UNC pathname of the printer or browse the network for it. Once you locate a valid printer, you are prompted to select the printer driver.

Regional Settings

Requires

NT Workstation or Server

Summary

The **Regional Settings** control panel administers language and region-specific settings on the local computer. If the computer is going to be used in a country other than one it was installed in, the control panel can be used to reconfigure the regional settings. Different *locales* that exist on the same computer can be toggled by special key sequences. A locale is a regional and language-specific collection of settings for the display of dates, currency, times and numbers, characters, and keyboard mappings.

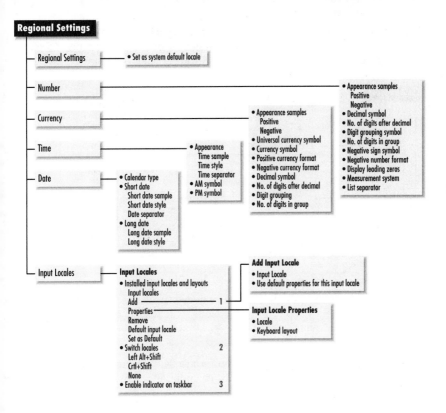

Regional Settings ── • Set as system default locale

Number

Currency

Time

Date
- Calendar type
- Short date
  Short date sample
  Short date style
  Date separator
- Long date
  Long date sample
  Long date style

• Appearance
  Time sample
  Time style
  Time separator
• AM symbol
• PM symbol

• Appearance samples
  Positive
  Negative
• Universal currency symbol
• Currency symbol
• Positive currency format
• Negative currency format
• Decimal symbol
• No. of digits after decimal
• Digit grouping
• No. of digits in group

• Appearance samples
  Positive
  Negative
• Decimal symbol
• No. of digits after decimal
• Digit grouping symbol
• No. of digits in group
• Negative sign symbol
• Negative number format
• Display leading zeros
• Measurement system
• List separator

Input Locales ── **Input Locales**
- Installed input locales and layouts
  Input locales
  Add ────────── 1
  Properties ────
  Remove
  Default input locale
  Set as Default
- Switch locales ────── 2
  Left Alt+Shift
  Crtl+Shift
  None
- Enable indicator on taskbar ── 3

Add Input Locale
- Input Locale
- Use default properties for this input locale

Input Locale Properties
- Locale
- Keyboard layout

Control Panel

---

1 Add [Input Locales-Installed input locales and layouts]

Add a new locale, in addition to the current one. For example, both EN English (United States) and FR French (Standard) can be installed on the same computer, and different users can switch to their preferred locale.

2 Switch locales [Input Locales]

Enable toggling between different locales by key sequences.

3 Enable indicator on taskbar [Input locales-Switch locales]

A two-letter locale code indicates the current locale on the taskbar. Clicking on the indicator switches locales.

SCSI Adapters

Requires

NT Workstation or Server

Summary

The **SCSI Adapters** control panel can add, configure, and remove SCSI and IDE controllers.

Note that there is no IDE control panel. You need to use the SCSI control panel for both IDE and SCSI controllers.

If you are adding new hardware, the **Resources** tab of the **Windows NT Diagnostics** tool is a good place to look for system-wide resource settings. Carefully choose the new settings to avoid conflicts with existing hardware.

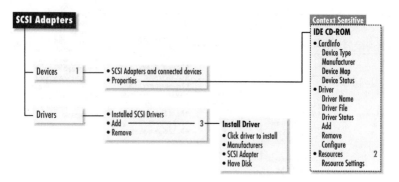

1 **Devices**

Double-clicking on a selected adapter will display all the devices connected to the adapter. For example, a SCSI adapter will display all disks, tapes, and CD-ROMs connected to its SCSI bus.

2 **Resources** [Devices-Properties]

Display IRQ and I/O port information for installed adapters or device specific information for a selected device. For example, if a SCSI disk is selected, the SCSI ID is displayed (as *Target ID*).

3 **Add** [Drivers]

Add a new adapter device driver.

Server

Requires

NT Workstation or Server
NT Server (for Replication Export)

Command-Line Equivalents

net file
net share
net session

Summary

The **Server** control panel gives detailed information about file sharing activity on the local computer. It can tell you which users are attached to the local computer and what files they are using. While the **Server Manager** administrative tool can manage computers on the network, the **Server** control panel can manage only the local computer. It also manages file replication to and from the computer, which is normally used to copy user logon scripts to other servers.

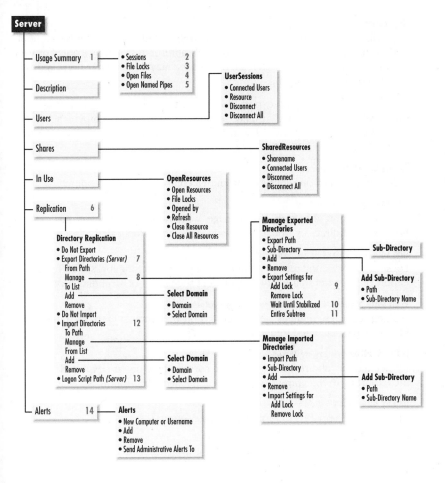

Control Panel

---

1 Usage Summary

Possible uses for the summary information include confirming that no one is using the computer before shutting it down and seeing how many licenses are required for client connections.

2 Sessions [Usage Summary]

Displays number of remotely connected users.

3 File Locks [Usage Summary]

Displays number of file locks by connected users. A file lock is created in order to prevent multiple users from overwriting the same file.

4 Open Files [Usage Summary]

Displays number of open files by connected users.

5 Open Named Pipes [Usage Summary]

Displays number of opened named pipes.

6 Replication

Replication is the process of exchanging copies of files with other NT computers on the network. The main use of replication is distributing copies of user information to each computer so that users may logon anywhere and still obtain their personal settings.

NT Server can import and export files. Workstation can only import files. Files (and subdirectories) are usually exported from one computer's *<winnt root>\SYSTEM32\REPL\EXPORT* directory to another computer's *<winnt root>\SYSTEM32\REPL\IMPORT.*

7 Export Directories [Replication]

(Server only) Turn on replication from this computer to other computers.

8 Manage [Replication-Export Directories]

For each export directory, the Manage window sets parameters that control how each subdirectory under the export directory is replicated.

9 Add Lock [Replication-Export Directories-Manage-Export Settings for]

Locks prevent a subdirectory from being replicated. Using locks, you can allow export of the parent directory, but prevent the export of a subdirectory.

10 Wait Until Stabilized [Replication-Export Directories-Manage-Export Settings for]

Waiting for a few minutes before replication may reduce network traffic if the files are being changed frequently.

11 Entire Subtree [Replication-Export Directories-Manage-Export Settings for]

By default, all subdirectories under the current directory are exported. To limit the exporting to the current subdirectory, uncheck this option.

12 Import Directories [Replication]

Allow other computers to replicate to this computer.

13 Logon Script Path [Replication]

Local path to directory where logon scripts are stored.

14 Alerts

This window allows you to send alerts to specific users or computers. Administrative alerts are messages that may be of interest to administrators, including security, disk space, printing problems, and more. If you are not logged in as administrator or are not logged in to the local computer, you may miss the alerts.

Services

Requires

NT Workstation or Server

Command-Line Equivalents

net continue
net pause
net start
net stop

Summary

The **Services** control panel can start, stop, and pause services, alter the startup type, and configure services for hardware profiles. After NT is installed, several services must be manually started before optional software can be used.

Unlike the **Devices** control panel, only installed services are listed. The Services control panel can control only an existing service. A service must be added using the **Network** control panel or other installation tool.

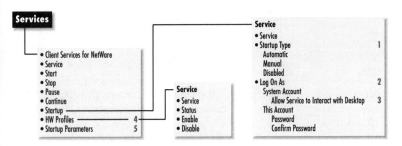

1 **Startup Type** [Startup]

The type determines what happens at boot time, as shown:

Automatic

Service will start every time the system is booted.

Manual

Service will be started only if a user, another service, or a program starts it. For example, the **Network DDE** service is started only if someone starts a program that requires it.

Disabled

Service cannot be started by a user, but could be started by the system if needed.

2 **Log On As** [Startup]

Normally, the services run with the permissions of the System Account, but some services may require the permissions of another user. For example, you may want to run a service with fewer permissions, so it cannot be used to exploit a potential security problem.

3 **Allow Service to Interact with Desktop** [Startup-Log On As-System Account]

Enable this option if the service needs to prompt a user for input. If the service tries to access the desktop for some reason (such as an error) and cannot, the service may hang or stop functioning.

4 **HW Profiles**

Once you have a created a hardware profile using the **System** control panel, you can determine which services should be started when using the profile. For example, if you created two profiles for a laptop for office and home use, you could turn off most of the network services for the home profile. Remember that the device drivers listed in the **Devices** control panel also have to be configured and running for the profile in order for the services to make use of them.

5 **Startup Parameters**

If the service needs parameters when it is started, these can be entered here. The backslash character (\) is an escape character and must be protected by another backslash. For example, if you wanted to pass the UNC name *NTSRV1* to a service, it would have to be typed as *NTSRV1*.

System

Requires

NT Workstation or Server

Summary

The **System** control panel is a catchall for settings and information that did not justify separate control panels. You can change environment variables, paging behavior, application priority, the startup menu, and create, copy, and delete hardware and user profiles.

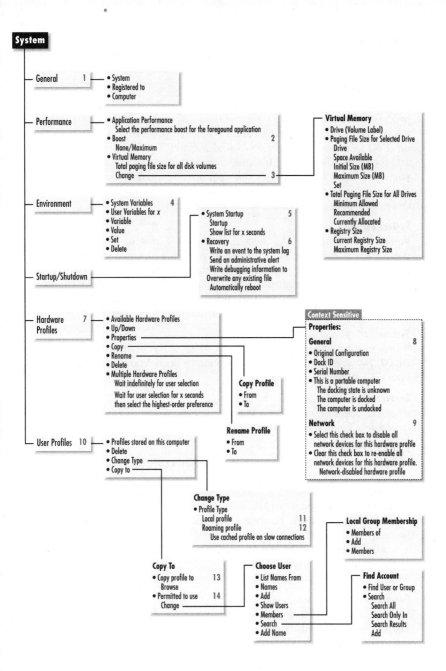

- General   1
  - • System
  - • Registered to
  - • Computer

- Performance
  - • Application Performance
    - Select the performance boost for the foreground application
  - • Boost   2
    - None/Maximum
  - • Virtual Memory
    - Total paging file size for all disk volumes
    - Change   3

- **Virtual Memory**
  - • Drive (Volume Label)
  - • Paging File Size for Selected Drive
    - Drive
    - Space Available
    - Initial Size (MB)
    - Maximum Size (MB)
    - Set
  - • Total Paging File Size for All Drives
    - Minimum Allowed
    - Recommended
    - Currently Allocated
  - • Registry Size
    - Current Registry Size
    - Maximum Registry Size

- Environment
  - • System Variables   4
  - • User Variables for x
  - • Variable
  - • Value
  - • Set
  - • Delete

  - • System Startup   5
    - Startup
    - Show list for x seconds
  - • Recovery   6
    - Write an event to the system log
    - Send an administrative alert
    - Write debugging information to
    - Overwrite any existing file
    - Automatically reboot

- Startup/Shutdown

- Hardware   7
  Profiles
  - • Available Hardware Profiles
  - • Up/Down
  - • Properties
  - • Copy
  - • Rename
  - • Delete
  - • Multiple Hardware Profiles
    - Wait indefinitely for user selection
    - Wait for user selection for x seconds
      then select the highest-order preference

  Copy Profile
  - • From
  - • To

  Context Sensitive
  Properties:

  General   8
  - • Original Configuration
  - • Dock ID
  - • Serial Number
  - • This is a portable computer
    - The docking state is unknown
    - The computer is docked
    - The computer is undocked

  Network   9
  - • Select this check box to disable all
    network devices for this hardware profile
  - • Clear this check box to re-enable all
    network devices for this hardware profile.
    Network-disabled hardware profile

  Rename Profile
  - • From
  - • To

- User Profiles   10
  - • Profiles stored on this computer
  - • Delete
  - • Change Type
  - • Copy to

Change Type
- • Profile Type
  - Local profile   11
  - Roaming profile   12
    - Use cached profile on slow connections

Local Group Membership
- • Members of
- • Add
- • Members

Copy To
- • Copy profile to   13
  - Browse
- • Permitted to use   14
  - Change

Choose User
- • List Names From
- • Names
- • Add
- • Show Users
- • Members
- • Search
- • Add Name

Find Account
- • Find User or Group
- • Search
  - Search All
  - Search Only In
  - Search Results
  - Add

---

1   **General**

Displays information about this computer. This would have been a great place to indicate whether the system was running Workstation or Server and what service packs are applied. (Service pack information is available in **Version** tab of **Windows NT Diagnostics** and the **Help-About Windows NT** menu item on most tools and control panels.)

---

2 Boost [Performance]
Change the priority of the foreground application. You may want to move the slider bar to **None** for servers that are not being used from the console.

3 Change [Performance-Virtual Memory]
Windows NT uses virtual memory, which allows the memory available to processes to be larger than the amount of physical memory (RAM) installed in the computer. Memory being used by inactive processes is paged out (stored on disk) to make room in the physical memory for active processes. The size and location of the paging file can affect system performance. For example, if you have several drives with different speeds, putting the page file on the fastest drive improves performance. Spreading the page file across several drives improves performance by distributing disk I/O.

4 System Variables [Environment]
Variables are used by the system and users to locate files and set various parameters at run time. For example, if you want to add a command in a new directory, you need to add the directory to the *Path* variable in order for the system to find the command. All the directories in the *Path* variable are searched in order when you are using the command line or the **Start-Run** menu. Changes take effect the next time an application is started.

5 System Startup [Startup/Shutdown]
When using a dual- or multiple-boot system, the startup menu (read from *BOOT.INI*) selects which operating system to boot. You can change the default operating system or timeout.

6 Recovery [Startup/Shutdown]
If an NT application crashes, you can tell the system to record the event or create debugging information.

7 Hardware Profiles
Hardware profiles are a way to manage different hardware configurations. The classic example is the laptop computer that needs different PC Cards to function depending on where it is being used. For example, it needs an Ethernet card when connected to a LAN, and a modem card when not connected to the LAN. A computer using hardware profiles presents you with a menu before booting NT (and before any **Startup** *BOOT.INI* menu). Once you have created a hardware profile using the **System** control panel, the **Devices** and **Services** control panels are used to customize which device drivers are loaded and which services are started for the specific profile.

8 General [Hardware Profiles-Properties]
Some laptops have a dock to plug into at a fixed location such as an office. The docking unit usually contains network interfaces or other features that are not required when the laptop is in an undocked state.

9 Network [Hardware Profiles-Properties]
As one of the most common uses of hardware profiles to switch between network and non-networked settings, this setting will turn off all network devices for the non-networked profile.

10 **User Profiles**

User profiles keep track of personal settings, such as the appearance of the Desktop and **Start** menu contents. You can set up multiple users with the same settings by copying user profiles from one user account to another.

11 **Local profile** [User Profiles-Change Type-Profile Type]

A local profile is associated with a specific computer.

12 **Roaming profile** [User Profiles-Change Type-Profile Type]

A roaming profile follows users regardless of what computer they are using.

13 **Copy profile to** [User Profiles-Copy To]

Copy the selected profile to a new location.

14 **Permitted to use** [User Profiles-Copy To]

Control which user or group can use the profile.

Tape Devices

Requires

NT Workstation or Server

Summary

The **Tape Device** control panel installs, configures, or removes tape devices from the local computer. This includes SCSI, IDE, floppy, and parallel port drives.

If you are adding new hardware, the **Resources** tab of the **Windows NT Diagnostics** tool is a good place to look for system-wide resource settings. Carefully choose the new settings to avoid conflicts with existing hardware.

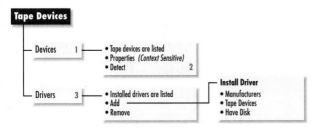

1 **Devices**

Displays a list of all detected tape devices.

2 **Detect** [Devices]

If you have just installed new tape hardware, the **Detect** button tells the system to try to find it and load the appropriate driver.

3 **Drivers**

Displays a list of all tape device drivers being used.

Telephony

Requires

NT Workstation or Server

Summary

The **Telephony** control panel configures many of the same modem properties as the **Modem** control panel. In addition, it can install, configure, and remove different telephony drivers.

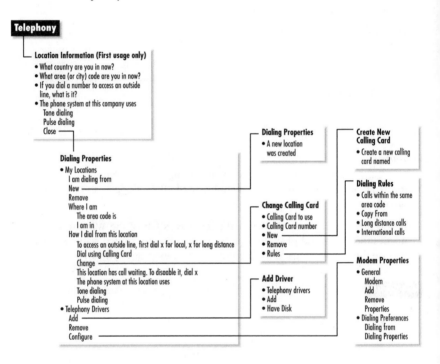

UPS

Requires

NT Workstation or Server

Summary

The **UPS** (uninterruptible power supply) control panel controls how Windows NT interacts with a UPS. A UPS is usually a battery. The NT computer can be configured to be automatically shut down by the UPS when the UPS battery runs low.

The UPS is typically connected to a COM port and can signal the computer about the status of line power and the battery. The UPS service is normally set for manual startup, but the **UPS** control panel will offer to start it for you the first time it is configured.

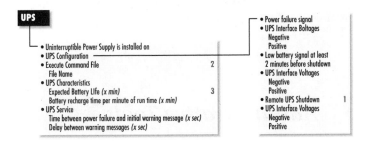

1 **Remote UPS Shutdown** [UPS Configuration]

If the UPS supports this feature, it can signal the computer to shutdown.

2 **Execute Command File**

Configures the UPS service to execute a command before system shutdown. The command must be in the *<winnt root>\SYSTEM32* directory and have a *.BAT, .CMD, .EXE,* or *.COM* extension.

3 **Expected Battery Life** [UPS Characteristics]

Shows expected runtime (in minutes) of a fully charged battery. In practice, you need to run several tests to tune the UPS settings before putting the NT computer into public use. This ensures the computer will gracefully shut down before the battery is completely drained. It also avoids unnecessary shutdowns if the UPS can last long enough to cover the power loss. If you add additional hardware to the computer after the initial UPS configuration, you should adjust the battery life expectations to reflect the increase in battery drain.

CHAPTER 3

Administrative Tools

The **Administrative Tools** manage user and group accounts, configure network services, and diagnose system and network problems. You will notice some overlap in functionality with the **Control Panel**, but the **Administrative Tools** usually offer the ability to manage other computers on the network, while the **Control Panel** manages the local machine only.

Nearly all of the NT administration tools are found in the **Administrative Tools** menu. The contents of the menu depend on what optional software is installed on the computer. Adding a service or protocol may install a corresponding administration tool. Some of the tools do not have shortcuts in the menu system when NT is first installed, but you are free to add your own to make them more accessible.

It is important to separate the role of the administrative tool from the service being administered. Most of the administrative tools have a generic **Select** menu or window listing servers that the tool detects. When you have the local computer selected, you are configuring a service running on the local computer. When you have the domain selected, you are configuring a service running on the PDC. When you have a remote computer selected, the administration tool is running on the local computer, but it is administering a service running on a remote computer. It is possible to use your computer exclusively for administering a remote service, with no local copy of the service running or configured.

Backup

Requires
>   NT Workstation or Server
>   Backup device

Command-Line Equivalents
>   *ntbackup*

Summary

The **Backup** tool backs up or restores file systems from tape media.

Only one mode of operation (either backup or restore) can be active at one time. Operations that would be invalid in the selected mode are inaccessible (grayed-out). The mode is toggled using the **Window** menu. Backup can also be run from the command line as *ntbackup*, allowing unattended operation.

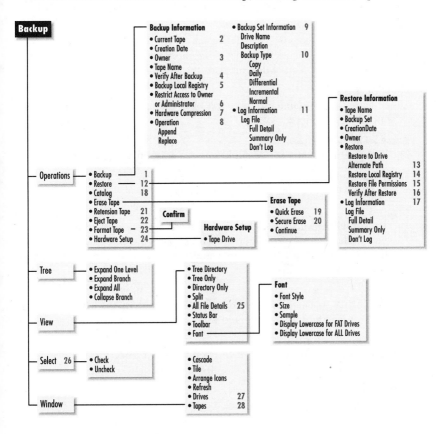

1   **Backup** [Operations]
    Backup selected disks or directories to tape.

2   **Current Tape** [Operations-Backup]
    The first time files are written to a tape, a header is created with a tape name, owner, and date. This can be used to confirm that you are using the correct tape.

3   **Owner** [Operations-Backup]
    Display the owner of the backup set. This can be used to restrict who can read the backup.

4   **Verify After Backup** [Operations-Backup]
    After the backup is completed, compare the files written to the tape with the files stored on disk.

5 **Backup Local Registry** [Operations-Backup]
Backup the Registry to the tape. This is essential if you want to be able to restore the system to exactly match the configuration at the time of backup.

6 **Restrict Access to Owner or Administrator** [Operations-Backup]
Allow only the owner or Backup Operators group members to read the tape. In reality, if users could gain access to the tape in a raw form, they may be able to read it regardless of the restriction. True security requires encryption.

7 **Hardware Compression** [Operations-Backup]
Turn on hardware compression. For example, some DDS-2 DAT drives support compression. Turning it on may store more data on the tape, but the tape can be read only by a drive that supports the same compression scheme.

8 **Operation** [Operations-Backup]
Either start at the beginning of the tape overwriting any existing backup sets, or append to existing sets.

9 **Backup Set Information** [Operations-Backup]
The name of the backup set. Multiple sets can exist on a single tape.

10 **Backup Type** [Operations-Backup-Backup Set Information]
Select one of the following backup types:

Copy
> Backup all specified files, but do not mark them as backed up. This prevents other backup operations (such as daily, incremental, and differential) from knowing that the files were backed up and compromising your backup strategy.

Daily
> Backup all specified files that have been modified on the same day as the backup. The files are not marked as backed up.

Differential
> Backup specified files that have been modified since the last normal or incremental backup. The files are not marked as backed up.

Incremental
> Backup specified files that have been modified since the last normal or incremental backup. The files are marked as backed up.

Normal
> Backup all specified files and mark them as backed up (default backup type).

11 **Log Information** [Operations-Backup]
Keep a logfile of everything that is backed up. This can be useful in determining when there are problems with the backup procedure. You can also use the logfile to determine which backup contains the file that you wish to restore.

12 **Restore** [Operations]
Read a backup off the tape and write it to a disk.

13 **Alternate Path** [Operations-Restore-Restore]
Restore to a path different from the one used in the backup set. This may be the cautious approach if you are unsure of the backup and do not want to risk overwriting files currently on the disk.

14 **Restore Local Registry** [Operations-Restore-Restore]
Overwrite current Registry with one on tape. This allows the current system to be restored to the exact condition it was in at the time of the backup.

15 **Restore File Permissions** [Operations-Restore-Restore]
If the same users and groups are in use on the current system as on the backup, keeping permissions maintains the same security settings. If the backup is from another system, you may wish to discard the old permissions.

16 **Verify After Restore** [Operations-Restore-Restore]
Check that the restored information matches the backup tape contents.

17 **Log Information** [Operations-Restore]
Keep a logfile of everything that is restored.

18 **Catalog** [Operations]
Display a listing of all backup sets and files on the backup tape. When the list of sets is displayed, select a specific set to list the individual files contained within the set. Note that this operation can take a long time to complete.

19 **Quick Erase** [Operations-Erase Tape]
Overwrite the tape header, leaving the rest of the tape undisturbed. This allows a tape to be quickly reused.

20 **Secure Erase** [Operations-Erase Tape]
Overwrite the entire tape contents. This may be important for security reasons.

21 **Retension Tape** [Operations]
If a tape is poorly wound, retensioning may help (rewinds the entire tape length).

22 **Eject Tape** [Operations]
Eject the tape from the drive (if the drive supports this operation). When running an unattended backup, ejecting the tape after a backup prevents the tape from being accidentally overwritten by subsequent backup operations.

23 **Format Tape** [Operations]
Previous information on the tape may confuse the tape drive or backup tool. Formatting the tape in the drive's native format may help.

24 **Hardware Setup** [Operations]
Select which backup device is being used.

25 **All File Details** [View]
When viewing a directory tree, show all information for a file.

26 **Select**
Select either backup mode (drives) or restore mode (tapes).

27 **Drives** [Window]
Displays a list of drives available for the backup operation.

28 **Tapes** [Window]
Displays a list of tapes available for the restore operation.

DHCP Manager

Requires

NT Server

TCP/IP protocol

Microsoft DHCP Server service

Summary

The **DHCP Manager** manages the **Dynamic Host Configuration Protocol** (DHCP) service. DHCP brings plug-and-play networking to TCP/IP. Normally, any computer that wants to use TCP/IP must be manually configured with at least an IP address, netmask, and default gateway. With DHCP, a computer can broadcast a DHCP request at boot time and obtain all required TCP/IP settings from a DHCP server. This has the effect of centralizing all TCP/IP administration on the DHCP server computer.

In addition to TCP/IP settings, DHCP can provide other information to DHCP clients, enabling the client to be generic and self-configuring regardless of the network it is connected to. For example, you could take a laptop computer to different office locations, connect it to the local network, and always obtain settings appropriate to the location.

A single DHCP server can hand out addresses for different networks. The DHCP addresses are managed in groups called *scopes*. A scope contains an address range for a single IP subnet. The subnet mask defines what addresses are in a scope. For example, all addresses within a single class-C network would be managed as a scope and the subnet mask (255.255.255.0) would apply to the entire scope.

In addition to handing out IP addresses, many different types of information can be supplied by DHCP. These are called DHCP *options*. DHCP options can be provided for a single scope or globally, meaning inclusive of all the scopes managed by a single DHCP server.

As with all broadcast-based protocols, there are special considerations when using DHCP across routers. If a DHCP server is not on the same LAN as the DHCP client, it will never hear the client requests. It is possible to configure a Windows NT server on the same LAN as the DHCP client to act as a DHCP relay and forward the requests to a DHCP server on another network. Some routers can also forward the DHCP requests on their own, as DHCP uses the same packet format as BOOTP, which is commonly supported by routers.

The current DHCP implementation also has problems with implementing redundancy and fault tolerance. DHCP servers do not coordinate information between servers (unlike WINS) and are not aware of each other. It is up to the administrator to come up with a scheme that provides a backup DHCP server if the main one should become unavailable. The most common way to do this is to allocate non-conflicting groups of IP addresses to different DHCP servers. For example, you could give addresses 1–127 to one DHCP server and 128–254 to another. If one DHCP server fails to respond, a second one can still provide a valid IP address to the client.

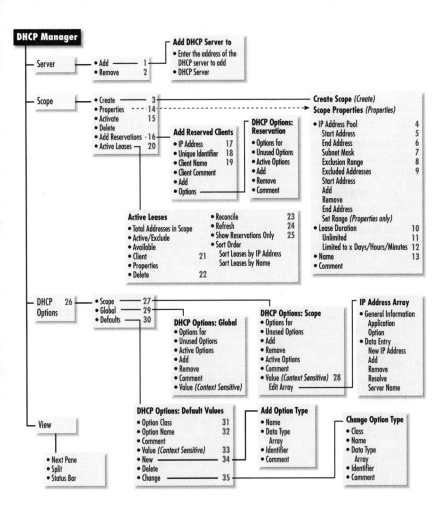

1   Add [Server]

Add a DHCP server to manage. If you want to manage a DHCP server running on a remote computer, enter the computer name or IP address of the remote computer. If the **Microsoft DHCP Server** service is running on the local computer, the DHCP server will automatically list it as *Local Machine* in the DHCP Servers window.

2   Remove [Server]

Remove a DHCP server. This removes only the management connection from DHCP Manager to a DHCP server; does not disturb DHCP server settings.

3   Create [Scope]

Create a new scope on the selected DHCP server.

4   IP Address Pool [Scope-Create]

A pool is a list of all possible IP addresses that could be handed out by DHCP. If you do not want to give out all the addresses within the subnet range, use the exclusion mechanism.

5 **Start Address** [Scope-Create-IP Address Pool]
First address in subnet. Usually this is 1, but it depends on subnet mask.

6 **End Address** [Scope-Create-IP Address Pool]
Last address in subnet. Usually this is 254, but it depends on subnet mask.

7 **Subnet Mask** [Scope-Create-IP Address Pool]
The subnet mask defines the network versus host portion of addresses.

8 **Exclusion Range** [Scope-Create-IP Address Pool]
The range of contiguous addresses to exclude from DHCP. If you want to add only a single address, type it in as the **Start Address** and hit **Add**.

9 **Excluded Addresses** [Scope-Create-IP Address Pool]
Individual or ranges of address that will not be available to DHCP clients.

10 **Lease Duration** [Scope-Create]
A DHCP client has to periodically renew the lease for an IP address. You can also force the client to give up the IP address.

11 **Unlimited** [Scope-Create-Lease Duration]
Allow the IP addresses to be used as long as the client requests them.

12 **Limited to** [Scope-Create-Lease Duration]
Release the IP address from the client after a specific time and put it back in the pool of available addresses.

13 **Name** [Scope-Create]
The name used to describe the scope within **DHCP Manager**.

14 **Properties** [Scope]
Edit an existing scope using same menus as **Scope-Create**.

15 **Activate** [Scope]
Activate an existing scope. A scope must be activated before DHCP will offer it to DHCP clients.

16 **Add Reservations** [Scope]
Always give a specific computer the same name. There may be some computers that need to keep a specific name to function. For example, if you are not using the **Microsoft DNS** server, you have to reserve IP addresses for your email, web, ftp, file, and DNS servers so they are always reachable by the same TCP/IP hostname. You can also put these computer IP addresses in the exclusion list for the scope or even leave them out of DHCP altogether.

17 **IP Address** [Scope-Add Reservations]
IP address that will always be given to this computer.

18 **Unique Identifier** [Scope-Add Reservations]
MAC-level address of computer network adapter (usually the Ethernet address).

19 **Client Name** [Scope-Add Reservations]
Name of computer. This name is known only within DHCP and does not change anything on the client.

20 **Active Leases** [Scope]
Display IP addresses that are in use by DHCP clients and reserved for specific computers.

21 Client [Scope-Active Leases]
Display all currently allocated IP addresses.

22 Delete [Scope-Active Leases]
Delete a lease, freeing up the IP address. If the client computer is still using the IP address, this could stop it from communicating via TCP/IP.

23 Reconcile [Scope-Active Leases]
Run a consistency check on the DHCP database. If you have a large DHCP installation, there may be old leases left by crashed computers that should be made available again.

24 Refresh [Scope-Active Leases]
Update the window with the latest information. DHCP leases can be changing constantly on a busy network.

25 Show Reservations Only [Scope-Active Leases]
Display only reserved IP addresses.

26 DHCP Options
Configure what types of information are provided to DHCP clients on a per-scope and global (every scope) level. The most commonly used DHCP options are as follows:

003 Router
The default gateway (router) for this subnet.

006 DNS Servers
List of three DNS servers.

015 Domain Name
DNS domain name for client.

044 WINS/NBNS Servers
List of IP addresses of WINS servers.

046 WINS/NBT Node Type
Node type for client. This controls how the client resolves computer names. It is usually set to h-node (0x8), which tries directly contacting a WINS server first and then broadcasting if one is unavailable. This reduces traffic on the local LAN. If the WINS client is contacting a WINS server over a WAN, you may wish to use the m-node (0x4), which tries broadcasts on the local LAN first, possibly reducing WAN traffic.

Setting up DHCP to supply these options allows a TCP/IP client to completely configure itself upon boot up or when dialing into to a RAS server.

27 Scope [DHCP Options]
Configure options for the selected scope. Transfer options from the Unused Options window to the Active Options window using the **Add** button.

28 Value [DHCP Options-Scope]
Once a DHCP option is added, edit the value of the option. If there are multiple values within an option, the **Edit Array** button allows you to enter them.

29 Global [DHCP Options]
Set options for all scopes active on selected DHCP server.

30 Defaults [DHCP Options]

Set defaults for all DHCP options being offered to DHCP clients. If there are option values that will be common to all scopes being offered by the DHCP server, setting the values here will save time as opposed to editing the values for each scope individually.

31 Option Class [DHCP Options-Defaults]

A group of DHCP options, normally **DHCP Standard Options**.

32 Option Name [DHCP Options-Defaults]

Specific option to change.

33 Value [DHCP Options-Defaults]

Current default value for option. Changing it here changes the default value for all scopes configured from this point forward.

34 New [DHCP Options-Defaults]

Add a custom DHCP value. The DHCP client has to be capable of using the new value for this to be of any use.

35 Change [DHCP Options-Defaults]

Edit an existing DHCP option.

Disk Administrator

Requires

NT Workstation or Server

Summary

The **Disk Administrator** tool creates and formats hard disk partitions and configures fault tolerance and disk management functions. These include:

Striping (requires NTFS)

Improves performance by spreading I/O across multiple disks.

Striping with parity (requires NTFS)

Improves performance and provides fault tolerance.

Mirroring (requires NTFS)

Provides fault tolerance by making multiple copies of data on different disks.

Volume sets (requires NTFS)

Allows creation of virtual partitions that may span multiple physical partitions and multiple drives.

All fault tolerance capabilities can be used on NT Workstation and Server, but they can be created only on the Server.

MS-DOS places some restrictions on what kind of partitioning you can use. If you are going to be using NT only to access the disks, you have many more options. MS-DOS allows you to have one primary partition and one extended partition. The extended partition can contain multiple logical drives. For example, the C: drive could be the primary partition, and the D:, E:, and F: drives could be within the extended partition.

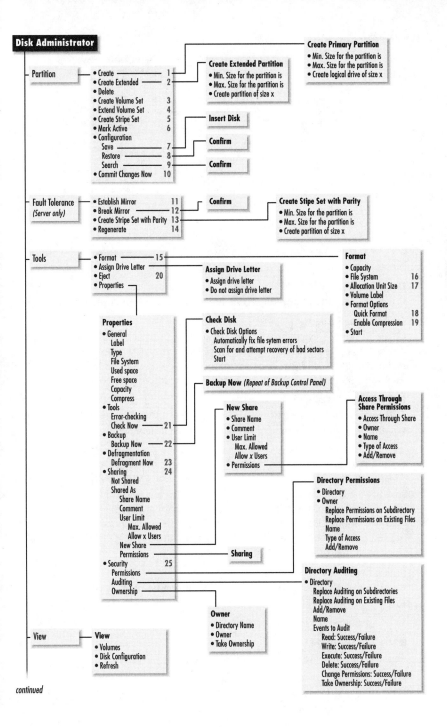

Disk Administrator

Partition
- Create — 1
- Create Extended — 2
- Delete
- Create Volume Set — 3
- Extend Volume Set — 4
- Create Stripe Set — 5
- Mark Active — 6
- Configuration
  Save — 7
  Restore — 8
  Search — 9
- Commit Changes Now — 10

Create Extended Partition
- Min. Size for the partition is
- Max. Size for the partition is
- Create partition of size x

Create Primary Partition
- Min. Size for the partition is
- Max. Size for the partition is
- Create logical drive of size x

Insert Disk

Confirm

Confirm

Fault Tolerance
(Server only)
- Establish Mirror — 11
- Break Mirror — 12
- Create Stripe Set with Parity — 13
- Regenerate — 14

Confirm

Create Stipe Set with Parity
- Min. Size for the partition is
- Max. Size for the partition is
- Create partition of size x

Tools
- Format — 15
- Assign Drive Letter
- Eject — 20
- Properties

Assign Drive Letter
- Assign drive letter
- Do not assign drive letter

Format
- Capacity
- File System — 16
- Allocation Unit Size — 17
- Volume Label
- Format Options
  Quick Format — 18
  Enable Compression — 19
- Start

Properties
- General
  Label
  Type
  File System
  Used space
  Free space
  Capacity
  Compress
- Tools
  Error-checking
  Check Now — 21
- Backup
  Backup Now — 22
- Defragmentation
  Defragment Now — 23
- Sharing — 24
  Not Shared
  Shared As
    Share Name
    Comment
    User Limit
      Max. Allowed
      Allow x Users
    New Share
    Permissions
- Security — 25
  Permissions
  Auditing
  Ownership

Check Disk
- Check Disk Options
  Automatically fix file sytem errors
  Scan for and attempt recovery of bad sectors
  Start

Backup Now *(Repeat of Backup Control Panel)*

New Share
- Share Name
- Comment
- User Limit
  Max. Allowed
  Allow x Users
- Permissions

Access Through Share Permissions
- Access Through Share
- Owner
- Name
- Type of Access
- Add/Remove

Directory Permissions
- Directory
- Owner
  Replace Permissions on Subdirectory
  Replace Permissions on Existing Files
  Name
  Type of Access
  Add/Remove

Sharing

Directory Auditing
- Directory
  Replace Auditing on Subdirectories
  Replace Auditing on Existing Files
  Add/Remove
  Name
  Events to Audit
    Read: Success/Failure
    Write: Success/Failure
    Execute: Success/Failure
    Delete: Success/Failure
    Change Permissions: Success/Failure
    Take Ownership: Success/Failure

Owner
- Directory Name
- Owner
- Take Ownership

View
View
- Volumes
- Disk Configuration
- Refresh

continued

Administrative Tools

Disk Administrator - *continuation*

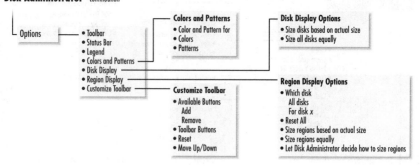

1 **Create** [Partition]

Create a partition. Only one is allowed in MS-DOS–compatible partitioning schemes.

2 **Create Extended** [Partition]

Create an extended partition. This can be divided into multiple logical drives.

3 **Create Volume Set** [Partition]

Create a virtual partition out of unpartitioned space on multiple physical drives. This allows partitions to span physical drives. For example, you could make one 2GB partition out of two 1GB drives. Select the first partition, and then hold down the CONTROL key while selecting unpartitioned areas.

4 **Extend Volume Set** [Partition]

Add more space to an existing volume set. Select the first partition or existing volume set, and then hold down the CONTROL key while selecting unpartitioned areas.

5 **Create Stripe Set** [Partition]

Create a partition that spreads I/O evenly over multiple drives. As striping spreads data over multiple drives, any failure of a single drive can result in the loss of portions of most files within the set. Striping decreases the reliability of data and should be combined with another scheme such as parity and mirroring. Select the first partition, and then hold down the CONTROL key while selecting unpartitioned areas.

6 **Mark Active** [Partition]

A partition has to be marked active before it can be used as a boot disk.

7 **Save** [Partition-Configuration]

Save current partitioning information to disk.

8 **Restore** [Partition-Configuration]

Replace current partitioning with a previously saved version.

9 **Search** [Partition-Configuration]

Search the hard drives for configuration information from another NT installation, overwriting the current configuration.

10 **Commit Changes Now** [Partition]
Commit changes to disk. This step is required before partitions can be modified.

11 **Establish Mirror** [Fault Tolerance]
(Server only) Create a mirror of an existing partition. All reads and writes of the current partition will also be made to the mirror.

12 **Break Mirror** [Fault Tolerance]
(Server only) Stop mirroring a partition. If one of the two partitions has failed, breaking the mirror allows you to start using the remaining disk as a replacement.

13 **Create Stripe Set with Parity** [Fault Tolerance]
(Server only) As the possibility of data loss is increased with striping, parity can increase reliability by allowing the re-creation of data if one of the stripe set drives fails.

14 **Regenerate** [Fault Tolerance]
(Server only) Use parity information to recreate a striped partition after a drive failure.

15 **Format** [Tools]
Format the selected partition. You must commit changes before the menu is enabled.

16 **File System** [Tools-Format]
Choose FAT or NTFS as the file system type. The following table lists some of the features on each:

Feature	FAT	NTFS
MS-DOS–compatible	YES	NO
Compression	NO	YES
Security	NO	YES
Mac support	NO	YES

17 **Allocate Unit Size** [Tools-Format]
(NTFS only) Choose block size for drive format. If you know that the drive is going to be used to store files of a certain size, you may get more usable drive space by modifying the block size. For example, if a drive is going to be used for large graphic files, a larger block size would be more efficient when allocating file space.

18 **Quick Format** [Tools-Format-Format Options]
Skip bad block detection pass.

19 **Enable Compression** [Tools-Format-Format Options]
(NTFS only) Compress drive, enabling more data to be stored.

20 **Eject** [Tools]
Eject the media (if supported by the device).

21 **Check Now** [Tools-Properties-Tools]
Run file integrity–checking utility on drive. The **Cancel** button does not stop the error checking once it has been started.

22 Backup Now [Tools-Properties-Backup]

Run **Backup** administrative tool (*ntbackup*) on drive.

23 Defragment Now [Tools-Properties-Defragmentation]

Run a defragmenting tool on drive (if one is installed).

24 Sharing [Tools-Properties]

Share drive on network. Same functionality as sharing windows in **Windows NT Explorer**, **File Manager**, or **Server Manager**.

25 Security [Tools-Properties]

Set file and directory permissions and auditing, or take ownership of a file or directory, on the selected drive.

DNS Manager

Requires

NT Server
TCP/IP protocol
Microsoft DNS Server service

Summary

The **DNS Manager** tool administers the **Domain Name System** (DNS). DNS is a networked, distributed database that manages the mapping of TCP/IP hostnames to IP addresses and IP addresses to hostnames. The inclusion of a DNS server in NT 4.0 enables NT to provide Internet services without having to rely on other non-NT platforms.

DNS data is complex and requires all entries to be in an exact format. **DNS Manager** acts as a front end to the DNS data files and ensures that the files are maintained in the correct format. You are still responsible for making sure that the data itself makes sense.

The following terms are used within **DNS Manager**:

- A *server* is the DNS service running on an NT computer.
- A *zone* is an administrative grouping of *domain* names.
- A *domain name* is a name that identifies an organization on the Internet. The DNS domain name has nothing to do with NT security domain names.
- A *record* is the individual unit of DNS data.

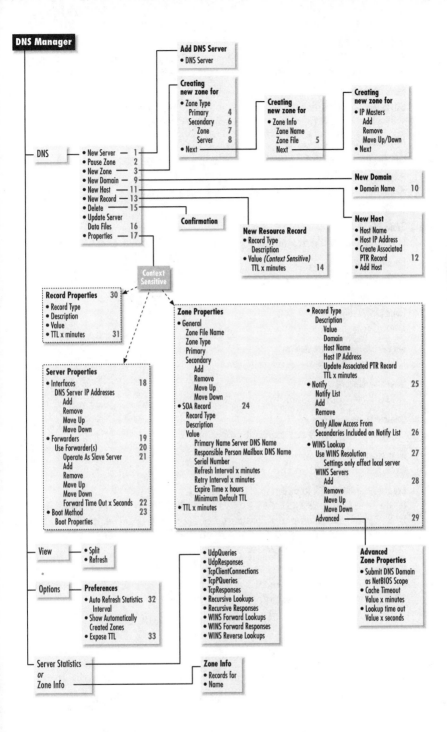

DNS Manager

Add DNS Server
- DNS Server

DNS
- New Server — 1
- Pause Zone — 2
- New Zone — 3
- New Domain — 9
- New Host — 11
- New Record — 13
- Delete — 15
- Update Server
  Data Files 16
- Properties — 17

**Creating
new zone for**
- Zone Type
  Primary   4
  Secondary   6
  Zone   7
  Server   8
- Next

**Creating
new zone for**
- Zone Info
  Zone Name
  Zone File   5
  Next

**Creating
new zone for**
- IP Masters
  Add
  Remove
  Move Up/Down
- Next

New Domain
- Domain Name   10

Confirmation

New Resource Record
- Record Type
  Description
- Value *(Context Sensitive)*
  TTL x minutes 14

New Host
- Host Name
- Host IP Address
- Create Associated
  PTR Record   12
- Add Host

**Context
Sensitive**

Record Properties   30
- Record Type
- Description
- Value
- TTL x minutes   31

Zone Properties
- General
  Zone File Name
  Zone Type
  Primary
  Secondary
    Add
    Remove
    Move Up
    Move Down
- SOA Record   24
  Record Type
  Description
  Value
    Primary Name Server DNS Name
    Responsible Person Mailbox DNS Name
    Serial Number
    Refresh Interval x minutes
    Retry Interval x minutes
    Expire Time x hours
    Minimum Default TTL
- TTL x minutes

- Record Type
  Description
  Value
  Domain
  Host Name
  Host IP Address
  Update Associated PTR Record
  TTL x minutes
- Notify   25
  Notify List
  Add
  Remove

  Only Allow Access From
  Secondaries Included on Notify List 26
- WINS Lookup
  Use WINS Resolution   27
    Settings only affect local server
  WINS Servers
    Add   28
    Remove
    Move Up
    Move Down
  Advanced   29

Server Properties
- Interfaces   18
  DNS Server IP Addresses
    Add
    Remove
    Move Up
    Move Down
- Forwarders   19
  Use Forwarder(s)   20
    Operate As Slave Server 21
    Add
    Remove
    Move Up
    Move Down
    Forward Time Out x Seconds 22
- Boot Method   23
  Boot Properties

**Advanced
Zone Properties**
- Submit DNS Domain
  as NetBIOS Scope
- Cache Timeout
  Value x minutes
- Lookup time out
  Value x seconds

View
- Split
- Refresh

Options

Preferences
- Auto Refresh Statistics 32
  Interval
- Show Automatically
  Created Zones
- Expose TTL   33

- UdpQueries
- UdpResponses
- TcpClientConnections
- TcpPQueries
- TcpResponses
- Recursive Lookups
- Recursive Responses
- WINS Forward Lookups
- WINS Forward Responses
- WINS Reverse Lookups

Server Statistics
or
Zone Info

Zone Info
- Records for
- Name

*Administrative
Tools*

1 **New Server** [DNS]
Add the ability to administer a DNS server. When used on the local computer, this has the effect of creating a new server if one does not currently exist.

2 **Pause Zone** [DNS]
Suspend answering queries for the selected zone. If a client queries the server while the zone is paused, it will get a "Query refused" error.

3 **New Zone** [DNS]
Create a new zone on the selected server.

4 **Primary** [DNS-New Zone-Zone Type]
A primary will be the authority for the zone and keep the master copy of all DNS information.

5 **Zone File** [DNS-New Zone-Next-Zone Info]
Name of disk file containing zone data.

6 **Secondary** [DNS-New Zone-Zone Type]
A secondary can answer queries for a zone, but it relies on a primary to give it the information.

7 **Zone** [DNS-New Zone-Zone Type-Secondary]
Zone for which a secondary is created.

8 **Server** [DNS-New Zone-Zone Type-Secondary]
IP address of primary server for zone.

9 **New Domain** [DNS]
Add a new domain name within selected zone.

10 **Domain Name** [DNS-New Domain]
Organization name. For example, *ora.com*.

11 **New Host** [DNS]
Create a single host record (an A or address record).

12 **Create Associated PTR Record** [DNS-New Host]
If the *IN-ADDR.ARPA* domain exists for the IP address, create a corresponding PTR record. For example, if hostname being added is *www.ora.com* with an IP address of 198.112.208.1, a PTR record for *www.ora.com* is created in the 208.112.198.IN-ADDR.ARPA domain.

13 **New Record** [DNS]
Create any kind of DNS record type, with the exception of Start of Authority (SOA). The most common types of records are:

A The address record maps a hostname with an IP address.

CNAME
The canonical name is an alias for another host.

MX The mail exchanger handles mail for the specified host.

NS The name server record lists name servers for the domain.

PTR
(Available only when adding records to a *IN-ADDR.ARPA* domain) The pointer record maps an IP address to a hostname.

14 **TTL** [DNS-New Record-Value]
    If **Options-Preferences-Expose TTL** is set, you can change the record's TTL.

15 **Delete** [DNS]
    The delete operation is context-sensitive, depending on what is selected (record, zone, or server). When you delete a server, you remove only the administrative connection, not the data.

16 **Update Server Data Files** [DNS]
    Synchronize the data on screen with what is stored on disk.

17 **Properties** [DNS]
    The **Properties** button is context-sensitive, depending on what is selected (record, zone, or server).

18 **Interfaces** [DNS-Properties]
    (For selected server) Select network interfaces DNS server will listen on.

19 **Forwarders** [DNS-Properties]
    (For selected server) Forwarders are other name servers that forward a request from the local name server to a remote name server.

20 **Use Forwarder(s)** [DNS-Properties-Forwarders]
    (For selected server) If you have a name server that cannot connect to the Internet directly (possibly for security or performance reasons), any queries the local name server cannot resolve can be forwarded to the name server with Internet access.

21 **Operate As Slave Server** [DNS-Properties-Forwarders-Use Forwarder(s)]
    (For selected server) Act as a simple redirector for DNS queries. When a query is received by the local name server, forward the request to the forwarder without checking any local data.

22 **Forward Time Out** [DNS-Properties-Forwarders-Use Forwarder(s)]
    (For selected server) Period of time to spend waiting for a response from each forwarder in the list.

23 **Boot Method** [DNS-Properties]
    (For selected server) The server can read boot information from either a disk file or the registry. If you want to change the boot method, you have to manually edit the registry. In the key *HKEY_LOCAL_MACHINE\SYSTEM\CurrentControlSet\Services\DNS\Parameters*, change the value of **EnableRegistryBoot** to 1 for booting from the registry and 0 for booting from a disk file.

24 **SOA Record** [DNS-Properties]
    (For selected zone) Edit field of Start Of Authority (SOA) record. This record tells other name servers how long data should be kept and when to get a new copy. If **Options-Preferences-Expose TTL** is set, you can change the TTL for the SOA record.

25 **Notify** [DNS-Properties]
    (For selected zone) Notify secondary servers if the information in a primary has changed.

26 **Only Allow Access From Secondaries Included on Notify List** [DNS-Properties-Notify]
    Normally, DNS primary servers do not place any restrictions on who is allowed to perform *zone transfers*. A zone transfer occurs when a secondary

downloads all the records for a zone in a single transaction. Setting this will cause the DNS server to reject a zone transfer unless the requesting secondary is listed in the **Notify List**. You should probably enable this restriction, as a complete list of DNS records may be useful to system hackers. DNS clients can still ask the DNS server for records one at a time. Note that setting this option also prevents the *nslookup* command from doing an *ls* of the domain.

27 **Use WINS Resolution** [DNS-Properties-WINS Lookup]
(For selected zone) If you are using DHCP to hand out IP addresses to computers, this raises an issue with TCP/IP hostnames. Hostnames are associated with an IP address and cannot be relied upon to always refer to the same computer in a DHCP environment. Computer names always refer to the same computer, as they are based on the MAC address of the network adapter, which is fixed. Microsoft's solution to this problem is to have the DNS server ask the WINS server for the current IP address of a computer. This convoluted process makes the DNS server data dynamic and compatible with a DHCP and WINS environment.

28 **Add** [DNS-Properties-WINS Lookup-WINS Servers]
Add a list of WINS servers to contact for the latest computer name and IP address mapping.

29 **Advanced** [DNS-Properties-WINS Lookup]
If you want to group computers according to a NetBIOS scope, this tells DNS to use the DNS domain name as the scope ID.

30 **Properties** [DNS]
(For selected record) The **Value** fields are context-sensitive depending on the selected record type.

31 **TTL** [DNS-Properties]
(For selected record) If **Options-Preferences-Expose TTL** is set, you can change the TTL for the record.

32 **Auto Refresh Statistics** [Options]
If you want to keep the statistics window open for monitoring DNS for a period of time, set how often the window should be updated (refreshed).

33 **Expose TTL** [Options]
You normally set all Time-To-Live (TTL) information in the SOA record, even though there is a TTL supplied for every record. You can change the TTL on a per-record basis if you expose the TTL.

Event Viewer

Requires

NT Workstation or Server

Summary

The **Event Viewer** tool lets you examine recorded system events. When something goes wrong, the first place to look for the cause is **Event Viewer**. **Event Viewer** can also be used to view security-related information if security auditing is enabled.

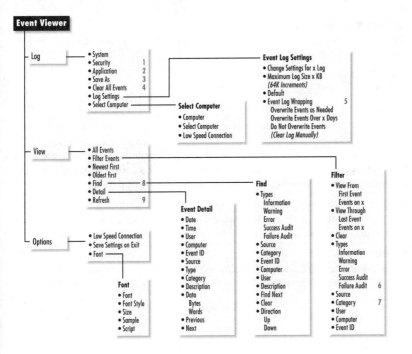

Event Viewer

- Log
  - System
  - Security   1
  - Application   2
  - Save As   3
  - Clear All Events   4
  - Log Settings
  - Select Computer

  Select Computer
  - Computer
  - Select Computer
  - Low Speed Connection

  Event Log Settings
  - Change Settings for x Log
  - Maximum Log Size x KB
    (64K Increments)
  - Default
  - Event Log Wrapping   5
    Overwrite Events as Needed
    Overwrite Events Over x Days
    Do Not Overwrite Events
    (Clear Log Manually)

- View
  - All Events
  - Filter Events
  - Newest First
  - Oldest first
  - Find   8
  - Detail
  - Refresh   9

  Event Detail
  - Date
  - Time
  - User
  - Computer
  - Event ID
  - Source
  - Type
  - Category
  - Description
  - Data
    Bytes
    Words
  - Previous
  - Next

  Find
  - Types
    Information
    Warning
    Error
    Success Audit
    Failure Audit
  - Source
  - Category
  - Event ID
  - Computer
  - User
  - Description
  - Find Next
  - Clear
  - Direction
    Up
    Down

  Filter
  - View From
    First Event
    Events on x
  - View Through
    Last Event
    Events on x
  - Clear
  - Types
    Information
    Warning
    Error
    Success Audit
    Failure Audit   6
  - Source
  - Category   7
  - User
  - Computer
  - Event ID

- Options
  - Low Speed Connection
  - Save Settings on Exit
  - Font

  Font
  - Font
  - Font Style
  - Size
  - Sample
  - Script

Administrative Tools

---

1   Security [Log]

Security logging (auditing) is not enabled by default. It must be enabled within another tool before anything is logged, as shown:

- User and group auditing is configured with the **Policies-Audit** menu of **User Manager**.

- Registry auditing is configured with the **Security Auditing** menu of **Regedt32**.

- File and directory auditing is configured with the **Security-Auditing** menu of **File Manager**.

- Printer auditing is configured with the **Properties-Security-Auditing** menu of the **Printers** control panel.

2   Application [Log]

The **Performance Monitor** can generate events in the application log using the alert mode.

3   Save As [Log]

In addition to the event log format (.EVT), it is possible to save events as text or comma-delimited text. This facilitates processing of the event logs by other programs such as Perl scripts.

4   Clear All Events [Log]

By clearing events, you are permanently removing previously recorded events from the disk.

5   Event Log Wrapping [Log-Log Settings]

Wrapping writes new events over the oldest events, wrapping around the log-file to the beginning.

6   Failure Audit [View-Filter Events-Types]

Repeated failures might indicate break-in attempts.

7   Category [View-Filter Events]

Category is enabled only when a specific *source* is selected. When security events are selected, the category scroll list contains security event types. These types correspond to the checkbox settings in the **Policies-Auditing** menu of **User Manager**, the **Security-Auditing** menu of *regedt32*, **File Manager**, and the **Properties-Security-Auditing** menu of the **Printers** control panel.

8   Find [View]

This is the same criteria available in the **View-Filter** menu, with the exception of time and date.

9   Refresh [View]

Since **Event Viewer** does not display events as they occur, you must continually refresh the display to see events that have occurred since **Event Viewer** was started.

File Manager

Requires

NT Workstation or Server

Command-Line Equivalents

cacls
net share
net use
net view

Summary

The **File Manager** tool is a browser for files and directories. It adds or deletes files and directories, manages share permissions, and makes connections to remote shares. It has an interface that dates back to Windows 3.x and Windows NT 3.x. Some people may prefer it to the object-oriented functionality of Windows NT **Explorer**, where files, printers, and control panels are all treated in a similar fashion.

One particularly confusing feature of **File Manager** is how it administers sharing for Microsoft Networking, Macintosh, and NetWare clients. Each has its own administration menu instead of a unified menu. A single NT directory could be shared by all three sharing mechanisms, but you then have to visit three different dialog boxes to administer the share. The sharing icon shows up only on directories being shared by Microsoft Networking, giving you no visual indication of any sharing going on under other protocols.

If **File Manager** is not part of your Administrative Tools menu, you can either add a shortcut to it (*<winnt root>\SYSTEM32\WINFILE.EXE*) or run it from the command line.

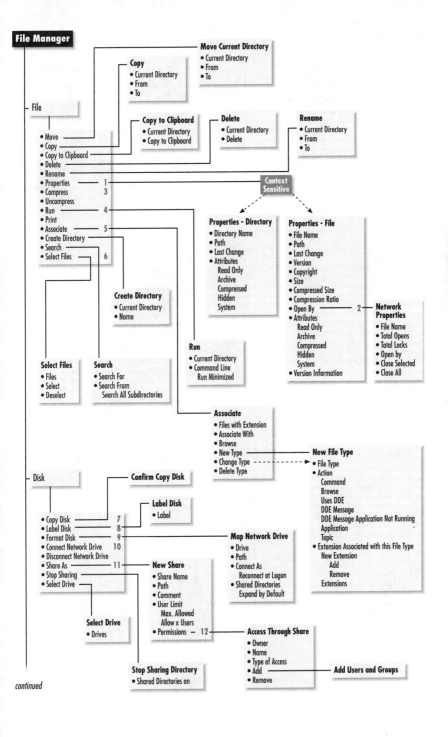

File Manager

Move Current Directory
• Current Directory
• From
• To

Copy
• Current Directory
• From
• To

Copy to Clipboard
• Current Directory
• Copy to Clipboard

Delete
• Current Directory
• Delete

Rename
• Current Directory
• From
• To

File
• Move
• Copy
• Copy to Clipboard
• Delete
• Rename
• Properties   1
• Compress   3
• Uncompress
• Run   4
• Print
• Associate   5
• Create Directory
• Search
• Select Files   6

Context Sensitive

Properties - Directory
• Directory Name
• Path
• Last Change
• Attributes
   Read Only
   Archive
   Compressed
   Hidden
   System

Properties - File
• File Name
• Path
• Last Change
• Version
• Copyright
• Size
• Compressed Size
• Compression Ratio
• Open By   2
• Attributes
   Read Only
   Archive
   Compressed
   Hidden
   System
• Version Information

Network Properties
• File Name
• Total Opens
• Total Locks
• Open by
• Close Selected
• Close All

Create Directory
• Current Directory
• Name

Select Files
• Files
• Select
• Deselect

Search
• Search For
• Search From
   Search All Subdirectories

Run
• Current Directory
• Command Line
   Run Minimized

Associate
• Files with Extension
• Associate With
• Browse
• New Type
• Change Type
• Delete Type

New File Type
• File Type
• Action
   Command
   Browse
   Uses DDE
   DDE Message
   DDE Message Application Not Running
   Application
   Topic
• Extension Associated with this File Type
   New Extension
   Add
   Remove
   Extensions

Disk

Confirm Copy Disk

Label Disk
• Label

• Copy Disk   7
• Label Disk   8
• Format Disk   9
• Connect Network Drive   10
• Disconnect Network Drive
• Share As   11
• Stop Sharing
• Select Drive

Map Network Drive
• Drive
• Path
• Connect As
   Reconnect at Logon
• Shared Directories
   Expand by Default

New Share
• Share Name
• Path
• Comment
• User Limit
   Max. Allowed
   Allow x Users
• Permissions   12

Access Through Share
• Owner
• Name
• Type of Access
• Add
• Remove

Add Users and Groups

Select Drive
• Drives

Stop Sharing Directory
• Shared Directories on

continued

File Manager - *continuation*

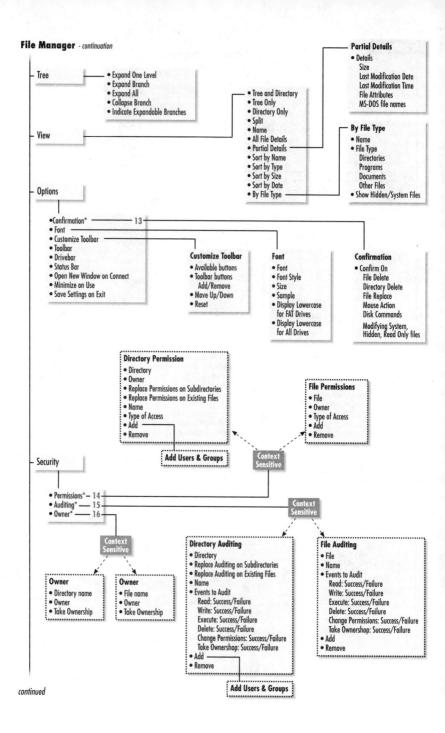

Partial Details
- Details
  - Size
  - Last Modification Date
  - Last Modification Time
  - File Attributes
  - MS-DOS file names

Tree
- Expand One Level
- Expand Branch
- Expand All
- Collapse Branch
- Indicate Expandable Branches

View
- Tree and Directory
- Tree Only
- Directory Only
- Split
- Name
- All File Details
- Partial Details
- Sort by Name
- Sort by Type
- Sort by Size
- Sort by Date
- By File Type

By File Type
- Name
- File Type
  - Directories
  - Programs
  - Documents
  - Other Files
- Show Hidden/System Files

Options
- Confirmation* — 13
- Font
- Customize Toolbar
- Toolbar
- Drivebar
- Status Bar
- Open New Window on Connect
- Minimize on Use
- Save Settings on Exit

Customize Toolbar
- Available buttons
- Toolbar buttons
  Add/Remove
- Move Up/Down
- Reset

Font
- Font
- Font Style
- Size
- Sample
- Display Lowercase for FAT Drives
- Display Lowercase for All Drives

Confirmation
- Confirm On
  - File Delete
  - Directory Delete
  - File Replace
  - Mouse Action
  - Disk Commands
  - Modifying System, Hidden, Read Only files

Directory Permission
- Directory
- Owner
- Replace Permissions on Subdirectories
- Replace Permissions on Existing Files
- Name
- Type of Access
- Add
- Remove

Add Users & Groups

File Permissions
- File
- Owner
- Type of Access
- Add
- Remove

Context Sensitive

Security
- Permissions* — 14
- Auditing* — 15
- Owner* — 16

Context Sensitive

Directory Auditing
- Directory
- Replace Auditing on Subdirectories
- Replace Auditing on Existing Files
- Name
- Events to Audit
  Read: Success/Failure
  Write: Success/Failure
  Execute: Success/Failure
  Delete: Success/Failure
  Change Permissions: Success/Failure
  Take Ownershop: Success/Failure
- Add
- Remove

File Auditing
- File
- Name
- Events to Audit
  Read: Success/Failure
  Write: Success/Failure
  Execute: Success/Failure
  Delete: Success/Failure
  Change Permissions: Success/Failure
  Take Ownershop: Success/Failure
- Add
- Remove

Context Sensitive

Owner
- Directory name
- Owner
- Take Ownership

Owner
- File name
- Owner
- Take Ownership

Add Users & Groups

continued

File Manager - *continuation*

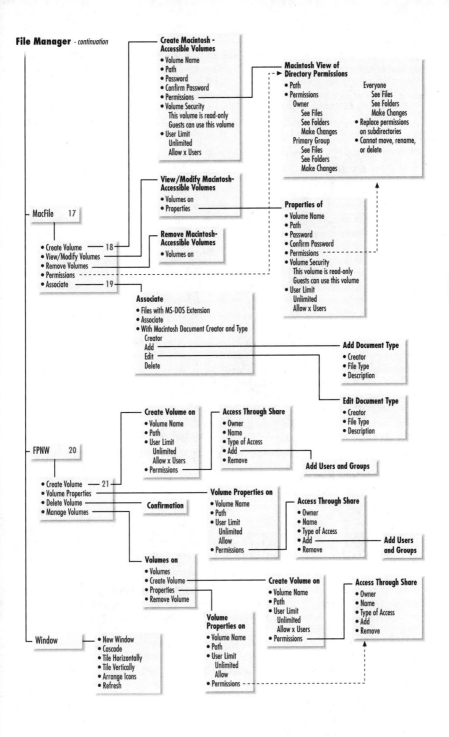

Create Macintosh - Accessible Volumes
- Volume Name
- Path
- Password
- Confirm Password
- Permissions
- Volume Security
  This volume is read-only
  Guests can use this volume
- User Limit
  Unlimited
  Allow x Users

Macintosh View of Directory Permissions
- Path
- Permissions
  Owner
    See Files
    See Folders
    Make Changes
  Primary Group
    See Files
    See Folders
    Make Changes

Everyone
  See Files
  See Folders
  Make Changes
- Replace permissions on subdirectories
- Cannot move, rename, or delete

View/Modify Macintosh-Accessible Volumes
- Volumes on
- Properties

MacFile   17

- Create Volume   18
- View/Modify Volumes
- Remove Volumes
- Permissions
- Associate   19

Remove Macintosh-Accessible Volumes
- Volumes on

Properties of
- Volume Name
- Path
- Password
- Confirm Password
- Permissions
- Volume Security
  This volume is read-only
  Guests can use this volume
- User Limit
  Unlimited
  Allow x Users

Associate
- Files with MS-DOS Extension
- Associate
- With Macintosh Document Creator and Type
  Creator
  Add
  Edit
  Delete

Add Document Type
- Creator
- File Type
- Description

Edit Document Type
- Creator
- File Type
- Description

Create Volume on
- Volume Name
- Path
- User Limit
  Unlimited
  Allow x Users
- Permissions

Access Through Share
- Owner
- Name
- Type of Access
- Add
- Remove

Add Users and Groups

FPNW   20

- Create Volume   21
- Volume Properties
- Delete Volume
- Manage Volumes

Confirmation

Volume Properties on
- Volume Name
- Path
- User Limit
  Unlimited
  Allow
- Permissions

Access Through Share
- Owner
- Name
- Type of Access
- Add
- Remove

Add Users and Groups

Volumes on
- Volumes
- Create Volume
- Properties
- Remove Volume

Volume Properties on
- Volume Name
- Path
- User Limit
  Unlimited
  Allow
- Permissions

Create Volume on
- Volume Name
- Path
- User Limit
  Unlimited
  Allow x Users
- Permissions

Access Through Share
- Owner
- Name
- Type of Access
- Add
- Remove

Window

- New Window
- Cascade
- Tile Horizontally
- Tile Vertically
- Arrange Icons
- Refresh

1 **Properties** [File]
View information about a file. View and edit attributes of the selected directory or file.

2 **Open By** [File-Properties]
If a file is selected and in use, the username(s) who have the file open are displayed. You also have the option of forcibly closing the file for each user.

3 **Compress** [File]
(NTFS only) Compress files or directories. If you compress a directory, you will be asked if you wish to compress all files and directories within the selected directory.

4 **Run** [File]
Run an executable or open a file. This is similar to the **Start-Run** menu, in that you can specify a UNC name to see the shares offered by a remote computer.

5 **Associate** [File]
Windows and DOS applications associate a file with an application by the filename extension. This dialog lets you edit the mapping of extensions to applications.

6 **Select Files** [File]
Select one or more files for an operation, such as deleting, compressing, and so on.

7 **Copy Disk** [Disk]
Copy the contents from one floppy disk to another.

8 **Label Disk** [Disk]
Label a floppy or hard disk.

9 **Format Disk** [Disk]
Format a floppy disk. You must use **Disk Manager** to format hard disks.

10 **Connect Network Drive** [Disk]
Connect to a share being offered by a remote computer.

11 **Share As** [Disk]
Offer selected directory as a share on local computer for Microsoft Networking clients. This is completely separate from the sharing offered by **Services for the Macintosh** (SFM) and **File and Print Services for NetWare** (FPNW).

12 **Permissions** [Disk-Share As]
Set permissions on share for remote users. The resulting permissions for a remote user are the more restrictive of either the share permissions (**Disk-Share As-Permissions**) or the file or directory permissions (**Security-Permissions**).

13 **Confirmation** [Options]
If you are confident that you always know what you are doing, you can turn off the confirmation dialog boxes when administering the file system.

14 **Permissions** [Security]
Set permissions on file or directory for locally logged-on users. The resulting permissions for a remote user are the more restrictive of either the share permissions (**Disk-Share As-Permissions**) or the file or directory permissions (**Security-Permissions**).

15 **Auditing** [Security]

Auditing files and directories allows you to record whenever a file is accessed (either successfully or unsuccessfully) by a specific user or group. The audited events are recorded in the **Event Viewer** security log and show the filename, username, domain name, and type of access. File auditing simply records what files are accessed by specific users. If the goal is to audit all user activity, use the **Policy-Audit** menu of **User Manager**.

16 **Owner** [Security]

Show change of ownership of a file or directory. The owner is always able to control the file, regardless of permissions settings. The owner is also able to lock out the administrator, unless the administrator takes ownership of the file.

17 **MacFile**

(Server only) Only present if **Services for the Macintosh** (SFM) is installed. Manage volumes that will be visible to Macintosh clients.

18 **Create Volume** [MacFile]

When you create a volume, you are sharing the NT directory using the AppleTalk protocol, allowing Macintosh clients to use it. This sharing is totally independent of file sharing under Microsoft Networking or **File and Print Services for NetWare** (FPNW).

19 **Associate** [MacFile]

Control how files are associated with applications. Windows NT (and all other versions of Windows) associate a file with an application based on the filename extension. Macintosh computers use two file attributes called *creator* and *type*. A proper association between application, file extension, and creator/type allows a single file to be shared by both Windows NT and Macintosh computers and enables users on either system to automatically start the correct application by double-clicking on the filename.

20 **FPNW**

(Server only) Only present if **File and Print Services for NetWare** (FPNW) is installed. Manage volumes that will be visible to Novell NetWare clients.

21 **Create Volume** [FPNW]

When you create a volume, you are sharing the NT directory using the IPX/SPX protocol, allowing Novell NetWare clients to use it. This sharing is totally independent of file sharing under Microsoft Networking or **Services for the Macintosh** (SFM).

Internet Service Manager

Requires

NT Workstation (Microsoft Peer Web Services)
NT Server (Microsoft Internet Information Server)

Summary

The **Internet Service Manager** administers web, Gopher, and ftp servers running on local or remote computers. Peer Web services is a subset of IIS that is licensed for only 10 users at a time. As Gopher has been replaced by the WWW, it is not documented here.

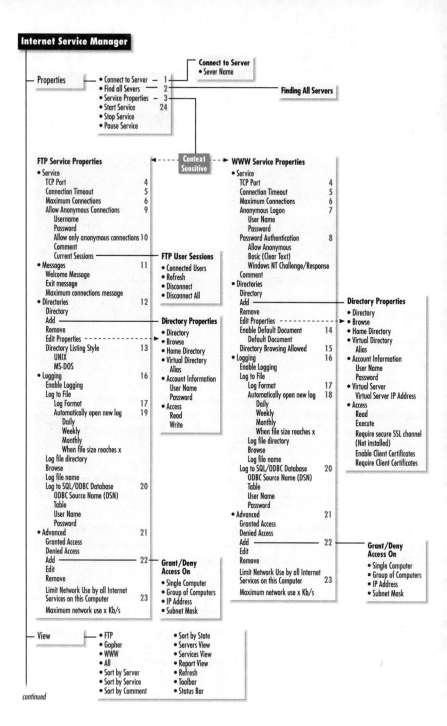

Internet Service Manager

Properties
- Connect to Server — 1
- Find all Severs — 2
- Service Properties — 3
- Start Service — 24
- Stop Service
- Pause Service

Connect to Server
- Sever Name

Finding All Servers

Context Sensitive

FTP Service Properties
- Service
  - TCP Port — 4
  - Connection Timeout — 5
  - Maximum Connections — 6
  - Allow Anonymous Connections — 9
    - Username
    - Password
    - Allow only anonymous connections — 10
    - Comment
    - Current Sessions
- Messages — 11
  - Welcome Message
  - Exit message
  - Maximum connections message
- Directories — 12
  - Directory
  - Add
  - Remove
  - Edit Properties
  - Directory Listing Style — 13
    - UNIX
    - MS-DOS
- Logging — 16
  - Enable Logging
  - Log to File
    - Log Format — 17
    - Automatically open new log — 19
      - Daily
      - Weekly
      - Monthly
      - When file size reaches x
  - Log file directory
  - Browse
  - Log file name
  - Log to SQL/ODBC Database — 20
    - ODBC Source Name (DSN)
    - Table
    - User Name
    - Password
- Advanced — 21
  - Granted Access
  - Denied Access
  - Add — 22
  - Edit
  - Remove
  - Limit Network Use by all Internet Services on this Computer — 23
  - Maximum network use x Kb/s

FTP User Sessions
- Connected Users
- Refresh
- Disconnect
- Disconnect All

Directory Properties
- Directory
- Browse
- Home Directory
- Virtual Directory
  - Alias
- Account Information
  - User Name
  - Password
- Access
  - Read
  - Write

WWW Service Properties
- Service
  - TCP Port — 4
  - Connection Timeout — 5
  - Maximum Connections — 6
  - Anonymous Logon — 7
    - User Name
    - Password
  - Password Authentication — 8
    - Allow Anonymous
    - Basic (Clear Text)
    - Windows NT Challenge/Response
  - Comment
- Directories
  - Directory
  - Add
  - Remove
  - Edit Properties
  - Enable Default Document — 14
    - Default Document
  - Directory Browsing Allowed — 15
- Logging — 16
  - Enable Logging
  - Log to File
    - Log Format — 17
    - Automatically open new log — 18
      - Daily
      - Weekly
      - Monthly
      - When file size reaches x
  - Log file directory
  - Browse
  - Log file name
  - Log to SQL/ODBC Database — 20
    - ODBC Source Name (DSN)
    - Table
    - User Name
    - Password
- Advanced — 21
  - Granted Access
  - Denied Access
  - Add — 22
  - Edit
  - Remove
  - Limit Network Use by all Internet Services on this Computer — 23
  - Maximum network use x Kb/s

Directory Properties
- Directory
- Browse
- Home Directory
- Virtual Directory
  - Alias
- Account Information
  - User Name
  - Password
- Virtual Server
  - Virtual Server IP Address
- Access
  - Read
  - Execute
  - Require secure SSL channel (Not installed)
  - Enable Client Certificates
  - Require Client Certificates

Grant/Deny Access On
- Single Computer
- Group of Computers
- IP Address
- Subnet Mask

Grant/Deny Access On
- Single Computer
- Group of Computers
- IP Address
- Subnet Mask

View
- FTP
- Gopher
- WWW
- All
- Sort by Server
- Sort by Service
- Sort by Comment
- Sort by State
- Servers View
- Services View
- Report View
- Refresh
- Toolbar
- Status Bar

continued

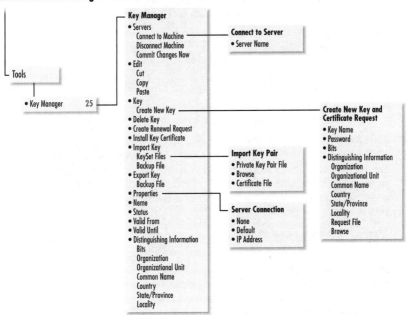

1 Connect to Server [Properties]
A server is a computer offering Internet services. When you connect to a server, you can administer the Internet services running on that computer.

2 Find all Servers [Properties]
Search the network for other servers and add them to the administration window.

3 Service Properties [Properties]
Edit properties for the selected service. A service is an Internet service, such as web, gopher, or ftp.

4 TCP Port [Properties-Service Properties-Service]
The TCP port that the service is accepting connections on. If you want to run multiple versions of a service on the same computer, you can use another port for the second service. Of course, remote clients will have to know the port number in advance to use the alternative service.

5 Connection Timeout [Properties-Service Properties-Service]
Disconnect idle users after specified time. Each client consumes resources on the server, regardless of whether it is actively transferring information.

6 Maximum Connections [Properties-Service Properties-Service]
Total number of clients that can be connected at the same time.

7 Anonymous Logon [Properties-Service Properties-Service]
(WWW service) Normally, the permissions of anonymous users are controlled by the *IUSR_<computername>* account. If you wish to restrict access to the web server, you can change the username to a regular account and use its permissions.

8 Password Authentication [Properties-Service Properties-Service]
(WWW service) Set type of authentication required to logon:

Allow Anonymous
No authentication needed.

Basic
Plain text authentication

Windows NT Challenge/Response
Use encrypted usernames and passwords

9 Allow Anonymous Connections [Properties-Service Properties-Service]
(FTP service) Allow ftp logons with username *anonymous* in addition to regular users. Users logged on anonymously are using the permissions of username *IUSR_<computername>*. The password has to match the one used by *IUSR_<computername>*. This is only used by the system, and is not typed in by an ftp user.

10 Allow only anonymous connections [Properties-Service Properties-Service]
(FTP service) Allow only anonymous ftp logons.

11 Messages [Properties-Service Properties]
(FTP service) Short messages can be displayed when ftp clients log on, log off, or are refused a connection due to too many ftp users. As ftp does not normally have a way to display text without downloading it, these messages can be used to inform users about events, usage rules, or recent changes to the site.

12 Directories [Properties-Service Properties]
Specify which directories are visible to remote user.

13 Directory Listing Style [Properties-Service Properties-Directories]
(FTP service) Select UNIX- or MS-DOS–style output for a directory listing. You should probably use UNIX-style output when offering an ftp site to the Internet, as this is still the most common.

14 Enable Default Document [Properties-Service Properties-Directories]
(WWW service) If a client does not specify a document in the request, display this document.

15 Directory Browsing Allowed [Properties-Service Properties-Directories]
(WWW service) Display a hypertext list of all the files in the directory.

16 Logging [Properties-Service Properties]
Log all HTTP or FTP transactions. Logging can be a very important issue for sites that charge based on the number of "hits" for a given document.

17 Log to File [Properties-Service Properties-Logging-Enable Logging]
Log WWW or FTP activity to a disk file.

18 Log Format [Properties-Service Properties-Logging-Enable Logging-Log to File]
(WWW service) You can log in in either Standard (EMWAC) or NCSA format. (Some may argue that NCSA is actually the more standard format.)

19 **Automatically Open New Log** [Properties-Service Properties-Logging-Enable Logging-Log to File]
(FTP service) Rotate log files based on date or log file size. This breaks logging information into manageable amounts for analysis.

20 **Log to SQL/ODBC Database** [Properties-Service Properties-Logging]
Log directly to a database using specified database, table, account, and password.

21 **Advanced** [Properties-Service Properties]
(Server only) Create a list of included or excluded hosts and networks that can or cannot connect to the service. This feature could be used to limit access to a non-public resource such as an internal web server.

22 **Add** [Properties-Service Properties-Advanced]
Add a specific host or entire subnet of hosts to the list of exceptions to the default access setting.

23 **Limit Network Use** [Properties-Service Properties-Advanced]
Set amount of data transferred to a specific number of kilobits/second. This could be used to prevent the system from being swamped by a single service or to save money on a metered Internet connection.

24 **Start Service** [Properties]
The selected services can be started, stopped, paused, and continued. The services can also be controlled on the local computer from the **Services** control panel or from the command line with *net start.*

25 **Key Manager** [Tools]
Manage encryption keys for Secure Sockets Layer (SSL) communication. See the section "Securing Data Transmissions with SSL" in the online IIS documentation for the procedure.

License Manager

Requires
    NT Server

Summary

The **License Manager** tool manages licensing for the local computer and remote computers. It centralizes administration of network-based licenses for the NT operating system itself and any optional software. The information will be only as honest and accurate as you make it, as most of the licensing is not strictly enforced.

Refer to the following figure for an illustration of the menu structure.

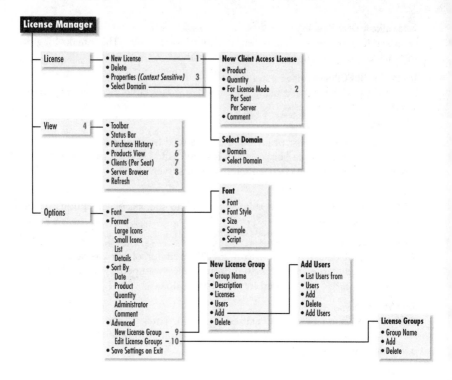

1 **New License** [License]

Add a new license for an existing product.

2 **For License Mode** [License-New License]

Select **Per Seat** or **Per Server** licensing mode.

3 **Properties** [License]

View clients using a product and purchase history of an existing product. Unlike the main **Clients** tab, you can revoke a license from a user.

4 **View**

Move selected tab view to foreground.

5 **Purchase History** [View]

Display of when and how many licenses were purchased for a product.

6 **Products View** [View]

Display of all licensed products.

7 **Clients (Per Seat)** [View]

Display users who have accessed products, either legitimately or illegitimately. This display is helpful when deciding how many licenses would be required to serve the demand.

8 **Server Browser** [View]

Select other domains and computers for which to administer licensing information.

9   **New License Group** [Options-Advanced]
    License groups allow you to associate licenses with specific users. Normally, licensing is based simply on the number of users, not a specific list of users. A group could be used to assure that only a certain group of users are allowed to use a product and prevents illegitimate users from consuming licenses.

10 **Edit License Groups** [Options-Advanced]
    Edit an existing group.

Migration Tool for NetWare

Requires

    NT Server
    IPX/SPX protocol
    Gateway Services for NetWare (GSNW) service
    NTFS partition (to retain NetWare file permissions)

Summary

    The **Migration Tool for NetWare** assists in moving accounts and files from an existing NetWare server to an NT server. All accounts and groups from the NetWare server are added to the domain of the target NT server.

    As there may be user and group name conflicts or problems with pathnames or filenames, the **Migration Tool** lets you run the migration in a read-only mode called a trial migration. This allows you to discover and resolve any problems before any data is transferred from the NetWare server to the NT server.

    You can create a text file that maps the NetWare user and group names to the desired NT domain user and group names in advance of the actual migration.

    The **Migration Tool** contains a logfile viewer that records all the results of the conversion attempts for later analysis.

    In practice, you will want to run a trial migration, examine the log files, fix the errors, and repeat until there are no serious problems. Only then should you run the actual migration.

    If the goal is to make the NT server act exactly like the NetWare server it replaces, you may wish to purchase **File and Print Services for NetWare** (FPNW), as it allows login scripts and NetWare-specific settings to be maintained for the clients.

    If you get the error message "The dynamic link library NWAPI32.dll could not be found," you probably have not installed **Gateway Services for NetWare** (GSNW).

    Refer to the following figure for an illustration of the menu structure.

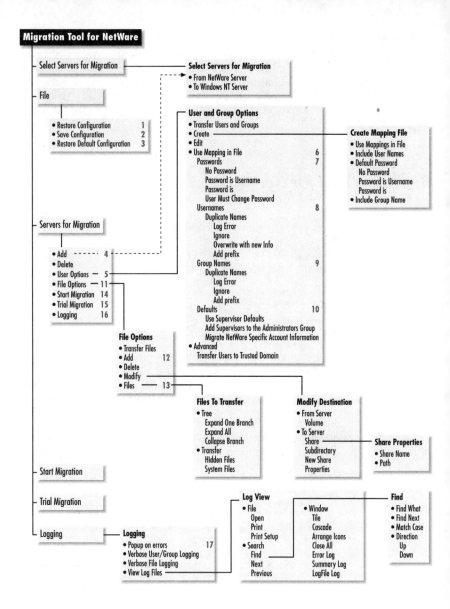

Migration Tool for NetWare

- Select Servers for Migration ────── **Select Servers for Migration**
  - From NetWare Server
  - To Windows NT Server

- File
  - Restore Configuration   1
  - Save Configuration   2
  - Restore Default Configuration   3

User and Group Options
- Transfer Users and Groups
- Create ──────────────────────────── **Create Mapping File**
- Edit   - Use Mappings in File
- Use Mapping in File   6   - Include User Names
  Passwords   7   - Default Password
    No Password   No Password
    Password is Username   Password is Username
    Password is   Password is
    User Must Change Password   - Include Group Name
  Usernames   8
    Duplicate Names
      Log Error
      Ignore
      Overwrite with new Info
      Add prefix
  Group Names   9
    Duplicate Names
      Log Error
      Ignore
      Add prefix
  Defaults   10
    Use Supervisor Defaults
    Add Supervisors to the Administrators Group
    Migrate NetWare Specific Account Information
- Advanced
  Transfer Users to Trusted Domain

- Servers for Migration
  - Add ----- 4
  - Delete
  - User Options — 5
  - File Options — 11
  - Start Migration   14
  - Trial Migration   15
  - Logging   16

File Options
- Transfer Files
- Add   12
- Delete
- Modify
- Files — 13

Files To Transfer
- Tree
  Expand One Branch
  Expand All
  Collapse Branch
- Transfer
  Hidden Files
  System Files

Modify Destination
- From Server
  Volume
- To Server
  Share ──────────────── **Share Properties**
  Subdirectory   - Share Name
  New Share   - Path
  Properties

- Start Migration

- Trial Migration

Log View
- File
  Open
  Print
  Print Setup
- Search
  Find
  Next
  Previous

- Window
  Tile
  Cascade
  Arrange Icons
  Close All
  Error Log
  Summary Log
  LogFile Log

Find
- Find What
- Find Next
- Match Case
- Direction
  Up
  Down

- Logging ──── **Logging**
  - Popup on errors   17
  - Verbose User/Group Logging
  - Verbose File Logging
  - View Log Files

---

1 Restore Configuration [File]

Use migration settings from a previous session.

2 Save Configuration [File]

Save current migration settings to disk.

3 Restore Default Configuration [File]

Reset all settings back to default.

4 Add [Servers for Migration]

Add a NetWare server and NT server pair for migration.

5   **User Options** [Servers for Migration]
Set options that control how users and groups are transferred.

6   **Use Mapping in File** [Servers for Migration-User Options]
Use a mapping file to map NetWare user and group names to NT names.

7   **Passwords** [Servers for Migration-User Options-Use Mapping in File]
Set a policy for the passwords on the migrated accounts.

8   **Usernames** [Servers for Migration-User Options-Use Mapping in File]
Choose how duplicate usernames should be handled.

9   **Group Names** [Servers for Migration-User Options-Use Mapping in File]
Choose how duplicate group names should be handled.

10   **Defaults** [Servers for Migration-User Options-Use Mapping in File]
Choose how many NetWare-specific settings to transfer.

11   **File Options** [Servers for Migration]
Control how files and directories are transferred.

12   **Add** [Servers for Migration-File Options]
Add source and destination directories for NetWare files transferred during the migration.

13   **Files** [Servers for Migration-File Options]
Specify individual directories and files to transfer or not transfer.

14   **Start Migration** [Servers for Migration]
Run an actual migration.

15   **Trial Migration** [Servers for Migration]
Run a trial migration, allowing errors to be fixed before the actual migration takes place.

16   **Logging** [Servers for Migration]
Control logging behavior. You should see every detail of the trial migration attempt to make sure there are no serious errors. When you are satisfied with the results of a trial migration, the verbose mode can be turned off.

17   **Popup on errors** [Servers for Migrations-Logging]
Pop up a dialog box when an error occurs during migration. This will be annoying if there are a large number of errors.

Network Client Administrator

Requires
NT Server

Summary
The **Network Client Administrator** is used to set up an NT server to support network booting of Windows and DOS computers. The most common use is creating boot floppies that another computer can boot from, and then get on the network and download installation files from the server. For example, if a computer does not have a local CD-ROM drive, it can be set up to install Windows NT Server, Windows NT Workstation, Windows 95, Windows for

Workgroups, or MS-DOS over the network. All you need is a network adapter and an NT Server somewhere on the network. You can also set up Windows or DOS computers to run completely diskless, downloading all their files over the network each time they are booted.

1 **Make Network Installation Startup Disk**

Create a floppy that enables a computer to get on the network and start installing Windows NT Server, Windows NT Workstation, Windows 95, Windows for Workgroups, or MS-DOS.

2 **Path** [Make Network Installation Startup Disk]

Path to directory where client boot files are stored. This can be the *CLIENTS* subdirectory of the Windows NT CD-ROM or a local hard disk. When network clients are booted from the floppy, they will try to access this path to obtain the client files on the server.

3 **Use Existing Path** [Make Network Installation Startup Disk]

The current location of the network client files. Network clients will try to use this directory when booted.

4 **Share Files** [Make Network Installation Startup Disk]

Create a new share name for the existing client file directory.

5 **Copy Files to New Directory and then Share** [Make Network Installation Startup Disk]

Copy files from the NT CD-ROM onto the local hard disk and share them.

6 **Use Existing Shared Directory** [Make Network Installation Startup Disk]

Tell clients to connect to another server and share name.

7 **Make Installation Disk Set**

The Installation Disk Set creates floppies that allow manual network installation of operating systems or optional software. The menus are identical to those in the previous option.

8 **Copy Client-based Network Administrator Tool**

Create a share that contains network administration tools for administering Windows NT from Windows NT Workstation, Windows NT Server, or Windows 95. The menus are similar to those in the previous option.

Network Monitor

Requires

NT Server

Network Monitor Tools and **Agent** service or **System Management Server** (SMS)

Command-Line Equivalents

netmon

Summary

The **Network Monitor** tool listens on network interfaces, captures network packets, and displays the packets in a raw form. It also provides network performance reports and can identify heavy network users.

This ability to listen on the network allows you see what is happening on the protocol level, which can be very helpful when debugging network problems. For example, if you have a problem printing from an NT server to a network printer, you can use **Network Monitor** to capture the entire transaction between the server and printer. You can then send the capture to Microsoft or the printer vendor, enabling them to play back the entire network transaction for debugging purposes.

The version of **Network Monitor** included in NT 4.0 Server does not allow the network interface to be put in *promiscuous mode*, severely limiting how the tool can be used. Normally, the network interface reads only network packets specifically addressed to it and packets addressed to everyone (broadcasts). Promiscuous mode allows the interface to read all network traffic, regardless of where it is addressed. The Microsoft **System Management Server** (SMS) product includes a version of **Network Monitor** that does allow promiscuous mode, but this must be purchased separately from the NT Server operating system. The limitations of the NT 4.0 Server version of **Network Monitor** confine it to monitoring broadcast traffic and traffic going to and from the local machine. It can also be used to monitor **Remote Access Service** (RAS) interfaces, providing a useful WAN analyzer function.

The **Monitoring Agent** service acts as a proxy for the **Network Monitor** tool. The **Monitoring Agent** runs on a remote computer and transmits captured network packets to the local computer running **Network Monitor**. You can create a central network monitoring station with a single copy of **Network Monitor** that receives captures from NT Workstation or NT Server computers running on remote LAN segments—similar in function to SNMP RMON devices, which sit on a remote network and interact with a centralized SNMP console.

Network Monitor understands all the network protocols supported by NT, including protocols used by RAS. It allows you to create filters that look for just the information you want or take action when a specific kind of network traffic is captured.

Network Monitor has two main modes of operation: a capture mode, where network traffic is read off the network, and a display mode, where captured data is displayed depending on various criteria. The menu choices are context-sensitive depending on the mode.

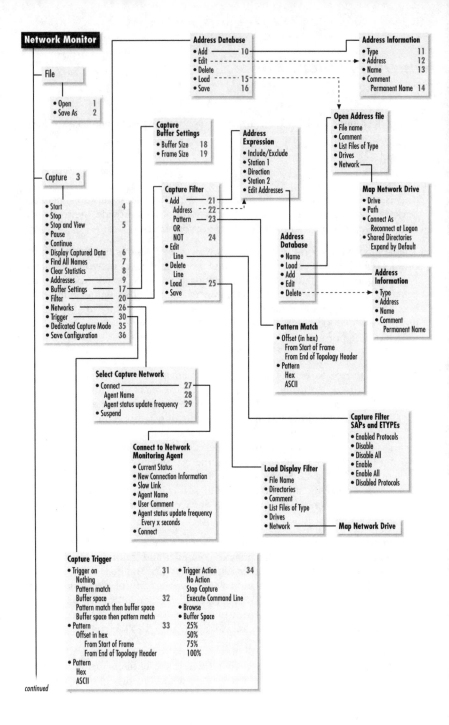

Network Monitor

File
- Open   1
- Save As   2

Capture   3
- Start   4
- Stop
- Stop and View   5
- Pause
- Continue
- Display Captured Data   6
- Find All Names   7
- Clear Statistics   8
- Addresses   9
- Buffer Settings   17
- Filter   20
- Networks   26
- Trigger   30
- Dedicated Capture Mode   35
- Save Configuration   36

Address Database
- Add   10
- Edit
- Delete
- Load   15
- Save   16

Address Information
- Type   11
- Address   12
- Name   13
- Comment
  Permanent Name   14

Capture Buffer Settings
- Buffer Size   18
- Frame Size   19

Address Expression
- Include/Exclude
- Station 1
- Direction
- Station 2
- Edit Addresses

Capture Filter
- Add   21
  Address   22
  Pattern   23
  OR
  NOT   24
- Edit
  Line
- Delete
  Line
- Load   25
- Save

Open Address file
- File name
- Comment
- List Files of Type
- Drives
- Network

Map Network Drive
- Drive
- Path
- Connect As
  Reconnect at Logon
- Shared Directories
  Expand by Default

Address Database
- Name
- Load
- Add
- Edit
- Delete

Address Information
- Type
- Address
- Name
- Comment
  Permanent Name

Pattern Match
- Offset (in hex)
  From Start of Frame
  From End of Topology Header
- Pattern
  Hex
  ASCII

Select Capture Network
- Connect   27
  Agent Name   28
  Agent status update frequency   29
- Suspend

Connect to Network Monitoring Agent
- Current Status
- New Connection Information
- Slow Link
- Agent Name
- User Comment
- Agent status update frequency
  Every x seconds
- Connect

Load Display Filter
- File Name
- Directories
- Comment
- List Files of Type
- Drives
- Network

Capture Filter SAPs and ETYPEs
- Enabled Protocols
- Disable
- Disable All
- Enable
- Enable All
- Disabled Protocols

Map Network Drive

Capture Trigger
- Trigger on   31
  Nothing
  Pattern match
  Buffer space   32
  Pattern match then buffer space
  Buffer space then pattern match
- Pattern   33
  Offset in hex
  From Start of Frame
  From End of Topology Header
- Pattern
  Hex
  ASCII

- Trigger Action   34
  No Action
  Stop Capture
  Execute Command Line
- Browse
- Buffer Space
  25%
  50%
  75%
  100%

continued

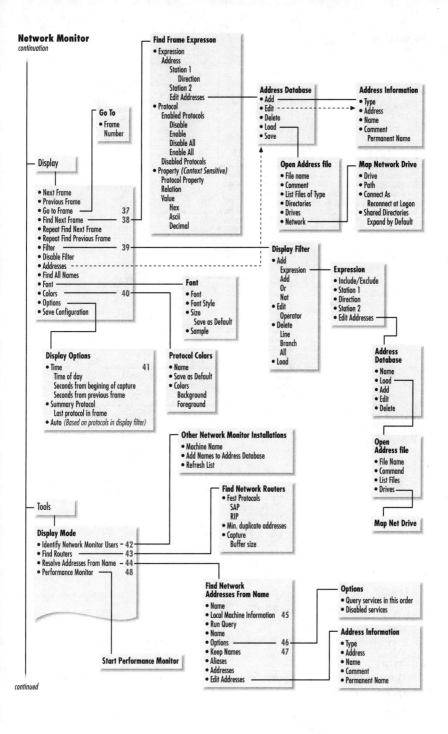

Network Monitor
continuation

Find Frame Expresson
- Expression
  Address
    Station 1
      Direction
    Station 2
    Edit Addresses
- Protocol
  Enabled Protocols
    Disable
    Enable
    Disable All
    Enable All
  Disabled Protocols
- Property *(Context Sensitive)*
  Protocol Property
  Relation
  Value
    Hex
    Ascii
    Decimal

Go To
- Frame
  Number

Display

- Next Frame
- Previous Frame
- Go to Frame 37
- Find Next Frame 38
- Repeat Find Next Frame
- Repeat Find Previous Frame
- Filter 39
- Disable Filter
- Addresses
- Find All Names
- Font
- Colors 40
- Options
- Save Configuration

Address Database
- Add
- Edit
- Delete
- Load
- Save

Address Information
- Type
- Address
- Name
- Comment
  Permanent Name

Open Address file
- File name
- Comment
- List Files of Type
- Directories
- Drives
- Network

Map Network Drive
- Drive
- Path
- Connect As
  Reconnect at Logon
- Shared Directories
  Expand by Default

Display Filter
- Add
  Expression
  Add
  Or
  Not
- Edit
  Operator
- Delete
  Line
  Branch
  All
- Load

Expression
- Include/Exclude
- Station 1
- Direction
- Station 2
- Edit Addresses

Font
- Font
- Font Style
- Size
  Save as Default
- Sample

Display Options
- Time 41
  Time of day
  Seconds from begining of capture
  Seconds from previous frame
- Summary Protocol
  Last protocol in frame
- Auto *(Based on protocols in display filter)*

Protocol Colors
- Name
- Save as Default
- Colors
  Background
  Foreground

Address Database
- Name
- Load
- Add
- Edit
- Delete

Open Address file
- File Name
- Command
- List Files
- Drives

Map Net Drive

Other Network Monitor Installations
- Machine Name
- Add Names to Address Database
- Refresh List

Find Network Routers
- Fest Protocols
  SAP
  RIP
- Min. duplicate addresses
- Capture
  Buffer size

Tools

Display Mode
- Identify Network Monitor Users – 42
- Find Routers 43
- Resolve Addresses From Name – 44
- Performance Monitor 48

Find Network Addresses From Name
- Name
- Local Machine Information 45
- Run Query
- Name
- Options 46
- Keep Names 47
- Aliases
- Addresses
- Edit Addresses

Options
- Query services in this order
- Disabled services

Address Information
- Type
- Address
- Name
- Comment
- Permanent Name

Start Performance Monitor

continued

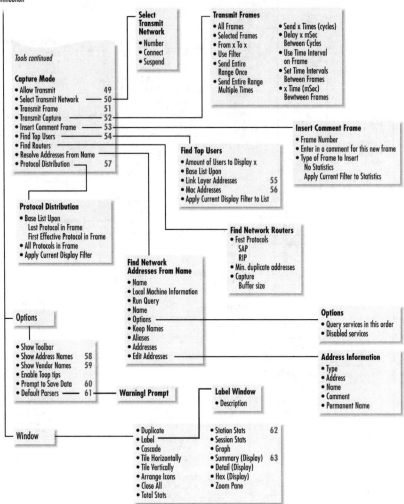

1 **Open** [File]

Open a previously saved network capture.

2 **Save As** [File]

Save a current capture to disk (stored as a *.CAP* file).

3 **Capture**

The **Capture** menu appears only when capturing data. The **Display** menu appears only when displaying captured data.

4 **Start** [Capture]

Start capturing network traffic.

5 **Stop and View** [Capture]
Stop capture and display capture window.

6 **Display Captured Data** [Capture]
Display capture window.

7 **Find All Names** [Capture]
Try to match addresses with computer names, improving readability of the capture display.

8 **Clear Statistics** [Capture]
Clear capture statistics.

9 **Addresses** [Capture]
Display all addresses in capture and allow new addresses to be added or current ones to be modified. The main goal here is to improve the readability of the capture data by associating familiar names with addresses. The address database can be saved and reused for other capture sessions.

10 **Add** [Capture-Addresses]
Add a new address to the address database.

11 **Type** [Capture-Addresses-Add]
Choose the type of address, which is either Ethernet, FDDI, IP, IPX/XNS, Token Ring, or VINES IP.

12 **Address** [Capture-Addresses-Add]
Add an address of the selected type. For Ethernet, use the Ethernet address of the network adapter from which you are trying capture traffic. For IP, use the IP address of the computer. The Ethernet address is useful, as it matches all traffic going to or from a computer, regardless of protocol. The problem with using Ethernet addresses is that they are only addressable on the local LAN. Any traffic from or to a computer on the other side of a router has the Ethernet address of the router, not the remote computer. You must use the higher level protocol address such as IP in this situation.

13 **Name** [Capture-Addresses-Add]
Add a name for the new entry. This name exists only with **Network Monitor** and is not known or used outside of it. For the network printer debugging example, you could name the NT server *ntserver* and the printer *printer* to make them obvious in capture data.

14 **Permanent Name** [Capture-Addresses-Add-Comment]
Store this computer name in the local address database. You will still have to save the address database to disk to keep the name from being lost upon exiting **Network Monitor**.

15 **Load** [Capture-Addresses]
Load a previously saved address database (an *.ADR* file).

16 **Save** [Capture-Addresses]
Save addresses in a disk file.

17 **Buffer Settings** [Capture]
The capture buffer is the amount of memory allocated for the captured data.

18 Buffer Size [Capture-Buffer Settings]

Set how much data can be captured in a single capture session.

19 Frame Size [Capture-Buffer Settings]

The network packets are within a structure called a frame. The beginning of the frame (the header) is usually the most interesting, as it contains all the protocol information such as source and destination addresses, options, checksums, and so on. The bulk of the packet is the data being sent in the packet. If you are only interested in the packet header, you can choose a frame size that encompasses just the header and the remainder of the frame will be discarded. This conserves buffer space, enabling more packets to be stored in the same size of capture buffer.

20 Filter [Capture]

A capture filter determines what types of network packets are captured. If a packet does not meet the criteria of the filter, it is discarded and not stored within the capture. A capture filter is different than a display filter in that a display filter limits which packets are displayed out of all those contained in the capture. Packets can be filtered based on source, destination, protocol, specific bit patterns present within the packet, and more.

21 Add [Capture-Filter]

Add a new rule to the filter.

22 Address [Capture-Filter-Add]

Capture traffic between an address on the left and an address on the right.

23 Pattern [Capture-Filter-Add]

Capture traffic matching patterns within the packet. This feature allows you to capture packets from any protocol (even ones unknown to **Network Monitor**), if you know what pattern to look for.

24 NOT [Capture-Filter-Add]

Add a boolean NOT expression to the rule. If you want to capture everything except the specified traffic, use this rule.

25 Load [Capture-Filter]

Load a previously saved filter (a *.CF* file).

26 Networks [Capture]

Attach network monitor to a different network interface. If the local computer has multiple network interfaces, they will be identified by different addresses. For some strange reason, the WAN interface used by RAS (normally a serial port going to a modem) lists an Ethernet interface with an address of all zeros.

27 Connect [Capture-Networks]

(SMS only) Selecting the interface named **REMOTE** connects **Network Monitor** to another computer running the **Monitoring Agent** service.

28 Agent Name [Capture-Networks-Connect]

(SMS only) Enter the name of the remote computer running **Monitoring Agent**.

29 Agent status update frequency [Capture-Networks-Connect]

Set how often the remote computer will send capture traffic to **Network Monitor**.

30 Trigger [Capture]

Network Monitor can be configured to perform some action based on an event or specific data it sees on the network. The event or data is a trigger.

31 Trigger On [Capture-Trigger]

Define criteria for a trigger to take place. A pattern match occurs when a captured packet matches a specific pattern. Buffer space is the amount of memory consumed by the capture.

32 Buffer Space [Capture-Trigger-Trigger On]

Set the amount of buffer space consumed before a trigger takes effect.

33 Pattern [Capture-Trigger]

Specify a pattern to look for in packets.

34 Trigger Action [Capture-Trigger]

Action to take if a trigger occurs. For example, you could run a program that pages the administrator when a specific type of network traffic appears.

35 Dedicated Capture Mode [Capture]

If the computer is dropping frames (failing to capture all packets), dedicated capture mode turns off all statistics displays, freeing up some resources for the capture process.

36 Save Configuration [Capture]

Save all current Network Monitor configuration settings to disk.

37 Go to Frame [Display]

Jump to a specific frame within the capture.

38 Find Next Frame [Display]

Search for frame based on address, protocol, or property (specify criteria).

39 Filter [Display]

Apply filter to display data. This is similar to a capture filter, but it does not discard filtered data.

40 Colors [Display]

Color-code display according to protocol.

41 Time [Display-Options]

Control how timestamps are represented in display window.

42 Identify Network Monitor Users [Tools]

(Capture mode only) Find other computers on the network running Network Monitor.

43 Find Routers [Tools]

(SMS only) Try to find all routers on the network. Routers are located using routing protocols and can then be added to an address database for future use.

44 Resolve Addresses From Name [Tools]

(SMS only) Try to find the corresponding addresses for computer name. This includes IP addresses for TCP/IP hostnames, Ethernet addresses for NetBIOS computer names, and so on. The name is looked up under each protocol running on the computer.

45 **Local Machine Information** [Tools-Resolve Addresses From Name]
Look up all addresses for the local computer.

46 **Options** [Tools-Resolve Addresses From Name]
Configure what types of name servers and databases should be used when looking up a name. Possibilities are:

DNS
    IP addresses

Local ADR Database
    MAC addresses stored in *DEFAULT.ADR* file

NetBIOS
    NetBIOS addresses (MAC addresses)

SAP
    IPX/SPX addresses

SMS
    System Management Server Database

47 **Keep Names** [Tools-Resolve Addresses From Name]
Store names in *DEFAULT.ADR* file which is loaded every time **Network Monitor** starts.

48 **Performance Monitor** [Tools]
Start **Performance Monitor**. This may be helpful if you want to monitor network performance of the local computer, remote computers, or both.

49 **Allow Transmit** [Tools]
(Display mode of SMS only) Enable transmit function. This allows **Network Monitor** to retransmit previously captured packets back on the network. This replaying of a sequence of packets can be used to test network-related problems. This is disabled by default, preventing mistakes. Note that this function could also be used in malicious ways.

50 **Select Transmit Network** [Tools]
(Display mode of SMS only) Select the network interface to receive traffic.

51 **Transmit Frame** [Tools]
(Display mode of SMS only) Send specified frame to selected network.

52 **Transmit Capture** [Tools]
(Display mode of SMS only) Send multiple frames to selected network.

53 **Insert Comment Frame** [Tools]
(Display mode only) Insert a comment into the capture output. This is a mechanism for annotating the captured data.

54 **Find Top Users** [Tools]
(Display mode of SMS only) Find the computers or network devices that generated the most network traffic during the capture. If you are wondering why the network is slow, this allows you to find which computers are using the network the most.

55 Link Layer Addresses [Tools-Find Top Users]

Use network address (such as IP address) to determine top users. If you count just MAC addresses, routers may be counted instead of the computer using the router.

56 MAC Addresses [Tools-Find Top Users]

Simply count MAC addresses. May distort information if traffic is crossing a router.

57 Protocol Distribution [Tools]

(Display mode of SMS only) Sort traffic by protocol type and show percentage of total traffic.

58 Show Address Names [Options]

Present address information is a user-friendly manner, matching computer names with addresses. For example, a broadcast address of FFFFFFFFFFFF could be displayed as BROADCAST, and 080009C76E6A could be displayed as the computer name NTSRV40. This should make reading captured data quicker and easier.

59 Show Vendor Names [Options]

Try to interpret vendor information from addresses. Every 12-byte Ethernet address contains a code number that indicates the manufacturer of the network adapter. For example, the address 080009C76E6A is displayed as HP C76E6A, indicating that the network adapter was made by Hewlett-Packard. This can be helpful when you are trying to match computers with their Ethernet addresses.

60 Prompt to Save Data [Options]

Prompt before allowing user to quit if there is unsaved data or settings.

61 Default Parsers [Options]

Parsers read packets and interpret their structure. When you enable a parser for a protocol, you are enabling **Network Monitor** to recognize and understand the packet format for that protocol. Disabling a parser will cause **Network Monitor** to treat the protocol type as unknown.

62 Stations Stats [Window]

Switch to capture mode, exposing **Capture** menu.

63 Summary [Window]

Switch to display mode, exposing **Display** menu.

Administrative Tools

Performance Monitor

Requires

NT Workstation or Server

Summary

Performance Monitor is used to generate graphs, reports, and logs of system activity from multiple computers. It can also be configured to notify users or run programs when a parameter reaches a user-defined threshold. Performance monitor can be used to tune systems and networks and to locate performance bottlenecks.

Performance Monitor has four modes of operation:

Chart

Graph system parameters over time. It can read data in real time from either the local computer or other computers over the network, or from recorded log files.

Alert

Set up triggers that depend on various criteria. A trigger can alert a user or run a program.

Log Record data from the local or remote computers to a disk file for later analysis.

Report

Generates reports based on data. This is useful for summarizing data and creating documents.

You can switch between modes without disrupting what is going on in other the modes.

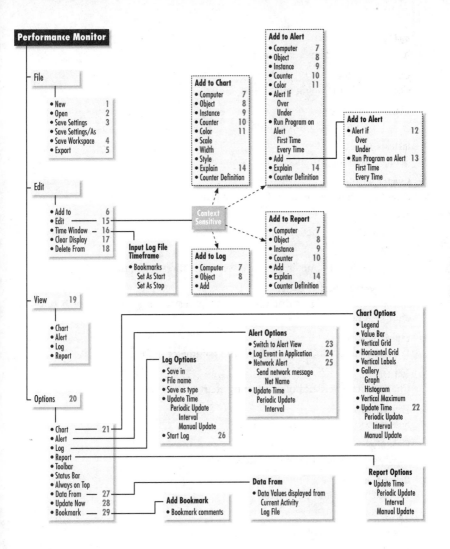

Performance Monitor

- File
  - • New — 1
  - • Open — 2
  - • Save Settings — 3
  - • Save Settings/As
  - • Save Workspace — 4
  - • Export — 5

- Edit
  - • Add to — 6
  - • Edit — 15
  - • Time Window — 16
  - • Clear Display — 17
  - • Delete From — 18

  Input Log File Timeframe
  - • Bookmarks
    - Set As Start
    - Set As Stop

- View — 19
  - • Chart
  - • Alert
  - • Log
  - • Report

- Options — 20
  - • Chart — 21
  - • Alert
  - • Log
  - • Report
  - • Toolbar
  - • Status Bar
  - • Always on Top
  - • Data From — 27
  - • Update Now — 28
  - • Bookmark — 29

Add to Chart
- • Computer — 7
- • Object — 8
- • Instance — 9
- • Counter — 10
- • Color — 11
- • Scale
- • Width
- • Style
- • Explain — 14
- • Counter Definition

Add to Alert
- • Computer — 7
- • Object — 8
- • Instance — 9
- • Counter — 10
- • Color — 11
- • Alert If
  - Over
  - Under
- • Run Program on Alert
  - First Time
  - Every Time
- • Add
- • Explain — 14
- • Counter Definition

Add to Alert
- • Alert if — 12
  - Over
  - Under
- • Run Program on Alert — 13
  - First Time
  - Every Time

Context Sensitive

Add to Report
- • Computer — 7
- • Object — 8
- • Instance — 9
- • Counter — 10
- • Add
- • Explain — 14
- • Counter Definition

Add to Log
- • Computer — 7
- • Object — 8
- • Add

Log Options
- • Save in
- • File name
- • Save as type
- • Update Time
  - Periodic Update
  - Interval
  - Manual Update
- • Start Log — 26

Alert Options
- • Switch to Alert View — 23
- • Log Event in Application — 24
- • Network Alert — 25
  - Send network message
  - Net Name
- • Update Time
  - Periodic Update
  - Interval

Chart Options
- • Legend
- • Value Bar
- • Vertical Grid
- • Horizontal Grid
- • Vertical Labels
- • Gallery
  - Graph
  - Histogram
- • Vertical Maximum
- • Update Time — 22
  - Periodic Update
  - Interval
  - Manual Update

Add Bookmark
- • Bookmark comments

Data From
- • Data Values displayed from
  - Current Activity
  - Log File

Report Options
- • Update Time
  - Periodic Update
  - Interval
  - Manual Update

1. **New** [File]
   Create a new chart, alert, log, or report.

2. **Open** [File]
   Use previously saved chart, alert, log, report, or *workspace* settings. The workspace is the combination of all mode settings.

3. **Save Settings** [File]
   Save current settings for a chart, alert, log, and report.

4. **Save Workspace** [File]
   Save settings for combined chart, alert, log, and report windows.

5. **Export** [File]
   Save data to disk in either Tab-Separated Variable (TSV) or Comma-Separated Variable (CSV) formats. The data file can then be imported to another application for further processing.

6 Add To [Edit]
Add a system parameter to monitor.

7 Computer [Edit-Add To]
Computer that is being monitored.

8 Object [Edit-Add To]
Select system object to monitor.

9 Instance [Edit-Add To]
Select a specific instance of the counter to monitor.

10 Counter [Edit-Add To]
Select a counter to monitor for this object.

11 Color [Edit-Add To]
Select a color for the chart line.

12 Alert if [Edit-Add To-Add]
Generate alert if counter goes over or under threshold value.

13 Run Program on Alert [Edit-Add To-Add]
Execute program or script upon alert, either the first time or each time the alert is generated.

14 Explain [Edit-Add To]
Pop up a help window describing the parameter being monitored.

15 Edit [Edit]
Change characteristics of an existing chart or alert.

16 Time Window [Edit]
Sets period of time to display data.

17 Clear Display [Edit]
Clear display, but do not delete data.

18 Delete From [Edit]
Delete the selected parameter.

19 View
Select mode of display.

20 Options
Options are specific to current mode.

21 Chart [Options]
Set graphing display options for chart.

22 Update Time [Options-Chart]
Either update report display on set intervals or by manually using **Options-Update Now** menu.

23 Switch to Alert View [Options-Alert]
Switch mode to Alert mode whenever an alert occurs.

24 Log Event in Application [Options-Alert]
Log alerts in application log of **Event Viewer**.

25 **Network Alert** [Options-Alert]
Send an alert to a specific user. The user has to be logged on the network or using a computer running the **Messenger** service.

26 **Start Log** [Options-Log]
Start logging data to disk.

27 **Data From** [Options]
Use current data or data stored in a logfile.

28 **Update Now** [Options]
Update display without waiting for next update interval.

29 **Bookmark** [Options]
Annotate points of interest in the logfile.

Remote Access Admin

Requires
NT Workstation or Server
Remote Access Service (RAS)

Command-Line Equivalents
rasadmin

Summary
The **Remote Access Admin** tool administers **Remote Access Service** (RAS) incoming and outgoing connections to the computer. (**Dial-Up Networking** configures outgoing connections.) It can also manage RAS on remote computers. If you select a remote computer or domain, all the configuration options pertain to the remote computer. **Remote Access Admin** can also send messages to connected RAS users. This may be useful for warning remote users about server downtime or other events.

In order to use **Remote Access Admin**, you must have configured at least one RAS port. This can be done using the **Network** control panel and selecting **Services-Remote Access Service-Properties-Configure**.

The Workstation version of RAS allows only one RAS connection at a time, while Server can support up to 256 simultaneous connections.

Refer to the following figure for an illustration of the menu structure.

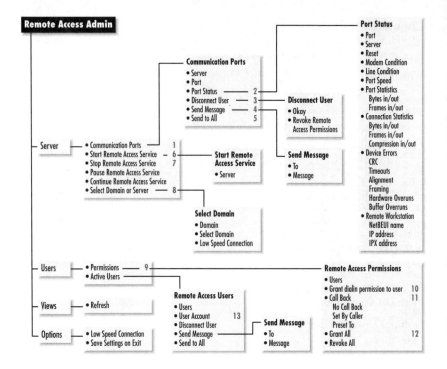

1 **Communication Ports** [Server]

Display information about RAS port usage (including virtual ports used by PPTP).

2 **Port Status** [Server-Communication Ports]

Display detailed communications statistics about a specific port. This can be used to verify that network addresses are being provided by the RAS server to the clients.

3 **Disconnect User** [Server-Communication Ports]

Disconnect user(s) from the RAS server, killing their session(s).

4 **Send Message** [Server-Communication Ports]

Send a message to specific users.

5 **Send to All** [Server-Communication Ports]

Send a message all connected users.

6 **Start Remote Access Service** [Server]

Start RAS service, enabling RAS connections. If you want the RAS service to always run or always be disabled, use the **Services** control panel.

7 **Stop Remote Access Service** [Server]

Stop the RAS service, killing any connected users and preventing new connections. This provides a means to prevent remote connections from taking place without disturbing permissions. You may wish to stop RAS during backups or other system maintenance.

8 **Select Domain or Server** [Server]

Select a remote domain or server on which to administer RAS.

9 **Permissions** [Users]

Determine which users are able to dial into the RAS server. If you have selected a domain, the permissions are set for the entire domain.

10 **Grant dialin permission to user** [Users-Permissions]

Allow selected user to call in to computer via RAS. Dial-in permissions can also be set in **User Manager for Domains** under the **User-Properties-Dialin** menu.

11 **Call Back** [Users-Permissions]

In order to reverse calling charges or enhance security, make an outgoing call to the remote user.

12 **Grant All** [Users-Permissions]

Give all users dial-in permissions.

13 **User Account** [Users-Active Users]

Dial-in permissions can also be set in **User Manager for Domains** under the **User-New User-Dialin** menu.

Rdisk

Requires

NT Workstation or Server

Command-Line Equivalents

rdisk

Summary

The **rdisk** utility is used to create emergency repair disks (ERD), which can be used to restore a damaged NT installation. The utility should be run each time there are significant changes to the system. This way, if you should have disk problems, you will be able to restore the system to its most recent configuration.

rdisk is not normally part of the **Administrative Tools** menu, but you can either add a shortcut to it (*<winnt root>\SYSTEM32\RDISK.EXE*) or run it from the command line.

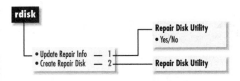

1 **Update Repair Info**

Exports current Registry settings into files in the *<winnt root>\REPAIR* directory.

Formats a floppy and copies the contents of the REPAIR directory to it.

Regedit

Requires

NT Workstation or Server

Command-Line Equivalents

regedit

Summary

The **Regedit** utility is the Windows 95–style Registry editor. Windows NT 4.0 also comes with the Windows NT 3.x–style **Regedt32** Registry editor (see comparison chart in the **Regedt32** description). The Registry editor is most commonly used to make small changes to the system configuration. For the most part, users interact with the Registry by using the administrative tools. The Registry editor lets you see the Registry in its raw form, bypassing the administrative tools. With this ability comes the hazard of creating invalid or useless Registry settings that may prevent an application from running or may even crash NT itself. NT has many settings and options that have no corresponding administrative interface. Using a Registry editor may be the only way to reach them.

Regedit is not normally part of the **Administrative Tools** menu, but you can either add a shortcut to it (*<winnt root>\REGEDIT.EXE*) or run it from the command line.

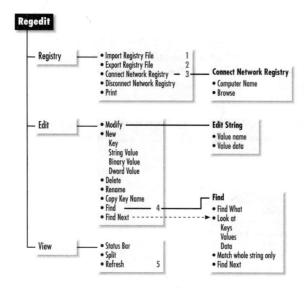

1 **Import Registry File** [Registry]
Read in Registry tree from a disk file, merging with current Registry information.

2 **Export Registry File** [Registry]
Write out selected Registry tree to a disk file.

3 **Connect Network Registry** [Registry]
Connect to another computer on the network and edit its Registry.

4 **Find** [Edit]
Search the Registry for a specific string that occurs in one of the keys, values, or data.

5 **Refresh** [View]
If some other program or user changes the Registry while you are you viewing it, you have to manually refresh the display in order see the most current information.

See the feature comparison chart in the **Regedt32** description.

Regedt32

Requires
NT Workstation or Server

Command-Line Equivalents
regedt32

Summary
The **Regedt32** utility is the Windows NT 3.x-style Registry editor. Windows NT 4.0 also comes with the Windows 95–style **Regedit** Registry editor (see comparison chart below). The Registry editor is most commonly used to make small changes to the system configuration. For the most part, users interact with the Registry by using the administrative tools. The Registry editor lets you see the Registry in its raw form, bypassing the administrative tools. With this ability comes the hazard of creating invalid or useless Registry settings that may prevent an application from running or may even crash NT itself. NT has many settings and options that have no corresponding administrative interface. Using a Registry editor may be the only way to reach them.

Note that **Regedt32** can administer security for the Registry, unlike **Regedit**. Keys and subkeys have permissions, much like directories in an NTFS file system. The security of the Registry is important, as allowing a user to change the Registry enables them to bypass the administrative tools, and possibly gain control of the system or seriously damage it. The Registry can also be edited remotely from other computers.

The **Regedt32** tool is not normally part of the **Administrative Tools** menu, but you can either add a shortcut to it (*<winnt root>\SYSTEM32\REGEDT32.EXE*) or run it from the command line.

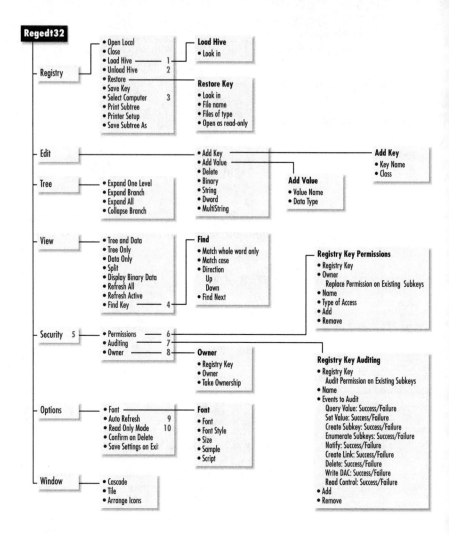

1 **Load Hive** [Registry]

Attach a hive (a Registry tree stored in a disk file) to the current Registry. The load operation works only on the **HKEY_USERS** and **HKEY_LOCAL_MACHINE** keys. Unlike a **Restore** or **Import** operation, **Load** does not merge data from the hive into the local Registry. This can be used to edit a hive from a remote machine by loading the hives off a network drive.

2 **Unload Hive** [Registry]

Detach a hive from the local Registry.

3 **Select Computer Registry**

Edit the Registry on another computer on the network.

4 **Find Key** [View]

Search the Registry for a key containing a given string.

5 Security

The NT Registry can set access control lists on Registry keys in the same manner as files and directories under NTFS. These permissions control which users and groups can edit which Registry keys.

6 Permissions [Security]

Assigns user and group permissions to selected key.

7 Auditing [Security]

Audit events on the selected key by the specific users and groups. The audited events appear in the security log of **Event Viewer**.

8 Owner [Security]

Take the ownership of selected key.

9 Auto Refresh [Options]

Update Registry display automatically as contents change.

10 Read Only Mode [Options]

Prevents any changes from taking place, allowing you to explore it without negative consequences.

The following table provides a comparison of **Regedt32** and **Regedit**.

Feature	Regedt32	Regedit
Load and unload hives	Yes	No
Searching for key, values, data	Keys only	Yes
Separate window for top level key	Yes	No
Read-only mode	Yes	No
Auto-refresh	Yes	No
Security administration	Yes	No
Import/Export from command line	No	Yes

Remoteboot Manager

Requires

NT Server
DLC Protocol
Remoteboot Service
NetBEUI Protocol

Summary

The **Remoteboot Manager** sets configuration options for computers that boot from the network (instead of their local hard drives). Computers can download their operating systems and obtain all their configuration information from an NT Server running the **Remoteboot** service. The **Remoteboot Manager** allows configuration of which operating system should be downloaded to a specific remoteboot client and which TCP/IP network settings should be used. The

Administrative Tools

operating system settings for clients are stored in profiles (which have nothing to do with hardware profiles or user profiles). The profile usually contains the operating system type and the brand and model of a network adapter; for example, Windows 95 3Com Etherlink III. You must specify TCP/IP settings and a profile as part of setting up each remoteboot client (or *workstation*). When a client is booted, the remoteboot service looks up its MAC-level address in the list of workstations and downloads the appropriate operating system, network adapter drivers, and TCP/IP settings.

If the **Remoteboot Manager** complains that the **Remoteboot Service** is not running, start it from the **Services** control panel or from the command line using:

```
net start "Remoteboot Service"
```

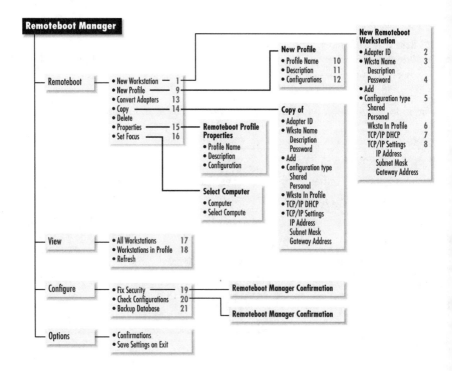

1   **New Workstation** [Remoteboot]
    Create a new record.

2   **Adapter ID** [Remoteboot-New Workstation]
    MAC-level address of network adapter on the client computer. This associates the following information with a specific client.

3   **Wksta Name** [Remoteboot-New Workstation]
    NetBIOS computer name of client.

4   **Password** [Remoteboot-New Workstation-Wksta Name]
    The password allows the client workstation to boot off the server. It is not related to any user of the workstation once it is booted.

5 **Configuration type** [Remoteboot-New Workstation]
Workstations either share a profile or use a specific one.

6 **Wksta In Profile** [Remoteboot-New Workstation-Configuration type]
Select a profile for new record. The options in the scroll list depend on what operating systems and adapters are supported by remoteboot.

7 **TCP/IP DHCP** [Remoteboot-New Workstation-Configuration type]
Have the client obtain the TCP/IP settings from a DHCP server.

8 **TCP/IP Settings** [Remoteboot-New Workstation-Configuration type]
Specify settings for the client.

9 **New Profile** [Remoteboot]
Create a new operating system and network adapter profile.

10 **Profile Name** [Remoteboot-New Profile]
Name for profile that will be used in scroll lists.

11 **Description** [Remoteboot-New Profile]
Description (should include operating system and network adapter type).

12 **Configurations** [Remoteboot-New Profile]
Select an existing profile to edit.

13 **Convert Adapters** [Remoteboot]
If you are able to boot a client workstation and get it on the network, you can add it to the remoteboot database by selecting it from the list. This may be preferable to typing in the Ethernet address manually.

14 **Copy** [Remoteboot]
Copy an existing record and modify it.

15 **Properties** [Remoteboot]
If a workstation is selected, allow editing of workstation settings. If a profile is selected, show current profile contents.

16 **Set Focus** [Remoteboot]
Select which computer to administer the remoteboot service on.

17 **All Workstations** [View]
Show all workstation records.

18 **Workstations in Profile** [View]
Show only those workstations with an associated profile.

19 **Fix Security** [Configure]
Modify disk and file permissions on local computer to allow for remoteboot operations.

20 **Check Configurations** [Configure]
Build configurations that can be downloaded by a remoteboot client. A configuration is a combination of an operating system and a network adapter driver.

21 **Backup Database** [Configure]
Write database and remoteboot settings to a disk file.

Server Manager

Requires

NT Server

Command-Line Equivalents

net computer

Summary

The **Server Manager** tool can manage domains, workgroups, or individual computers. It controls domain membership, status of domain controllers, file sharing, file replication, and the determination of who receives administrative alerts. **Server Manager** also allows you to disconnect users and processes using network resources. **Server Manager** includes the functionality of several control panels, including **FPNW**, **MacFile**, **Server**, **Services**, and some features of **Windows NT Explorer**. It may help to think of **Server Manager** as a networked control panel, as it can operate the control panels on remote computers. If you have permissions set up correctly, it should be possible for you to administer any NT machine on the network from any NT computer.

Properties for
- Usage Summary
  Sessions
  Open Files
  File Locks
  Open Named Pipes
- Description
- Users
- Shares
- In Use
- Replication
- Alerts

User Sessions on
- Connected Users
- Resource
- Disconnect
- Disconnect All

Shared Resources on
- Sharename
- Connected Users
- Disconnect
- Disconnect All

Open Resources on
- Open Resources
- File Locks
- Opened by
- Refresh
- Close Resource
- Close All Resources

Manage Exported Directories
- Export Path
- Sub-Directory
- Add
- Remove
- Export Settings for
  Add Lock
  Remove
  Wait Until Stabilized
  Entire Subtree

Add Sub-Directory
- Path
- Sub-Directory Name

Add Sub-Directory
- Path
- Sub-Directory Name

Alerts on
- New Computer or
  Username
- Add
- Remove
- Send Administrative
  Alerts To

Directory Replication on
- Do Not Export
- Export Directories
  From Path
  Manage
  Too List
  Add
  Remove
- Do Not Import
- Import Directories
  To Path
  Manage
  From List
  Add
  Remove
- Logon Script Path

Select Domain
- Domain
- Select Domain

Manage Imported Directories
- Imprt Path
- Sub-Directory
- Add
- Remove
- Import Settings for
  Add Lock
  Remove Lock

Select Domain
- Domain
- Select Domain

Shared Directories
- Shared Directories on
- New Share
- Properties
- Stop Sharing

New Share
- Share Name
- Path
- Comment
- User Limit
  Max. Allowed
  Allow x Users
- Permissions

Access Through Shared Permissions
- Access Through Share
- Owner
- Name
- Type of Access
- Add
- Remove

Add Users and Groups
- List Names From
- Names
- Add
- Show Users
- Members
- Search
- Add Names
- Type of Access

Share Properties
- Share Name
- Path
- Comment
- User Limit
  Max. Allowed
  Allow x Users
- Permissions

Computer

- Properties   1
- Shared Directories 2
- Services   3
- Send Message   4
- Promote to Primary
  Domain Controller   5
- Synchronize Entire Domain 6
- Add to Domain   7
- Remove from Domain 8
- Select Domain   9

Send Message
- To users connected to
- Message

Services on
- Service
- Start
- Stop
- Pause
- Continue
- Startup
- HW Profiles
- Startup Parameters

Service on
- Service
- Startup Type
  Automatic
  Manual
  Disabled
- Log On As
  System Account
    Allow Service to
    Interact with Desktop
  This Account
    Password
    Confirm Password

Add Computer to Domain
- Computer Type
  Windows NT Workstation or Server
  Windows NT Backup Domain Controller
- Add
- Computer Name

Select Domain
- Domain
- Select Domain
- Low Speed Connection

Service on
- Service   • Enable
- Status   • Disable

continued

Server Manager
continued

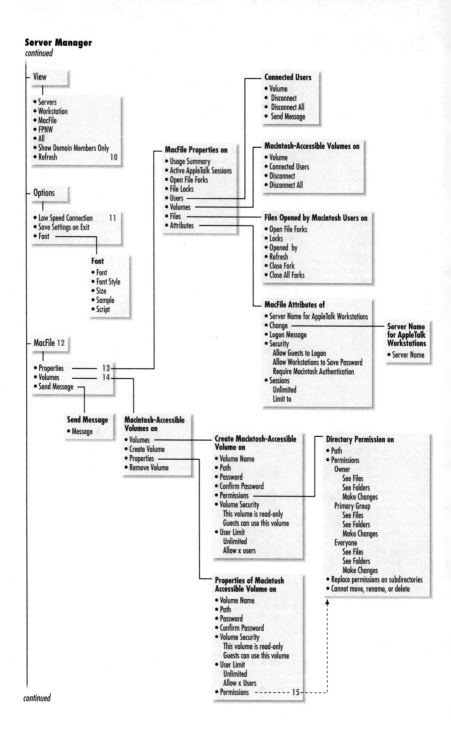

View
- Servers
- Workstation
- MacFile
- FPNW
- All
- Show Domain Members Only
- Refresh   10

Options
- Low Speed Connection   11
- Save Settings on Exit
- Font

Font
- Font
- Font Style
- Size
- Sample
- Script

MacFile 12
- Properties ———— 13
- Volumes ———— 14
- Send Message

Send Message
- Message

MacFile Properties on
- Usage Summary
- Active AppleTalk Sessions
- Open File Forks
- File Locks
- Users ————
- Volumes
- Files ————
- Attributes

Connected Users
- Volume
- Disconnect
- Disconnect All
- Send Message

Macintosh-Accessible Volumes on
- Volume
- Connected Users
- Disconnect
- Disconnect All

Files Opened by Macintosh Users on
- Open File Forks
- Locks
- Opened by
- Refresh
- Close Fork
- Close All Forks

MacFile Attributes of
- Server Name for AppleTalk Workstations
- Change ————
- Logon Message
- Security
  Allow Guests to Logon
  Allow Workstations to Save Password
  Require Macintosh Authentication
- Sessions
  Unlimited
  Limit to

Server Name for AppleTalk Workstations
- Server Name

Macintosh-Accessible Volumes on
- Volumes ————
- Create Volume
- Properties ————
- Remove Volume

Create Macintosh-Accessible Volume on
- Volume Name
- Path
- Password
- Confirm Password
- Permissions ————
- Volume Security
  This volume is read-only
  Guests can use this volume
- User Limit
  Unlimited
  Allow x users

Properties of Macintosh Accessible Volume on
- Volume Name
- Path
- Password
- Confirm Password
- Volume Security
  This volume is read-only
  Guests can use this volume
- User Limit
  Unlimited
  Allow x Users
- Permissions ---------- 15 ------

Directory Permission on
- Path
- Permissions
  Owner
    See Files
    See Folders
    Make Changes
  Primary Group
    See Files
    See Folders
    Make Changes
  Everyone
    See Files
    See Folders
    Make Changes
- Replace permissions on subdirectories
- Cannot move, rename, or delete

continued

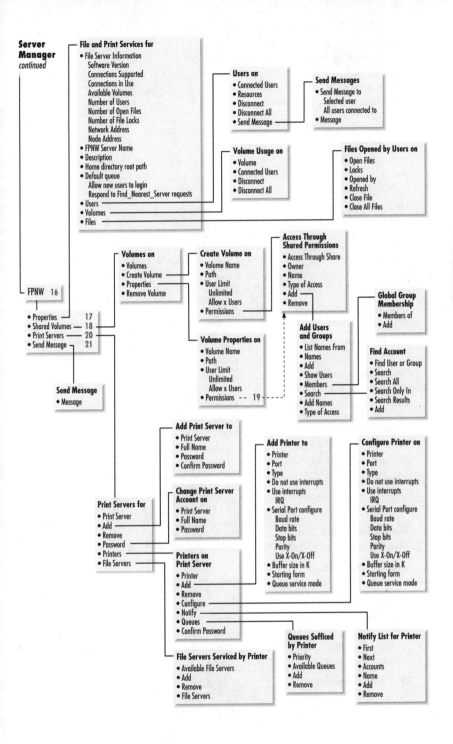

Server Manager
continued

File and Print Services for
- File Server Information
  Software Version
  Connections Supported
  Connections in Use
  Available Volumes
  Number of Users
  Number of Open Files
  Number of File Locks
  Network Address
  Node Address
- FPNW Server Name
- Description
- Home directory root path
- Default queue
  Allow new users to login
  Respond to Find_Nearest_Server requests
- Users
- Volumes
- Files

Users on
- Connected Users
- Resources
- Disconnect
- Disconnect All
- Send Message

Send Messages
- Send Message to
  Selected user
  All users connected to
- Message

Volume Usage on
- Volume
- Connected Users
- Disconnect
- Disconnect All

Files Opened by Users on
- Open Files
- Locks
- Opened by
- Refresh
- Close File
- Close All Files

FPNW   16

- Properties ——— 17
- Shared Volumes — 18
- Print Servers —— 20
- Send Message — 21

Volumes on
- Volumes
- Create Volume
- Properties
- Remove Volume

Create Volume on
- Volume Name
- Path
- User Limit
  Unlimited
  Allow x Users
- Permissions

Access Through Shared Permissions
- Access Through Share
- Owner
- Name
- Type of Access
- Add
- Remove

Global Group Membership
- Members of
- Add

Send Message
- Message

Volume Properties on
- Volume Name
- Path
- User Limit
  Unlimited
  Allow x Users
- Permissions — 19

Add Users and Groups
- List Names From
- Names
- Add
- Show Users
- Members
- Search
- Add Names
- Type of Access

Find Account
- Find User or Group
- Search
- Search All
- Search Only In
- Search Results
- Add

Add Print Server to
- Print Server
- Full Name
- Password
- Confirm Password

Add Printer to
- Printer
- Port
- Type
- Do not use interrupts
- Use interrupts
  IRQ
- Serial Port configure
  Baud rate
  Data bits
  Stop bits
  Parity
  Use X-On/X-Off
- Buffer size in K
- Starting form
- Queue service mode

Configure Printer on
- Printer
- Port
- Type
- Do not use interrupts
- Use interrupts
  IRQ
- Serial Port configure
  Baud rate
  Data bits
  Stop bits
  Parity
  Use X-On/X-Off
- Buffer size in K
- Starting form
- Queue service mode

Change Print Server Account on
- Print Server
- Full Name
- Password

Print Servers for
- Print Server
- Add
- Remove
- Password
- Printers
- File Servers

Printers on Print Server
- Printer
- Add
- Remove
- Configure
- Notify
- Queues
- Confirm Password

File Servers Serviced by Printer
- Available File Servers
- Add
- Remove
- File Servers

Queues Sufficed by Printer
- Priority
- Available Queues
- Add
- Remove

Notify List for Printer
- First
- Next
- Accounts
- Name
- Add
- Remove

Administrative Tools

1 Properties [Computer]
Shows what is being used and who is using it on the selected computer. It allows you to view what resources the computer is providing from several different perspectives, including what users are using, what resources are being offered, and what resources are in use.

See the **Server** control panel.

2 Shared Directories [Computer]
Administer file sharing for Microsoft Networking clients. You can start and stop sharing, and set permissions for sharing and view sharing activity on the selected computer.

3 Services [Computer]
See the **Services** control panel.

4 Send Message [Computer]
Send a popup text message to all users connected to the selected computer. This is handy for warning users about downtime, and so on. The user has to be connected to receive the message.

5 Promote to Primary Domain Controller [Computer]
If the Primary Domain Controller (PDC) is unavailable for a period of time, this menu option can be used to promote a Backup Domain Controller (BDC) to a PDC.

6 Synchronize Entire Domain [Computer]
Synchronize account databases with the PDC for this domain. BDCs periodically synchronize with the PDC, but this command can be used to force an immediate synchronization without waiting for the next scheduled one. This may be helpful after restoring communications between BDC and PDC after network problems or machine downtime. Also see the /sync option for the *net accounts* command.

7 Add to Domain [Computer]
Add computer to current domain. A computer must be a domain member to take part in domain security.

8 Remove from Domain [Computer]
Break security relationship between computer and domain.

9 Select Domain [Computer]
Select which domain to administer.

10 Refresh [View]
The display of computers shows only what is current for the last refresh, which occurs when **Server Manager** is started or when the computer being managed is changed. The **Refresh** menu option manually updates the display to the most current information.

11 Low Speed Connection [Options]
Reduce the amount of information transferred between the computer being managed and computer running **Server Manager**. For example, the display is not refreshed after **Server Manager** starts. It has to be manually refreshed to reflect any changes.

12 **MacFile**
Administer volumes for Macintosh clients. Only present if **Services for the Mac-intosh** (SFM) is installed.

13 **Properties** [MacFile]
See **MacFile** control panel.

14 **Volumes** [MacFile]
Administer shares being offered to Macintosh clients.

15 **Permissions** [MacFile-Volumes-Properties]
Set permissions for share. Note that these permissions apply only to Macintosh clients.

16 **FPNW**
Administer volumes for NetWare clients. Only present if **File and Print Services for NetWare** (FPNW) is installed.

17 **Properties** [FPNW]
See **FPNW** control panel.

18 **Shared Volumes** [FPNW]
Administer shares being offered to NetWare clients.

19 **Permissions** [FPNW-Shared Volumes-Properties]
Set permissions for share. Note that these permissions apply only to NetWare clients.

20 **Print Servers** [FPNW]
Administer NetWare print servers being offered to NetWare clients.

21 **Send Message** [FPNW]
Send message to attached NetWare clients.

System Policy Editor

Requires
  NT Server

Summary
  The **System Policy Editor** tool can be used to set restrictions and defaults for users, groups, computers, or entire domains. It allows an administrator to control what a user can and cannot do in excruciating detail. If you want a certain type of behavior on a group of computers to be enforced, such as preventing users from altering their systems or limiting what they can run, a policy can be created to accomplish this. It may help to think of the policy editor as a user-friendly front end to the Registry, as all the policy settings are actually stored in the Registry. The policy editor can either edit the Registry of the local computer or create a policy on a domain controller which will download the policy to a client computer and modify its Registry.

  Policy templates describe possible policy settings to the policy editor. An administrator or vendor can add customized policies by creating templates.

  Policies can be replicated between domain controllers just like other account information, such as user profiles and logon scripts.

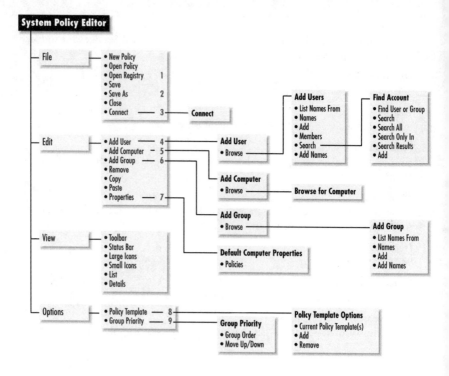

System Policy Editor

- File
  - • New Policy
  - • Open Policy
  - • Open Registry   1
  - • Save
  - • Save As   2
  - • Close
  - • Connect   3 —— **Connect**

- Edit
  - • Add User   4
  - • Add Computer   – 5
  - • Add Group   6
  - • Remove
  - • Copy
  - • Paste
  - • Properties   7

  Add User
  - • Browse

  Add Computer
  - • Browse —— **Browse for Computer**

  Add Group
  - • Browse

  Add Users
  - • List Names From
  - • Names
  - • Add
  - • Members
  - • Search
  - • Add Names

  Find Account
  - • Find User or Group
  - • Search
  - • Search All
  - • Search Only In
  - • Search Results
  - • Add

  Add Group
  - • List Names From
  - • Names
  - • Add
  - • Add Names

- View
  - • Toolbar
  - • Status Bar
  - • Large Icons
  - • Small Icons
  - • List
  - • Details

  Default Computer Properties
  - • Policies

- Options
  - • Policy Template   8
  - • Group Priority   9

  Group Priority
  - • Group Order
  - • Move Up/Down

  Policy Template Options
  - • Current Policy Template(s)
  - • Add
  - • Remove

1   Open Registry [File]
Edit Registry on local machine.

2   Save As [File]
Save current policy. If creating a policy for client computers of a domain controller (DC), save the policy as *NTCONFIG.POL* in the *<winnt root>\SYSTEM32\REPL\EXPORT* directory of the DC.

3   Connect [File]
Connect to a remote computer (and edit the remote computer's Registry).

4   Add User [Edit]
Add user to current policy.

5   Add Computer [Edit]
Add computer to current policy.

6   Add Group [Edit]
Add group to current policy.

7   Properties [Edit]
Edit policy for selected object (user or computer).

8   Policy Template [Options]
Read policy from template. A template contains a description of all the settings that could be enabled or disabled within the Registry. You can create your own templates or add application-specific templates.

Group Priority [Options]

If a user is in multiple groups that have different policies, the order of the groups determine which policy takes effect first.

Task Manager

Requires

NT Workstation or Server

Summary

The **Task Manager** tool displays information about programs and processes running on the local computer. It is very useful for finding out why your computer is running slowly, as it indicates which processes are consuming the most system resources. **Task Manager** can also start new processes or kill existing ones.

To run **Task Manager**, press CONTROL-ALT-DELETE and select **Task Manager** or right-click on the Task Bar.

Task Manager is not normally part of the **Administrative Tools** menu, but you can either add a shortcut to it (*<winnt root>\SYSTEM32\TASKMGR.EXE*) or run it from the command line.

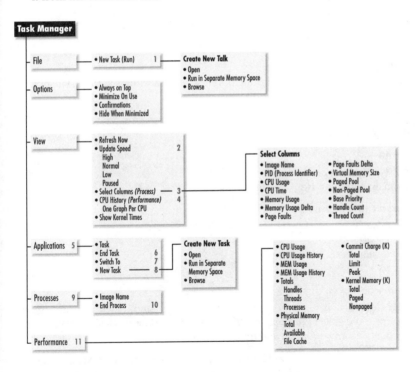

1 **New Task (Run)** [File]

Start a new command or application.

2 **Update Speed** [View]
Set how often display is updated.

3 **Select Columns** [View]
(Processes view only) Select which process attributes should be displayed.

4 **CPU History** [View]
(Performance view only) Show CPU usage over time.

5 **Applications**
Display all running applications. Applications are processes usually started by the user and interact with the desktop. An application that is not responding has hung for some reason and can be killed with **End Task**.

6 **End Task** [Applications]
Terminate selected application.

7 **Switch To** [Applications]
Change foreground application to selected application.

8 **New Task** [Applications]
Start new command.

9 **Processes**
Display all running processes. Processes include applications, services, kernel services, and so on.

10 **End Process** [Processes]
Terminate selected process

11 **Performance**
Graphical display of CPU, and memory usage, and various system statistics.

User Manager

Requires
NT Workstation or Server
Domain controller (for domain management)

Command-Line Equivalents
net accounts
net group
net localgroup
net user

Summary
User Manager is used for creating, modifying, and deleting users, global groups, and local groups. It also controls account policies, group rights, account security auditing, and trust relationships.

On an NT server configured as a domain controller (DC), **User Manager** will be named **User Manager for Domains**. If it is on an NT Workstation or a non-DC NT Server, the tool is called **User Manager** and some of the options listed below are not present or enabled. You need a DC to administer global groups, trust relationships, and other domains.

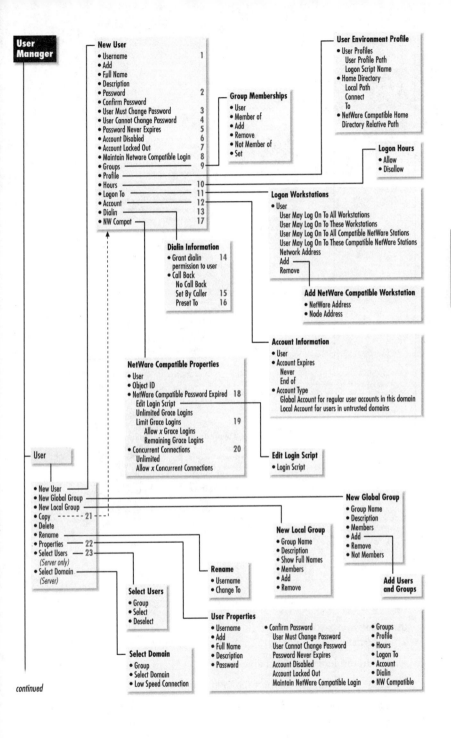

User Manager

New User
- Username   1
- Add
- Full Name
- Description
- Password   2
- Confirm Password
- User Must Change Password   3
- User Cannot Change Password   4
- Password Never Expires   5
- Account Disabled   6
- Account Locked Out   7
- Maintain Netware Compatible Login   8
- Groups   9
- Profile
- Hours   10
- Logon To   11
- Account   12
- Dialin   13
- NW Compat   17

Group Memberships
- User
- Member of
- Add
- Remove
- Not Member of
- Set

User Environment Profile
- User Profiles
  - User Profile Path
  - Logon Script Name
- Home Directory
  - Local Path
  - Connect
  - To
- NetWare Compatible Home Directory Relative Path

Logon Hours
- Allow
- Disallow

Logon Workstations
- User
  - User May Log On To All Workstations
  - User May Log On To These Workstations
  - User May Log On To All Compatible NetWare Stations
  - User May Log On To These Compatible NetWare Stations
  - Network Address
  - Add
  - Remove

Dialin Information
- Grant dialin permission to user   14
- Call Back
  - No Call Back
  - Set By Caller   15
  - Preset To   16

Add NetWare Compatible Workstation
- NetWare Address
- Node Address

Account Information
- User
- Account Expires
  - Never
  - End of
- Account Type
  - Global Account for regular user accounts in this domain
  - Local Account for users in untrusted domains

NetWare Compatible Properties
- User
- Object ID
- NetWare Compatible Password Expired   18
  - Edit Login Script
  - Unlimited Grace Logins
  - Limit Grace Logins   19
    - Allow x Grace Logins
    - Remaining Grace Logins
- Concurrent Connections   20
  - Unlimited
  - Allow x Concurrent Connections

Edit Login Script
- Login Script

User
- New User
- New Global Group
- New Local Group
- Copy   21
- Delete
- Rename
- Properties   22
- Select Users   23
  (Server only)
- Select Domain
  (Server)

New Global Group
- Group Name
- Description
- Members
- Add
- Remove
- Not Members

New Local Group
- Group Name
- Description
- Show Full Names
- Members
- Add
- Remove

Add Users and Groups

Rename
- Username
- Change To

Select Users
- Group
- Select
- Deselect

Select Domain
- Group
- Select Domain
- Low Speed Connection

User Properties
- Username
- Add
- Full Name
- Description
- Password
- Confirm Password
- User Must Change Password
- User Cannot Change Password
- Password Never Expires
- Account Disabled
- Account Locked Out
- Maintain NetWare Compatible Login
- Groups
- Profile
- Hours
- Logon To
- Account
- Dialin
- NW Compatible

continued

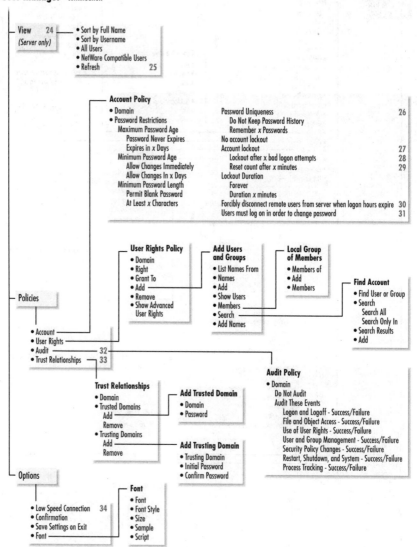

View 24
(Server only)
- Sort by Full Name
- Sort by Username
- All Users
- NetWare Compatible Users
- Refresh 25

Account Policy
- Domain
- Password Restrictions
  - Maximum Password Age
    - Password Never Expires
    - Expires in *x* Days
  - Minimum Password Age
    - Allow Changes Immediately
    - Allow Changes In *x* Days
  - Minimum Password Length
    - Permit Blank Password
    - At Least *x* Characters

Password Uniqueness 26
  Do Not Keep Password History
  Remember *x* Passwords
No account lockout
Account lockout 27
  Lockout after *x* bad logon attempts 28
  Reset count after *x* minutes 29
Lockout Duration
  Forever
  Duration *x* minutes
Forcibly disconnect remote users from server when logon hours expire 30
Users must log on in order to change password 31

User Rights Policy
- Domain
- Right
- Grant To
- Add
- Remove
- Show Advanced User Rights

Add Users and Groups
- List Names From
- Names
- Add
- Show Users
- Members
- Search
- Add Names

Local Group of Members
- Members of
- Add
- Members

Find Account
- Find User or Group
- Search
  - Search All
  - Search Only In
- Search Results
- Add

Policies

- Account
- User Rights
- Audit 32
- Trust Relationships 33

Trust Relationships
- Domain
- Trusted Domains
  - Add
  - Remove
- Trusting Domains
  - Add
  - Remove

Add Trusted Domain
- Domain
- Password

Add Trusting Domain
- Trusting Domain
- Initial Password
- Confirm Password

Audit Policy
- Domain
  - Do Not Audit
  - Audit These Events
    - Logon and Logoff - Success/Failure
    - File and Object Access - Success/Failure
    - Use of User Rights - Success/Failure
    - User and Group Management - Success/Failure
    - Security Policy Changes - Success/Failure
    - Restart, Shutdown, and System - Success/Failure
    - Process Tracking - Success/Failure

Options

- Low Speed Connection 34
- Confirmation
- Save Settings on Exit
- Font

Font
- Font
- Font Style
- Size
- Sample
- Script

---

1   **Username** [User-New User]

The username has to conform to the following rules:

- Maximum length of 20 characters.

- Cannot contain any of the following characters: \ / | [ ] : ; | =,+*?<>

- Cannot match any existing username or group within current domain or local computer. The username will be used to identify the user account in all subsequent operations.

---

2   **Password** [User-New User]
The password has to conform to the following rules:

- Passwords are case-sensitive.

- You can leave the password field blank if you wish.

- Maximum password length is 14 characters.

- Minimum password length is determined by **Policies-Account-Minimum Password Length**.

3   **User Must Change Password at Next Logon** [User-New User]
This is useful if you want to force people to change passwords without requiring your intervention. Users are prompted the next time they log in and are required to enter the current password before being allowed to change it.

4   **User Cannot Change Password** [User-New User]
If an account is shared among a number of people, preventing the password from being changed prevents a single user from locking out the others.

5   **Password Never Expires** [User-New User]
Prevents password from expiring, regardless of the account expiration policy settings.

6   **Account Disabled** [User-New User]
Disabling an account prevents the account from being used, but the account information is still maintained. Some good accounts to disable would be template accounts or accounts which are currently unused.

7   **Account Locked Out** [User-New User]
Normally this option is inaccessible. An account can be locked out if too many bad password attempts are made. An administrator can manually unlock an account in this state by selecting the checkbox. The criteria for locking out accounts is set in **Policies-Account**.

8   **Maintain NetWare Compatible Login** [User-New User]
Requires NT Server and **File and Print Services for NetWare** (FPNW). Allows a NetWare client user to login.

9   **Groups** [User-New User]
The *primary group* provides account and group information to be used by other non-Windows NT systems.

10 **Hours** [User-New User]
Only present on Server when configured as domain controller (DC). Restrict user to specific login hours.

11 **Logon To** [User-New User]
Only present on Server when configured as domain controller (DC). Restrict which computers a user can logon to.

12 **Account** [User-New User]
Only present on Server when configured as domain controller (DC). Set expiration time and account type (global or local).

13 Dialin [User-New User]

Requires **Remote Access Service**. Allow or disallow dial-up users to logon.

14 Grant dialin permission to user [User-New User-Dialin]

Allow a RAS user to dial-in. The dial-in permissions for a user can also be set in the **Remote Access Admin** tool in **Users-Permissions**.

15 Set By Caller [User-New User-Dialin-Call Back]

Callers enter their current phone number, hang up, and the system calls them back. This is useful for roving employees who frequently change locations and want the calling charges reversed.

16 Preset To [User-New User-Dialin-Call Back]

A preset call-back number provides both increased security (by calling a known number) and calling charge reversal.

17 NW Compat [User-New User]

Requires NT Server and **File and Print Services for NetWare** (FPNW). Configure settings for users logging in from NetWare clients.

18 NetWare Compatible Password Expired [User-New User-NW Compat]

Force NetWare client users to change their password on next logon.

19 Limit Grace Logins [User-New User-NW Compat-NetWare Compatible Password Expired]

Limit number of times users can login with their password expired.

20 Concurrent Connections [User-New User-NW Compat]

Limit number of simultaneous connections a user can make to the server.

21 Copy [User]

When copying a group, all members of the original group are copied to the new group, but permissions and rights of original group are not.

22 Properties [User]

If there are multiple user accounts selected, the list of users is displayed, and user-specific fields such as *username, full name,* and *description* are disabled.

23 Select Users [User]

(Server and Domain Controller only) Select which user(s) to administer. This option can be used to administer several accounts at one time by using group membership. When you select or deselect groups, you are selecting or deselecting all the members of the groups for the desired administrative operation (**Delete** or **Properties**).

24 View

(Server and DC only) Sort user accounts by various criteria.

25 Refresh [View]

Refreshes display of account and group information to reflect current database. If **User Manager** is running while account and group information is changed from somewhere else (using command line *net user* commands or over the network, for example), the changes are not displayed in User Manager in real time. You have to manually refresh the display to make sure you are seeing the most current information.

26 Password Uniqueness [Policies-Account-Password Restrictions]

The number of previous passwords that the system tracks. If users are notified that their password is about to expire, they may change their password to an

---

intermediate value, and then immediately resume the original password. The password history remembers previous passwords and stops this practice.

27 **Account lockout** [Policies-Account-Password Restrictions]
The bottom half of the form sets options that prevent someone from trying to break account security by using brute force methods or automated attacks. The reasoning behind these options is that people or programs trying to guess account passwords are likely to generate more bad logins than the legitimate user who makes an occasional mistake.

28 **Lockout after x bad logon attempts** [Policies-Account-Password Restrictions-Account lockout]
This is called *Lockout Threshold* in the *net accounts* command.

29 **Reset count after x minutes** [Policies-Account-Password Restrictions-Account lockout]
The period of time that bad logon attempts are counted in. This is called *Lockout Observation Window* in the *net accounts* command.

30 **Forcibly disconnect** [Policies-Account-Password Restrictions]
Log users off the server if their logon time is exceeded while they are logged on to the server.

31 **Users must log on in order to change password** [Polices-Account-Password Restrictions]
Requires administrator intervention before users can access their account.

32 **Audit** [Policies]
The audited events are logged in the **Log-Security** log of **Event Viewer**.

33 **Trust Relationships** [Policies]
(Server and DC only) Establish trust relationships with other domains. Users from a trusted domain are allowed to use resources on the local domain without having a local domain account. Local domain users are allowed to use resources on a trusting domain without having an account within that domain.

34 **Low Speed Connection** [Options]
(Server and DC only) If you are using a slow link (such as a dial-up modem) for remote administration, setting this minimizes the amount of information transferred over the link.

Windows NT Diagnostics

Requires
NT Workstation or Server

Summary
The **Windows NT Diagnostics** tool displays a variety of information about a computer, including both software and hardware information. It is a read-only tool and cannot make changes to any of the displayed information. One of the more powerful features is the ability to display information about other computers on the network—you can see what IRQ is being used by the sound card in a computer located in another country! You can also tell what protocols are loaded and what services are running. This feature should greatly enhance your ability to debug problems with remote computers. You can produce reports that describe all the hardware and software settings for remote computers and the local computer. Note that the **Drives** and **Memory** tabs are not available when examining a computer over the network.

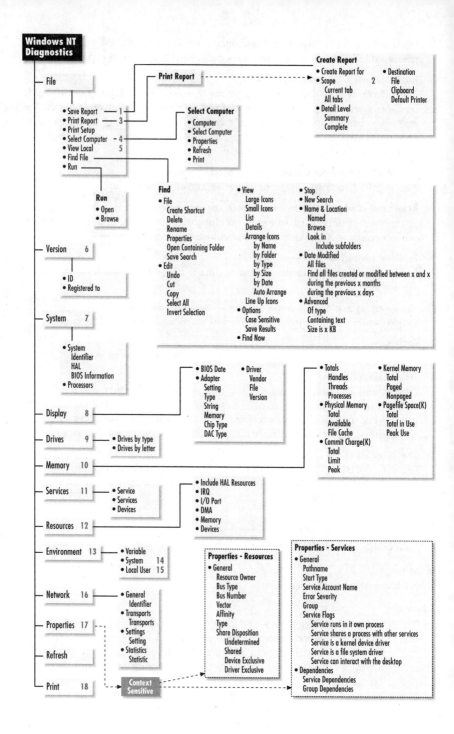

Windows NT Diagnostics

- File
  - Save Report — 1
  - Print Report — 3
  - Print Setup
  - Select Computer — 4
  - View Local — 5
  - Find File
  - Run

Print Report

Create Report
- Create Report for
- Scope — 2
  - Current tab
  - All tabs
- Detail Level
  - Summary
  - Complete
- Destination
  - File
  - Clipboard
  - Default Printer

Run
- Open
- Browse

Select Computer
- Computer
- Select Computer
- Properties
- Refresh
- Print

Find
- File
  - Create Shortcut
  - Delete
  - Rename
  - Properties
  - Open Containing Folder
  - Save Search
- Edit
  - Undo
  - Cut
  - Copy
  - Select All
  - Invert Selection
- View
  - Large Icons
  - Small Icons
  - List
  - Details
  - Arrange Icons
    - by Name
    - by Folder
    - by Type
    - by Size
    - by Date
    - Auto Arrange
    - Line Up Icons
  - Options
    - Case Sensitive
    - Save Results
  - Find Now
- Stop
- New Search
- Name & Location
  - Named
  - Browse
  - Look in
    - Include subfolders
- Date Modified
  - All files
  - Find all files created or modified between x and x
    - during the previous x months
    - during the previous x days
- Advanced
  - Of type
  - Containing text
  - Size is x KB

- Version — 6
  - ID
  - Registered to

- System — 7
  - System
    - Identifier
    - HAL
    - BIOS Information
  - Processors

- Display — 8
  - BIOS Date
  - Adapter
    - Setting
    - Type
    - String
    - Memory
    - Chip Type
    - DAC Type
  - Driver
    - Vendor
    - File
    - Version

- Drives — 9
  - Drives by type
  - Drives by letter

- Memory — 10
  - Totals
    - Handles
    - Threads
    - Processes
  - Physical Memory
    - Total
    - Available
    - File Cache
  - Commit Charge(K)
    - Total
    - Limit
    - Peak
  - Kernel Memory
    - Total
    - Paged
    - Nonpaged
  - Pagefile Space(K)
    - Total
    - Total in Use
    - Peak Use

- Services — 11
  - Service
  - Services
  - Devices

- Resources — 12
  - Include HAL Resources
  - IRQ
  - I/O Port
  - DMA
  - Memory
  - Devices

- Environment — 13
  - Variable
  - System — 14
  - Local User — 15

- Network — 16
  - General
    - Identifier
  - Transports
    - Transports
  - Settings
    - Setting
  - Statistics
    - Statistic

- Properties — 17

- Refresh

- Print — 18

Context Sensitive

Properties - Resources
- General
  - Resource Owner
  - Bus Type
  - Bus Number
  - Vector
  - Affinity
  - Type
  - Share Disposition
    - Undetermined
    - Shared
    - Device Exclusive
    - Driver Exclusive

Properties - Services
- General
  - Pathname
  - Start Type
  - Service Account Name
  - Error Severity
  - Group
  - Service Flags
    - Service runs in it own process
    - Service shares a process with other services
    - Service is a kernel device driver
    - Service is a file system driver
    - Service can interact with the desktop
- Dependencies
  - Service Dependencies
  - Group Dependencies

1 **Save Report** [File]
Save a text report about the currently selected computer.

2 **Scope** [File-Save Report]
The scope determines what system attributes are included in the report. This can be a single tab or all tabs.

3 **Print Report** [File]
Send report to printer, using same criteria as **File-Save Report-Scope**.

4 **Select Computer** [File]
Select another computer from the network to examine. The **Disk** and **Memory** tabs are unavailable when viewing remote computers.

5 **View Local** [File]
Examine the local computer.

6 **Version**
Displays information about the operating system, including OS version, service packs, and serial numbers. This is one of the few places where NT tells you if it is Workstation or Server.

7 **System**
Display hardware information about processor and BIOS.

8 **Display**
Display current display drivers, screen size, color depth, and refresh frequency.

9 **Drives**
Display drive capacity and current usage and file system type (FAT or NTFS). Network drives connected to the local computer are also listed.

10 **Memory**
Display various memory statistics for the local computer.

11 **Services**
Show status of services and devices (device drivers).

12 **Resources**
Display resources in use by installed hardware, including IRQ, I/O Port, DMA, and Memory.

13 **Environment**
Environment variables are used to provide settings to programs at run-time. For example, if you change the **Path** variable, all programs started after the change obtain the new value.

14 **System** [Environment]
Display system environment settings.

15 **Local User** [Environment]
Display environment for user running **Windows NT Diagnostics**.

16 **Network**

Display the following types of information:

General

General information about the account you are using to log in, including username, domain name, and rights. Also shows list of logged in users. The ability to see who is logged onto a remote computer is useful, and provides a similar function to the *finger* program.

Transports

Transports are network protocols. The transport name is a combination of protocol name, network adapter model, and number of adapters within the computer. See the following table for examples.

Transport	Description
NetBT_AMDPCN1	TCP/IP (NetBIOS over TCP/IP) AMD PCNet Ethernet 1
NetBT_SMCISAA	TCP/IP SMC ISA Ethernet 1
Nbf_E1001	NetBEUI (NetBEUI Frame) Intel Pro100 1
NwlnkNB	IPX/SPX

If the transport shows up in the list, it indicates that the network protocol is installed and bound to the network adapter. Combining this list with the list of resources and services gives you some idea of what a remote computer is doing on the network, although in an obscure manner.

The address is the MAC-level address of each network adapter. This is handy for mapping MAC addresses to computer names, as you frequently have to know a remote computer's MAC address when administering WINS and DHCP or running the Network Monitor.

Settings

Various system settings. Most cannot be directly manipulated by the user and should not be changed unless you really know what you are doing.

Statistics

Various system statistics, including network, disk, and memory.

17 **Properties**

The properties tab is context-sensitive according to what tab is being viewed. For **Services**, it displays a general description of the service or a list of other services that the selected service requires to run (dependencies). For **Resources**, it displays details about a selected resource.

18 **Print**

Identical to **File-Print Report**.

Windows NT Explorer

Requires

NT Workstation or Server

Command-Line Equivalents

cacls
net share
net use
net view

Summary

The **Windows NT Explorer** is a browser that treats the desktop, networks, computers, drives, directories, and files as objects. This is different from **File Manager**, which understands only file systems.

The **Windows NT Explorer** should not to be confused with **Internet Explorer**, even though they are starting to converge on the same functionality.

Note that even though **Explorer** is supposed to replace **File Manager** in NT 4.0, Explorer has no administrative control over file sharing for the Macintosh (SFM) or NetWare (FPNW). You could use **Server Manager** for this task.

Refer to the following figure for an illustration of the menu structure.

Administrative Tools

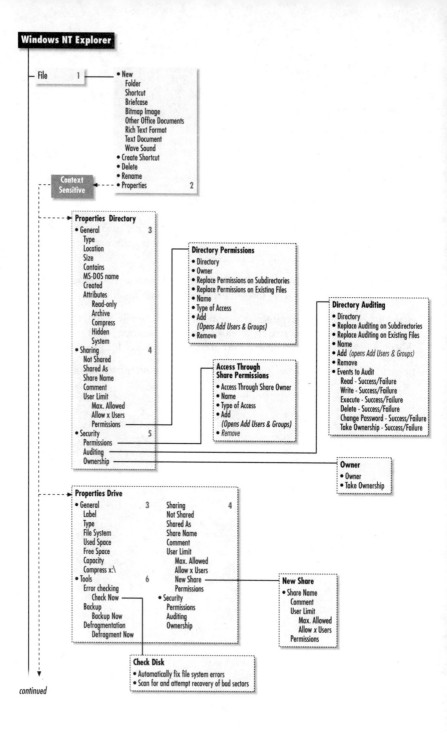

Windows NT Explorer

File 1
- New
  - Folder
  - Shortcut
  - Briefcase
  - Bitmap Image
  - Other Office Documents
  - Rich Text Format
  - Text Document
  - Wave Sound
- Create Shortcut
- Delete
- Rename
- Properties 2

Context Sensitive

Properties Directory
- General 3
  - Type
  - Location
  - Size
  - Contains
  - MS-DOS name
  - Created
  - Attributes
    - Read-only
    - Archive
    - Compress
    - Hidden
    - System
- Sharing 4
  - Not Shared
  - Shared As
  - Share Name
  - Comment
  - User Limit
    - Max. Allowed
    - Allow x Users
  - Permissions
- Security 5
  - Permissions
  - Auditing
  - Ownership

Directory Permissions
- Directory
- Owner
- Replace Permissions on Subdirectories
- Replace Permissions on Existing Files
- Name
- Type of Access
- Add
  - *(Opens Add Users & Groups)*
- Remove

Access Through Share Permissions
- Access Through Share Owner
- Name
- Type of Access
- Add
  - *(Opens Add Users & Groups)*
- Remove

Directory Auditing
- Directory
- Replace Auditing on Subdirectories
- Replace Auditing on Existing Files
- Name
- Add *(opens Add Users & Groups)*
- Remove
- Events to Audit
  - Read - Success/Failure
  - Write - Success/Failure
  - Execute - Success/Failure
  - Delete - Success/Failure
  - Change Password - Success/Failure
  - Take Ownership - Success/Failure

Owner
- Owner
- Take Ownership

Properties Drive
- General 3   Sharing 4
  - Label   Not Shared
  - Type   Shared As
  - File System   Share Name
  - Used Space   Comment
  - Free Space   User Limit
  - Capacity   Max. Allowed
  - Compress x:\   Allow x Users
- Tools 6   New Share
  - Error checking   Permissions
    - Check Now   • Security
  - Backup   Permissions
    - Backup Now   Auditing
  - Defragmentation   Ownership
    - Defragment Now

New Share
- Share Name
  - Comment
  - User Limit
    - Max. Allowed
    - Allow x Users
  - Permissions

Check Disk
- Automatically fix file system errors
- Scan for and attempt recovery of bad sectors

continued

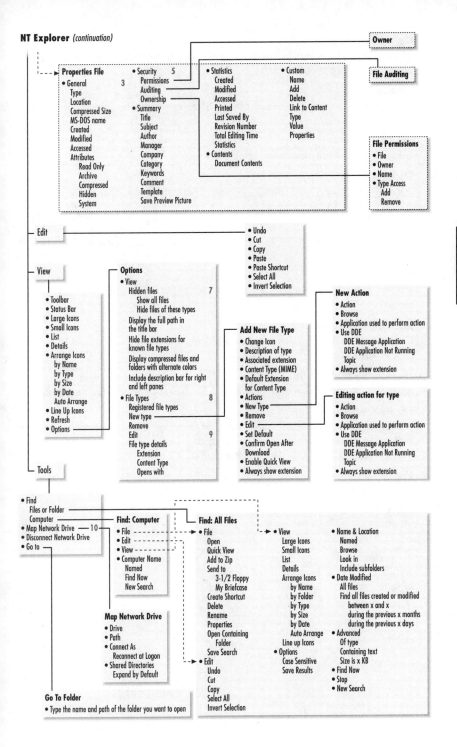

Owner

File Auditing

Properties File
• General   3
  Type
  Location
  Compressed Size
  MS-DOS name
  Created
  Modified
  Accessed
  Attributes
    Read Only
    Archive
    Compressed
    Hidden
    System

• Security   5
  Permissions
  Auditing
  Ownership
• Summary
  Title
  Subject
  Author
  Manager
  Company
  Category
  Keywords
  Comment
  Template
  Save Preview Picture

• Statistics
  Created
  Modified
  Accessed
  Printed
  Last Saved By
  Revision Number
  Total Editing Time
  Statistics
• Contents
  Document Contents

• Custom
  Name
  Add
  Delete
  Link to Content
  Type
  Value
  Properties

File Permissions
• File
• Owner
• Name
• Type Access
  Add
  Remove

Edit
• Undo
• Cut
• Copy
• Paste
• Paste Shortcut
• Select All
• Invert Selection

View

Options
• View
  Hidden files   7
    Show all files
    Hide files of these types
  Display the full path in
  the title bar
  Hide file extensions for
  known file types
  Display compressed files and
  folders with alternate colors
  Include description bar for right
  and left panes
• File Types   8
  Registered file types
  New type
  Remove
  Edit   9
  File type details
    Extension
    Content Type
    Opens with

• Toolbar
• Status Bar
• Large Icons
• Small Icons
• List
• Details
• Arrange Icons
  by Name
  by Type
  by Size
  by Date
  Auto Arrange
• Line Up Icons
• Refresh
• Options

Add New File Type
• Change Icon
• Description of type
• Associated extension
• Content Type (MIME)
• Default Extension
  for Content Type
• Actions
• New Type
• Remove
• Edit
• Set Default
• Confirm Open After
  Download
• Enable Quick View
• Always show extension

New Action
• Action
• Browse
• Application used to perform action
• Use DDE
  DDE Message Application
  DDE Application Not Running
  Topic
• Always show extension

Editing action for type
• Action
• Browse
• Application used to perform action
• Use DDE
  DDE Message Application
  DDE Application Not Running
  Topic
• Always show extension

Tools

• Find
  Files or Folder
  Computer
• Map Network Drive — 10
• Disconnect Network Drive
• Go to

Find: Computer
• File
• Edit
• View
• Computer Name
  Named
  Find Now
  New Search

Find: All Files
• File
  Open
  Quick View
  Add to Zip
  Send to
    3-1/2 Floppy
    My Briefcase
  Create Shortcut
  Delete
  Rename
  Properties
  Open Containing
    Folder
  Save Search
• Edit
  Undo
  Cut
  Copy
  Select All
  Invert Selection

• View
  Large Icons
  Small Icons
  List
  Details
  Arrange Icons
    by Name
    by Folder
    by Type
    by Size
    by Date
    Auto Arrange
  Line up Icons
• Options
  Case Sensitive
  Save Results

• Name & Location
  Named
  Browse
  Look in
  Include subfolders
• Date Modified
  All files
  Find all files created or modified
    between x and x
    during the previous x months
    during the previous x days
• Advanced
  Of type
  Containing text
  Size is x KB
• Find Now
• Stop
• New Search

Map Network Drive
• Drive
• Path
• Connect As
  Reconnect at Logon
• Shared Directories
  Expand by Default

Go To Folder
• Type the name and path of the folder you want to open

1 **File**

The options under the **File** menu are context-sensitive according to the type of object being explored.

2 **Properties** [File]

Edit properties of the selected object. The object can be a computer, drive, directory, or file.

3 **General** [File-Properties]

General information about the selected object.

4 **Sharing** [File-Properties]

(Drives and directories only) Sharing permissions for the entire drive or selected directory.

5 **Security** [File-Properties]

(Files and directories only) File and directory permissions for locally logged-on users.

6 **Tools** [File-Properties]

(Drives only) Run **Check Disk** (*chkdsk*), **Backup** (*ntbackup*), or a disk defragmenter.

7 **Hidden Files** [View-Options-View]

Control which files are displayed or hidden depending on filename extensions or file attributes.

8 **File Types** [View-Options]

Associate an application and icon with a file based on the filename extension.

9 **Edit** [View-Options-File Types]

Change application used to open file. For example, if you want to prevent the registry from being accidentally being updated by a *.REG* file, you can change the application from **Regedit** to something safer, such as Notepad.

10 **Map Network Drive** [Tools]

Map a remote share to a local drive letter.

WINS Manager

Requires

    NT Server
    Windows Internet Name Service

Summary

The **WINS Manager** tool configures the **Windows Internet Name Service** (WINS). It can manage both local WINS servers and servers running on remote computers. The WINS server is a name server that maps NetBIOS computer names (not TCP/IP hostnames) to IP addresses.

Multiple WINS servers can be interconnected, allowing servers to share information. This sharing process is *replication*, and WINS servers that share are called replication partners. When data is being replicated from one computer to another, and the sending computer initiates the transfer, then it is called a *push* partner. If the receiving computer initiates the transfer, then it is called a *pull* partner.

There is no NT security relationship between replication partners. The only thing preventing a foreign WINS server from copying all the WINS data is the replication settings.

The main uses of WINS are mapping dynamic IP addresses obtained from DHCP to computer names and enabling browsing on remote networks. When DHCP hands out an IP address for a given computer, other computers must know the current IP address in order to communicate with it. They can ask the WINS server for the IP address for a given computer name. When browsing remote networks, broadcasts are stopped by routers between the networks. This prevents computers on one network from finding computers on the other. A WINS server on each network collects all the computer names and IP addresses. The WINS servers coordinate information among themselves, so that any WINS server knows about all the other WINS servers. When a computer wants to communicate with another computer, it asks the closest WINS server for the computer IP address. This mechanism works across routers because it uses direct communication between the computer and WINS server instead of broadcasts.

The WINS Manager contains a plethora of options that may scare off the new user. In most cases, you should only need to do the following:

- Create a server (**Server-Add WINS Server**).

- Add replication partners (**Server-Replication Partners-Add**).

- Set the partners for push and pull (**Server-Replication Partners-Pull Partner** and **Server-Replication Partners-Push Partner**).

Administrative Tools

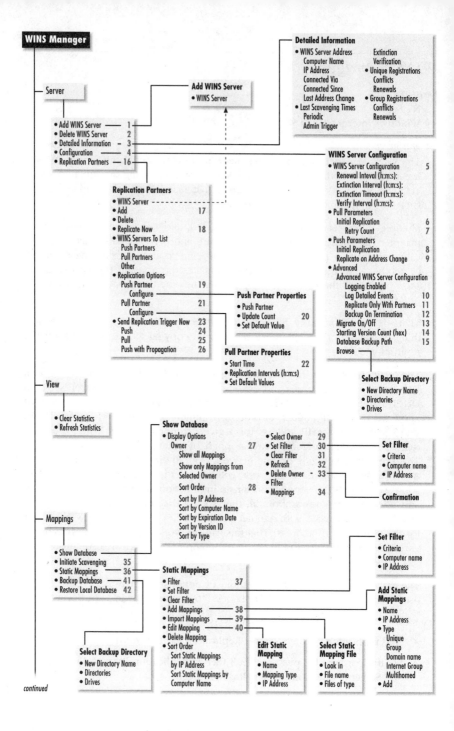

WINS Manager

Server
- Add WINS Server — 1
- Delete WINS Server — 2
- Detailed Information — 3
- Configuration — 4
- Replication Partners — 16

Add WINS Server
- WINS Server

Detailed Information
- WINS Server Address
  Computer Name
  IP Address
  Connected Via
  Connected Since
  Last Address Change
- Last Scavenging Times
  Periodic
  Admin Trigger

  Extinction
  Verification
- Unique Registrations
  Conflicts
  Renewals
- Group Registrations
  Conflicts
  Renewals

Replication Partners
- WINS Server
- Add — 17
- Delete
- Replicate Now — 18
- WINS Servers To List
  Push Partners
  Pull Partners
  Other
- Replication Options
  Push Partner — 19
    Configure
  Pull Partner — 21
    Configure
- Send Replication Trigger Now — 23
  Push — 24
  Pull — 25
  Push with Propagation — 26

Push Partner Properties
- Push Partner
- Update Count — 20
- Set Default Value

Pull Partner Properties
- Start Time — 22
- Replication Intervals (h:m:s)
- Set Default Values

WINS Server Configuration
- WINS Server Configuration — 5
  Renewal Inteval (h:m:s):
  Extinction Interval (h:m:s):
  Extinction Timeout (h:m:s):
  Verify Interval (h:m:s):
- Pull Parameters
  Initial Replication — 6
    Retry Count — 7
- Push Parameters
  Initial Replication — 8
  Replicate on Address Change — 9
- Advanced
  Advanced WINS Server Configuration
  Logging Enabled
  Log Detailed Events — 10
  Replicate Only With Partners — 11
  Backup On Termination — 12
  Migrate On/Off — 13
  Starting Version Count (hex) — 14
  Database Backup Path — 15
  Browse

Select Backup Directory
- New Directory Name
- Directories
- Drives

View
- Clear Statistics
- Refresh Statistics

Show Database
- Display Options
  Owner — 27
  Show all Mappings
  Show only Mappings from
  Selected Owner
  Sort Order — 28
  Sort by IP Address
  Sort by Computer Name
  Sort by Expiration Date
  Sort by Version ID
  Sort by Type

- Select Owner — 29
- Set Filter — 30
- Clear Filter — 31
- Refresh — 32
- Delete Owner — 33
- Filter
- Mappings — 34

Set Filter
- Criteria
- Computer name
- IP Address

Confirmation

Mappings
- Show Database
- Initiate Scavenging — 35
- Static Mappings — 36
- Backup Database — 41
- Restore Local Database — 42

Static Mappings
- Filter — 37
- Set Filter
- Clear Filter
- Add Mappings — 38
- Import Mappings — 39
- Edit Mapping — 40
- Delete Mapping
- Sort Order
  Sort Static Mappings
  by IP Address
  Sort Static Mappings by
  Computer Name

Set Filter
- Criteria
- Computer name
- IP Address

Add Static Mappings
- Name
- IP Address
- Type
  Unique
  Group
  Domain name
  Internet Group
  Multihomed
- Add

Select Backup Directory
- New Directory Name
- Directories
- Drives

Edit Static Mapping
- Name
- Mapping Type
- IP Address

Select Static Mapping File
- Look in
- File name
- Files of type

continued

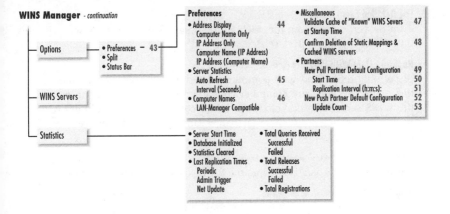

WINS Manager - *continuation*

- Options
  - Preferences — 43
    - Split
    - Status Bar
- WINS Servers
- Statistics

Preferences
- Address Display   44
  Computer Name Only
  IP Address Only
  Computer Name (IP Address)
  IP Address (Computer Name)
- Server Statistics
  Auto Refresh   45
  Interval (Seconds)
- Computer Names   46
  LAN-Manager Compatible

- Miscellaneous
  Validate Cache of "Known" WINS Severs   47
  at Startup Time
  Confirm Deletion of Static Mappings &   48
  Cached WINS servers
- Partners
  New Pull Partner Default Configuration 49
  Start Time   50
  Replication Interval (h:m:s):   51
  New Push Partner Default Configuration 52
  Update Count   53

- Server Start Time
- Database Initialized
- Statistics Cleared
- Last Replication Times
  Periodic
  Admin Trigger
  Net Update

- Total Queries Received
  Successful
  Failed
- Total Releases
  Successful
  Failed
- Total Registrations

1 Add WINS Server [Server]

When the local computer name or IP is used, a local WINS server is created. If a remote computer name or IP is used, you merely add the ability to administer the remote server but don't add or delete the server. If you are not going to remotely administer a remote server, you do not need to add it.

2 Delete WINS Server [Server]

Either delete the local server or delete the ability to administer a remote server.

3 Detailed Information [Server]

Display settings and statistics for a selected server. The **Connected Via** value shows the protocol being used to communicate between the WINS Manager and the WINS server. The protocol is usually NetBIOS for the local server and TCP/IP for any remote servers.

4 Configuration [Server]

Sets various parameters for the selected server that determine how long information lives in its database and how it communicates with other WINS servers.

5 WINS Server Configuration [Server-Configuration]

Renewal is the process of clients contacting the WINS server and saying "I'm still here." Normally, clients do this every two days. When a client is not heard from for the **Renewal Interval**, the client is marked released.

6 Initial Replication [Server-Configuration-Pull Parameters]

When this WINS server is started, pull data from all known replication partners. Also replicate if any replication-related configuration changes are made.

7 Retry Count [Server-Configuration-Pull Parameters-Initial Replication]

Number of times to try pulling data from partner. If the retry count is exceeded, the WINS server will wait for a period of time before trying again.

8 Initial Replication [Server-Configuration-Push Parameters]

Push data to known replication partners when WINS service is started.

9 Replicate on Address Change [Server-Configuration-Push Parameters]

Push data whenever an IP address within the database changes.

10 Log Detailed Events [Server-Configuration-Advanced]

Turn on verbose logging for WINS in the system log of **Event Viewer**. Use this only for debugging purposes.

11 Replicate Only With Partners [Server-Configuration-Advanced]

Allow only replication with computers listed in the replication partners list. If this is not checked, any computer (possibly over the Internet) can connect to the WINS server and download the list of computers. This could aid potential hackers by giving away internal names and show what services are being offered to the network.

12 Backup on Termination [Server-Configuration-Advanced]

Backup the WINS database when the WINS server is manually stopped.

13 Migrate On/Off [Server-Configuration-Advanced]

Overwrite old records with newest information when there are conflicts.

14 Starting Version Count [Server-Configuration-Advanced]

Sets the starting version number of records created by selected WINS server. As higher version numbers are treated as newer, incrementing the version number above other WINS servers will cause this WINS server's records to take precedence over others.

15 Database Backup Path [Server-Configuration-Advanced]

Directory path used for WINS database backup files.

16 Replication Partners [Server]

A replication partner is another WINS server that exchanges information with the administered WINS server.

17 Add [Server-Replication Partners]

Adding a server makes it a partner.

18 Replicate Now [Server-Replication Partners]

Start replication now instead of waiting for normally replication interval.

19 Push Partner [Server-Replication Partners-Replication Options]

Make selected server a push partner.

20 Update Count [Server-Replication Partners-Replication Options-Push Partner-Configure]

Number of new records that should be accumulated before notifying replication partners. This setting will affect how much network traffic is generated by replication.

21 Pull Partner [Server-Replication Partners-Replication Options]

Make selected server a pull partner.

22 Start Time [Server-Replication Partners-Replication Options-Pull Partner-Configure]

Specify start time of replication.

23 Send Replication Trigger Now [Server-Replication Partners]

If you do not want to wait for the next scheduled replication, you can manually induce one. All the following settings apply only to the manual replication, not the normal scheduled operation.

24 Push [Server-Replication Partners-Send Replication Trigger Now]

Manually notify all push partners to start replicating.

---

25 Pull [Server-Replication Partners-Send Replication Trigger Now]
Manually notify all pull partners to start replicating.

26 Push with Propagation [Server-Replication Partners-Send Replication Trigger Now]
If the selected WINS server obtains new records, it should tell its partners to pull the new records from it. This way, a change is propagated from WINS server to WINS server. If this is not checked, the WINS sever does not notify its partners of changes.

27 Owner [Mappings-Show Database-Display Options]
The owner of a record is the WINS server that created it. Either show records created by all WINS servers or a specific server.

28 Sort Order [Mappings-Show Database-Display Options]
Sort the **Mappings** display by various criteria.

29 Select Owner [Mappings-Show Database]
Select which WINS server records to display. The highest ID is the highest version number used so far by the WINS server.

30 Set Filter [Mappings-Show Database]
If you have a large number of database entries, the filter can be used to limit the display to specific computer names or IP addresses. The filter uses wildcards to match computer names or IP address. For example, *ntserver** could match *ntserver1* or *ntserver2.*and *198.112.209.** could match any address starting with *198.112.209.* The **Filter** settings affect the display in **Mappings-Static Mappings** and **Mappings-Show Database**.

31 Clear Filter [Mappings-Show Database]
Disable filter, displaying all names.

32 Refresh [Mappings-Show Database]
Update display to most current information.

33 Delete Owner [Mappings-Show Database]
Delete all database entries made by specified WINS server. This can be used to delete old entries when a WINS server has been removed.

34 Mappings [Mappings-Show Database]
The mappings display shows all records stored in the WINS database. The other **Show Database** options control which records are displayed and in what order. The database fields are as follows:

<Icon>
An icon indicating a unique name (a single computer) or a group name.

<NetBIOS name>
NetBIOS computer name (not TCP/IP hostname).

<IP address>
IP address associated with computer name.

Mapping type
A is an active mapping and S is static.

Expiration date
Indicates when record will expire.

Version ID
> Number assigned to records that indicates when the record was created. If a record has a higher version number than one stored on another WINS server, the higher version record is newer and should replace the older record.

35 Initiate Scavenging [Mappings]
Manually purge old information from the WINS database. This is normally done automatically by the system at regular intervals.

36 Static Mappings [Mappings]
Static mappings are permanent entries in the WINS database. Normally, computer names and addresses are learned dynamically from the network. If you know a computer is always going to remain at the same IP address, you can create a static mapping for it.

37 Filter [Mappings-Static Mappings]
If you have large numbers of static mappings, the filter can be used to limit the display to specific computer names or IP addresses. The **Filter** settings affect the display in **Mappings-Static Mappings** and **Mappings-Show Database**.

38 Add Mappings [Mappings-Static Mappings]
Add a new static mapping.

39 Import Mappings [Mappings-Static Mappings]
Read in mappings from a text file in the *LMHOSTS* format.

40 Edit Mapping [Mappings-Static Mappings]
Edit an existing mapping.

41 Backup Database [Mappings]
Copy current WINS database to disk.

42 Restore Local Database [Mappings]
Read in a WINS database backup file from disk.

43 Preferences [Options]
The preferences window determines not only how WINS database information is displayed, but also default settings for new replication partners and various other settings.

44 Address Display [Options-Preferences]
Settings to determine how WINS server addresses appear in the various windows of WINS Manager.

45 Auto Refresh [Options-Preferences-Server Statistics]
Update the Statistics window automatically at the specified interval.

46 Computer Names [Options-Preferences]
Only accept computer names that meet LAN Manager conventions (15-character name, plus 1 character that indicates name type).

47 Validate Cache [Options-Preferences-Miscellaneous]
Check to make sure each WINS server is contacted when WINS is started.

48 Confirm Deletion [Options-Preferences-Miscellaneous]
Ask for confirmation when deleting a static mapping or when a cached WINS server is deleted.

49 **New Pull Partner Default Configuration** [Options-Preferences-Partners]
Set defaults for any pull partners added from this point on.

50 **Start Time** [Options-Preferences-Partners-New Pull Partner Default Configuration]
When to start replication.

51 **Replication Interval** [Options-Preferences-Partners-New Pull Partner Default Configuration]
How often to replicate.

52 **New Push Partner Default Configuration** [Options-Preferences-Partners]
Set defaults for any pull partners added from this point forward.

53 **Update Count** [Options-Preferences-Partners-New Push Partner Default Configuration]
How many updates on administered WINS server should take place before notifying remote WINS servers about the new information.

CHAPTER 4

Accessories

Several of the accessories can be useful to the NT administrator when connecting to remote computers and network devices. The accessories are available in the **Start-Programs-Accessories** menu.

Calculator

Requires

NT Workstation or Server

Summary

The **Calculator** accessory can be used to do base conversions between binary (base 2), octal (base 8), hexadecimal (base 16), and decimal (base 10) numbers. These can be useful for various system administration tasks, especially when calculating network masks and subnetting.

To enable base conversions, change to **Scientific** under the **View** menu. Select which base (**Hex**, **Dec**, **Oct**, or **Bin**) you want convert from and input the number. Then select the base that you want to convert to and the number will be converted.

Many non-Microsoft operating systems represent netmasks using hexadecimal numbers. For example, if someone tells you that the netmask for your network was fffffe0, you cannot type this directly into the NT TCP/IP configuration, as NT requires you to enter the netmask in decimal. You can use the calculator to convert the number for you by following these steps:

1. As the netmask represents four different numbers, you cannot convert the entire number all at once. You must first break the number into octets. This gives you:

   ```
   ff ff ff e0
   ```

2. Select the **Hex** button and type in `ff`.

3. Select the **Dec** button and 255 is printed.

4. Select the **Hex** button and type in `e0`.

5. Select the **Dec** button and 224 is printed.

6. Your netmask converted to decimal is:

   ```
   255.255.255.224
   ```

Dial-Up Networking

Requires
   NT Workstation or Server
   Remote Access Service (RAS)

Command-Line Equivalents
   rasdial
   rasphone

Summary

The **Dial-Up Networking** accessory configures outgoing RAS sessions from the local computer. It creates entries that describe a remote site, including which port and device to use, phone numbers, and security settings. Configuration settings are associated with an *entry*, which is normally the name of the remote site to which you wish to connect.

The configuration of Dial-Up Networking is highly biased towards PPP connections, but this is a good thing, as most people will be using PPP.

As administering RAS can be quite complicated, it has an entire chapter devoted to it; see Chapter 5, *RAS and DUN*.

Refer to the following figure for an illustration of the menu structure.

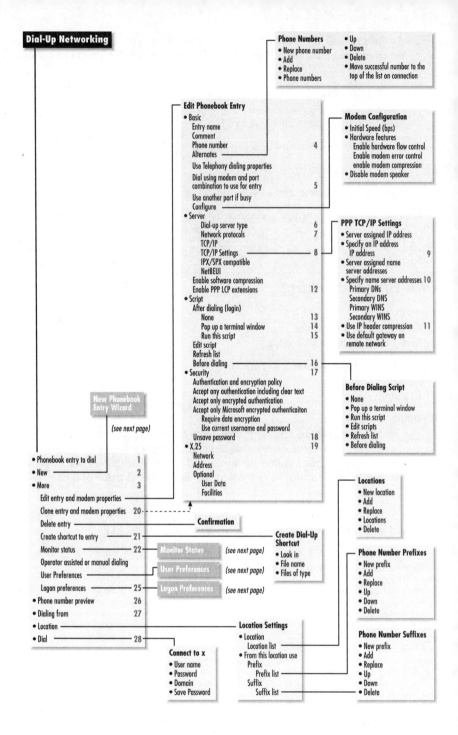

Phone Numbers
- New phone number
- Add
- Replace
- Phone numbers
- Up
- Down
- Delete
- Move successful number to the top of the list on connection

Edit Phonebook Entry
- Basic
  - Entry name
  - Comment
  - Phone number   4
  - Alternates
  - Use Telephony dialing properties
  - Dial using modem and port combination to use for entry   5
  - Use another port if busy
  - Configure
- Server
  - Dial-up server type   6
  - Network protocols   7
  - TCP/IP
  - TCP/IP Settings   8
  - IPX/SPX compatible
  - NetBEUI
  - Enable software compression
  - Enable PPP LCP extensions   12
- Script
  - After dialing (login)
    - None   13
    - Pop up a terminal window   14
    - Run this script   15
  - Edit script
  - Refresh list
  - Before dialing   16
- Security   17
  - Authentication and encryption policy
  - Accept any authentication including clear text
  - Accept only encrypted authentication
  - Accept only Microsoft encrypted authenticaiton
    - Require data encryption
    - Use current username and password
  - Unsave password   18
- X.25   19
  - Network
  - Address
  - Optional
    - User Data
    - Facilities

Modem Configuration
- Initial Speed (bps)
- Hardware features
  - Enable hardware flow control
  - Enable modem error control
  - enable modem compression
- Disable modem speaker

PPP TCP/IP Settings
- Server assigned IP address
- Specify an IP address
  - IP address   9
- Server assigned name server addresses
- Specify name server addresses   10
  - Primary DNs
  - Secondary DNS
  - Primary WINS
  - Secondary WINS
- Use IP header compression   11
- Use default gateway on remote network

Before Dialing Script
- None
- Pop up a terminal window
- Run this script
- Edit scripts
- Refresh list
- Before dialing

New Phonebook Entry Wizard

(see next page)

- Phonebook entry to dial   1
- New   2
- More   3
  - Edit entry and modem properties
  - Clone entry and modem properties   20
  - Delete entry
  - Create shortcut to entry   21
  - Monitor status   22
  - Operator assisted or manual dialing
  - User Preferences
  - Logon preferences   25
- Phone number preview   26
- Dialing from   27
- Location
- Dial   28

Confirmation

Monitor Status *(see next page)*

User Preferences *(see next page)*

Logon Preferences *(see next page)*

Create Dial-Up Shortcut
- Look in
- File name
- Files of type

Locations
- New location
- Add
- Replace
- Locations
- Delete

Phone Number Prefixes
- New prefix
- Add
- Replace
- Up
- Down
- Delete

Location Settings
- Location
  - Location list
- From this location use
  - Prefix
    - Prefix list
  - Suffix
    - Suffix list

Connect to x
- User name
- Password
- Domain
- Save Password

Phone Number Suffixes
- New prefix
- Add
- Replace
- Up
- Down
- Delete

Dial-Up Networking *(continuation)*

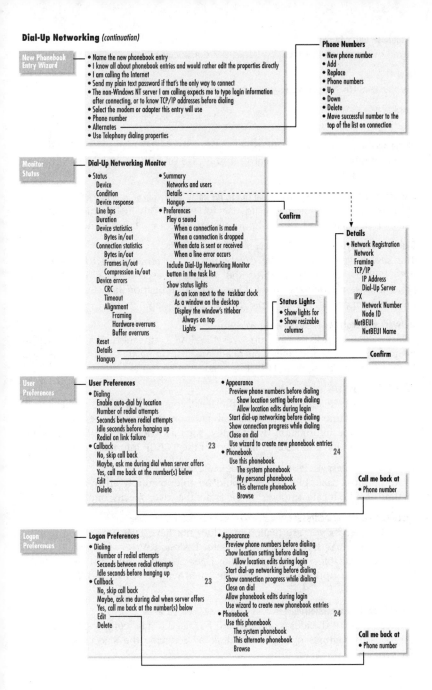

New Phonebook Entry Wizard
- Name the new phonebook entry
- I know all about phonebook entries and would rather edit the properties directly
- I am calling the Internet
- Send my plain text password if that's the only way to connect
- The non-Windows NT server I am calling expects me to type login information after connecting, or to know TCP/IP addresses before dialing
- Select the modem or adapter this entry will use
- Phone number
- Alternates
- Use Telephony dialing properties

Phone Numbers
- New phone number
- Add
- Replace
- Phone numbers
- Up
- Down
- Delete
- Move successful number to the top of the list on connection

Monitor Status

Dial-Up Networking Monitor
- Status
  Device
  Condition
  Device response
  Line bps
  Duration
  Device statistics
    Bytes in/out
  Connection statistics
    Bytes in/out
    Frames in/out
    Compression in/out
  Device errors
    CRC
    Timeout
    Alignment
      Framing
      Hardware overruns
      Buffer overruns
  Reset
  Details
  Hangup
- Summary
  Networks and users
  Details - - - - - - - - - - - - - -
  Hangup
- Preferences
  Play a sound
    When a connection is made
    When a connection is dropped
    When data is sent or received
    When a line error occurs
  Include Dial-Up Networking Monitor button in the task list
  Show status lights
    As an icon next to the taskbar clock
    As a window on the desktop
    Display the window's titlebar
      Always on top
    Lights

Confirm

Status Lights
- Show lights for
- Show resizable columns

Details
- Network Registration
  Network
  Framing
  TCP/IP
    IP Address
    Dial-Up Server
  IPX
    Network Number
    Node ID
  NetBEUI
    NetBEUI Name

Confirm

User Preferences

User Preferences
- Dialing
  Enable auto-dial by location
  Number of redial attempts
  Seconds between redial attempts
  Idle seconds before hanging up
  Redial on link failure
- Callback   23
  No, skip call back
  Maybe, ask me during dial when server offers
  Yes, call me back at the number(s) below
  Edit
  Delete
- Appearance
  Preview phone numbers before dialing
    Show location setting before dialing
    Allow location edits during login
  Start dial-up networking before dialing
  Show connection progress while dialing
  Close on dial
  Use wizard to create new phonebook entries
- Phonebook   24
  Use this phonebook
    The system phonebook
    My personal phonebook
    This alternate phonebook
    Browse

Call me back at
- Phone number

Logon Preferences

Logon Preferences
- Dialing
  Number of redial attempts
  Seconds between redial attempts
  Idle seconds before hanging up
- Callback   23
  No, skip call back
  Maybe, ask me during dial when server offers
  Yes, call me back at the number(s) below
  Edit
  Delete
- Appearance
  Preview phone numbers before dialing
  Show location setting before dialing
    Allow location edits during login
  Start dial-up networking before dialing
  Show connection progress while dialing
  Close on dial
  Allow phonebook edits during login
  Use wizard to create new phonebook entries
- Phonebook   24
  Use this phonebook
    The system phonebook
    This alternate phonebook
    Browse

Call me back at
- Phone number

Accessories

1 **Phonebook entry to dial**
Name of entry. All the Dial-Up settings are associated with the entry name.

2 **New**
Invoke **Dial-Up Networking** wizard for creating entries.

3 **More**
Modify existing entry.

4 **Phone number** [More-Edit entry and modem properties-Basic]
Phone number(s) to dial for entry. In the case of a PPTP entry, this will be an IP address or hostname.

5 **Dial using modem and port combination to use for entry** [More-Edit entry and modem properties-Basic]
Modem and port combination to use for entry. With PPTP, this will be the *RASPPTPM* device and a virtual port named *VPNx* (*x* is the port number).

6 **Dial-up server type** [More-Edit entry and modem properties-Server]
The server type describes the capabilities of the remote site you are dialing into. PPP has the most features and should be used if possible. The other types impose restrictions on what protocols and functionality is available over the RAS connection. For example, SLIP is TCP/IP-only.

7 **Network protocols** [More-Edit entry and modem properties-Server]
Select which protocols can run over the RAS connection. For best performance, select only the ones you need. Most anything that can be done over NetBEUI can be done over TCP/IP instead.

8 **TCP/IP Settings** [More-Edit entry and modem properties-Server]
Configure TCP/IP information that the local computer will use while it connects to the remote system. The ideal situation is when the remote systems provides all the information dynamically, such as when using DHCP. In some cases, you will have to enter some or all of the TCP/IP information manually.

9 **Specify an IP address** [More-Edit entry and modem properties-Server-TCP/IP Settings]
Even the most basic PPP server should be able to supply an IP address automatically to the local computer. If this is not the case, specify one here.

10 **Specify name server addresses** [More-Edit entry and modem properties-Server-TCP/IP Settings]
If the PPP server you are dialing into does not have DHCP or a similar functionality, you may have to manually enter DNS and WINS server addresses. If DHCP is available, setting the "006 DNS Servers" and "044 WINS/NBNS Servers" DHCP options will supply the client with the DNS and WINS server addresses.

11 **Use IP header compression** [More-Edit entry and modem properties-Server-TCP/IP Settings]
Request that IP header compression be used. This compression scheme improves throughput over the PPP link by reducing the size of headers on each packet.

12 **Enable PPP LCP extensions** [More-Edit entry and modem properties-Server]
Enable PPP features such as multilink and callback. Multilink allows multiple PPP sessions to be combined in parallel, adding to the total bandwidth for the connection. Callback is the ability of the remote end of the PPP connection to call back the local end, reversing phone charges or increasing security. The Link Control Protocol (LCP) is a subprotocol of PPP and is used to negotiate PPP options and test the link between the PPP client and server. Note that setting this option does not necessarily mean that the options will work; it only tells the PPP client to ask the PPP server if it supports the extensions.*

13 **None** [More-Edit entry and modem properties-Script-After dialing]
When using a PPP connection, use one of the of PPP authentication methods selected in the **Security** tab (as opposed to scripting or manual input).

14 **Pop up a terminal window** [More-Edit entry and modem properties-Script-After dialing]
Bring up a terminal window after dialing that allows you to type in information manually to the remote device. This is useful when logging into remote sites for which you have not yet written a script.

15 **Run this script** [More-Edit entry and modem properties-Script-After dialing]
Run a script stored in an *.SCP* or *SWITCH.INF* file.

16 **Before Dialing** [More-Edit entry and modem properties-Script]
Pop-up terminal window or run script before dialing.

17 **Security** [More-Edit entry and modem properties]
See the section entitled "PPP authentication" in Chapter 5, *RAS and DUN*.

18 **Unsave password** [More-Edit entry and modem properties-Security]
If you have previously saved the password when dialing, this causes the computer to forget it.

19 **X.25** [More-Edit entry and modem properties]
Configure connection to X.25 network.

20 **Clone entry and modem properties** [More]
Copy all the settings of an existing entry to a new entry.

21 **Create shortcut to entry** [More]
Create a shortcut on the desktop that will dial entry.

22 **Monitor status** [More]
Bring up Dial-Up Networking monitor. This allows you to monitor the performance of a session and set preferences for the monitor appearance on the desktop.

23 **Callback** [More-User preferences]
Callback is the ability for a remote system to call you back after you initially connect. This can be used to increase security or reverse calling charges.

---

*See RFC1570, "PPP LCP Extensions," RFC1700, "Assigned Numbers," and "Debugging PPP" in Chapter 5, *RAS and DUN*, for information about LCP and IPCP codes.

24 **Phonebook** [More-User preferences]

Change phonebooks. Phonebooks store lists of entries and include all the information related to connecting to an entry. Phonebooks are normally stored in the *<winnt root>\SYSTEM32\RAS* directory. The system phonebook is the default phonebook and is called *RASPHONE.PBK*. If you create a personal phonebook, it will be the first eight characters of your username followed by a *.PBK* extension. For example, the **Administrator** accounts personal phonebook would be called *ADMINIST.PBK*. Creating a personal phonebook allows you to move your private information from system to system without disturbing any existing phonebooks. You can also specify a file outside of the *RAS* directory with the **Browse** button.

25 **Logon preferences** [More]

These settings apply if you select the **Logon using Dial-Up Networking** box from the initial console logon.

26 **Phone number preview**

Phone number to be dialed for selected entry. In the case of a PPTP connection, this will be an IP address or hostname.

27 **Dialing from**

Selection location to dial from. If you use the computer in multiple locations, you can set location-specific prefix and suffix dialing strings. These include codes to get outside lines, disable call waiting, credit card numbers, and so on.

28 **Dial**

Dial selected entry. If any entry is active, the button changes to **Hang Up**.

HyperTerminal

Requires

NT Workstation or Server

Summary

The **HyperTerminal** accessory is a replacement for the generic COM program that allows simple terminal emulation and file transfer (*Xmodem, Ymodem, Zmodem,* and *Kermit*). It is also useful for testing modems and writing RAS scripts.

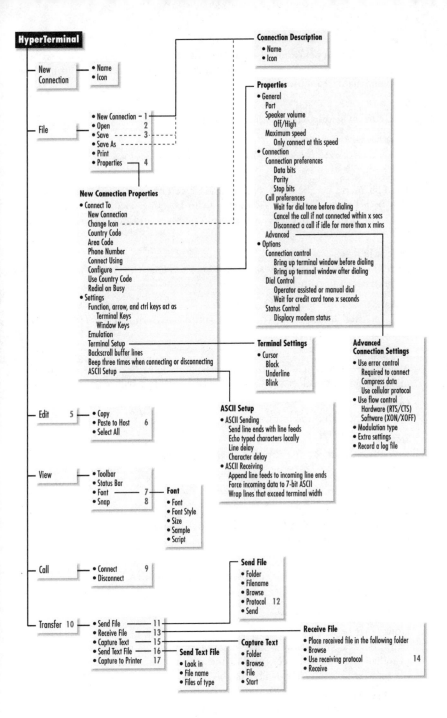

HyperTerminal

New Connection
- Name
- Icon

Connection Description
- Name
- Icon

File
- New Connection – 1
- Open   2
- Save   3
- Save As
- Print
- Properties   4

Properties
- General
  Port
  Speaker volume
    Off/High
  Maximum speed
    Only connect at this speed
- Connection
  Connection preferences
    Data bits
    Parity
    Stop bits
  Call preferences
    Wait for dial tone before dialing
    Cancel the call if not connected within x secs
    Disconnect a call if idle for more than x mins
  Advanced
- Options
  Connection control
    Bring up terminal window before dialing
    Bring up termnal window after dialing
  Dial Control
    Operator assisted or manual dial
    Wait for credit card tone x seconds
  Status Control
    Display modem status

New Connection Properties
- Connect To
  New Connection
  Change Icon
  Country Code
  Area Code
  Phone Number
  Connect Using
  Configure
  Use Country Code
  Redial on Busy
- Settings
  Function, arrow, and ctrl keys act as
    Terminal Keys
    Window Keys
  Emulation
  Terminal Setup
  Backscroll buffer lines
  Beep three times when connecting or disconnecting
  ASCII Setup

Terminal Settings
- Cursor
  Block
  Underline
  Blink

Advanced Connection Settings
- Use error control
  Required to connect
  Compress data
  Use cellular protocol
- Use flow control
  Hardware (RTS/CTS)
  Software (XON/XOFF)
- Modulation type
- Extra settings
- Record a log file

Edit   5
- Copy
- Paste to Host   6
- Select All

ASCII Setup
- ASCII Sending
  Send line ends with line feeds
  Echo typed characters locally
  Line delay
  Character delay
- ASCII Receiving
  Append line feeds to incoming line ends
  Force incoming data to 7-bit ASCII
  Wrap lines that exceed terminal width

View
- Toolbar
- Status Bar
- Font   7
- Snap   8

Font
- Font
- Font Style
- Size
- Sample
- Script

Call
- Connect   9
- Disconnect

Send File
- Folder
- Filename
- Browse
- Protocol 12
- Send

Transfer 10
- Send File   11
- Receive File   13
- Capture Text   15
- Send Text File 16
- Capture to Printer 17

Send Text File
- Look in
- File name
- Files of type

Capture Text
- Folder
- Browse
- File
- Start

Receive File
- Place received file in the following folder
- Browse
- Use receiving protocol   14
- Receive

Accessories

1   **New Connection** [File]

Create new connection. Enter a name for session, select icon, phone, and port settings.

2 **Open** [File]

Open existing **HyperTerminal** configuration settings (.*HT*) files. Can also open .*TRM* terminal files created with the Windows Terminal accessory from previous versions of Windows NT.

3 **Save** [File]

Save current settings in a session (.*HT*) file.

4 **Properties** [File]

Edit name for session, select icon, phone, and port settings.

5 **Edit**

The **Edit** menu can be used to copy and paste text from a HyperTerminal session between applications. This feature can be quite useful when transferring small amounts of text between the local computer and the computer to which you are connected.

6 **Paste to Host** [Edit]

Paste the clipboard to the session window, sending it to the remote system as if you typed it in manually.

7 **Font** [View]

Set font used for session. You may want to use **Terminal** when DEC-specific characters are being used.

8 **Snap** [View]

Adjust size of terminal window automatically. Right-click mouse in active terminal session and select **View-Snap**. Terminal window will resize to fit.

9 **Connect** [Call]

Connect and dial number of remote computer.

10 **Transfer**

Upload or download files from local computer to remote computer.

11 **Send File** [Transfer]

Upload file from local computer to remote computer.

12 **Use receiving protocol** [Transfer-Send File]

Protocol used for upload. You must choose a protocol supported by both the local computer and the remote computer.

13 **Receive File** [Transfer]

Download file from remote computer to local computer.

14 **Protocol** [Transfer-Receive File]

Protocol used for download.

15 **Capture Text** [Transfer]

Capture text coming from remote computer and save to a file. This serves as a primitive file transfer mechanism if the remote computer does not support a file transfer protocol. This will probably work only for 7-bit ASCII data.

16 **Send Text File** [Transfer]

Upload text file from local computer to remote computer.

17 **Capture to Printer** [Transfer]

Copy everything received from remote computer to printer.

Telnet

Requires
NT Workstation or Server
TCP/IP protocol

Command-Line Equivalents
telnet

Summary
The **Telnet** accessory creates an interactive session on a remote computer using TCP/IP. It allows you to log onto a remote computer and type commands using a text-based interface. In order for you to telnet to a remote computer, it must be running a telnet server. Windows NT does not supply a telnet server as part of the base operating system, but there are several third-party products available. The **Telnet** accessory can also be started from the command line.

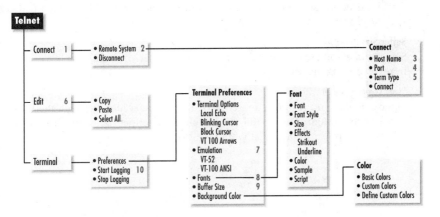

1 Connect

To connect to or disconnect from a remote system. The **Telnet** accessory remembers previous remote systems and includes them in the menu.

2 Remote System [Connect]

Specify remote system for connection.

3 Host Name [Connect-Remote System]

The TCP/IP hostname or IP address of the remote system.

4 Port [Connect-Remote System]

The TCP/IP port on the remote system you are connecting to. Normally, this is the telnet port (23), but you can also telnet to other services that have text based commands, such as SMTP (25), NNTP (119), etc. The scroll list contains some predefined entries of services for testing, but you can always type in your own port number. For example, to connect to an HTTP server, try port 80. The *SERVICES* file in *<winnt root>\SYSTEM32\DRIVERS\ETC* contains the mapping of port numbers to names.

5 **TermType** [Connect-Remote System]

When connecting to a remote system, the **TermType** name is sent to the telnet server on the remote system. This ensures that the telnet server and telnet client are both using the same terminal emulation. Changing the TermType has no effect on the terminal emulation being used by the **Telnet** program, which is controlled by **Terminal-Preferences**.

6 **Edit**

The **Edit** menu can be used to copy and paste text from a telnet session between applications. This feature can be quite useful when transferring small amounts of text between different systems.

7 **Emulation** [Terminal-Preferences]

Type of emulation used by local side of telnet connection. The DEC VT100 is one of the most common terminal types used to communicate with UNIX and VMS systems, network equipment, and text-based browsers, such as Lynx. To use anything more complicated than VT100 (for example, IBM 3270 emulation), you will have to use a third-party application.

8 **Fonts** [Terminal-Preferences]

Set font used for session. User may want to use the **Terminal** font when DEC-specific characters are being used.

9 **Buffer Size** [Terminal-Preferences]

Set size of scroll area. This is the amount of text that you will be able to scroll in reverse using the scrollbar.

10 **Start Logging** [Terminal]

Open a logfile and record a transcript of all communication between the local and remote system. This useful for writing RAS scripts. Be aware that passwords may appear in plain text within the logfile.

CHAPTER 5

RAS and DUN

The **Remote Access Service** (RAS) allows computers to make network connections to each other using telephone lines.

Windows 3.11, Windows 95, and Windows NT Workstation and Server can call out to another computer or communications server. Windows NT Workstation and Server can accept calls from any of these OS types. In most cases, the type of connection between the computers will be the Point-to-Point Protocol (PPP) running over an analog phone line, but RAS also supports the Serial Line Internet Protocol (SLIP), X.25, and ISDN connections.

This chapter describes the network protocols used by RAS, and how to install, configure, and start the RAS services. The syntax of RAS scripting languages is documented along with examples of their usage.

RAS Protocols

A RAS connection running PPP can support the TCP/IP, IPX/SPX, and NetBEUI protocols simultaneously. For example, you may browse a remote network and share files using NetBEUI, browse the World Wide Web using TCP/IP, and access a Novell NetWare file server using IPX—all over a single dial-up RAS connection.

The SLIP protocol is TCP/IP-only and does not support the multitude of options available in PPP. It has fallen out of favor for these reasons and can be avoided in most situations.

The NetBEUI protocol will not generally be able to run over the RAS connection unless you have a Microsoft operating system at both ends of the connection. NetBIOS functions such as file sharing, printing, and NetBIOS name service can all be made to work over either a TCP/IP-only PPP or a SLIP connection using NetBIOS over TCP/IP (NBT).

PPTP

NT 4.0 also supports the Point-to-Point Tunneling Protocol (PPTP). This allows the creation of Virtual Private Networks (VPN) using the Internet. PPTP creates a virtual "tunnel" between your computer and a remote NT server (or communications server that understands PPTP). This tunnel is encrypted, enabling you to send sensitive data over the Internet. The main reasons to use PPTP are security and lowering remote access costs. PPTP may save you money if you are able to use the Internet to connect remote sites instead of private leased lines.

RAS Components

You may be confused by how the different components of RAS are named and administered. Previous to NT 4.0, RAS referred to both the client and server side of a connection. Typically, the client side is doing the dialing, and the server side is receiving calls. In NT 4.0, the client side of RAS is called Dial-Up Networking (DUN), which is buried in the **Programs-Accessories** menu. DUN looks similar to the Windows 95 implementation but is different in operation and configuration. The server side, the **Remote Access Service**, is administered by the **Remote Access Admin** tool and the **Services-Remote Access Service-Properties** menu of the **Network** control panel. This book uses the term RAS to describe the entire Remote Access functionality, and DUN for the client side of RAS.

Installing RAS

To install RAS under NT Server or Workstation, use the **Services-Add** button of the **Network** control panel and select **Remote Access Service**.

Dial-Up Networking will prompt you to install it the first time you try to run it unless it is already installed.

To install the Point-to-Point Tunneling Protocol (PPTP), use the **Protocols-Add** button of the **Network** control panel. Installing PPTP also installs RAS if it is not already installed.

Overview of a RAS session

To illustrate how the DUN side of RAS works, let us assume you are a typical NT user who wants to log in to the Internet using your local ISP. To initiate the connection:

1. Start Dial-Up Networking.

2. Select an entry name from the scroll list.

3. Click on the **Dial** button.

4. Enter username and password into the dialog box.

5. After this point, the local computer should log onto the remote RAS server and start the network connection (see Figure 5-1).

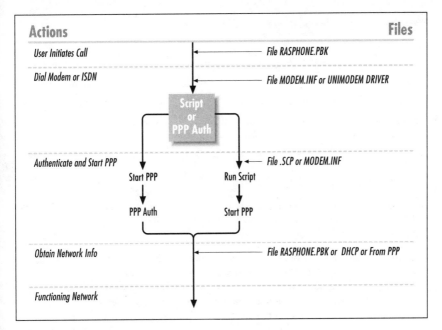

Figure 5-1: RAS session startup

There are several processes needed for a successful start of the DUN session. The first is authentication, the process of proving to the remote site that you are a legitimate user. The second is configuring the network, which usually involves getting network information from the remote site to configure the local computer.

PPP Authentication

If you are using PPP, you should be able to use PPP authentication protocols to authenticate your RAS connection to the remote device. An authentication protocol is a set of standards for exchanging logon name and password information between the two network devices.

The most common PPP authentication protocols are the Password Authentication Protocol (PAP) and the Challenge Handshake Authentication Protocol (CHAP). PAP is a simple protocol that sends your username and password to the remote system. The exchange of passwords between client and server are in clear text and could be snooped by a third party listening in on the connection. CHAP is more secure in that the password information is encrypted before it is sent over the PPP connection. Shiva PAP (SPAP), a Shiva-specific version of PAP, improves on PAP by encrypting the password before sending it to the remote system. Microsoft has its own version of CHAP that encrypts the password using a different scheme. This is called MS-CHAP and is generally available only for Microsoft products. If you do not control both ends of your RAS connection, ask the person in charge of the remote end what PPP authentication protocols are supported.

The PPP client and PPP server negotiate to find a common authentication protocol. You can limit the choices in order to enhance security. The choice of PPP authentication protocol is made in the DUN **Security** tab, as shown in Table 5-1.

Table 5-1: PPP Authentication Protocol Selection

Setting	Allowed authentication protocols
Accept any authentication including clear text	PAP, CHAP, SPAP, MS-CHAP
Accept only encryped authentication	SPAP, CHAP, or MS-CHAP
Accept only Microsoft encrypted authentication	MS-CHAP

Authentication Using Scripting

If you are using SLIP or are logging in to a remote device which does not support a PPP authentication protocol, you are going to need a script to provide the authentication information.

A script fools a remote computer or device into thinking that you are typing in a username, password, or other logon information, while it is actually done by your computer. Scripting automates the logon procedure and makes it possible for your computer to reconnect a failed connection without user intervention; or, it can even establish connections via the *at* command scheduler service.

Normally, getting DUN to log in to a Microsoft RAS server is simple and pretty much works out of the box. Configuration is done by clicking on a few check-boxes and typing in names and phone numbers for the remote sites.

The situation becomes more complicated if you are trying to use a non-Microsoft product on one side of the connection. For example, most Internet Service Providers (ISPs) are not using Microsoft NT RAS servers to provide dial-up connectivity for their customers. They typically use specialized "comm-servers" that run vendor-specific and proprietary operating systems. Some of these comm-servers are starting to support RAS, but there are still a huge number that offer generic PPP dial-up support. Some of these authenticate PPP users by using a UNIX-like login and password prompts. For example:

```
Login: <username>
Password: <password>

#$$(&*%@)wS@#
<ppp session starts>
```

These prompts were originally intended to be used by humans who were logging in to character-based terminal sessions. Then programs such as UNIX UUCP (UNIX-to-UNIX Copy) started to use the same authentication mechanism to login, but did so by pretending to be a human user and entering the username and password via a program.

As the login/password prompts varied among different systems and vendors, a scripting "language" was used to describe the different login/password procedures for each remote computer. In UUCP terminology, the scripting functionality is called a chat script. Chat scripts are similar in function to macros or scripts that terminal emulators or *Comm programs* provide to automate the login to a BBS or other remote computer system.

Microsoft supports two different scripting languages in NT 4.0. The first consists of the *SWITCH.INF*-style scripts that appeared in NT 3.5x. The second is the Windows 95–style scripts contained in files with the *.SCP* extension. If you have existing scripts from NT 3.51 or Windows 95, you should not need to modify them for NT 4.0. If you are writing a script from scratch on 4.0, it is probably better to use the Windows 95–style *.SCP* scripting language, as it has many more features. For example, the *SWITCH.INF* language has no time-out functionality, so it will wait forever if something goes wrong. The *.SCP* scripting language also has more traditional program-flow structures that should be familiar to even the casual programmer. If you are logging in to an ISP or company remote-access facility, chances are that someone else has already written a script in one of the languages that you can use.

If you are setting up Dial-Up Networking to log in to a non-Microsoft PPP server for the first time, it is worth seeing if the Microsoft-supplied *Generic Login* script will work without any further customization. It should handle the most common login name and password prompts.

Note that it is possible to hardcode your username and password into the scripts themselves. This would eliminate having to type the information each time you use DUN, but your account would be wide open to anyone who gains access to the script files.

Configuring the Network

Your computer has to obtain several pieces of information before it can start communicating via TCP/IP with other computers. This information includes an IP address for the client side of the connection, a list of DNS servers, and possibly a list of WINS servers.

PPP has the ability to obtain an IP address from a PPP server and give it to the dial-in client, but getting DNS and WINS server information to the client requires functionality external to PPP.

IP addresses are usually handed out dynamically by the device you are calling. This means that your IP address (and possibly the TCP/IP hostname) could be different each time you dial in. The IP addresses can come either from a pool of addresses handed out by the remote PPP device or via DHCP.

In order to look up hostnames on the Internet (such as when using a web browser) you also need the address of one or more DNS servers. Some communications servers (including NT RAS) supply this automatically to the dial-in clients via DHCP, and others require you to type the information into DUN using the **Server-TCP/IP** tab.

If you want to browse the remote network you are dialing into using Microsoft networking, you need a WINS server IP address in the **Server-TCP/IP** tab. You can either type one in or have it supplied by DHCP.

Debugging PPP

When a PPP connection is first started, the two ends of the connection negotiate lots of options, trying to find a common set that they both support. If you are having trouble connecting with PPP, there are several tools available for debugging. The first is a logfile generated by DUN that records all PPP packets going to and from the local computer and the remote device. The second is the **Network Monitor** application, which can "listen" on the PPP interface and record all traffic going over the PPP link.

In order to understand the PPP information, you have to have a detailed explanation of PPP readily available. Good sources for descriptions of the protocol are the Internet Request For Comments (RFC) documents available on the Internet. The following Internet RFCs cover PPP:

> RFC1661   *The Point to Point Protocol (PPP)*
> RFC1700   *Assigned Numbers* (PPP Protocol Field Assignments section)

You should easily be able to find RFCs on many web and ftp sites. One of the official sites is *http://ds.internic.net/ds/*. The Southwest Free Software Organization site at *http://www.freesoft.org* has an especially nice RFC display.

You really do not have to understand the protocol completely in order to spot problems. If you cannot find the error, at least you will be able to produce a logfile that you can show to someone who does understand PPP.

PPP Logging

Locate the key *SYSTEM\CurrentControlSet\Services\RasMan\PPP* and change **Logging** from 0 to 1. This will create a file called *PPP.LOG* in the *<winnt root>\SYSTEM32\RAS* directory.

To debug a PPP session, first enable logging and then initiate the PPP connection. When the connection fails or exits, examine *PPP.LOG* to see what happened.

```
more < PPP.LOG
Line up event occurred on port 0
FsmInit called for protocol = c021, port = 0
FsmReset called for protocol = c021, port = 0
FsmThisLayerStarted called for protocol = c021, port = 0
<PPP packet sent at 02/06/1997 11:14:12:436
<Protocol = LCP, Type = Configure-Req, Length = 0x26, Id = 0x0, Port = 0
<C0 21 01 00 00 24 02 06 00 00 00 00 05 06 00 00  |.!...$.........|
<5B D5 07 02 08 02 0D 03 06 11 04 06 4E 13 09 03  |[...........N...|
<00 AA 00 A5 84 EF                                |......         |

>PPP packet received at 02/06/1997 11:14:12:597
>Protocol = LCP, Type = Configure-Req, Length = 0x24, Id = 0x1, Port = 0
>C0 21 01 01 00 22 01 04 05 F2 02 06 00 0A 00 00  |.!..."..........|
>03 0C C0 27 01 00 00 03 00 00 00 0E 05 06 64 03  |...'.........d.|
>1E 2A 08 02                                      |.*..           |
```

```
<PPP packet sent at 02/06/1997 11:14:12:597
<Protocol = LCP, Type = Configure-Nak, Length = 0xe, Id = 0x1, Port = 0
<C0 21 03 01 00 0C 03 08 C0 27 01 00 00 01        |.!.......'....  |

>PPP packet received at 02/06/1997 11:14:12:597
>Protocol = LCP, Type = Configure-Reject, Length = 0x16, Id = 0x0, Port = 0
>C0 21 04 00 00 14 0D 03 06 11 04 06 4E 13 09 03 |.!..........N...|
>00 AA 00 A5 84 EF                                |......          |
```

What you are seeing is a trace of every PPP packet going to and from your computer to the remote PPP device. The *Protocol* and *Type* fields tell you what is going on. The data in the packets is presented in both hexadecimal and ASCII.

One of the most common failures you may have when setting up a new PPP connection is with the negotiation of an authentication Protocol. This is controlled on the client side of RAS by the **Security** tab of Dial-Up Networking. Both ends of the PPP connection try to find a common mechanism for authentication. The Dial-Up Networking **Security** tab places various restrictions on the allowable authentication protocols.

The PPP session should try to negotiate the most secure protocol first, and if this fails, try the second best, and so on. In reality, not every device that speaks PPP handles the authentication protocol negotiation gracefully, leading to interoperability problems between different vendor devices.

Use the most secure protocol, which will normally be **Accept only encrypted authentication**. If both ends are Microsoft products, you could use MS-CHAP.

For authentication failures, the most interesting part of the *PPP.LOG* file is going to be the section starting with *Authentication phase*. For example:

```
Authenticating phase started
<PPP packet sent at 02/06/1997 15:05:04:169
<Protocol = SHIVA PAP, Type = Protocol specific, Length = 0x28, Id = 0x0, Port = 0
<C0 27 06 00 00 26 01 05 65 61 70 02 15 31 5C 5C |.'...&..eap..1\\|
<0B 11 3D 73 9F C7 2A 49 EB 67 64 7C A4 89 D5 5D |..=s..*I.gd|...]|
<03 04 00 01 04 04 00 01                          |........        |

>PPP packet received at 02/06/1997 15:05:04:389
>Protocol = SHIVA PAP, Type = Protocol specific, Length = 0x8, Id = 0x0, Port = 0
>C0 27 02 00 00 06 00 00                          |.'......        |

FsmThisLayerUp called for protocol = c027, port = 0
```

This DUN client is configured with the **Accept only encryption authentication** option, which accepts either SPAP, CHAP, or MS-CHAP. From this sequence, you can see that the local computer tried using the SPAP (Shiva PAP) authentication protocol, and the remote PPP device accepted it. You can see that protocol c027 succeeded from the lines' referrals to Shiva PAP and *FsmThisLayerUp*. In RFC 1700, c027 is listed as the Shiva Password Authentication Protocol or SPAP.

c021	Link Control Protocol
c023	Password Authentication Protocol
c025	Link Quality Report
c027	**Shiva Password Authentication Protocol**
c029	CallBack Control Protocol (CBCP)

```
c081            Container Control Protocol
c223            Challenge Handshake Authentication Protocol
c225            RSA Authentication Protocol
c227            Extensible Authentication Protocol
c26f            Stampede Bridging Authorization Protocol
c281            Proprietary Authentication Protocol
c283            Proprietary Authentication Protocol
c481            Proprietary Node ID Authentication Protocol
```

The next example shows a failure:

```
Authenticating phase started
>PPP packet received at 02/06/1997 14:28:11:617
>Protocol = CHAP, Type = Protocol specific, Length = 0x1a, Id = 0x1, Port = 0
>C2 23 01 01 00 18 08 32 F9 F9 ED 00 1E 4D 60 6F  |.#.....2.....M'o|
>70 60 2F 74 66 73 74 2D 6E 62                     |ora-login:.    |

<PPP packet sent at 02/06/1997 14:28:11:617
<Protocol = CHAP, Type = Protocol specific, Length = 0x21, Id = 0x1, Port = 0
<C2 23 02 01 00 1F 10 94 40 30 22 05 A5 DF 43 1E  |.#......@0"...C.|
<E0 85 54 8B 0F CA 64 48 4F 4D 45 5C 70 63 65 61  |..T...dHOMEcea|
<70                                               |p              |

>PPP packet received at 02/06/1997 14:28:11:757
>Protocol = CHAP, Type = Protocol specific, Length = 0x1b, Id = 0x1, Port = 0
>C2 23 04 01 00 19 49 6E 76 61 6C 69 64 20 43 48  |.#...Invalid CH|
>41 50 20 72 65 73 70 6F 6E 73 65                  |AP response    |

Auth Protocol c223 terminated with error 7
FsmThisLayerDown called for protocol = c021, port = 0
```

The "Protocol = CHAP" and the message "Invalid CHAP response" are clues to
what is wrong. From looking at RFC1700, you can tell that "Auth Protocol c223" is
CHAP. The next step is to examine the remote device you are calling and find out
why it does not speak CHAP.

Network Monitor and PPP

The Network Monitor is normally used to capture network traffic from a LAN
interface, such as an Ethernet adapter. It is also possible to use it as a "WAN
Analyzer" by listening on serial interface used by RAS and capturing packets from
the PPP session. It is most useful during the initial negotiation between DUN and
the remote device, as this is where errors are likely to occur. Follow these steps to
locate errors:

1. Start **Network Monitor**.

2. Select interface to capture traffic from. Under the **Capture-Networks** menu,
   click on the Ethernet interface with all zeros for the **Current Address** (see Figure 5-2).

3. Start the capture. Select **Capture-Start**.

4. Start DUN.

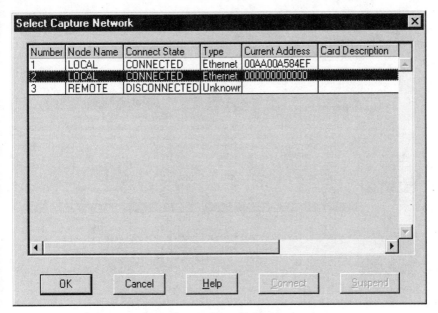

Figure 5-2: Selecting serial interface in Network Monitor

5. Dial the entry that is to be debugged.

6. When the connection fails, go back to **Network Monitor** and select **Capture-Stop and View**.

7. Step through each packet and look for errors, especially with "Reject" in the *Description* field (see Figure 5-3).

Keep in mind that the PPP device that you are calling in to is likely to have an ability to debug the PPP negotiation process, enabling the PPP connection to be debugged from either side of the conversation.

Also realize that you are unlikely to be the first person to discover a new PPP problem between devices and you should search the Internet, web sites, and Usenet newsgroups before paying for help.

Writing Scripts

Writing a script is pretty easy most of the time. These steps outline the process:

1. Connect to the remote system using **Terminal Window** or **Hyperterminal**.

2. Write down what the remote system sends and what you have to type.

3. Create the script in *SWITCH.INF* or *.SCP* language.

4. Associate the script with the dial-up entry by using the **Script** tab and selecting the script name from the **Run this script** scroll list.

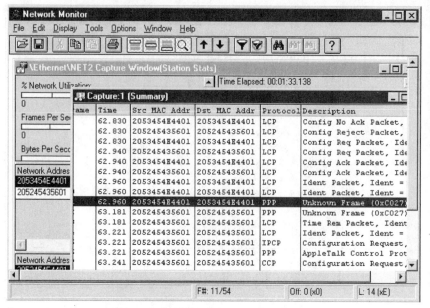

Figure 5-3: Capture of PPP traffic from RAS session

5. Test the script.

6. If the script fails, turn on *DEVICE.LOG* debugging and correct errors.

The following example shows how scripts can log into a Shiva LanRover using prompts to authenticate and start the PPP session. Have the manual available, so you know what to type at each prompt. (The LanRover can be configured to authenticate and start PPP automatically, but this configuration illustrates script features nicely.)

1. A new phonebook entry is created by starting up **Dial-Up Networking**, selecting **New**, and filling out the form.

2. Under the **Script** tab, select **Pop up a terminal window**.

3. Dial entry.

4. When the connection is made, the terminal window appears, but no prompt is seen from the remote system.

5. After hitting ENTER twice, the login prompt appears:

   @ Userid:

6. Type your username and hit ENTER.

7. The next prompt appears:

   Password?

8. Type your password and hit ENTER.

9. Another prompt appears:

```
Shiva LanRover/8E, Version 4.0.2 96/05/07
lanrover>
```

10. Type in **ppp** and hit ENTER.

11. The PPP session then starts:

```
Exiting shell, starting PPP
@3~$#$&~$#$#$%#^$#
```

12. At this point, you can continue to logon by clicking the **Done** button.

From information collected during the terminal session, a script can be created. The following is a sample *SWITCH.INF* script:

```
; interactive lanrover entry
[lanrover]
; needs two returns before prompt appears
COMMAND=<cr>
COMMAND=<cr>
OK=<match>"Userid:"
LOOP=<ignore>
COMMAND=<username><cr>
OK=<match>"assword?"
LOOP=<ignore>
COMMAND=<password><cr>
; have to explicitly start ppp
OK=<match>"anrover>"
LOOP=<ignore>
COMMAND="ppp"<cr>
; ignore anything from here on
OK=<ignore>
```

And here is a sample *.SCP* script:

```
proc main
transmit "^M"
transmit "^M"
waitfor "Userid:"
transmit $USERID
transmit "^M"
waitfor "assword?"
transmit $PASSWORD
transmit "^M"
waitfor "anrover>"
transmit "ppp^M"
endproc
```

Either of these scripts can be associated with the phonebook entry by using the **Script** tab and selecting the script name from the **Run this script** scroll list.

Debugging Scripts

Unlike Windows 95, NT does not supply a "step through script" function that allows you to execute your script one line at a time and watch it interact with the remote system. When running *.SCP* scripts, it does pop up the terminal window as the script executes, but this usually exits too quickly for you to catch the reason for failures. DUN does offer a form of post mortem analysis by recording the interaction between the client (your NT machine running dial-up networking) and the server (the comm-server you are logging into) in a log file, called *<winnt root>\SYSTEM32\RAS\DEVICE.LOG*. You have to specifically enable logging in the Registry in order for this to work.

In *KEY_LOCAL_MACHINE\SYSTEM\CurrentControlSet\Services\RasMan\Parameters*, change the value for *Logging* from 0 to 1. You do not need to reboot the system for this to take effect, just exit and restart Dial-Up Networking.

Try dialing the entry you are debugging. After it fails or terminates, examine the *DEVICE.LOG* file:

```
Remote Access Service Device Log  01/09/1997  09:54:55
-------------------------------------------------------------
Port: Command to Device:
Port: Response from Device:netblazer login:
Port: Command to Device:eap
Port: Echo from Device :eap
Port: Response from Device:
Password:
Port: Command to Device:foo
Port: Echo from Device :
Lo
Port: Response from Device:gin incorrect.
netblazer login:
```

The "Command to Device" lines are text being sent from your computer to the remote computer. The "Response from Device" is what the remote computer sends back. The "Echo from Device" is simply the text you are sending being echoed back by the remote device. The actual exchange would look like this:

```
Your Computer          Remote Computer
-------------------------------------------------------------
<nothing>
                       netblazer login:
eap
                       Password:
foo
                       Login incorrect.
```

The echo is normally turned on for everything except passwords. This is another holdover from human interaction, where you expect to see what you are typing. The "Login incorrect" message coming from the comm-server in the "Response from Device" indicates that either the username or password is incorrect and this is the reason the script is failing. Keep in mind that the *DEVICE.LOG* file may contain your password in clear-text (the password is "foo" in the example).

SWITCH.INF

The *SWITCH.INF* file contains multiple scripts in the scripting language first introduced in NT 3.x.

Section header

Section headers are used to delineate individual scripts within the *SWITCH.INF*. This is different from the Windows 95 scripting language, where each script is stored in a separate *.SCP* file. The header is simply a name enclosed in brackets:

```
[myscript]
```

Anything following the header is assumed to be script commands until the next header or the end of file.

The name within the brackets appears in the scroll list **Run this script** in the **Script** tab of Dial-Up Networking.

COMMAND

COMMAND is used to send text to the remote computer or device. It does not add a carriage-return character, so one must be added with the *<cr>* macro.

```
COMMAND=string<cr>
```

As each *COMMAND* statement takes about two seconds to execute, an empty statement such as:

```
COMMAND=
```

serves as a way to insert time delays into the script.

The sequence:

```
COMMAND=P
COMMAND=P
COMMAND=P
```

is equivalent to:

```
COMMAND=PPP
```

but each character is separated by a two-second delay in the first sequence. This method could be used to communicate with extremely slow devices.

OK

The *OK* command's main purpose is to look for a specific response from the remote computer or device. Most of the time this will be a prompt for the username or password.

```
OK=<match>"ogin:"
```

This *OK* command will try to match the string "ogin:" in any response coming from the remote device. The *<match>* macro is case-sensitive, so using the string "ogin:" will match either "Login:" or "login:".

LOOP

The *LOOP* command is usually combined with the *OK* command and has the effect of a conditional loop. The *LOOP* ignores any text coming from the remote device until something matching the *OK* command is found.

```
OK=<match>"ogin:"
LOOP=<ignore>
```

This *OK* and *LOOP* combination is useful for skipping through greeting messages or other text irrelevant to the login process. For example, if your Internet provider has a message of the day that is printed before the login prompt:

```
Welcome to Joe Bob's ISP
System down at 5pm tonight for repairs

          *********************************

login:
```

The *OK/LOOP* combination would ignore all the text until it found the "login:" prompt.

Response Commands

The response commands deal with processing output from the remote device.

CONNECT=response <macro>
> The *CONNECT* command looks for a connect message from the communications device, indicating a successful connection. This is primarily used when talking to PAD devices in the *PAD.INF* file.

ERROR=response <macro>
> If the script is looking for a specific error message, the *ERROR* keyword will tell DUN to look for this error message and notify the user that an error has occurred.

ERROR_DIAGNOSTICS=response <diagnostics>
> If the script encounters an error message, RAS will try to interpret what it means and inform the user.

NoResponse
> Do not expect any response from the remote device.

Macros

Macros are used to match or send special characters when sending text to or receiving text from the remote device.

<cr>
> Send carriage return character.

<lf>
> Send line feed character.

<match>string
> Look for *string* in output from remote device and exit loop. The *<match>* macro will find the string anywhere in the output (it does not have to be by

itself) and is case-sensitive. For these reasons, *<match>Login:* would fail to match "login:", but using "ogin:" matches either case.

<?>

Wildcard character for *<match>* macro that matches any single character. For example, *<match>"<?>ogin:"* could be used to match "Login:" or "login:".

<hXX>

Refer to character via position in ASCII character set by hex number (XX). This is useful for describing non-printing characters, such as *NUL*, which could be matched with *<h00>*. The ASCII code for a carriage return is 13 in base 10 and 0D in base 16. This could be represented by *<h0d>* in a script.

<ignore>

Ignore the responses from the remote system.

<diagnostics>

Interpret response from the remote system as an error diagnostic message and display it to user.

<username>

Supply username from **Connect To** dialog box. Not supported in SLIP sessions.

<password>

Supply password from **Connect To** dialog box. Not supported in SLIP sessions.

Comments

Comments can be used to annotate scripts to make them easier to maintain. A comment is started by a semicolon as the first character on the line:

```
;
; LanRover requires 2 carriage-returns before prompting for username
; (expecting PPP/ARA?)
;
```

Further Info

There are several files in the *<winnt root>\SYSTEM32\RAS* directory:

RASPHONE.HLP

Windows Help file for RAS

SWITCH.INF

Sample scripts for modems and ISDN TAs

PAD.INF

Sample scripts for PAD/X.25 devices

Windows 95 SCP Scripts

The Windows 95 Dial-Up Networking scripting language is supported under NT 4.0. In fact, you should be able to reuse any scripts you wrote for Windows 95 on NT 4.0 without modification.

The Windows 95 scripting language uses separate files ending with the extension *.SCP* for each script. This different than the *SWITCH.INF* scripting language, which stores multiple scripts within the same file.

The Windows 95 scripting language is "richer" in that it is more like a traditional programming language, with program-flow structures, variables, types, and so on. Another advantage over *SWITCH.INF*-scripts is a time-out capability that permits the script writer to handle unresponsive connections and other communications failure conditions gracefully.

Script Structure

All scripts must have a main procedure, delimited by *proc* and *endproc*, that can contain variable declaration and commands.

```
proc main
      variable declaration
      commands
endproc
```

Variables

Variables are either user- or system-defined names for holding values during the execution of the script. Variable names must begin with a letter or underscore character, but can contain mixed-case letters, numbers, and underscores. Be sure to avoid using any of the scripting language commands as variable names. These are called "reserved words," in that they are unavailable for use within the script.

Variable Data Types

The Windows 95 scripting language variables support the concept of *type*, which defines the kind of data contained in the variable and operations that can be performed on it.

Type	Description
Integer	A negative or positive whole number
String	One or more characters enclosed in double quotation marks
Boolean	Only possible values are *TRUE* or *FALSE*

Variable declaration and assignment

Variables are declared with a type the first time they appear in the script:

```
integer          timeout
```

Variables are assigned values using an expression:

```
timeout   =   10
```

Variables can also be declared and assigned in the same statement:

```
integer          timeout = 10
```

Predefined variables

The system provides several variables as a way for scripts to check for a common condition at run-time. They are read-only, meaning that you can query their value, but not alter it.

Name	Type	Description
$USERID	String	The username of the account making the connection. This is taken from the *User* field of the **Connect To** dialog box.
$PASSWORD	String	The password of the account making the connection. This is taken from the *Password* field of the **Connect To** dialog box.
$SUCCESS	Boolean	If a script command succeeds, this is set to *TRUE*, otherwise it is *FALSE*.
$FAILURE	Boolean	If a script command fails, this is set to *TRUE*, otherwise it is *FALSE*.

String literals

String literals are used to represent characters or strings that would be difficult to use because they contain nonprinting characters or characters that may be interpreted by the scripting language (instead of taken literally).

String	Name	Description
^*char*	Caret translation	Used to represent non-printing ASCII characters.
<cr>	Carriage return	
<lf>	Line feed	
\"	Double quotation mark	Protects or quotes the double quotation mark from being interpreted as the beginning or end of a string.
\^	Caret	Prevents character following carat from being interpreted as a caret translation.
\<	Less-than sign	
\\	Single backslash	

Expressions

Expressions are operations that yield a result which can be assigned to a variable or evaluated.

Operator	Type	Valid Data Types
–	Unary minus	
!	One's complement	
*/	Multiplicative	Integer
+–	Additive	Integer, string (+ only)
<><=>=	Relational	Integer
== !=	Equality	Integer, string, boolean
and	Logical AND	Boolean
or	Logical OR	Boolean

Comments

The comment character for scripts is the semi-colon. Anything following the comment character is ignored by the script processor.

```
;
; Here is a comment
```

Keywords

Keywords define the structure of the script and declare variable *type*.

proc	**proc** *name*
	Beginning of procedure. Scripts must have at least a *main* procedure.
	Example
	```proc main```

endproc	**endproc**
	End of procedure. When used to end procedure *main*, PPP (or SLIP) will be started.

integer	**integer** *name [= value]*
	Declare *name* as type integer and optionally assign it a *value*.

Example

```
integer nLoginTimeout = 3
```

---

string *name [= value]*   string

Declare *name* as type string and optionally assign it a *value.*

Example

```
string szPW = "password:"
```

---

boolean *name [= value]*   boolean

Declare *name* as type boolean and optionally assign a *value.*

Example

```
boolean bUseSlip = FALSE
```

Commands

Commands control the flow of the script or perform some function on a variable.

---

if/then   if/then

Execute *commands* if *condition* is TRUE.

Usage

```
if condition then
commands
endif
```

Example

```
if FALSE == $SUCCESS then
    goto TryAgain
endif
```

---

goto *label*   goto

Jump to *label* and resume execution. Used to escape out of program
flow structures.

→

Usage

```
goto label
label:
```

Example

```
commands...
goto Bailout
more commands...

Bailout:
    ; Something isn't responding. Halt the script
    ; and let the user handle it manually.

    set screen keyboard on
    halt
```

delay

delay

Pause script execution for *seconds* seconds.

Usage

```
delay seconds
```

Example

```
; Delay for 2 seconds first to make sure the
; host doesn't get confused when we send the
; two carriage returns.

delay 2
transmit "^M^M"
```

waitfor

waitfor

A form of a case statement that waits for output from remote device and jumps to labels based on the output or a timeout. The system variable *$SUCCESS* is set to *TRUE* if a label is matched by output and set to *FALSE* if *time* expires before any output is received.

Usage

```
waitfor string [,matchcase][then label
        {, string [matchcase] then label } ]
[ until time ]
```

Example

```
; Wait for the login prompt before entering
; the user ID, timeout after x seconds

waitfor szLogin then DoLogin
        until nLoginTimeout
```

while/do

while/do

Execute *commands* while *condition* is TRUE.

Usage

```
while condition do
commands
endwhile
```

Example

```
; Attempt to login at most 'nTries' times

while 0 < nTries do

  transmit "^M"
  nTries = nTries - 1   ; decrement nTries

endwhile
```

halt

halt

Cease executing script, without terminating terminal window.

Example

```
BailOut:
  ; Something isn't responding.  Halt the script
  ; and let the user handle it manually.

  set screen keyboard on
  halt
```

Functions

getip *[value]*

getip

Obtain IP address from remote device. If multiple IPs are received, parse output using *position* to index the list.

→

	Options 　　[*position*] 　　　　Optional index into array of IP addresses. *Example* 　　set ipaddr getip 2
set port	**set port** *[options]* Set communications parameters of terminal window session, overriding current settings for phonebook entry. *Options* 　　databits *bits* 　　　　Set number of databits to 5, 6, 7, or 8. 　　parity *type* 　　　　Set parity to none, odd, even, mark, or space. 　　stopbits *bits* 　　　　Set stopbits to 1 or 2. *Example* 　　; Set the port settings so we can wait for 　　; non-gibberish text. 　　set port databits 7 　　set port parity even
set screen keyboard	**set screen keyboard** *value* Either allow or disallow keyboard input in terminal window during script execution. *Options* 　　on | off 　　　　Toggle keyboard input on or off. *Examples* 　　set screen keyboard on
set ipaddr	**set ipaddr** *value* Set IP address for current session.

Options

> `value` IP address or variable containing IP address.

Example

```
set ipaddr getip 2
```

---

transmit *[string]*

Send *string* to remote device.

Options

> `string [,raw]`
>> Optional *raw* keyword is used when *string* contains characters that could be interpreted by script.

Example

```
transmit $USERID, raw
transmit "/go:pppconnect^M"
```

Reserved Words

The following reserved words are part of the script language and cannot be used as variable names:

```
and boolean databits delay do endif endproc endwhile even FALSE
getip goto halt if integer ipaddr keyboard mark matchcase none
odd off on or parity port proc raw string then transmit TRUE
until waitfor while
```

Further Info

There are several files in the *<winnt root>\SYSTEM32\RAS* directory:

RASPHONE.HLP
> Windows Help file for RAS.

SCRIPT.DOC
> Script documentation in Word format.

CIS.SCP, PPPMENU.SCP, SLIP.SCP, and SLIPMENU.SCP
> Sample SCP scripts.

PPTP

The Point-to-Point Tunneling Protocol can be used to create encrypted *tunnels* between computers separated by networks, enabling sites and users to connect in a low-cost and secure manner.

Tunneling

The tunnel can create a path for several protocols to run over a protocol of a different type. This is called *encapsulation,* as the network traffic entering one end of the tunnel is encapsulated within the protocol native to the intermediate network and unencapsulated on the other end of the tunnel. The most common example of tunneling would be carrying IPX, NetBEUI, and TCP/IP over a TCP/IP-only network (such as the Internet). See Figure 5-4 for a diagram of this example.

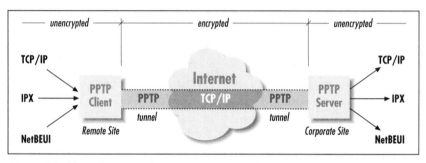

Figure 5-4: Tunneling over the Internet using PPTP

Encryption

If you are using your own dedicated ("leased") lines between sites or dialing into your company RAS server, you are not likely to be worried about a third party intercepting traffic. The act of sending traffic over the Internet brings up potential security problems. If you were conducting business or transferring sensitive data between sites using the Internet, someone could intercept the traffic and analyze it. PPTP encrypts traffic, preventing the packets from being read if they are snooped by a third party.

Cost

Many companies have created large and complex in-house dial-up facilities for remote workers to dial into. Some companies use dedicated lines to link their sites, resulting in large, recurring facilities costs. Tunneling over the Internet may allow remote workers or sites to use the Internet in place of expensive company-owned facilities.

Dial-Up Versus Dedicated

Nearly all descriptions of PPTP describe its use only in regard to dial-up situations. It is possible to use PPTP over a previously existing network connection, such as a dedicated connection to the Internet. If you can reach a PPTP server, you simply "dial" into it using its IP address. The PPTP session runs on top of the existing connection.

Installing PPTP

PPTP is installed as a protocol using the **Protocol-Add** button of the **Network** control panel. The only installation option is the number of Virtual Private Network (VPN) ports. Each end of each PPTP session requires a VPN port. VPN ports do not have to have a corresponding physical RAS port (COM port). They exist in software only. If you have only one PPTP session on your computer, you need only one VPN port. A RAS server requires as many VPN ports as might possibly be in use simultaneously, both incoming and outgoing.

Once you have installed a VPN port, RAS and DUN treat it as if it were a physical port. The only difference is that an IP address or hostname is used instead of a phone number when calling the remote site.

Using PPTP

In most cases, you will being using PPTP over a dial-up RAS connection to an ISP. You should first establish the RAS session to the ISP using DUN to dial the modem or ISDN entry. Once you are connected to the ISP, you can use DUN to dial the PPTP entry, which runs on top of the conventional RAS session.

If you have a dedicated connection to the Internet or use a device that behaves as if it were permanently connected, you can skip the modem dialing entirely, and initiate the PPTP session on top of the existing Internet connection.

Using PPTP over a dedicated connection means using RAS, even though you are not using RAS to create the initial connection. It may look a little silly to have the RAS modem monitor lights flashing and a baud rate of 10,000,000 when using PPTP over an Ethernet LAN.

Other Tunnel Products

The market has yet not selected a winner in the tunnel area. Microsoft is pushing PPTP and several vendors are adding support for it, including US Robotics, Ascend, and 3Com. The main competition for PPTP is L2F (Layer 2 Forwarding), promoted by Cisco Systems, Shiva, and Nortel. Digital Equipment Corporation also has a tunneling product for Windows NT and Windows 95, called AltaVista Tunnel.

Files Used by RAS

There are several files that RAS uses to accomplish the logon procedure. They are stored in the directory *<winnt root>\SYSTEM32\RAS*.

- When DUN is started, it reads the system phonebook file (*RASPHONE.PBK*) or a user-specified phonebook for a list of possible entries to dial. The phonebook file supplies all the settings for the particular entry to DUN, including the device being used to dial, the phone number, the networking and authentication protocols, and so on.

- If the device being used to connect is a modem, the modem type is looked up in the *MODEM.INF* file. Any commands or features unique to the particular modem are found here.

- If the device is a PAD (used for packet networks such as x.25) the Network or PAD type is looked up in the *PAD.INF* file.

- When dialing into a non-RAS computer or communications server using a script, the script associated with the phonebook entry is read from either the *SWITCH.INF* file or a standalone script in a .SCP file.

For the RAS server side of the connection, accepting calls from remote computers, the RAS service reads the *MODEM.INF* file for any modems it has configured. The permissions for users allowed to dial in is maintained by either **Remote Access Admin** or **User Manager for Domains**.

MODEM.INF

The role of the *MODEM.INF* file is to abstract interaction with modems so software can control modem characteristics in a generic manner, without the user supplying details about the specific brand, model, or type of modem.

Previous to NT 4.0, all modems had to be described in the *MODEM.INF* file. In NT 4.0, the Universal Modem Driver (Unimodem) is used if the modem supports it. NT 4.0 still supports the *MODEM.INF* for backwards compatibility with non-Unimodem capable modems.*

If your modem does not support Unimodem or is not listed in *MODEM.INF*, check if the modem manufacturer distributes a *MODEM.INF* entry on media that came with the modem or from a web site or BBS. You could also add your own entries to *MODEM.INF*, but you should think seriously about buying a new modem or one that complies with industry standards.

File Description

Most modems made today still use the original AT command set that came from Hayes. The big problem is that each manufacturer has expanded on the original command set in their own proprietary way. There is also the concept of registers, which are general purpose NVRAM settings that can be used to store highly modem-specific settings. The meaning of the registers may change between firmware revisions of the same modem!

For example, here is a fragment of the *MODEM.INF* that describes the US Robotics Sportster:

```
[US Robotics Sportster 14400]
CALLBACKTIME=10
DEFAULTOFF=compression
MAXCARRIERBPS=19200
```

*You can manually configure RAS to use *MODEM.INF* instead of Unimodem by editing the Registry. See KB article #Q150808.

```
MAXCONNECTBPS=38400
<speaker_on>=M1
<speaker_off>=M0
<hwflowcontrol_on>=&H1&R2
<hwflowcontrol_off>=&H0&R1
<compression_on>=&K1
<compression_off>=&K0
<protocol_on>=&M4
<protocol_off>=&M0
<autodial_on>=ATDT
<autodial_off>=ATD


DETECT_STRING=ATI3<cr>
DETECT_RESPONSE=Sportster 14,400


COMMAND_INIT=AT&F&C1&D2 V1 S0=0 S2=128 S7=55<cr>
COMMAND_INIT=AT<hwflowcontrol><protocol><compression><speaker>&B1<cr>
COMMAND_DIAL=<autodial><phonenumber><cr>
CONNECT=\
<cr><lf>CONNECT <carrierbps><cr><lf>
CONNECT_EC=\
<cr><lf>CONNECT <carrierbps>/ARQ<cr><lf>
```

By assigning tags to various functions, such as turning compression on or off with *compression_on* and *compression_off*, software using the modem does not have to know that the USR Sportster uses *&K1* for this function, while the Cardinal 14400 uses *%C0*.

Software can also dynamically detect the type of installed modem using the *DETECT_STRING*. If it sends the *ATI3* command to the modem and gets Sportster 14,400 back, it knows what type of modem is installed. This creates a plug and play capability for modems.

The *COMMAND_INIT* string is similar to the init strings required by comm programs or fax software. The *COMMAND_INIT* typically resets the modem to the factory defaults (usually *&F*) and then changes anything that should be different from the factory default setting. By returning to the factory defaults each time you use it, the modem always starts with a clean configuration.

The modem can tell the software what speed and type of connection it has made with the *CONNECT* message. This allows DUN or RAS to inform the user about the baud rate, bits per second (BPS), compression, error control, and so forth used during the connection to a remote computer or device. The *CONNECT* message is the same one you see when dialing a modem manually.

RASPHONE.PBK

The *RASPHONE.PBK* (RAS phonebook) file contains entries that describe sites to which Dial-Up Networking can connect. Each phonebook entry contains phone numbers, security, and network settings. Users can create multiple phonebook files and they are available to Dial-Up Networking as long as they have the *.PBK* filename extension. The file *RASPHONE.PBK* is the default phonebook and will be used unless you specify an alternative. You can select alternative phonebooks in the GUI version of Dial-Up Networking by selecting **More-User Preferences** and the **Phonebook** tab. From the command line, you can dial using alternate phone-books with the *rasphone* or *rasdial* commands.

For example, assume the alternate phonebook file is called *MYOWN.PBK* and the entry name is **ora**. The *rasphone* command can specify an alternate phonebook using the *-f* flag and the phonebook entry using the *-d* flag:

```
rasphone -f myown.pbk -d ora
```

The *rasdial* command takes the entry name, followed by the */phonebook:* flag and the name of the alternate phonebook.

```
rasdial ora /phonebook:myown.pbk
```

File Description

You should be able modify anything you need in the phonebook by using the DUN GUI. As the phonebook file is just a text file, it is possible to edit it by hand. It is safer to modify an existing entry than to try to create your own from scratch. If you do modify the phonebook file directly using an editor, you will have to quit and restart DUN for your changes to take effect.

Entries in the phonebook file are started by an entry name in brackets. The entry name is followed by a list of parameters and values that have been set by the Dial-Up Networking GUI:

```
[ora]
Description=This is a comment
AutoLogon=0
DialParamsUID=17651351
UsePwForNetwork=0
BaseProtocol=1
Authentication=-1
ExcludedProtocols=0
LcpExtensions=1
DataEncryption=0
SwCompression=1
UseCountryAndAreaCodes=0
AreaCode=
CountryID=1
CountryCode=1
SkipNwcWarning=0
SkipDownLevelDialog=0
DialMode=1
DialPercent=90
DialSeconds=120
HangUpPercent=50
HangUpSeconds=120
IdleDisconnectSeconds=0
SecureLocalFiles=0
CustomDialDll=
CustomDialFunc=
AuthRestrictions=0
IpPrioritizeRemote=1
IpHeaderCompression=1
```

```
IpAddress=0.0.0.0
IpDnsAddress=0.0.0.0
IpDns2Address=0.0.0.0
IpWinsAddress=0.0.0.0
IpWins2Address=0.0.0.0
IpAssign=1
IpNameAssign=1
IpFrameSize=1006
```

Most values are toggled on or off by setting them to 1 or 0. The *Ip* values are expected to be supplied dynamically at connection time.

This is followed by *MEDIA* and *DEVICE* sections that describe the communications device to be used for the connection:

```
MEDIA=serial
Port=COM2
OtherPortOk=1
Device=Courier V.Everything
ConnectBPS=115200

DEVICE=modem
PhoneNumber=18005551212
PromoteAlternates=1
HwFlowControl=1
Protocol=1
Compression=1
Speaker=1
```

If the entry uses a script, there is another *DEVICE* entry that has either the path-name of a Windows 95–style script:

```
DEVICE=switch
Type=D:\WINNT35\System32\ras\ora.scp
```

or the name of an entry in the *SWITCH.INF* file:

```
DEVICE=switch
Type=netblazer
```

An entry for PPTP has the following *MEDIA* and *DEVICE* fields:

```
MEDIA=rastapi
Port=VPN1
OtherPortOk=1
Device=RASPPTPM

DEVICE=rastapi
PhoneNumber=208.26.94.11
PromoteAlternates=1
```

PAD.INF

The *PAD.INF* file contains descriptions of various PAD (Packet Assembler/Deassembler) devices and networks that RAS can connect to, which are typically X.25.

The *PAD.INF* file use the same scripting language as *SWITCH.INF*. The following is a script to connect to the SprintNet packet network:

```
[SprintNet, Standard]

DEFAULTOFF=
MAXCARRIERBPS=9600
MAXCONNECTBPS=9600

; The next two lines ignore logon banners.
COMMAND=
OK=<ignore>

; The @ characters sets the SprintNet PAD for 8 databit communication.
COMMAND=@
NoResponse

; The D character requests a 9600 speed.
COMMAND=D<cr>
; We don't care about the response, so we ignore it (unless modem has hung up).
ERROR_NO_CARRIER=<match>"NO CARRIER"
OK=<ignore>

; A carriage return to initialize the PAD read/write buffers.
COMMAND=<cr>
ERROR_NO_CARRIER=<match>"NO CARRIER"
OK=<ignore>

; Set the first half of X.3 settings on the PAD which make it work well with RAS.
COMMAND=SET 1:0,2:0,3:0,4:1,5:0,6:1,7:0,8:0,9:0,10:0<cr>
ERROR_NO_CARRIER=<match>"NO CARRIER"
OK=<ignore>

; Set the other half of X.3 parameters.
COMMAND=SET 12:0,13:0,14:0,15:0,16:0,17:0,18:0,19:0,20:0,22:0<cr>
ERROR_NO_CARRIER=<match>"NO CARRIER"
OK=<ignore>

; Finally try to call RAS X25 server.
COMMAND=C <x25address>*<UserData><cr>
CONNECT=<match>" CONNECT"
ERROR_NO_CARRIER=<match>"NO CARRIER"
ERROR_DIAGNOSTICS=<cr><lf><Diagnostics>
ERROR_DIAGNOSTICS=<lf><cr><lf><Diagnostics>
```

CHAPTER 6

Using the Command Line

The command line is not just for old DOS users. Many useful commands exist only in a command-line form. Some commands are just quicker to type than traversing several menu trees and selecting an item with the mouse. If you have to do an administrative task several times or maybe even hundreds of times, it is well worth the effort to see if the task can be automated by creating batch files containing commands.

One problem with the commands is their uneven matching of functionality with the GUI tools. Some settings and options seem to be available from either the GUI or the command line, but not both. In some cases, the same options have different names, depending on where they are set (GUI or command line).

As a general rule, the commands are less forgiving of mistakes than their GUI equivalents. Once you combine this feature with batch file automation, it becomes possible to "trash" your computer's configuration quickly with simple mistakes.

You will also notice some inconsistencies with the way options or arguments are used with the commands. Most of the older DOS commands use the forward slash character followed by the option name. The TCP/IP commands and those with a UNIX and POSIX heritage use a dash and a single option letter. Some of these have options that are case-sensitive, unlike traditional DOS commands. Ex-UNIX users may be frustrated by the different options that the NT versions of UNIX commands use, as many of the changes seem unwarranted.

This book assumes that you know your way around DOS and do not need a refresher course on how to use the *dir* command. Only those commands that are unique to Windows NT or are of interest to the administrator are described.

net Commands

The *net* commands control services, user and group accounts, file and printer sharing, and tell you what your computer is doing on the network.

net accounts

The *net accounts* command is used to control settings and policies that affect all accounts on a system or domain. It performs many of the same functions as the **Policies-Account** menu option in **User Manager**.

Options

none   Displays settings that are controlled by *net accounts* with their current values.

/domain   When run on NT Workstation, this forces the operation to take place on the PDC for the default domain. This is the default option for NT Server, and is unnecessary.

/forcelogoff:[*minutes*|NO]
   If an account expires or a restriction on logon time goes in effect while a user is logged on, this option specifies the number of minutes before the user is automatically logged off. Setting this to *NO* lets users stay logged on indefinitely (but they cannot log back on once they have exited the current session).

/lockoutdur:*minutes*
   Sets lockout duration. This is the number of minutes a user is locked out of the system after entering a certain number (the lockout threshold) of unsuccessful logon attempts.

/lockoutthr:[*attempts*|NEVER]
   Sets lockout threshold. This is the number of unsuccessful logon attempts allowed before a user lockout takes effect. Setting it to *NEVER* disables the lockout mechanism entirely.

/lockoutwin:*minutes*
   Sets lockout observation window. This is the amount of time during which unsuccessful logon attempts are counted. If the lockout threshold is exceeded within the lockout window, the user is locked out (for the lockout duration).

/maxpwage:[*days*|UNLIMITED]
   Sets maximum number of days for which a password is valid before expiring (default is 90). The number of days can range from 1 to 49710 and cannot be less than *minpwage*. If *UNLIMITED* is specified, no limit is enforced.

/minpwage:*days*
   Sets minimum number of days between password changes (default is 0). The number of days can range from 1 to 49710 and cannot be more than *maxpwage*. If 0 is specified, no limit is enforced.

/minpwlen:*characters*
   Sets minimum number of characters required in passwords. This can range from 0 to 14 (default is 6). The longer a password, the more

difficult it is to crack. Users will rebel with poor passwords if you make the password requirements unreasonable.

/sync   Synchronize account databases with Primary Domain Controller (PDC) for this domain. Backup Domain Controllers (BDC) periodically synchronize with the PDC, but this command can be used to force an immediate synchronization without waiting for the next scheduled one. This may be helpful after restoring communications between BDC and PDC after network problems or computer downtime.

/uniquepw:*password_changes*

Sets minimum number of password changes before a password can be reused (maximum of 8). The main purpose of this option is to prevent lazy users from changing their passwords to some intermediate value and then immediately back to the original, which would circumvent any security gained by forcing password changes in the first place.

Examples

Set the minimum number of characters allowed in a password to 5 and the number of password changes required before a password can be reused to 3:

```
net accounts /minpwlen:5 /uniquepw:3
```

Set the lockout threshold to 5, the lockout duration to 1 hour, and the lockout observation window to 1 hour:

```
net accounts /lockoutthr:5 /lockoutdur:60 /lockoutwin:60
```

Notes

The main purpose of the lockout values is to prevent automated or "brute force" attacks. If someone tried many break-in attempts in a short period of time, the lockout values would slow this type of attack to the point where it becomes impractical and increases the chance of detection.

The *lockoutdur, lockoutthr,* and *lockoutwin* options seem to be undocumented, at least in the Microsoft-supplied help text.

See Also

net localgroup
net group
net user

GUI Equivalents

User Manager, Policies-Account

---

net computer

net computer *[options]*

The *net computer* command adds or deletes computers (NT workstations and servers) from the current domain. A computer must be a member of the domain to participate in domain security.

→

net computer

←

Options

computername
>   UNC name of computer being added or deleted

/add   adds *computername* to domain database

/del   deletes *computername* from domain database

Examples

Add computer *ntwks* to domain:

```
net computer \\ntwks /add
```

Delete computer *ntwks* from domain:

```
net computer \\ntwks /del
```

Notes

This command runs only on an NT server.

GUI Equivalents

Server Manager, Computer

Requires

NT Server

---

net config server   net config server *[options]*

The *net config server* command can set several parameters that control the **Server** service. The **Server** service provides resources to other computers over the network, such as file sharing, printing, and so on.

Options

none   Display current settings for **Server** service on current computer.

/autodisconnect:*minutes*
>   By default, users are disconnected from the server when their session is inactive for 15 minutes. The possible values for *autodisconnect* are –1 to 65355, with –1 indicating that a session should never be disconnected. As a session consumes resources on the server, autodisconnecting idle users would lessen the load on the server and keep client licenses from running out.

/srvcomment:*"comment"*
>   The *commment* can be used to describe the server's function or location when the server name appears in a list. The comment is displayed in the *remark* field in the output of the *net view* command and the description field in **Server Manager**, in addition to other places.

/hidden:[yes|no]
>   By default, the server name shows up in any listing of servers. You can suppress this by setting */hidden* to *yes.*

Examples

```
net config server

Server Name                  \\ICA
Server Comment               This is a SRVCOMMENT

Software version             Windows NT 3.51
Server is active on          NetBT_NdisWan6 (000000000000)
Nbf_NdisWan4 (524153480003) Nbf_NdisWan3 (524153480002)
NetBT_E1007 (00aa00a584ef) Nbf_E1007 (00aa00a584ef)

Server hidden                Yes
Maximum Logged On Users      Unlimited
Maximum open files per session 2048

Idle session time (min)      15
The command completed successfully.
```

The fields are as follows:

Field	Description
Server Name	UNC name of server
Server Comment	Value of *srvcomment*
Software version	NT version
Server is active on	List of interfaces that server service is bound to
Server hidden	Value of *hidden*
Maximum Logged On Users	Limited to 10 for NT Workstation; unlimited for Server
Maximum open files per session	
Idle session time (min)	Value of *autodisconnect*

See Also

   net config workstation

Requires

   NT Workstation or Server

---

net config workstation

`net config workstation [options]`

The *net config workstation* command can set several parameters for the **Workstation** service that deal with communications (COM) devices.

Options

   none   Display current settings for the **Workstation** service.

→

/charcount:*bytes*

> Set number of bytes that are collected (buffered) before they are sent to COM device. This can range from 0 to 65535 bytes and defaults to 16 bytes. If *chartime* is also set, whatever value is reached first is used (number of bytes read or milliseconds past).

/chartime:*msec*

> Set number of milliseconds the system should pause after collecting data before sending it to the COM device. This can range from 0 to 6535000 milliseconds and defaults to 250 milliseconds. If *charcount* is also set, whatever value is reached first is used (number of bytes read or milliseconds past).

/charwait:*seconds*

> Set number of seconds the system waits for a COM device to become available. This can range from 0 to 65535 seconds and defaults to 3600 seconds.

Examples

```
net config workstation

Computer name                        \\ICA
User name                            Administrator

Workstation active on                NetBT_NdisWan6 (000000000000)
Nbf_NdisWan4 (524153480003)          Nbf_NdisWan3 (524153480002)
NetBT_E1007 (00AA00A584EF)           Nbf_E1007 (00AA00A584EF)
Software version                     Windows NT 3.51

Workstation domain                   HOME
Logon domain                         HOME

COM Open Timeout (sec)               3600
COM Send Count (byte)                16
COM Send Timeout (msec)              250
The command completed successfully.
```

The fields are as follows:

Field	Meaning
Computer name	UNC name of computer
User name	Account currently logged in
Workstation active on	List of network interfaces that workstation service is bound to
Software version	NT version and release number
Workstation domain	Domain that workstation service is running in
Logon domain	Domain that you are currently logged on to
COM Open Timeout (sec)	Value of *charwait*
COM Send Count (byte)	Value of *charcount*
COM Send Timeout (msec)	Value of *chartime*

See Also

    net config server

GUI Equivalents

    Windows NT Diagnostics, Network

Requires

    NT Workstation or Server

---

net continue

net continue servicename

The *net continue* command resumes a service that was paused by *net pause*.

Options

    servicename

        Specify the service to be resumed.

Examples

    Continue the "LPDSVC" service:

```
net continue "LDPSVC"
The TCP/IP Print Server service was continued successfully.
```

Notes

    Service names that contain spaces have to be quoted. Unlike *net start, net continue* does not show the current status of services.

See Also

    net start
    net stop
    net pause

GUI Equivalents

    Services control panel, **Continue**
    Windows NT Diagnostics, Services

Requires

    NT Workstation or Server

Using the Command Line

---

net file

net file [options]

The *net file* command can be used to close shared files and remove file locks. NT will sometimes indicate that a file is still in use even if the user or application that opened it is no longer present.

Options

none	List opens files and lock status.
id	With no further arguments, display file referenced by *id* in detail.
/close	Close open file and removes lock.

$\rightarrow$

Examples

For this example, the directory *D:\TEMP* was shared on a Windows NT server and the file *REG.PL* was opened on a Windows 95 computer by user *eap* (using **Notepad**).

List all open files:

```
net file
ID   Path            User name   # Locks
6    D:\temp\REG.PL      EAP       0
```

List a specific file in detail:

```
net file 6
File ID     6
User name   EAP
Locks    0
Path        D:\temp\REG.PL
Permissions   R
```

Close a specific file:

```
net file 6 /close
The command completed successfully.
```

Confirm the results:

```
net file
There are no entries in the list.
```

See Also

net share
net session
net use
net view

GUI Equivalents

Server Manager, Properties-In Use
Server control panel

Requires

NT Workstation or Server

---

net group   net group [options]

The *net group* command creates or deletes global groups and adds or deletes users from global groups.

Options

none   Display all the global groups on the system or domain.

---

group-name
>   Display all the members of a group.

username(s)
>   A space-separated list of usernames that the */add* or */delete* operation is being performed on.

/add   Create a new group or adds users to named group.

/comment:*"comment"*
>   Add a 48-character comment field associated with the group.

/delete   Delete an existing group or remove users from named group.

/domain   When run on NT Workstation, this forces the operation to take place on the PDC for the default domain.

Examples

Create a new group:

```
net group "Domain Game Players" /add  /comment:"Group for Game Players"
```

Add users *eap* and *larryc* to an existing group:

```
net group "Domain Game Players" /add eap larryc
```

Delete a user from the group:

```
net group "Domain Game Players" /delete eap
```

Delete a group:

```
net group "Domain Game Players" /delete
```

Notes

Users have to exist before you can add them to groups.

The dual use of the command for deleting groups and removing users from groups can be surprising. For example, if you want to delete some group members, but forget to include them on the */delete* command, you delete the group itself.

See Also

> *net accounts*
> *net localgroup*
> *net user*

GUI Equivalents
User Manager, User

Requires
NT Workstation or Server

net help net help *[options]*

The *net help* command prints out the help message for a *net* command.

Options

none   Prints out all *net help* topics.

services Prints a listing of system services available for starting, pausing, continuing, and stopping via *net* commands.

syntax   Describes help message conventions for indicating which command-line arguments are required, optional, or of a certain format.

Examples

net help can be invoked as an argument to any *net* command as */help* on the command line:

    net pause /help

As many of the help messages are longer than a single screen, you can pipe the message through the *more* command:

    net help services | more

Notes

Some of the help messages are not very helpful.

See Also

net helpmsg

GUI Equivalents

Any **Help** button.

Requires

NT Workstation or Server

---

net helpmsg net helpmsg *[message-number]*

The *net helpmsg* command displays a more detailed description of an error message when given the error message number. The four-digit error message number is generated when a *net* command fails in some manner.

Options

message-number
         Message number from error message.

Examples

Type a command that fails:

    net send administrator

The error message is then displayed:

```
Sending files is no longer supported.
More help is available by typing NET HELPMSG 3777
```

Look up the detailed description with *net helpmsg*:

```
net helpmsg 3777

Sending files is no longer supported.
EXPLANATION
The NET SEND command no longer sends files.
ACTION
Type the message you wish to send on the same line as NET SEND.
```

Notes

For most of the simple or common errors, *net helpmsg* does not give any more information than the original error message.

See Also

net help

Requires

NT Workstation or Server

---

net localgroup

net localgroup [options]

The *net localgroup* command creates or deletes local groups and adds or deletes users from local groups.

Options

none   Displays all the local groups on the system or domain.

group-name
            Displays all the members of a group.

username(s)
            A space-separated list of usernames or global group names on which the */add* or */delete* operation is being performed. When adding users from a domain other than the current domain, preface the username with the other domain name.

/add   Creates a new group or adds users or global group to named local group.

/comment:"comment"
            Add a 48-character comment field associated with the group.

/delete   Delete an existing group or remove users or global groups from named group.

/domain   When run on NT Workstation and on a standalone Server, this forces the operation to take place on the PDC for the default domain.

$\rightarrow$

Examples

Create a new local group called Game Players:

```
net localgroup "Game Players" /add  /comment:"Local Group for Game Players"
```

Add users *eap* and *larryc* and global group Domain Game Players to the existing local group Game Players:

```
net localgroup "Game Players" /add eap larryc "Domain Game Players"
```

Add a user (*steve*) from another domain (*WEST*):

```
net localgroup "Game Players" /add WEST\steve
```

Delete user *eap* from the group:

```
net localgroup "Game Players" /delete eap
```

Delete the group itself:

```
net localgroup "Game Players" /delete
```

Notes

Users have to exist before you can add them to groups.

The dual use of the command for deleting groups and users can be surprising. For example, if you want to delete some group members, but forget to include them on the */delete* command, you delete the group itself.

See Also

net accounts
net group
net user

GUI Equivalents

User Manager, User

Requires

NT Workstation or Server

---

net name net name [options]

The *net name* command administers the list of names (or aliases) that are valid recipients of messages sent using the **Messenger** service.

Options

none	Display current list of messaging names on computer. This is usually the name of the computer and the user(s) currently logged onto it.
/add	Add a messaging name to a computer.
/delete	Delete a messaging name from a computer.

Examples

Display list of messaging names:

```
net name

Name
--------------------------------------------------------
VECTRA
ADMINISTRATOR
The command completed successfully.
```

Add a new name:

```
net name eap /add
The message name EAP was added successfully.
```

Confirm new name:

```
net name

Name
--------------------------------------------------------
VECTRA
ADMINISTRATOR
EAP
The command completed successfully.
```

Delete a name:

```
net name eap /delete
EAP was deleted successfully.
```

Confirm deletion:

```
net name

Name
--------------------------------------------------------
VECTRA
ADMINISTRATOR
The command completed successfully.
```

Using the
Command Line

Notes

The */add* option is not required. Just typing *net name <newname>* will add the name. Names have to be unique within the current usernames and computer names.

See Also

net send

Requires

NT Workstation or Server
The Messenger Service must be running on any computer that sends or receives messages.

net pause

The *net pause* command pauses a service, but does not terminate it. The service can be resumed with the *net continue* command.

Options

    `service` Specifies the service to be paused.

    `/help`   Displays a list of services that could be paused. This list does not indicate the current status of the services (running, paused, and so forth).

Examples

Pause a service:

```
net pause lpdsvc
The TCP/IP Print Server service was paused successfully.
```

Continue a service:

```
net continue lpdsvc
The TCP/IP Print Server service was continued successfully.
```

Notes

Service names containing spaces have to be quoted.

See Also

net continue
net start
net stop

GUI Equivalents

Services control panel, **Pause**
Server Manager, Computer-Services

Requires

NT Workstation or Server

---

net print

The *net print* command administers printer queues. It can display the current contents of a printer queue and manipulate individual print jobs within a queue.

Options

    `\\computer`

                UNC name for computer that is sharing the printer queues.

    `share-name`

                Name of printer share.

    `job`   Numeric print job ID.

    `/delete` Deletes a job from the printer queue

`/hold`   Holds a job in the printer queue, preventing it from printing.

`/release` Releases a held job in the printer queue, permitting it to print.

Examples

Examine print queue *DeskJet* on computer named *ICA*:

```
net print \\ica\DeskJet

Printers at \\ica

Name            Job #  Size   Status
-------------------------------------------------------
DeskJet Queue          1 jobs      *Printer Active*
   Administrator         5  1170041   Printing
```

This output shows a single job (Job #5), 1170041 bytes long, sent by user *Administrator*, being printed on the *DeskJet* queue.

Put the job on hold:

```
net print \\ica 5 /hold
```

Release the job:

```
net print \\ica 5 /release
```

Delete the job:

```
net print \\ica 5 /delete
```

Notes

Print job IDs are unique across queues on the same computer, so you do not need to specify the printer queue name, only the name of the computer on which the queue resides.

If you specify a nonexistent job ID, the resulting error message is less than helpful:

```
net print \\ica 99 /delete
System error 87 has occurred.

The parameter is incorrect.
```

The status field does not indicate whether the job is being held or not.

See Also

net session
net share
net use
net view

GUI Equivalents

Printers control panel

Requires

NT Workstation or Server

net send

The *net send* command sends a text message to users and computers on the network. The **Messenger** service running on the message recipients' computers will pop up a dialog box containing the message.

Options

name   Sends message to *name*.

*   Sends message to all members of sender's group.

/domain[:domain-name]
        Sends message to all domain members of domain or workgroup name. If *domain-name* is omitted, current domain is implied.

/users Sends message to all users currently connected to server.

Examples

Send a message to a single name:

    net send larryc "want to chow?"

Send a broadcast message to everybody using the server:

    net send /users "system will be going down for repair at 5pm tonight"

Notes

You could send a message to a computer name if you don't know who is currently logged onto it (or do not care.) A user must be logged on to receive the message.

See Also

net name

GUI Equivalents

Server Manager, Computer-Send Message

Requires

NT Workstation or Server
Messenger Service

---

net session

The *net session* command either displays information about current sessions or disconnects sessions. A session could be a shared file, printer, or the like, that is being used by another computer.

Options

none   Lists current sessions.

\\computer
        UNC name of remote computer.

/delete Disconnects session, closing open files in the process. If used with a computer name, it closes only sessions from the named computer. If used without a computer name, it closes all sessions.

Examples

List all active sessions:

```
net session
Computer    User name    Client Type    Opens    Idle time
\\pc248     larryc       Windows 4.0    1        00:00:07
```

List a single session in detail:

```
net session \\pc248
User name     larryc
Computer      pc248
Guest logon   No
Client type   Windows 4.0
Sess time     00:05:06
Idle time     00:05:06
```

Disconnect a single session:

```
net session \\pc248 /delete
This session from PC248 has open files.

Do you want to continue this operation? (Y/N) [N]: y
The command completed successfully.
```

The command warns you if the client has some open files. You could use *net file* to see what files are open and make a more informed decision. The *Idle time* field may also be useful, as it specifies that long ago someone was using the session.

See Also

net file
net share
net use
net view

GUI Equivalents

Server Manager, Properties-Users
Server control panel, **Users**

Requires

NT Workstation or Server

---

net share   net share [options]

The *net share* command administers network shares. It displays current shares, creates shares, and deletes shares.

Options

none   Displays all active shares of the server service.
sharename
            Displays details about *sharename*.
directory
            Sets directory to be shared.

→

/delete   Discontinues sharing of *sharename*.

/remark:"*comment-text*"
> Comment text that can be used to describe share.

/unlimited
> Removes any limit on the number of users that can simultaneously use the share.

/users:*max-users*
> Sets a limit on the number of users that can simultaneously use the share.

Examples

Display information about all shares on server:

```
net share

Share name   Resource                               Remark
-----------------------------------------------------------------------------
ADMIN$       C:\WINNT35                             Remote Admin
IPC$                                                Remote IPC
C$           C:\                                    Default share
NETLOGIN     C:\WINNT35\system32\Repl\Import        Logon server share
temp         C:\temp                                Test Share
```

Display information about a single share:

```
net share C$

Share name     C$
Path           C:\
Remark         Default share
Maximum users  No limit
Users          PC248
```

Create a share (with a 10-user limit):

```
net share temp=C:\temp /users:10 /remark:"10 people can use this"
temp was shared successfully.

net share temp

Share name     temp
Path           C:\temp
Remark         10 people can use this
Maximum users  10
Users
```

See Also

net file
net session
net use
net view

GUI Equivalents

Windows NT Explorer, File-Properties-Sharing
File Manager, Disk-Share As
Server Manager, Properties-Shared Directories
Server, Shares

Requires

NT Workstation or Server

---

net start

net start *[options]*

The *net start* command starts a service or displays a list of currently running services.

Options

none   Displays a list of services that are currently started on this computer.

servicename
         Starts service *servicename*.

Examples

Get a listing of currently running services:

```
net start

        FILE SERVER FOR MACINTOSH
        FTP SERVER
        LPDSVC
        NET LOGON
        NETWORK DDE
        NETWORK DDE DSDM
        NT LM SECURITY SUPPORT PROVIDER
        REMOTEBOOT
        REMOTE ACCESS SERVER
        SCHEDULE
        SERVER
        SIMPLE TCP/IP SERVICES
        WORKSTATION
```

Start the **LPDSVC** service:

```
net start LPDSVC
The TCP/IP Print Server service is starting.
The TCP/IP Print Server service was started successfully.
```

See Also

net stop
net continue
net pause

GUI Equivalents

Services control panel, **Start**
Server Manager, Computer-Services-Start
Windows NT Diagnostics, Services

→

Using the Command Line

net start

Requires

NT Workstation or Server

---

net statistics

net statistics *[options]*

The *net statistics* command displays various counters and values for the **Workstation** and **Server** services.

Options

```
workstation
```
Display statistics for Workstation service.

```
server    Display statistics for Server service.
```

Examples

```
net statistics workstation
Workstation Statistics for \\VECTRA

Statistics since 9/17/96 1:25 AM

    Bytes received                                626
    Server Message Blocks (SMBs) received         7
    Bytes transmitted                             1077
    Server Message Blocks (SMBs) transmitted      7
    Read operations                               0
    Write operations                              8
    Raw reads denied                              0
    Raw writes denied                             0

    Network errors                                0
    Connections made                              2
    Reconnections made                            0
    Server disconnects                            0

    Sessions started                              2
    Hung sessions                                 0
    Failed sessions                               0
    Failed operations                             0
    Use count                                     2
    Failed use count                              0

net statistics server
Server Statistics for \\VECTRA

Statistics since 9/17/96 1:25 AM

    Sessions accepted              1
    Sessions timed-out             0
    Sessions errored-out           1
```

```
Kilobytes sent                      1
Kilobytes received                  1

Mean response time (msec)           0

System errors                       0
Permission violations               0
Password violations                 0

Files accessed                      0
Communication devices accessed      0
Print jobs spooled                  0

Times buffers exhausted

  Big buffers                       0
  Request buffers                   0
```

GUI Equivalents

Windows NT Diagnostics, Network-Statistics

Requires

NT Workstation or Server

---

net stop

<code>net stop [options]</code>

The *net stop* command terminates a service.

Options

/help   Displays a list of installed services.

servicename

     Stops *servicename*.

Examples

```
net stop snmp
The SNMP Service is stopping.
The SNMP Service was stopped successfully.
```

Notes

Unlike *net start, net stop* does not show the current status of services.

net start can be used to display the currently running services.

See Also

net start
net pause
net continue

GUI Equivalents

Services control panel, **Services-Stop**
Server Manager, Computer-Services-Stop

→

net stop

 ←

Requires

NT Workstation or Server

---

net time   net time [options]

The *net time* command can either query the time and date from another computer or synchronize the current computer's time with that of another computer.

Options

\\computer-name

UNC name of remote computer to query or synchronize with.

/domain[:domainname]

Domain name to synchronize with, or current domain, if not specified.

/set   Synchronizes local system time with remote computer or domain.

/yes   Do not ask for user confirmation when using the */set* option.

Examples

Query the time on *pc248*:

```
net time \\pc248
Current time at \\pc248 is 9/17/96 1:44 PM
```

Synchronize the current computer's time to *pc248*:

```
net time \\pc248 /set
Current time at \\pc248 is 9/17/96 1:44 PM
The current local clock is 9/17/96 1:42 AM
Do you want to set the local computer's time to match the time
at \\pc248 (Y/N) [Y]: y
```

Notes

The */yes* option is helpful when the *net time* command is used within a batch file. The */yes* option seems to be undocumented.

Requires

NT Workstation or Server

---

net use   net use [options]

The *net use* command administers local connections to network resources, such as shared directories and printers. It controls the client side of resources provided by a server.

Options

none   Display any shares being used by the local computer.

devicename
> The name of the device to which a network resource will be connected. For example, this would be a drive and pathname for a shared directory or an lpt device for a shared printer.

*computername**sharename*
> Network resource for connection.

volume   Volume name of NetWare server for connection.

password Password for password-protected shares (password appears in clear text on command line).

*   Forces prompting for password-protected shares (password is not echoed as it is typed).

/delete Disconnects a network resource.

/home   Connects a user to their home directory on the server.

/persistent:[yes|no]
> A *yes* value will make the connection to a network resource persistent, which means the system will try to keep the connection alive from this point forward and will be automatically reconnected after reboots. A *no* value indicates that if the current connection is broken, no attempt will be be made to reconnect. Even with the *no* value set, any connections that are present at the time of a reboot will be reconnected.

/user:[*domain*\\]*username*
> Forces the connection be made by *username*, regardless of who is running the command. If a domain name is also supplied, the connection is made in that domain instead of the current domain.

Examples

Display list of currently connected network drives:

```
net use
New connections will be remembered.


Status   Local   Remote              Network
-------------------------------------------------------------------
         F:      \\NWSRV312\SYS      NetWare or Compatible Network
OK       G:      \\pceap\tmp         Microsoft Windows Network
         Y:      \\NWSRV312\SYS      NetWare or Compatible Network
         Z:      \\NWSRV312\SYS      NetWare or Compatible Network
```

This display shows three connections to a Novell server and one to a Windows 95 computer.

Find the name of a share to connect to on the computer *pceap*:

```
net view \\pceap
Shared resources at \\pceap

Eric Pearce

Share name   Type   Used as     Comment
-------------------------------------------------------------
TMP          Disk   G:
VISIO        Disk
```

→

Connect to a the share *VISIO* on *pceap* to drive *h:*

```
net use h: \\pceap\visio
The command completed successfully.
```

Delete the share to *h:*

```
net use h: /delete
h: was deleted successfully.
```

Notes

Be sure to use quotation marks for any computer name or share name that contains spaces.

See Also

net share
net file
net session
net view

GUI Equivalents

Windows NT Explorer, Tools-Map Network Drive
File Manager, Disk-Connect Network Drive

Requires

NT Workstation or Server

---

net user   net user [options]

The *net user* command can create, modify, and delete user accounts.

Options

none   Display all usernames that exist on system or domain.
username List account attributes for *username.*

All of the following options must include the username as the first argument:

password Set account password to *password.*
*   Interactively prompt for password (without displaying typed characters).
/active:[yes|no]
          Activate (enable) or deactivate (disable) account.
/add   Add account for *username.*
/comment:"comment-text"
          Add a 48-character comment field associated with the account.
/countrycode:ccode
          Turn on localized text for county code, *ccode.* A *ccode* of 0 uses the default country code.

/delete   Delete account for *username*. *Warning:* This command does not ask for confirmation!

/domain   When run on NT Workstation, this option forces the operation to take place on the PDC for the default domain. This is the default for NT Server, and is unnecessary.

/expires:[*date*|NEVER]
Set expiration date for account or disable expiration completely with reserved word *NEVER*. The date can be entered in various formats: month names spelled out, abbreviated, or in numeric form. The order of month and day is determined by country code. Years can be either two or four digits long. Fields can be separated by commas or slashes. For example: 12/18/66, 18/12/66, Dec/18/66, December/18/1966, or Dec,18,1966. Note that an account expiration is different than a password expiration, which is controlled by the *net accounts* command or the **User Manager Policies-Account** menu.

/fullname:"*full-name*"
Full name of user.

/homedir:*homedirpath*
Set home directory path.

/homedirreq:[yes|no]
Determine whether a home directory is required.

/passwordchg:[yes|no]
Determine whether users are allowed to change their own password. If used on an account shared by a group of people, this would prevent a single person from locking others out by changing the password.

/passwordreq:[yes|no]
Determine whether a password is required for the account.

/profilepath:*profilepath*
Set pathname of user profile.

/scriptpath:*scriptpath*
Pathname of user logon script.

/times:[*times*|ALL]
Set time of day and day of week at which user can logon. The time and day format is expressed as a series of ranges in one-hour increments of 12- or 24-hour time. When using 12-hour time, specify AM or PM. Specify the day or a range of days, a comma, and then a time range. Each day and time entry should be separated from other day and time entries by semicolons. The name of day can be abbreviated, but only to two characters. The reserved word *ALL* allows a logon at all times (the default) and a blank argument disables logons entirely.

/usercomment:"*comment-text*"
Add an additional comment field. This is displayed only in the command-line *net user* form, not in **User Manager**.

/workstations:*workstation*[,*workstation*]
Comma-separated list of workstations that user can login from (maximum of eight). If list is * or blank, user can logon from any workstation (the default behavior).

$\rightarrow$

net user

←

Examples

Add a single account:

```
net user larryc /add
```

Multiple options can be combined in the same *net user* command:

```
net user larryc /add /comment:"Larry's Account" /homedir:"c:\users\larryc" \
/expires:never /fullname:"Larry Chapman" /passwordreq:yes /homedirreq:yes
```

Set the logon times for *larryc* to 10:00 AM to 4:00 PM on Sunday, and 9:00 AM to 6:00 PM for the rest of the week:

```
net user larryc /times:su,10:00-16:00;monday-saturday,9am-6pm
```

Notes

As the *net user* command does not ask for confirmation, you can do a lot of damage to the user database if you are not careful.

An account has to exist before you can modify it.

net user can be used to set most (but not all) of the account option settings present in **User Manager**. As with **User Manager**, the default settings for accounts are determined by account policies, available under either **Policies-Account** or the *net accounts* command.

It is possible to use **User Manager** and the *net user* commands simultaneously. If you have the **User Manager** running while issuing a *net user* command, you will have to manually select **View-Refresh** to refresh the on-screen display of account information to the latest version.

The */times* option can be confusing. Each time you use *net user* with the */times* option, you are overwriting the previous setting, not adding to the times that someone can logon. You have to make sure that all the logon times are completely specified within a single */times* command. Confirm your settings by typing the *net user* command with only the username as an argument and examine the "Logon hours allowed" output.

See Also

net accounts
net group
net localgroup

GUI Equivalents

User Manager

Requires

NT Workstation or Server

The *net view* command displays available resources on the network. This can include domains, servers, shared directories, and printers.

Options

none   Display list of servers in local domain.

\\computername
            Display list of shares on *computername*.

/domain[:domainname]
            Display a list of domains, or computers within a specified *domain-name*.

/network:nw
            Display list of servers in a Novell NetWare network. If a server name is specified, resources on that computer are displayed.

Examples

Display list of computers offering resources:

```
net view
Server name     Remark
-----------------------------------------------------
\\ICA
\\PCEAP         Eric Pearce
```

Examine a specific computer (*ica*):

```
net view \\ica
Shared resources at \\ica

Share name     Type      Used as    Comment
-----------------------------------------------------
DeskJet        Print     HP DeskJet 660C
I386           Disk
NETLOGON       Disk      Login server share
temp           Disk      Temporary Share
```

The *Used as* field displays the drive letter or print device to which a share is connected.

Display list of domains and workgroups:

```
net view /domain
Domain
-----------------------------------------------------
HOME
OFFICE
```

Display list of computers in domain or workgroup *OFFICE*:

```
net view /domain:OFFICE
Server name     Remark
-----------------------------------------------------
\\ICA
```

$\rightarrow$

net view

←

Display list of Novell NetWare servers:

```
net view /network:nw
Resources on NetWare or Compatible Network
--------------------------------------------------
\\NWSRV312
```

Examine a specific NetWare server (*NWSRV312*):

```
net view /network:nw \\nwsrv312
Shared resources at \\nwsrv312
--------------------------------------------------
Disk      \\NWSRV312\SYS
```

Notes

File or printer sharing must be turned on for shares to appear in browse lists.

You must have permission to browse a server that has NT domain security implemented on it. If you do not have an account on the server, your ability to browse will depend on the rights of the guest account.

See Also

net file
net session
net share
net use

GUI Equivalents

File Manager
Network Neighborhood
Windows NT Explorer

Requires

NT Workstation or Server

TCP/IP Commands

The TCP/IP commands all use TCP/IP (as opposed to NetBEUI) in some manner. Most of the commands originated on UNIX systems and behave in a manner similar to their UNIX counterparts. Their main uses are communicating with TCP/IP-based systems such as UNIX or debugging TCP/IP network problems.

---

arp   arp [options]

The *arp* command manipulates the Address Resolution Protocol cache. Once an IP address is mapped to a hardware address using the ARP protocol, the entry is cached so that is it readily available for any future communication.

Options

-a [IP-address]
> Display contents of entire ARP cache or just the entry for *IP-address*. If there are multiple network interfaces, the *-N* option can limit the display to the ARP entries for a specific interface.

-d IP-address [Interface-address]
> Delete the ARP entry for *IP-address*. The *Interface-address* can be specified if there are multiple network interfaces.

-g
> Identical to *-a*.

-s IP-address hardware-address [Interface-address]
> Manually add an entry to the ARP cache. The *IP-address* and *hardware-address* pair stays in the cache after the system reboots and never times out.

-N [Interface-address]
> Prints the ARP entries for the interface *Interface-address*. If an interface is not specified, uses the first one found.

Examples

Check the ARP cache:

```
arp -a
No ARP Entries Found
```

Force an ARP broadcast to take place:

```
ping -n 1 nugget

Pinging nugget [10.0.0.15] with 32 bytes of data:

Reply from 10.0.0.15: bytes=32 time<10ms TTL=255
```

Check ARP cache again:

```
arp -a

Interface: 10.0.0.3 on Interface 2
  Internet Address      Physical Address      Type
    10.0.0.15           08-00-20-10-3e-a8     dynamic
```

Manually add an ARP entry:

```
arp -s 10.0.0.1 00-AA-00-A5-84-EF
arp -a

Interface: 10.0.0.3 on Interface 2
  Internet Address      Physical Address      Type
    10.0.0.1            00-AA-00-A5-84-EF     static
    10.0.0.15           08-00-20-10-3e-a8     dynamic
```

Note that the manually added entry is type *static*.

$\rightarrow$

Delete an entry from the cache from a specific interface:

- Find the interface IP address with *ipconfig*:

```
ipconfig

Windows NT IP Configuration

Ethernet adapter AMDPCN1:
        IP Address. . . . . . . . . : 10.0.0.5    <-- IP address of Interface
        Subnet Mask . . . . . . . . : 255.255.255.0
        Default Gateway . . . . . . : 10.0.0.254

Ethernet adapter NdisWan5:
        IP Address. . . . . . . . . : 0.0.0.0
        Subnet Mask . . . . . . . . : 0.0.0.0
        Default Gateway . . . . . . :
```

- Delete the entry 10.0.0.1 from interface 10.0.0.5:

```
arp -d 10.0.0.1 10.0.0.5
```

Notes

Normally cached entries will time out in a matter of minutes (10 by default). Entries created with the *-s* flag are always available, enabling them to be used for *proxy-arp* situations. In proxy-arp, one computer responds for another when it sees a broadcast for a hardware address. This allows the proxy computer to intercept network traffic and forward it to another interface (such as a modem). This method is sometimes used for directing traffic to a host connected to the LAN via PPP or SLIP.

See Also

ipconfig

Requires

NT Workstation or Server

---

finger   `finger [options]`

The *finger* command queries a remote computer for a list of currently logged on users.

Options

`@hostname`
    Name of remote computer to query.

`username` Ask for information for just this user.

`-1`   Display more detailed information about users.

Examples

Query the entire computer *nugget*:

```
finger @nugget
[nugget]

Login     Name            TTY       Idle   When       Where
eap       Eric A Pearce   console          Mon 07:15
eap       Eric A Pearce   pts/0            Mon 07:16
eap       Eric A Pearce   pts/1     19     Mon 07:16
```

Each line indicates a separate logon (which are all the same user in this example).

Query a specific user in detail on *nugget*:

```
finger -l eap@nugget

[nugget]

Login name: eap                    In real life: Eric A Pearce
Directory: /home/eap               Shell: /usr/bin/tcsh
On since Oct 21 07:15:38 on console
11 seconds Idle Time
No unread mail
No Plan.

Login name: eap                    In real life: Eric A Pearce
Directory: /home/eap               Shell: /usr/bin/tcsh
On since Oct 21 07:16:04 on pts/0
11 seconds Idle Time

Login name: eap                    In real life: Eric A Pearce
Directory: /home/eap               Shell: /usr/bin/tcsh
On since Oct 21 07:16:04 on pts/1
18 minutes Idle Time
```

It is possible to bounce the *finger* request off a third party computer using the syntax *@host1@host2*.

```
finger eap@nugget.west.ora.com@ora.com

[ora.com]
[nugget.west.ora.com]

<normal finger output>
```

Notes

The output of the *finger* command is totally dependent on the remote computer and varies with different operating systems.

If you get a "connection refused" error, the remote host is not running the server side of *finger*. Many sites are disabling the finger server to limit information that could be used for break-in attempts.

→

Requires

NT Workstation or Server
TCP/IP protocol

---

ftp

The *ftp* command is the standard TCP/IP utility for transferring files from one computer to another. It can be run interactively from the command line or in a batch mode. The *ftp* command is the client side of the ftp connection. The ftp server is part of the **Peer Web Services** on NT Workstation and **Microsoft Internet Server** (IIS) on NT Server. It is administered using **Internet Service Manager**.

Options

hostname Remote host for connection.

-a   Use any local interface as the end point of the data connection. *ftp* normally starts a *control* connection going from the local computer to the remote computer for ftp commands. A second connection, called the *data* connection, goes from the remote computer back to the local computer and is used for the actual file transfer.

-d   Turn on debugging. Display all ftp commands being sent between the ftp client on the local computer and the ftp server on remote computer. *Note:* This option displays the password in plain text.

-g   Disables filename *globbing*. Globbing is the wildcard expansion that normally takes place on the command-line shell. Turning this off allows wildcard characters to be used within local filenames or pathnames without interpretation by the shell.

-i   Turn off prompting when transferring multiple files. Otherwise, you are asked to manually confirm every file before it is transferred.

-n   Turn off autologon when *ftp* is started. Normally the ftp client prompts for a username to begin the logon. Turning this off establishes a control connection to the remote host, but nothing else.

-s:*filename*
     Use *filename* as source for subsequent ftp commands. This can be used to run *ftp* in a batch mode. *Note:* This file may contain the ftp password in plain text!

-w:*windowsize*
     Set the amount of data that can be transferred before a confirmation is required from the receiving end of the connection (the *window* size). In theory, increasing this could improve throughput on a reliable connection.

-v   Turn off display of responses from remote end of connection.

ftp Commands

Only the most commonly used commands are listed. Type *help* at the ftp> prompt for the complete list.

---

ascii Set ASCII file transfer type. This is the default file transfer type and should be used when transferring ASCII text files. It automatically performs the translations between different operating system conventions for text files.

binary Set binary *image* file transfer type. This will transfer a file byte-for-byte with no conversions. Use this mode for anything other than plain ASCII text.

bye End ftp session.

cd *remote-directory*
Change directory on remote computer.

dir [*remote-directory*][*local-file*]
Directory listing of current remote directory or directory specified. If a local file is specified, the directory list is stored in the file instead of displayed on the screen.

get *remote-file* [*local-file*]
Transfer *remote-file* to local computer. The local copy of the file will be renamed to *local-file* if one is specified.

hash Print a hash character (#) for every 2048 bytes transferred. This provides entertainment while waiting for large or slow file transfers and assures you that something is indeed happening.

help [*command*]
Print a listing of all *ftp* commands understood by the local ftp client. If *command* is specified, give a short description of the command.

lcd *local-directory*
Change directory on local computer.

ls [*remote-directory*][*local-file*]
See *dir* command.

mget *remote-files*
Get multiple files from the remote computer.

mput *local-files*
Send multiple files to remote computer.

open *computer* [*port*]
Open an *ftp* command connection to *computer*. *ftp* normally does this for you, unless you specified *-b* on the command line. The *port* number is the TCP port number of the remote ftp server (usually 21).

prompt Toggle prompting for user confirmation (default is on).

pwd Print working directory—display the name of the current directory on the remote computer.

quit End ftp session.

remotehelp [*command*]
Print a listing of all *ftp* commands understood by the remote *ftp* server. If *command* is specified, give a short description of the command.

user *username*
Log onto remote host with username *username*. You are prompted for a password.

→

Examples

Run *ftp* in an interactive mode and transfer the file */etc/hosts* from host *nugget* to *\temp\hosts* on the local computer:

```
ftp nugget
Connected to nugget.
220 nugget FTP server (UNIX(r) System V Release 4.0) ready.
User (nugget:(none)): eap
331 Password required for eap.
Password:password
230 User eap logged in.
ftp> cd /etc
250 CWD command successful.
ftp> lcd \temp
Local directory now D:\temp
ftp> get hosts
200 PORT command successful.
150 ASCII data connection for hosts (nugget:1068) (192 bytes).
226 ASCII Transfer complete.
200 bytes received in 0.00 seconds (200000.00 Kbytes/sec)
ftp> quit
221 Goodbye.
```

Here is an *ftp* trick for reading text files on a remote computer without storing them locally. You can use a dash as the local filename, which will transfer the file to Standard Out, printing it on the screen. This is handy for quickly scanning a *README* or index file on an ftp site.

```
ftp> cd /etc
250 CWD command successful.
ftp> get hosts -
200 PORT command successful.
150 ASCII data connection for hosts (10.0.0.3),1034 (232 bytes).
#
# Internet host table
#
127.0.0.1 localhost
10.0.0.1 ica
10.0.0.3 vectra2
10.0.0.15 nugget loghost
226 ASCII Transfer complete.
242 bytes received in 0.18 seconds (1.34 Kbytes/sec)
ftp>
```

To run *ftp* in a batch mode:

1. Run through the entire ftp session manually and record what commands you needed to type.

2. Put the commands in a text file.

3. Start the ftp session with the *-s* option and the command file path.

Example text file containing *ftp* commands (*ftp.dat*) that logs in to a UNIX host and transfers the */etc/hosts* file to the *temp* directory on the local computer:

```
open nugget
user eap
password
cd /etc
lcd \temp
get hosts
quit
```

Example of batch mode *ftp* using text file:

```
ftp -n -v -s:ftp.dat
ftp> open nugget
ftp> user eap
ftp>
ftp> cd /etc
ftp> lcd \temp
Local directory now D:\temp
ftp> get hosts
ftp> quit
```

The batch mode *ftp* can then be run via the *at* command if you need to perform a file transfer regularly without user intervention.

Notes

The *ftp* commands are an odd mix due to their UNIX heritage and support of different operating systems. The filenames and output of the directory listing commands can be confusing when *ftp*ing files between different operating systems. For example, one system may use a forward slash (/) in pathnames instead of a backslash (\), require drive letters, have spaces within filenames, and so on.

The * wildcard matches the "." and ".." directories when used with the *mget* and *mput* commands. This seems like the wrong thing to do.

See Also

Internet Service Manager

Requires

NT Workstation for *ftp* server (Peer Web Services)
NT Server for *ftp* server (Internet Information Server)
TCP/IP protocol

The *hostname* command displays the TCP/IP hostname of the local computer.

Examples

```
hostname
vectra
```

Notes

Your computer can have a different name on the network for each protocol.
The name usually referred to as the "computer name" is listed in the **Computer
Name** field of the **Network** control panel. The TCP/IP hostname is set in the
Protocols-TCP/IP-DNS-Host Name menu of the **Network** control panel. The
hostname name defaults to the computer name, but it does not have to be the
same.

Requires

NT Workstation or Server
TCP/IP protocol

---

ipconfig   ipconfig [options]

The *ipconfig* command displays the current TCP/IP settings on the command line.
It is handy for quickly checking the TCP/IP configuration and debugging problems
with DHCP.

Options

none   Displays a short summary of TCP/IP settings for the network
adapters.

/all   Verbose display of TCP/IP settings.

/renew [adapter]
Request a new IP address from the DHCP server. This does not necessarily mean you will get one different than last time.

/release [adapter]
Notify the DHCP server that you no longer want the current IP
address and that it is available for reuse. This disables TCP/IP on the
local computer until a new address is obtained.

Examples

Summary display:

```
ipconfig
Windows NT IP Configuration
```

```
Ethernet adapter AMDPCN1:

        IP Address. . . . . . . . . : 10.0.0.5
        Subnet Mask . . . . . . . . : 255.255.255.0
        Default Gateway . . . . . . : 10.0.0.254

Ethernet adapter NdisWan5:

        IP Address. . . . . . . . . : 0.0.0.0
        Subnet Mask . . . . . . . . : 0.0.0.0
        Default Gateway . . . . . . :
```

This computer has one Ethernet card installed, with an interface named *AMDPCN1*. The *NdisWan5* interface is the one used by RAS (a serial port connected to a modem, in this example).

Detailed display from computer without DHCP enabled:

```
ipconfig/all
Windows NT IP Configuration

        Host Name . . . . . . . . . : vectra.eap.com
        DNS Servers . . . . . . . . : 198.112.214.1
                                      204.148.49.1
        Node Type . . . . . . . . . : Hybrid
        NetBIOS Scope ID. . . . . . :
        IP Routing Enabled. . . . . : Yes
        WINS Proxy Enabled. . . . . : No
        NetBIOS Resolution Uses DNS : Yes

Ethernet adapter AMDPCN1:

        Description . . . . . . . . : AMD PCNET Family Ethernet Adapter
        Physical Address. . . . . . : 08-00-09-BB-61-AE
        DHCP Enabled. . . . . . . . : No
        IP Address. . . . . . . . . : 10.0.0.5
        Subnet Mask . . . . . . . . : 255.255.255.0
        Default Gateway . . . . . . : 10.0.0.254
        Primary WINS Server . . . . : 10.0.0.1

Ethernet adapter NdisWan5:

        Description . . . . . . . . : NdisWan Adapter
        Physical Address. . . . . . : 00-00-00-00-00-00
        DHCP Enabled. . . . . . . . : No
        IP Address. . . . . . . . . : 0.0.0.0
        Subnet Mask . . . . . . . . : 0.0.0.0
        Default Gateway . . . . . . :
```

→

Detailed display from computer with DHCP enabled:

```
Windows NT IP Configuration

        Host Name . . . . . . . . . : vectra2
        DNS Servers . . . . . . . . :
        Node Type . . . . . . . . . : Broadcast
        NetBIOS Scope ID. . . . . . :
        IP Routing Enabled. . . . . : No
        WINS Proxy Enabled. . . . . : No
        NetBIOS Resolution Uses DNS : No

Ethernet adapter AMDPCN1:

        Description . . . . . . . . : AMD PCNET Family Ethernet Adapter
        Physical Address. . . . . . : 08-00-09-BB-61-AE
        DHCP Enabled. . . . . . . . : Yes
        IP Address. . . . . . . . . : 10.0.0.21
        Subnet Mask . . . . . . . . : 255.255.255.0
        Default Gateway . . . . . . :
        DHCP Server . . . . . . . . : 10.0.0.1
        Lease Obtained. . . . . . . : Monday, October 28, 1996 12:28:29 PM
        Lease Expires . . . . . . . : Thursday, October 31, 1996 12:28:29 PM
```

Release current IP address from DHCP-enabled computer:

```
ipconfig /release
Windows NT IP Configuration

IP address 10.0.0.21 successfully released for adapter "ADMPCN1"

ipconfig
Windows NT IP Configuration
Ethernet adapter AMDPCN1:

        IP Address. . . . . . . . . : 0.0.0.0
        Subnet Mask . . . . . . . . : 0.0.0.0
        Default Gateway . . . . . . :
```

Get a new IP address for DHCP-enabled computer:

```
ipconfig /renew
Windows NT IP Configuration
Ethernet adapter AMDPCN1:

        IP Address. . . . . . . . . : 10.0.0.21
        Subnet Mask . . . . . . . . : 255.255.255.0
        Default Gateway . . . . . . :
```

Field Description

Host name

The TCP/IP hostname (not the computer name used by other protocols, even though they may be the same).

DNS servers

A list of up to three Domain Name Servers. If the first DNS server is unreachable, the second is tried, and so on. If all three DNS servers are unreachable, the lookup fails.

Node type

Describes how NetBIOS name resolution takes place (via broadcast, point-to-point, or a combination of both).

Scope ID

A way to group computers on a network. If a scope ID is specified, only computers with the same scope ID can communicate with each other via NetBIOS over TCP/IP (NBT). Has nothing to do with a DHCP Scope.

IP routing enabled

This host routes IP packets from one interface to another (interfaces include serial ports to modems, and so on).

WINS proxy enabled

This host forwards NetBIOS name resolution requests to a WINS server.

NetBIOS resolution uses DNS

This host tries to resolve NetBIOS names by using the Domain Name System.

Network adapter name

The name of the network adapter, which is a combination of the brand name, model name, and the number of interfaces installed in the computer.

Description

Adapter manufacturer and model.

Physical address

The hardware or MAC-level address.

DHCP enabled

This host uses DHCP to obtain an IP address.

IP address

Current IP address for this interface.

Subnet mask

Mask describing what part of the IP address is the network address and what part is the host address.

Default gateway

IP address where any traffic for unknown networks should be sent.

DHCP server

IP address of DHCP server found by this host.

Lease obtained

Time and date when this IP address was obtained from DHCP server.

Lease expires

Time and date when this IP address will expire (only if there is no further

→

communication with the DHCP server).

See Also
arp
ping
nbtstat
netstat

GUI Equivalents
Network control panel, **Protocols-TCP/IP**

Requires
NT Workstation or Server
TCP/IP protocol

---

lpq   lpq [options]

The *lpq* command queries a TCP/IP host or printer running the LPD protocol for the printer queue contents and status.

Options
-S print_server

        Name or IP address of remote TCP/IP host that provides printer queue.

-P printer

        Name of print queue on remote host.

-l   Prints a more verbose message.

Examples
Query printer queue *DeskJet* on host *ica*:

```
lpq -S ica -P DeskJet

        Windows NT LPD Server
          Printer DeskJet

Owner          Status   Jobname       Job-id  Size  Pages Priority
-----------------------------------------------------------------
Administrator  Printing hosts           4      0     0    1
```

If you have a TCP/IP printer queue on the local computer, you can query it by using *localhost* as the server name:

```
lpq -S localhost -P DeskJet
```

Notes

It would be nice to have the *LPRM* command implemented.

See Also

lpr

GUI Equivalents

Printers control panel, **Open**

Requires

NT Workstation or Server
TCP/IP protocol

---

lpr

`lpr [options]`

The *lpr* command prints to a TCP/IP-based printer or computer running the LPD printing protocol.

Options

`file` File to be printed.

`-S print_server`
Name or IP address of remote TCP/IP host to receive print job.

`-P printer`
Name of print queue on remote host.

`-C class` The *class* name is typically the name of the host that the print job originated on. The *-C* option can be used to specify another name. This name appears on the banner or burst page that separates print jobs (if one is enabled). If a printer is shared by many users, the class name can help identify the output.

`-J job` The *job* name is typically the filename of the file being printed. The *-J* option can be used to change this. The job name will appear on the banner or burst page that separates print jobs (if one is enabled).

`-o option`
Set type of file being printed. The default is plain ASCII text. Use *-ol* when the file is already in a printer language such as PCL or Post-Script.

`-x` Turn on a backwards-compatibility mode for printing to systems running older versions of Sun Microsystem's SunOS.

`-d` Normally there are two files transmitted as part of each print job. The first is a control file that describes the print job and the second is the data file, which contains the data being printed. The *-d* option sends the data file before the control file.

→

lpr

←

Examples

Print the file *hosts* on the printer *DeskJet*, which is a queue on the host *ica*:

```
lpr -S ica -P DeskJet hosts
```

Notes

The *-o* option may be helpful if you have problems printing certain documents. The printer may just print out the contents of a file without interpreting the printer language in which the file is encoded.

For example, if the first several lines of the file look like this:

```
%!PS-Adobe-2.0
%%Creator: dvips 5.495 Copyright 1986, 1992 Radical Eye Software
%%Title: proposal.dvi
%%CreationDate: Fri Feb 19 08:09:04 1993
%%Pages: 15
```

it is a PostScript document and should be printed with *-ol* to prevent the printer from treating it as plain text. Any document starting with **%!** is probably PostScript.

See Also

lpq

Requires

NT Workstation or Server
TCP/IP protocol

---

nbtstat

nbtstat [options]

The *nbtstat* command administers the mapping of NetBIOS names to IP addresses. This mapping enables NetBIOS over TCP/IP (NBT). NBT communication can take place over a TCP/IP-only network connection such as between two LANs on the opposite sides of a router or even across the Internet. *nbtstat* can display various statistics about current names, add or delete names from the NetBIOS name cache, and query remote computers for their NetBIOS information.

Options

none   Print help screen.

-a *computer-name*

Display the NetBIOS name table of the computer *computer-name*.

-A *IP-address*

Display the NetBIOS name table of the computer with IP address *IP-address*.

-c   Display name cache of remote computer names and their IP addresses.

-n	Display NetBIOS name table of the local computer.
-R	Remove any cached names and load contents of *LMHOSTS* file into cache.
-r	Display statistics about NetBIOS name resolution. Name resolution takes place either by broadcast (asking every computer on the LAN) or by contacting a name server (such as WINS).
-S	Display current NetBIOS sessions. Remote computers are listed by their IP addresses.
-s	Display current NetBIOS sessions. Remote computers are listed by their NetBIOS names.
interval	Repeat *nbtstat* command every *interval* seconds until manually terminated with CONTROL-C.

Examples

Manually tell the local system about another system that is reachable using NBT (NetBIOS over TCP/IP), using the following steps:

Check current cache:

```
nbtstat -c

No names in cache
```

Add remote system to *LMHOSTS* file:

```
edit \winnt\system32\drivers\etc\lmhosts
    <add entry>
type \winnt\system32\drivers\etc\lmhosts
10.0.0.1      ica    #PRE    #DOM:HOME
```

Rebuild cache:

```
nbtstat -R

Successful purge and preload of the NBT Remote Cache Name Table.
```

Check cache again:

```
nbtstat -c

Node IP Address: [10.0.0.21] Scope Id: []

            NetBIOS Remote Cache Name Table

    Name          Type      Host Address    Life [sec]
    -------------------------------------------------------
    ICA       <03> UNIQUE    10.0.0.1          -1
    ICA       <00> UNIQUE    10.0.0.1          -1
    ICA       <20> UNIQUE    10.0.0.1          -1
```

→

nbtstat

←

Display NBT name table for computer *ica*:

```
nbtstat -a ica

          NetBIOS Remote Machine Name Table

    Name                Type        Status
    ---------------------------------------------
    ICA           <00>  UNIQUE      Registered
    ICA           <20>  UNIQUE      Registered
    HOME          <00>  GROUP       Registered
    HOME          <1C>  GROUP       Registered
    HOME          <1B>  UNIQUE      Registered
    ICA           <03>  UNIQUE      Registered
    ADMINISTRATOR <03>  UNIQUE      Registered
    HOME          <1E>  GROUP       Registered
    INet~Services <1C>  GROUP       Registered
    HOME          <1D>  UNIQUE      Registered
    IS~ICA........<00>  UNIQUE      Registered

    MAC Address = 00-AA-00-A5-84-EF
```

Display sessions using NetBIOS names:

```
nbtstat -s
              NetBIOS Connection Table

    Local Name         State   In/Out  Remote Host        Input   Output
    --------------------------------------------------------------------------
    VECTRA2     <03>   Listening
    VECTRA2     <00>   Connected  Out  ICA          <20>   3KB     2KB
```

Display sessions using IP addresses:

```
nbtstat -S
              NetBIOS Connection Table

    Local Name         State   In/Out  Remote Host        Input   Output
    --------------------------------------------------------------------------
    VECTRA2     <03>   Listening
    VECTRA2     <00>   Connected  Out  10.0.0.1            3KB     2KB
```

Requires

NT Workstation or Server
TCP/IP protocol

The *netstat* command displays the status of TCP/IP network connections to and from the local computer. It can be used to verify which TCP and UDP services are being offered to other computers and who is currently using them.

Options

none   Show all active TCP connections and their connection status.

-a   Show all active TCP connections and UDP ports that are accepting connections.

-e   Display statistics for the network interface. This can be combined with protocol statistics by using the *-s* option.

-n   Do not try to resolve IP addresses into hostnames or convert port numbers to symbolic names. If there is a problem with DNS, this will prevent long delays waiting for DNS timeouts. The symbolic port names are from the *<system root>\SYSTEM32\DRIVERS\ETC\SERVICES* file.

-p protocol
    Limit display to specified protocol. Possible protocol types for the statistics display (*-s*) are *icmp*, *ip*, *tcp*, and *udp*. The display of connections and listening ports is limited to *tcp* and *udp*.

-r   Display TCP/IP routing table contents.

-s   Display statistics for each protocol.

interval Continuously redisplay *netstat* output every *interval* seconds. Type CONTROL-C to quit. This is handy if you want to observe changes in (almost) real time while something is happening on the network.

Fields

Proto
    Protocol in use (either TCP or UDP).

Local address
    Address and port pair for local side of connection. The address is always the local computer hostname or IP address. If *netstat* cannot find the port number in the *services* file or the lookup is disabled with the *-n* option, the port number is printed. If the address or port number is unknown or not yet established, an asterisk is displayed.

Foreign address
    Address and port pair for remote side of connection. The foreign address is usually a remote host, but it does not have to be (two applications running on the local computer can use the network to talk to each other). No foreign address is displayed for the **UDP** protocol.

State
    The state that the TCP connection is currently in. The possible values are:

LISTEN:
    TCP is waiting for a connection at this port.

→

ESTABLISHED:

There is an active TCP connection at this port.

The following are states in the three-way close of a TCP connection:

FIN_WAIT_1
CLOSE_WAIT
FIN_WAIT_2
LAST_ACK
TIME_WAIT
CLOSED

You might see these states if one end of the TCP connection is still waiting to hear from the other end. The states will also depend on which side of the connection initiated the close.

Examples

Show active TCP connections and available UDP ports:

```
netstat -a

Active Connections

  Proto  Local Address       Foreign Address      State
  TCP    ica:1043            nugget:ftp           CLOSE_WAIT
  TCP    ica:80              nugget:32772         ESTABLISHED
  TCP    ica:1026            localhost:1028       ESTABLISHED
  TCP    ica:1028            localhost:1026       ESTABLISHED
  UDP    ica:1027            *:*
  UDP    ica:echo            *:*
  UDP    ica:1031            *:*
  UDP    ica:discard         *:*
  UDP    ica:daytime         *:*
  UDP    ica:1038            *:*
  UDP    ica:qotd            *:*
  UDP    ica:chargen         *:*
  UDP    ica:name            *:*
  UDP    ica:domain          *:*
  UDP    ica:135             *:*
  UDP    ica:snmp            *:*
  UDP    ica:domain          *:*
  UDP    ica:bootp           *:*
  UDP    ica:nbname          *:*
  UDP    ica:nbdatagram      *:*
```

From the first TCP line, we can tell that there is an *ftp* connection between the local computer and the host *nugget*. The local computer initiated the session, as the port being used on the remote computer is the *ftp* port (21). The status of *CLOSE_WAIT* indicates that the connection is in the process of shutting down. The second TCP line has a connection from the host *nugget* to the WWW server on the local computer (port 80). Most of following UDP ports result from installing **Simple TCP Services**.

Display active TCP connections with DNS and *SERVICES* file resolution turned off:

```
netstat -n

Active Connections

   Proto  Local Address        Foreign Address       State
   TCP    10.0.0.1:1043        10.0.0.15:21          CLOSE_WAIT
   TCP    10.0.0.1:80          10.0.0.15:32772       ESTABLISHED
   TCP    127.0.0.1:1026       127.0.0.1:1028        ESTABLISHED
   TCP    127.0.0.1:1028       127.0.0.1:1026        ESTABLISHED
```

Notes

It would be nice if *netstat* could display TCP ports on local host that are in the LISTEN state.

Do not confuse with *net statistics*!

See Also

nbtstat
ping
route print
tracert

Requires

NT Workstation or Server
TCP/IP protocol

---

nslookup   nslookup [options]

The *nslookup* command queries DNS name servers. It is primarily used to confirm that DNS is configured properly and working, but it can be used for finding out various types of DNS information for any host on the Internet. *nslookup* has two modes of operation: it either makes a single query and exits, or goes in an interactive mode where multiple queries can be made. Most of the *nslookup* options can be specified either on the command line or at the interactive mode prompt.

Options

none   Go into interactive mode and wait for user input.

-command Run an *nslookup* command (see list below). If a command does not follow the hyphen character, go into interactive mode after processing any other command-line options.

hostname|IP-address
        TCP/IP hostname or IP address to lookup in DNS.

DNS-server
        Use *DNS-server* instead of default. The three default nameservers are specified in the **Protocols-TCP/IP Protocol-DNS** tab of the **Network** control panel.

→

nslookup

←

Commands

help   List all available *nslookup* commands.

exit   Exit interactive mode.

finger [*username*]

Run the *finger* command to print a list of users logged on to the current host. If *username* is specified, *finger* just this user.

ls [-a|-d|-t *type*] *domain* [> *filename*]

List all members of *domain*. If the redirection symbol (>) and *filename* are specified, store the output in the file instead of printing it on the screen. The *-a* option displays canonical names and aliases (CNAME) records. The *-d* option displays all record types. The *-t* option displays *type* records (A, CNAME, MX, MS, PTR, HINFO, and so on).

lsserver *server*

Change the default DNS server to *server*, looking up the name of *server* using the initial server.

root   Set default server to the *root* name server. This is compiled into the *nslookup* command as *ns.nic.ddn.mil*.

server *server*

Change the default DNS server to *server*, looking up the name of *server* using the current server.

view *file*

Display an *ls* output file on the screen.

set *option*|all

Toggle an option to be used for subsequent *nslookup* commands. If *all* is specified, display all the current settings and their values.

The following are arguments to the *set* command. Once an option has been set, it remains in effect until it is cancelled with the *no* command.

class=*class*

Set query class to *class*. Possible values are *IN* (Internet), *CHAOS*, *HESIOD*, or *ANY*. Not likely to be used outside of MIT.

debug

Print debugging information while lookup is taking place. This is helpful if you are trying to figure out why a lookup is failing.

d2 Print even more debugging information.

defname

Append domain name to each query. By default, *nslookup* appends the current domain name to any unqualified hostname before looking it up. This works most of the time, as most queries are for local hosts. You can turn this off by unsetting *defname* or by appending a period to the end of the hostname.

domain=*domainname*

Set default domain name to *domainname*. This name will be appended to all queries if *defname* is set. The default domain name is normally set in the **Protocols-TCP/IP Protocol-DNS** tab of the **Network** control panel.

`ignore`

Ignore network errors.

`port=port`

Set TCP/UDP port number to use for contacting the name server (default is 53). If you were running an experimental version of a nameserver on a nonstandard port, you could use this to tell *nslookup* which port the server is using.

`querytype=type`

Set type of record to query for (by default, this is *A* (address)). Possible record types are A, CNAME, MX, NS, PTR, SOA, or ANY.

`recurse`

Recursively make query, asking each name server to ask other name servers until the answer is found.

`search`

Use list of domains set with *srchlist*. Try query with each domain name appended.

`srchlist=domain1[/domain2/.../domain6]`

Try appending up to six different domains when making query. The first domain in the search list is used as the default domain.

`timeout=seconds`

Set timeout for query to *seconds* seconds.

`type=type`

Same as *querytype*.

`vc` Use *virtual circuit* to name server. This has the effect of using TCP for queries that would normally use UDP.

Examples

Go into interactive mode:

```
nslookup
Default Server: SanFrancisco01.POP.InterNex.Net

>
```

Tell *nslookup* to look for *A* (address) records:

```
> set q=a
```

Lookup up the address for the host *www.whitehouse.gov*:

```
> www.whitehouse.gov

Server:  SanFrancisco01.POP.InterNex.Net
Address:  205.158.3.50

Non-authoritative answer:
Name:    www.whitehouse.gov
Addresses:  198.137.240.92, 198.137.240.91
```

→

The "Non-authoritative answer" message indicates that the DNS information has been cached from a previous query and the DNS server did not consult the actual name servers for the domain being looked up.

Tell *nslookup* to look for *PTR* (pointer) records:

```
> set q=ptr
```

Lookup up the *PTR* record for the host *198.137.240.91* in the *in-addr.arpa* domain:

```
> 91.240.137.198.in-addr.arpa

Server:  SanFrancisco01.POP.InterNex.Net
Address:  205.158.3.50

Non-authoritative answer:
91.240.137.198.in-addr.arpa     name = www1.whitehouse.gov
```

Notes

Do not confuse TCP/IP domain names with NT security domain names.

The *ls* may fail to work on domains other than your own. Running *ls* attempts a DNS *zone transfer* of the domain, which means opening a TCP connection to the DNS server and downloading the entire domain database in a single transaction (as opposed to the normal method of looking up one host at a time). Most sites that are concerned about security are going to block this from happening, as a listing of every computer within an organization could be used for automating break-in attempts.

Another security-related trend is the removal of the *HINFO* type record. In the past this was used to store the OS name and version of a host. As this information could be used to customize an attack on the host, most people are no longer going to make this information public.

See Also

DNS & BIND, Second Edition (1996), Albitz and Liu, O'Reilly & Associates

GUI Equivalents

Network Monitor (SMS version) Display-Resolve Addresses from Name

Requires

NT Workstation or Server
TCP/IP protocol

---

ping   `ping [options]`

The *ping* command is used to test TCP/IP connectivity. If you can *ping* another host or gateway, this proves you can communicate with it and that TCP/IP is configured correctly.

Options

`target`	Computer or gateway whose connectivity you want to test.
`-a`	Resolve IP addresses to hostnames in output.
`-n count`	Send *count* number of echo packets (default is 4).
`-l size`	Set size of echo packet data field (default is 32 bytes, maximum is 65527 bytes).
`-t`	Continuously ping host until manually interrupted with CTRL-C.
`-f`	Set *Do not Fragment* flag in echo packet header. This stops gateways from breaking echo packet into multiple smaller packets.
`-i ttl`	Set *Time to Live* field in echo packet header to *ttl*. Each gateway will decrement the *ttl* by 1. If it reaches 0, the packet will be discarded. The default *ttl* is 128.
`-v tos`	Set *Type of Service* field in Echo packet header to *tos*.
`-r count`	Set the *Record Route option*, which stores the IP address of each gateway the packet goes through on its way to and from the target. The number of routes recorded is set to *count* (a value from 1 to 9).
`-s count`	Record a timestamp for each gateway that the packet goes through. The number of timestamps recorded is set by *count*.
`-j IP-list`	
	Use *IP-list* as a *loose source-route* for the echo packet. In source routing, the route the packet should take is specified at the source, instead of making routing decisions one hop at a time. It is a *loose* route in that not every hop is specified, while a *strict* route would have every hop specified. The maximum number of IP addresses that can be specified is 9.
`-k IP-list`	
	Use *IP-list* as a *strict source-route* for the echo packet. In source routing, the route the packet should take is specified at the source, instead of making routing decisions one hop at a time. It is a *strict* route in that every hop is specified, while a *loose* route would not have to have every hop specified. The maximum number of IP addresses that can be specified is 9.
`-w timeout`	
	Wait *timeout* milliseconds to get a reply from an echo packet before sending the next one. Default is 1000 milliseconds (1 second).

Examples

See if you can reach the President:

```
ping whitehouse.gov

Pinging whitehouse.gov [198.137.241.30] with 32 bytes of data:

Reply from 198.137.241.30]: bytes=32 time=220ms TTL=245
Reply from 198.137.241.30]: bytes=32 time=220ms TTL=245
Reply from 198.137.241.30]: bytes=32 time=220ms TTL=245
Reply from 198.137.241.30]: bytes=32 time=220ms TTL=245
```

$\rightarrow$

ping

←

Notes

ping works by sending ICMP echo packets from the local computer to the remote target(s) and waiting for a reply. If replies are received, this proves that the target(s) are reachable and functioning on the network. There are several reasons why a *ping* could fail:

- There could be a problem with DNS. Try specifying the target via its IP address instead of the hostname. It is possible to *ping* a target computer via its NetBIOS name if you have the **Enable DNS for Windows Resolution** button checked in the TCP/IP configuration, so using an IP address will bypass any name resolution problem.

- There could be a routing problem. Try the *tracert* command to see if you can at least get out of your LAN.

- Some types of computers (such as the Apple Macintosh) can be configured so that their TCP/IP stacks are unloaded when not in use. In this scenario, the computer will only respond to a *ping* if someone happens to running a TCP/IP application on the computer while you are *ping*ing it.

See Also

arp
ipconfig
nbtstat
netstat
route

Requires

NT Workstation or Server
TCP/IP protocol

---

rcp   rcp [options]

The *rcp* command is remote copy, which can copy files and directories over a TCP/IP connection to another computer. There is no authentication mechanism, so the remote computer must be configured to trust the local computer.

Options

    -a   Use ASCII transfer mode (the default.) This changes end-of-line characters in ASCII files from UNIX format to MS-DOS format or vice versa, depending on the direction of the copy operation.

    -b   Use binary or image transfer mode. Use this for any binary or data that should be transferred without modification.

    -h   Also transfer hidden files. By default, these are ignored by *rcp* and not copied.

-r   Recursively copy all subdirectories and files.

[hostname[.username]]:
            Specify source hostname and destination hostname with an optional
            username (if different than currently logged-in user).

source-files
            Filename or pathname of files that should be copied.

destination-directory
            Pathname of destination directory. The destination directory is
            stored under the home directory of the user, unless it is an absolute
            path (preceded with "/" or "\").

Examples

Copy a directory from the local computer to a remote UNIX computer:

```
rcp -r \winnt35\system32\drivers\etc nugget.eap:/tmp
```

This recursively copies the contents of the \WINNT35\SYSTEM32
\DRIVERS\ETC directory to the *nugget* computer as user *eap* and store the
directory as */tmp/etc*.

Copy a directory from the remote UNIX computer to the local computer:

```
rcp -r nugget.eap:/tmp/etc \users\default
```

This will recursively copy the contents of the */tmp/etc* directory on the *nugget*
computer to the local directory \USERS\DEFAULT. The copy operation is performed by user *eap* on the *nugget* computer.

Notes

Windows NT provides only the client side of the remote copy protocol, so you
can initiate the copy from NT to a UNIX system, but not the other way around.
The *rcp* command is from the Berkeley UNIX "R" commands, which are
acknowledged to have security problems.

The most common "trust" mechanism on the UNIX side of the connection is
the *.rhosts* file stored in the UNIX user's home directory. This contains a list of
remote hostnames and usernames that should be allowed to run commands as
if they were the UNIX user (without being asked for a password!).

The *rcp* command syntax can be used to initiate a third party copy where the
initiating user is on a third computer and is not logged onto either the source
or destination computer. Both the source and destination computers would
have be non-NT systems, as an NT system cannot be instructed to copy files to
or from another NT computer via *rcp*.

Requires

NT Workstation or Server
TCP/IP protocol

rexec

The *rexec* command is remote execute. It executes commands on a remote host. The commands are limited to non-interactive commands that do not need further input from the user and do not require full-screen access. *rexec* prompts for the username and password and passes this on (in plain text) to the remote computer.

Options

hostname Name of remote computer to execute command.

command Command to be executed on the remote computer. If it contains spaces or special characters, enclose it in quotation marks.

-l username
Username that command should be run by on the remote computer.

-n Redirect standard input of command to the *NULL* device. Use this for commands that are to be run interactively.

Examples

Get a directory listing on the UNIX system *nugget*:

```
rexec nugget -l eap "ls ~"
Password (nugget:): password
Russ
TeX.ps
audio-tape.ps    <directory listing is printed>
nt-book
doc
eap.ps
```

Notes

Windows NT provides only the client side of the remote execution protocol, so you can execute UNIX commands from NT, but not the other way around. The *rexec* command is from the Berkeley UNIX "R" commands, which are acknowledged to have security problems.

Requires

NT Workstation or Server
TCP/IP protocol

route

The *route* command manipulates the TCP/IP routing table for the local computer.

Options

-f Delete (flush) all routes from the routing table. Use this option with caution, as this may stop the computer from communicating with others or break your own communication with the computer if you are accessing it over the network.

-p	Make any manually added route permanent across reboots. By default, route changes are lost.
add	Add a route.
print	Print current routing table (on the screen).
delete	Delete a route.
change	Modify an existing route.
destination	
	The host or network that is reachable via *gateway*.
gateway	The router or gateway to be used for traffic going to *destination*.
mask netmask	
	Specifies the subnet mask for a *destination*. If this option is omitted, a mask of 255.255.255.255 is used.
metric metric	
	Specifies a metric for the *gateway*. If there are multiple routes to a *destination*, the metric provides a mechanism for indicating which route is preferred. The route with the lowest metric is used unless it is becomes unavailable, and then the next lowest metric takes over. The metric is typically the number of network hops or gateways between the local computer and the destination, but this is not mandatory.

Examples

Display the current route table:

```
route print
```

```
Active Routes:
  Network Address          Netmask  Gateway Address      Interface  Metric
        10.0.0.0      255.255.255.0       10.0.0.14       10.0.0.14      1
       10.0.0.14    255.255.255.255       127.0.0.1       127.0.0.1      1
  10.255.255.255    255.255.255.255       10.0.0.14       10.0.0.14      1
       127.0.0.0          255.0.0.0       127.0.0.1       127.0.0.1      1
       224.0.0.0          224.0.0.0       10.0.0.14       10.0.0.14      1
 255.255.255.255    255.255.255.255       10.0.0.14       10.0.0.14      1
```

Add a default gateway:

```
route add 0.0.0.0 10.0.0.200
```

This sends any traffic that does not match any of the existing routes to the gateway at 10.0.0.200.

Check route table again:

```
route print
```

```
Active Routes:
  Network Address          Netmask  Gateway Address      Interface  Metric
         0.0.0.0    255.255.255.255      10.0.0.200       10.0.0.14      1
        10.0.0.0      255.255.255.0       10.0.0.14       10.0.0.14      1
       10.0.0.14    255.255.255.255       127.0.0.1       127.0.0.1      1
  10.255.255.255    255.255.255.255       10.0.0.14       10.0.0.14      1
       127.0.0.0          255.0.0.0       127.0.0.1       127.0.0.1      1
       224.0.0.0          224.0.0.0       10.0.0.14       10.0.0.14      1
 255.255.255.255    255.255.255.255       10.0.0.14       10.0.0.14      1
```

$\rightarrow$

Notes

The *route* command has rather terse error messages that give little guidance about what might be wrong with what you are trying to do. For example:

```
route add 10.0.0.1 mask 255.255.255.0 10.0.0.2 metric 1
The route addition failed: 87

net helpmsg 87

The parameter is incorrect.
```

The *change* command seems somewhat useless. As you have to specify several fields to identify the route you wish to change, you are prevented from modifying these fields. You might as well add a new route and delete the old one.

It would be nice to know more about how the routes were created, as in the flags column available in the UNIX version of *netstat*.

See Also

netstat
ping
RIP Routing Protocol
tracert

Requires

NT Workstation or Server
TCP/IP protocol
RIP for Internet Protocol *service (for routing)*

---

rsh

The *rsh* command executes commands on a remote host. The commands are mostly limited to non-interactive commands that do not need further input from the user nor do they require full-screen access. There is no authentication mechanism, so the remote computer must be configured to trust the local computer.

Options

`hostname` Name of remote TCP/IP system.

`-l username`
> Username by which command should be run on remote system.

`-n`   Redirect standard input to *NULL* device. Use this for commands that are expecting to be run interactively.

`command` Command to execute on remote system. Make sure to quote the command if it contains spaces or special characters that could be interpreted by the local shell.

Examples

Get a directory listing on the UNIX system *nugget* and redirect it to the local file *unix-ls*:

```
rsh nugget -1 eap "ls ~" > unix-ls
```

Let's see what we got:

```
type unix-ls
Russ
TeX.ps
audio-tape.ps
nt-book
doc
eap.ps
```

Output a listing of the local system directory to a file on the UNIX system:

```
dir | rsh nugget -1 eap "cat > /tmp/nt-ls"
Terminal read: The pipe has been ended.
```

Start up a shell on UNIX system:

```
rsh nugget
rsh: remote terminal session not supported.
```

Try another approach:

```
rsh nugget /bin/csh -i
Warning: no access to tty; thus no job control in this shell...
nugget % id
uid=101(eap) gid=100
nugget % exit
```

Notes

Windows NT provides only the client side of the remote shell protocol, so you can execute UNIX commands from NT, but not the other way around. The *rsh* command is from the Berkeley UNIX "R" commands, which are acknowledged to have security problems.

The *-l* option specifies the username that exists on the remote system, not the local one.

The most common "trust" mechanism on the UNIX side of the connection is the *.rhosts* file stored in the UNIX user's home directory. This contains a list of remote hostnames and usernames that should be allowed to run commands as if they were the UNIX user (without being asked for a password!).

See Also

rexec
rlogin
telnet

Requires

NT Workstation or Server
TCP/IP protocol

telnet

The *telnet* command creates an interactive shell session on a remote computer. See the GUI section for documentation on the GUI interface to *telnet*.

It is possible to give the *telnet* command some options from the DOS prompt. These are helpful if you are trying to debug TCP/IP services on the local computer or remote computers.

Options

`hostname` Name of remote computer to connect to.

`port` Name or number of TCP port to connect to. By default, *telnet* connects to port 23, as this is where telnet servers are listening. You can specify alternate ports to connect to such as 25 for SMTP or 80 for HTTP. The *<system root>\SYSTEM32\DRIVERS\ETC\SERVICES* file lists some of the common port numbers and service names.

Examples

To connect to the SMTP mail server on host *storm.eop.gov* and expand the *postmaster* alias:

```
telnet storm.eop.gov smtp

220 Storm.EOP.GOV -- Server ESMTP (PMDF V5.0-7 #6879)
expn postmaster
250-<fox_J@EOP.GOV>
250-<postmaster@Whitehouse.GOV>
250 <mailadmin@a1.eop.gov>
quit
221 Bye received. Goodbye.
```

To check to see that the web server is operating correctly on the local computer:

```
telnet localhost 80

telnet session starts...

GET /
<!doctype html public "-//IETF//DTD HTML//EN">
<HTML>

<HEAD>
<BODY BACKGROUND="/samples/images/backgrnd.gif">
<TITLE>Microsoft Internet Information Server</TITLE>
</HEAD>

<BODY BGCOLOR="FFFFFF">
<CENTER>
<IMG SRC="/samples/images/h_logo.gif" ALIGN="BOTTOM" ALT="Microsoft
Internet Information Server">
```

If you cannot see what you are typing in the *telnet* session, turn on **Local Echo** in **Terminal-Preferences-Terminal Options** menu.

NT supplies only the client side of *telnet,* but a telnet server is included in NT Server Resource Kit.

GUI Equivalents

Telnet

Requires

NT Workstation or Server
TCP/IP protocol

---

tftp   tftp [options]

The *tftp* (Trivial File Transfer Protocol) command uses the UDP protocol. *tftp* is rarely used interactively by users. Its most common use is downloading boot images to computers or network devices that lack local storage.

Options

- i   Transfer file in *image* mode. Use this to transfer binary files, such as executables, boot images, and so forth. If not specified, the transfer mode is ASCII, which tries to convert end-of-line conventions according to the type of systems between which the file is being transferred.

hostname The remote host to or from which you want to transfer the file. It must be running a tftp server for you to connect to it.

get|put   Either *get* a file from the remote computer or *put* a local file on the remote computer. Some implementations require the files on the remote computer to be writable by anyone for them to be transferred in either direction.

source-file [destination-file]
          Name of file to be transferred. If a *destination-file* name is specified, rename *source-file* to *destination-file.*

Examples

Transfer the binary file *bootfile* from a remote host named *sun* and rename it *bootfile.sun* on the local computer:

```
tftp -i sun get bootfile bootfile.sun
Transfer successful: 224 bytes in 1 second, 224 bytes/s
```

Notes

tftp was intended to provide an easy-to-implement and compact way to transfer files. As it uses UDP, there is no guarantee of the file transfer succeeding or the data arriving intact. It also lacks an authentication mechanism. This is fine for the simple LAN environment where *tftp* is used to download boot images or configuration files, but it is not suitable for Internet applications.

→

Using the Command Line

tftp
←

See Also

ftp

Requires

NT Workstation or Server
TCP/IP protocol

---

tracert

<code>tracert [options]</code>

The *tracert* command can be used to "trace the route" that IP packets take between the local system and a remote system. The remote system does not have to be a computer; it can be a router or any type of system that implements ICMP. This is helpful in solving connectivity or routing problems, as *tracert* can determine where on the network the problem is occurring.

Options

`target`   The destination whose connectivity you are checking. This can be either a TCP/IP hostname or an IP address.

`-d`   Do not try to resolve IP addresses into hostnames. This is helpful if there is also a problem with DNS.

`-h max_hops`

Cease after encountering *max_hops* hops trying to reach the target (default is 30).

`-i ip-list`

Use *ip-list* as a *loose source-route*. In source routing, the route the packet should take is specified at the source, instead of routing decisions being made while the packet is in transit, one hop at a time. It is a *loose* route, in that not every hop is specified, while a *strict* route would have every hop specified.

`-w timeout`

Number of milliseconds to wait for a reply before going onto the next hop.

Examples

Normal trace route:

```
tracert nic.near.net

Tracing route to nic.near.net [192.52.71.4]
over a maximum of 30 hops:

  1    10 ms   <10 ms   <10 ms  router.foo.xo.com [208.89.78.253]
  2    40 ms    20 ms    30 ms  SanFrancisco01-Max1.POP.InterNex.Net [205.158.3.52]
  3   120 ms    30 ms    30 ms  SanFrancisco01-rtr.POP.InterNex.Net [205.158.3.49]
  4    30 ms    40 ms    30 ms  205.158.2.37
  5    30 ms    50 ms   431 ms  region-1A-rtr-fddi.InterNex.Net [205.158.0.4]
  6    60 ms    60 ms    60 ms  mae-west.SanFrancisco.mci.net [198.32.136.12]
  7   230 ms   291 ms   240 ms  core1-hssi3-0.SanFrancisco.mci.net [204.70.1.205]
```

```
  8    571 ms     *       121 ms   core2-hssi-3.Boston.mci.net [204.70.1.10]
  9    130 ms    261 ms   140 ms   core2-hssi-2.Boston.mci.net [204.70.1.2]
 10    130 ms    140 ms   131 ms   core.Boston.mci.net [204.70.4.137]
 11    120 ms    150 ms   141 ms   border1-fddi-0.Boston.mci.net [204.70.2.34]
 12    150 ms    151 ms   140 ms   nearnet.Boston.mci.net [204.70.20.6]
 13    320 ms    241 ms   160 ms   cambridge2-cr3.bbnplanet.net [192.233.33.10]
 14    311 ms    360 ms     *      cambridge2-cr2.bbnplanet.net [199.92.129.2]
 15      *       831 ms   711 ms   cambridge1-cr1.bbnplanet.net [192.233.149.201]
 16    430 ms     *       240 ms   cambridge1-cr5.bbnplanet.net [206.34.78.31]
 17      *       140 ms   161 ms   nic.near.net [192.52.71.4]

Trace complete.
```

Trace route with DNS turned off:

```
tracert -d 192.52.71.4

Tracing route to 192.52.71.4 over a maximum of 30 hops

  1    <10 ms    <10 ms   <10 ms   208.89.78.253
  2    280 ms     50 ms    30 ms   205.158.3.52
  3     31 ms     30 ms    30 ms   205.158.3.49
  4     90 ms     50 ms    40 ms   205.158.2.37
  5     40 ms     40 ms    40 ms   205.158.0.4
  6     50 ms     50 ms    40 ms   198.32.136.12
  7     60 ms    230 ms   301 ms   204.70.1.205
  8    130 ms    150 ms   250 ms   204.70.1.2
  9    121 ms      *      310 ms   204.70.1.2
 10    180 ms    160 ms   221 ms   204.70.4.137
 11    320 ms    311 ms   150 ms   204.70.2.34
 12    301 ms    230 ms   250 ms   204.70.20.6
 13    561 ms    491 ms   861 ms   192.233.33.10
 14    531 ms    461 ms   380 ms   199.92.129.2
 15    862 ms    420 ms   631 ms   192.233.149.201
 16    370 ms    491 ms   601 ms   206.34.78.31
 17    501 ms    491 ms   530 ms   192.52.71.4

Trace complete.
```

Failed trace route:

```
tracert 10.0.0.1

Tracing route to 10.0.0.1 over a maximum of 30 hops

  1    <10 ms    <10 ms    10 ms   router.foo.xo.com [208.89.78.253]
  2     60 ms     20 ms    30 ms   SanFrancisco01-Max1.POP.InterNex.Net [205.158.3.52]
  3    210 ms     30 ms    30 ms   SanFrancisco01-rtr.POP.InterNex.Net [205.158.3.49]
  4     30 ms     30 ms    40 ms   205.158.2.37
  5    150 ms     40 ms    40 ms   region-1A-rtr-fddi.InterNex.Net [205.158.0.4]
  6    260 ms    350 ms   341 ms   agis-internex.santaclara.agis.net [206.62.13.17]
  7      *         *        *      Request timed out.
  8      *         *        *      Request timed out.
  9      *         *        *      Request timed out.
 10      *         *        *      Request timed out.
 11      *         *        *      Request timed out.
 12      *         *        *      Request timed out.
```

→

13	*	*	*	Request timed out.
14	*	*	*	Request timed out.
15	*	*	*	Request timed out.

For this example, the target address of the non-existent network 10 is used to generate a failure. If you see this with a valid destination, you can be pretty sure there is a routing problem with the last hop.

Notes

The *tracert* command comes from UNIX, where it is called *traceroute*. It works by utilizing the *ttl* (Time To Live) to field the ICMP echo packet. At each router or gateway, the *ttl* value is decremented before being passed on to the next hop. When an echo packet reaches an IP device with a value of 0, the device should send back an ICMP Time Exceeded packet to the source. *tracert* starts with a *ttl* of 1 and then increments it by 1 for every 3 packets sent. The 3 packets get one hop farther each time, and print out the name of each router until they reach the final destination or their *ttl* runs out.

Several things can go wrong with this process:

- There are routers that do not implement ICMP correctly. These may not appear in *tracert* output.

- There could be a problem resolving the IP address of the target or intermediate router. If DNS is not working on the local computer or there are IP addresses without a proper DNS PTR record, *tracert* may hang for several minutes trying to resolve each address. You can turn off use of DNS with -*d* option.

- There may be a routing loop or other problem. If you see the *tracert* output endlessly cycling back and forth between a pair of router addresses, there may be a routing problem. *tracert* has served its purpose in this case, but you can limit it to a reasonable number of hops using the -*h* option.

See Also

arp
ping
netstat
nbtstat
route

Requires

NT Workstation or Server
TCP/IP protocol

System Administration Commands

The System Administration commands deal with installing NT, making backups, setting file permissions, and checking system performance.

---

at

The *at* command schedules commands or *jobs* to run at a later time. The jobs can run just once or be executed regularly at certain times or days of the week.

Options

`none`	Display current *at* jobs.
`\\computer-name`	
	Name of remote computer to run the *at* job on.
`id`	Numeric *at* job identifier.
`/delete`	Delete *at* job referred to by *id*. If an *id* is not specified, all jobs on the current computer are removed.
`/yes`	Turn off prompting for confirmation before deleting job.
`time`	Set time when job is supposed to be run. Use 24-hour syntax.
`/interactive`	
	Enable interaction between an *at* job and a logged-in user.
`/every:date[,date]`	
	Run job every date listed. A date is either a day of the week (M/T/W/Th/F/S/Su) or a numeric day of the month (1–31). If *date* is not specified, it defaults to the current date.
`/next:date[,date]`	
	Run job on the next occurrence of *date*. If *date* is not specified, it defaults to the current dateday of month.
`command`	Command or batch file to be run by *at*. Enclose the command in quotes if it contains spaces.

Examples

Synchronize the time with the system *ICA* every day at midnight:

```
at 00:00 /every:M,T,W,Th,F,S,Su "cmd net time \\ica /set /yes"
Added a new job with job ID = 0
```

Check the *at* job queue:

```
at

Status ID  Day              Time       Command Line
-------------------------------------------------------------------
        0  Each M T W Th F S Su  12:00 AM   "cmd net time \\ica /set /yes"
```

Using the Command Line

Delete the *at* job id 0:

```
at 0 /delete

at
There are no entries in the list.
```

Create *at* jobs for running backups at midnight:

```
at 00:00 /every:Su "cmd ntbackup backup d:\ /a /v"
at 00:00 /every:M,T,W,Th,F,S "cmd ntbackup backup d:\ /a /v /t incremental"
```

The first job does a full backup of *D:* every Sunday, and the second does an incremental every day of the week except for Sunday.

Notes

If you get the following message:

```
at
The service has not been started.
```

you need to start the **Schedule** service:

```
net start schedule
The Schedule service is starting.
The Schedule service was started successfully.
```

at does not start the command interpreter automatically, so *cmd* has to be specified as the first command when running something other than an executable file.

If a remote computer or file system is used within an *at* command, use the UNC name (*computername**sharename*) instead of drive letters.

Requires

Schedule Service NT Workstation or Server

---

attrib

The *attrib* command changes or displays current attributes of files.

Options

filename File to be changed or examined.

none   Display attributes for specified file.

+r   Set read-only attribute. Useful for protecting users against themselves.

-r   Clear read-only attribute.

+a   Set archive attribute. Handy for marking files to be backed up.

-a   Clear archive attribute.

+s	Set system attribute.
-s	Clear system attribute.
+h	Set hidden attribute.
-h	Clear hidden attribute.
/s	Set or display attributes recursively on current directory.

Examples

List attributes of *C:\boot.ini* file:

```
attrib C:\boot.ini
A   S R    C:\boot.ini
```

From this, we can tell that *boot.ini* has the *archive, system,* and *read-only* attributes set.

Clear the *system* and *read-only* attributes so that the file may be edited:

```
attrib -s -r C:\boot.ini
 check them again...
attrib -s -r C:\boot.ini
A          C:\boot.ini
```

Edit the *boot.ini* file, then restore the previous attributes:

```
attrib +s +r C:\boot.ini
```

Requires

NT Workstation or Server

---

backup

backup [options]

The *backup* command is a very simple backup program that can write to disks or floppy drives. You will probably want to use the **Backup** administrative tool for doing system backups (it can also be run from the command line as *ntbackup*).

Options

source	Files or directories to be backed up.
destination-drive	
	Drive letter of drive used to hold backup.
/a	Appends current backup to an existing backup. The default is to overwrite any existing backup.
/d:*date*	Backup only those files that have been modified on or after *date*.
/f[:*size*]	
	backup automatically detects an unformatted disk and formats it, but the */f* option always forces a format before starting the backup. If *size* is specified, format according to this size instead of the default for the drive.

→

Using the Command Line

The possible values of *size* are listed in the following table:

Size, value, aliases	Sides	Density	Media
160 160k 160kb	SS	DD	5.25
180 180k 180kb	SS	DD	5.25
320 320k 320kb	DS	DD	5.25
360 360k 360kb	DS	DD	5.25
720 720k 720kb	DS	DD	5.25
1200 1200k 1200kb 1.2 1.2m 1.2mb	DD	QD	5.25
1440 1440k 1440kb 1.44 1.44m 1.44mb	DD	QD	3.50
2880 2880k 2880kb 2.88 2.88m 2.88mb	DD	QD	3.50

/l[:[*drive*:[*pathname*:]*logfile*]]
: Create a logfile containing a list of files that are backed up. If *drive* and/or *path* are specified, write the logfile in *path* on *drive*. The default is the root directory of the source drive. If *logfile* is specified, use *logfile* instead of *BACKUP.LOG*. The logfile will append to an existing file. Each backup is separated by a time and date stamp in the logfile.

/m
: Backup only those files that have been modified since the last backup. Disables *archive* attribute after file is backed up.

/s
: Recursively backup directories.

/t:*time*
: Backup only those files that have been modified on or after *time*.

Examples

Recursively backup the *C:\temp* directory to the floppy drive and keep a log file in *C:\temp.log*:

```
backup /s /l:C:\temp\temp.log c:\temp\ica a:

Insert backup diskette 01 in drive A:

WARNING! Files in the target drive
A: root directory will be erased
Press any key to continue . . .

*** Backing up files to drive A: ***
Diskette Number: 01

Logging to file C:\TEMP\TEMP.LOG

\TEMP\ICA\GNU\CYGWIN.DLL

Insert backup diskette 02 in drive A:

WARNING! Files in the target drive
A: root directory will be erased
```

```
*** Backing up files to drive A: ***
Diskette Number: 02

\TEMP\ICA\GNU\CYGWIN.DLL
\TEMP\ICA\GNU\GREP.EXE
\TEMP\ICA\GNU\STRINGS.EXE
\TEMP\ICA\TEMP\21TO22.EXE

backup continues...
```

Examine the logfile:

```
type temp.log
10/30/1996  16:00:31
001  \TEMP\ICA\GNU\CYGWIN.DLL
002  \TEMP\ICA\GNU\CYGWIN.DLL
002  \TEMP\ICA\GNU\GREP.EXE
002  \TEMP\ICA\GNU\STRINGS.EXE
002  \TEMP\ICA\TEMP\21TO22.EXE
```

The logfile contains the list of backed-up files, along with the floppy disk number and a date and time stamp.

See Also

> *ntbackup*
> *restore*

Requires

NT Workstation or Server

---

cacls   cacls [options]

The *cacls* command administers Access Control Lists (ACLs) for files and directories. It offers much finer control over ACLs than the GUI tools, such as **Windows NT Explorer** and **File Manager**, but it has more a complex view of permissions.

Options

filename(s)

> Display ACLs for filenames(s).

/t   Apply changes recursively. Change ACLs of specified files in current
          directory and any subdirectories.

/e   Add changes to ACL instead of overwriting previous ACL.

/c   Continue changing ACLs even when there are errors.

/g *username:right*

> Grant *username* one of the following *rights*: R for read, C for change
> (write), or F for full control.

→

←

/r username
> Revoke rights from *username*.

/p username:right
> Replace previous *right* for *username* with a new *right*. The values for rights are: N for none, R for read, C for change (write), or F for full control.

/d username
> Set user rights to NONE, explicitly denying access to the resource and overriding all other permissions for the user.

Examples

Display the ACL for the directory *D:\users\eap*:

```
cacls D:\users\eap
```

```
d:\users\eap Everyone:(CI)R                      <line 1>
             BUILTIN\Administrators:(CI)C        <line 2>
             BUILTIN\Account Operators:(CI)C     <line 3>
             NT AUTHORITY\SYSTEM:(OI)(IO)F       <line 4>
             NT AUTHORITY\SYSTEM:(CI)F           <line 5>
             HOME\eap:(OI)(IO)F                  <line 6>
             HOME\eap:(CI)F                      <line 7>
```

There are several concepts you need to understand before being able to decipher *cacls* output:

- A *Container* is a directory.

- An *Object* is a file.

- To *inherit* means to take the same rights as the parent directory.

- (OI) is *Object Inherit*. Files (*Objects*) created under this directory will inherit this right.

- (CI) is *Container Inherit*. Directories (*Containers*) created under this directory will inherit this right.

- (IO) is *Inherit Only*. This right does not apply to this directory; it only specifies what would be the inherited rights for subdirectories.

The following explanations apply for the previous example:

- Line 1: Group **Everyone** has read (R) access to the current directory and subdirectories.

- Lines 2 and 3: Built-in Groups **Administrators** and **Account Operators** have create (C) access to the current directory and subdirectories

- Line 4: **System** has Inherit-Only full control (F) access for files.

- Line 5: **System** has full control (F) access to current directory and subdirectories.

- Line 6: User *eap* in the *HOME* domain has Inherit-Only full control to files.

- Line 7: User *eap* in the *HOME* domain has full control for directory and subdirectories.

Now that was easy, right?

Give user *larryc* create rights to the *EAP* directory and any subdirectory without disturbing other ACL information:

```
cacls D:\users\eap /g larryc:C /e /t
processed dir: d:\users\eap
```

Check the rights again:

```
cacls D:\users\eap
d:\users\eap Everyone:(CI)R
             BUILTIN\Administrators:(CI)C
             BUILTIN\Account Operators:(CI)C
             NT AUTHORITY\SYSTEM:(OI)(IO)F
             NT AUTHORITY\SYSTEM:(CI)F
             HOME\eap:(OI)(IO)F
             HOME\eap:(CI)F
             HOME\larryc:(OI)(CI)C
```

Sometimes you will be prompted for confirmation for the *cacls* command:

```
cacls D:\users\eap /p larryc:f /t
Are you sure (Y/N)?
```

You can bypass this confirmation by sending a *Y* character to the *cacls* command using *echo*:

```
echo Y|cacls D:\users\eap /p larryc:f /t
Are you sure (Y/N)?processed dir: d:\users\eap
```

Make sure there is no space between the *Y* and the pipe (|) command.

Notes

The **File Manager** and **Windows NT Explorer** tend to be rather blunt tools for changing permissions. If you want to make subtle changes (especially without overwriting previous settings), mastering the *cacls* syntax is a good idea.

GUI Equivalents

Windows NT Explorer
File Manager

Requires

NT Workstation or Server
NTFS partition

chkdsk

The *chkdsk* command verifies file system integrity.

Options

none	Run *chkdisk* on the current drive.
drive:	Run *chkdsk* on drive *drive*.
pathname	Name of file(s) that *chkdsk* should try to verify.
/f	Try to fix any errors, instead of just reporting them. If an active drive is specified, *chkdsk* will run on the next reboot.
/v	Verbose mode. Print the name of every file processed.
/r	Find bad sectors and try to recover data. If an active drive is specified, *chkdsk* will run on the next reboot.

Examples

Run *chkdsk* on current drive:

```
chkdsk
The type of the file system is NTFS.
Warning! F parameter not specified
Running CHKDSK in read-only mode.

CHKDSK is verifying files...
File verification completed.
CHKDSK is verifying indexes...
Index verification completed.
CHKDSK is verifying security descriptors...
Security descriptor verification completed.

   240943 kilobytes total disk space.
     2575 kilobytes in 164 user files.
       34 kilobytes in 27 indexes.
     2877 kilobytes in use by the system.
     2416 kilobytes occupied by the logfile.
   235457 kilobytes available on disk.

      512 bytes in each allocation unit.
   481886 total allocation units on disk.
   470914 allocation units available on disk.
```

Notes

The "security descriptors" message appears only when checking an NTFS partition.

GUI Equivalents

Disk Administrator, Tools-Properties-Tools-Check Now
Windows NT Explorer, Properties-Tools-Check Now

Requires

NT Workstation or Server

cmd

The *cmd* command starts the command-line shell.

Options

none	Start up new command shell.
command	Run command in new NT command shell.
/a	Use ANSI output.
/c	Execute *command* and then exit.
/k	Execute *command* and continue running shell.
/q	Turn off echo.
/u	Use Unicode output.
/t *fb*	Set foreground color to *f* and background color to *b*. Colors are described by numeric codes in the same manner as the DOS *colors* command.
/x	Turn on Windows NT extensions to DOS command shell (the default). This affects the operation of the following commands: *del, erase, cd, chdir, md, mdir, prompt, color, pushd, popd, set, call, set local, endlocal, if, for, call, shift, goto, start, assoc,* and *ftype.*
/y	Turn off Windows NT extensions.

Requires

NT Workstation or Server

---

convert

The *convert* command converts a drive partition from FAT to NTFS. It requires either that you run the *convert* command from a drive other than the one being converted or it will do the conversion after the next reboot.

Options

drive	Drive that is going to be converted.
/fs:ntfs	Convert to NTFS
/v	Verbose display of messages from conversion process.
/nametable:*filename*	Create a table of filenames that need to be changed when converting from FAT to NTFS. This option seems to be invalid. It is contained in the NT help system but does not work.

Examples

Convert drive C: (a drive in use) from FAT to NTFS:

```
convert C: /fs:ntfs
The type of the file system is FAT. Convert cannot gain
exclusive access to the C: drive, so it cannot convert it now.
Would you like to schedule it to be converted the next time
the system restarts (Y/N)? yes
The conversion will take place automatically the next time the
```

→

system restarts.

Convert drive F: (not in use) from FAT to NTFS:

```
convert F: /fs:ntfs /v
The type of the file system is FAT.
Determining disk space required for filesystem conversion
Total disk space:                240943 kilobytes.
Free space on volume:            237612 kilobytes.
Space required for conversion:     3145 kilobytes.
Converting file system
InetPub.
    ftproot.
    gophroot.
    scripts.
        iisadmin.
            adv.htr.
            advaddd.htr.
            advadddu.htr.
            advaddg.htr.
            advaddgu.htr.
            advded.htr.
    <listing continues...>
        dialer.exe.
        hypertrm.exe.
        Windows Messaging.
            mlset32.exe.
            mlshext.dll.
Conversion complete
```

Requires

NT Workstation or Server

---

diskperf

diskperf [options]

The *diskperf* command turns disk performance counters on or off. In order for **Performance Monitor** to display disk performance data, the counters must be turned on.

Options

none	Display current status of performance counters (on or off).
-y[E]	Turn on performance counters. If you want to monitor the performance of single disks within a stripe set, use the *E* flag.
-n	Turn off performance counters.
computer-name	
	Run *diskperf* command on remote computer *computer-name*.

Examples

Examine local computer for current settings:

```
diskperf
```

```
Disk Performance counters on this system are currently set to never start.
```

Turn on Performance counters:

```
diskperf -y
```

```
Disk Performance counters on this system are now set to start at boot.
This change will take effect after the system is restarted.
```

Notes

The *-yE* option allows striped or mirrored disk set performance to be monitored for each individual drive in the set. If the *E* option is not specified, only the performance of the entire set is monitored.

See Also

Performance Monitor
Disk Administrator

Requires

NT Workstation or Server

---

ntbackup

<code>ntbackup [options]</code>

The *ntbackup* command can be used to backup the entire computer to tape media. It allows several different types of backup operations, including a full system backup, backing up only files that have changed since a previous backup, and backup of the system registry. Not all of the operations are available from the command line. You will have to use the GUI version to restore files. The main reason for the command-line version is the ability to do unattended backups using the *at* command.

Options

none	Starts the GUI version of *ntbackup*.
backup	The operation being performed (the only other valid operation is ejecting the tape).
eject	Eject tape (if tape drive supports operation).
path	A list of one or more directories that should be backed up.
/a	Append this backup set to previous backup sets that exist on backup media. The default action is to overwrite (replace).
/v	Verify the backup (read back the backup and compare it with the disk files).
/r	Restricts access to backup tape to owner, Administrator, and Backup Operators Group.
/d text	Use *text* as a description of the backup set on the tape.

$\rightarrow$

/b   Backup the Registry of the local computer as part of the backup set. The drive containing the Registry must be specified as part of the backup. You cannot use this option to backup a remote computer's Registry.

/hc:[on|off]

     Turn hardware compression on or off (for drives that support this).

/nopoll   Erase tape. This prompts the user for confirmation, so this command should not be used in an *at* job or batch file.

/missingtape

     Tell *ntbackup* that part of tape backup set is missing and to treat every tape as an individual backup.

/t type   Specifies backup *type*. *Type* can be one of the following:

copy

     Backup all specified files, but do not mark them as backed up. This prevents other backup operations (such as daily, incremental, and differential) from knowing that the files were backed up and disturbing your backup strategy.

daily

     Backup all specified files that have been modified on the same day as the backup. Does not mark files as backed up.

differential

     Backup specified files that have been modified since last normal or incremental backup. Files are not marked as backed up.

incremental

     Backup specified files that have been modified since last normal or incremental backup.

normal

     Backup all specified files and mark them as backed up (default type). By using a combination of backup types, you can tailor the backup strategy to what is most important to you: fast backups, less frequent tape changing, or fast restores.

/l logfile

     Store a logfile in *filename*. The logfile will contain a list of all files and directories backed up and any errors.

/e   Store only error information in logfile.

/tape:[drive]

     Tape device to use for backup. If you have more than one drive, you can specify a drive by a *drive* number (0–9).

Examples

Backup the entire *D:\temp* directory, verify the backup after it is completed, label the backup set as "temp dir", and store a log in *backup.log*:

```
ntbackup backup d:\temp /v /d "temp dir" /l "backup.log"
```

After some files in *D:\temp* have modified, do an incremental backup and append it to the previous backup set:

```
ntbackup backup d:\temp /v /d "temp dir" /l "backup.log" /t incremental
```

Create *at* jobs for running backups at midnight:

```
at 00:00 /every:Su "cmd ntbackup backup d:\ /a /v"
at 00:00 /every:M,T,W,Th,F,S "cmd ntbackup backup d:\ /a /v /t incremental"
```

The first job does a full backup of *D:* every Sunday, and the second does an incremental every day of the week except for Sunday.

Notes

When running *ntbackup* from within a batch file, only directory names can be specified on the command line. No wildcard characters can be used within the batch file.

The incremental, daily, and normal backup types clear the *A* (archive) attribute on the directory or file being backed up. If the file is modified or a new file is created, it will have the archive attribute set, enabling *ntbackup* to find it for the next incremental, daily, or differential operation.

See Also

attrib
backup
restore

GUI Equivalents

Backup

Requires

NT Workstation or Server

---

rdisk

The *rdisk* command creates Emergency Repair Disks (ERDs) that can be used to recover a damaged NT installation.

Options

none	Start up Emergency Repair Disk dialog box.
/s	Bypass confirmation and save system configuration information to *<winnt root>\REPAIR* directory. Then prompt user about creating an ERD.
/s-	Just save system configuration to repair directory and exit (without prompt for ERD).

Notes

<winnt root>/REPAIR directory, which is the same action as selecting the **Update Repair Info** button. Once this is done, the contents of the directory can be copied to the ERD floppy. If the */s* option is specified, the SAM and SECURITY hives are also backed up to the *<winnt root>/REPAIR* directory and are available for copying to the ERD.

→

rdisk

←

Requires

NT Workstation or Server

---

regedit

regedit *[options]*

The *regedit* command is the Windows 95–style Registry editor. It has several useful command-line options for reading or writing Registry files.

Options

`none`   Start GUI version

`/s`   Run *regedit* silently, suppressing informational messages. This is useful when *regedit* is run from a script or batch file.

`source-file`
    Import Registry file, merging or adding new information.

`/e`   Export Registry contents into *filename*. The optional *regpath* can be used to limit the output to a specific Registry key.

Examples

Export contents of *HKEY_LOCAL_MACHINE\SYSTEM\CurrentControlSet* to file *ccs.reg*:

```
regedit /e ccs.reg HKEY_LOCAL_MACHINE\SYSTEM\CurrentControlSet
```

The resulting text file can be edited with any text editor:

```
REGEDIT4

[HKEY_LOCAL_MACHINE\SYSTEM\CurrentControlSet]

[HKEY_LOCAL_MACHINE\SYSTEM\CurrentControlSet\Control]
"WaitToKillServiceTimeout"="20000"
"CurrentUser"="USERNAME"
"SystemStartOptions"=""


        continues...
```

It can then be imported back into the Registry:

```
regedit ccs.reg
```

Notes

It is extremely easy to make mistakes when using **Explorer** to browse Registry data files. For example, if you happen to double-click on a file with a *.reg* extension, the file will be imported into the Registry without any warning or confirmation.

Normally, *regedit* will produce a popup message saying "Information in *filename* has been successfully entered into the Registry" when a file has been imported. The */s* option is useful for suppressing this when *regedit* is run from a script or batch file.

See Also

Regedt32

Requires

NT Workstation or Server

---

restore   restore [options]

The *restore* command restores files from a backup made with the *backup* command.

Options

source-drive
> Drive that contains backup to be restored.

destination-drive
> Drive where backup should be restored.

destination-path
> Path where backup files will be restored. This has to be identical to the path used when creating the backup.

filename(s)
> A list of filenames that you wish restored. If none are specified, all files in the backup will be restored.

/s   Recursively restore directories.

/p   Ask user for confirmation before overwriting any read-only files or files with *archive* attribute set.

/b:date Restore only those files last modified on or before *date*.

/a:date Restore only those files last modified on or after *date*.

/e:time Restore only those files last modified at or before *time*.

/t:time Restore only those files last modified at or after *time*.

/m   Restore those files last modified since last backup.

/n   Restore those files that would not overwrite any files on destination drive.

/d   Print a list of files contained in the backup that match *filename(s)*. You have to specify a *destination-drive* even though nothing is written to it.

Examples

Recursively restore backup from floppy onto drive *D:*

```
restore a: d: /s
Insert backup diskette 01 in drive A:
Press any key to continue . . .
*** Files where backed up 10-30-1996 ***
*** Restoring files from drive A: ***
Diskette: 01
```

$\rightarrow$

```
\TEMP\ICA\GNU\CYGWIN.DLL
\TEMP\ICA\GNU\GREP.EXE
\TEMP\ICA\GNU\STRINGS.EXE

Insert backup diskette 02 in drive A:
Press any key to continue . . .
Diskette: 02

\TEMP\ICA\GNU\STRINGS.EXE
\TEMP\ICA\TEMP\21TO22.EXE
```

See Also
backup
ntbackup

Requires
NT Workstation or Server

---

start

The *start* command starts applications from the command line. It has several options that control the appearance, environment, and priority for the application.

Options

`none`	Open an application line window.
`application [parameters]`	
	Run *application* with optional *parameters.*
`window title`	
	Set title of application line window.
`/dpath`	Specify startup directory for application.
`/i`	Pass existing environment to new window.
`/min`	Start window minimized.
`/max`	Start window maximized.
`/separate`	
	Start 16-bit application in separate memory space.
`/shared`	Start 16-bit application in shared memory space.
`/low`	Start application with a low priority (idle class).
`/normal`	Start application with a normal priority (normal class).
`/high`	Start application with a high priority (high class).
`/realtime`	
	Start application with a higher priority (realtime class).
`/wait`	Start application and return control to the existing window until the application finishes.
`/b`	Start application in existing window.

Examples

Start a new window with the title "keepalive" and run the *ping* command:

```
start "keepalive" ping -t microsoft.com
```

Requires

NT Workstation or Server

---

winnt

The *winnt* command is the 16-bit NT installation utility. It can be used to install Windows NT on a computer currently running MS-DOS, Windows 3.1, Windows for Workgroups, or Windows 95. It is usually executed from the CD-ROM installation media or a network drive. It is possible to automate most of the NT installation process by using *winnt* to read various datafiles that specify information that would normally have to be entered by hand.

Options

/b　　　Copy boot files to hard drive instead of floppies: this takes less time than loading multiple floppies at boot time. The help file indicates that /b requires the /s option, but this is apparently not true.

/c　　　Do not check boot floppies for amount of free space before copying boot files to them.

/e: *command*
　　　Run *command* after installation is complete.

/f　　　Do not verify boot floppies after they are created.

/i:*inf-file*
　　　Use specified *.INF* file *inf-file* for installation. Default is *dosnet.inf.*

/ox　　　Force creation of boot floppies (the default).

/u[:*script-file*]
　　　Use settings of current NT installation for upgrade process, allowing it to run unattended. If a *script-file* or Uniqueness Database File (UDF) is specified, read settings from this file instead of the current system. This option requires that you specify the location of the NT installation files with /s.

/r:*directory*
　　　Creates *directory* on installed system.

/rx:*directory*
　　　Copies *directory* to installed system.

/s:*directory*
　　　Location of NT installation files.

/t:*drive-letter*
　　　Drive *drive-letter* should be used to store temporary files used during installation.

/x　　　Do not create boot floppies.

→

Examples

Install NT 4.0 on an Intel-based PC from a CD-ROM (D:), using unattended mode and floppy-less installation:

```
cd d:\i386
winnt /b /u /s:d:\i386
```

See Also

Microsoft Windows NT Workstation Resource Kit:
    Chapter 2, *Customizing Setup*, and Appendix A, *Answer Files and UDFs*
sysdiff utility

Requires

NT Workstation or Server

---

winnt32

The *winnt32* command is the 32-bit NT installation utility. It can be used to upgrade a computer currently running Windows NT to a newer version. It is usually executed from the CD-ROM installation media or network drive. It is possible to automate most of the NT installation by using *winnt32* to read various data files that specify information that would normally be hand-entered.

Options

/b
    Copy boot files to hard drive instead of floppies. This saves time over loading multiple floppies at boot time.

/e: *command*
    Run *command* after installation is complete.

/i:*inf-file*
    Use specified *.INF* file *inf-file* for installation. Default is *dosnet.inf*.

/ox
    Force creation of boot floppies (the default).

/u[:*script-file*]
    Use settings of current NT installation for upgrade process, allowing it to run unattended. If a *script-file* or Uniqueness Database File (UDF) is specified, read settings from this file instead of the current system. This option requires that you specify the location of the NT installation files with */s*.

/r:*directory*
    Creates *directory* on installed system.

/s:*directory*
    Location of NT installation files.

/t:*drive-letter*
    Drive *drive-letter* should be used to store temporary files used during installation.

/x
    Do not create boot floppies.

Upgrade an Intel-based PC from NT 3.51 to 4.0 from CD-ROM (D:), using unattended mode with current NT settings:

```
cd d:\i386
winnt32 /b /u
```

See Also

Microsoft Windows NT Workstation Resource Kit:
> Chapter 2, *Customizing Setup*, and Appendix A, *Answer Files and UDFs*
sysdiff utility

Requires

NT Workstation or Server

RAS Commands

The RAS commands administer Dial-Up Networking and RAS functions. This
includes starting, stopping, and checking the status of RAS connections.

---

rasadmin   rasadmin [options]

The *rasadmin* command can control the startup behavior of the **Remote Access
Admin** administrative tool.

Options

none   Start up **Remote Access Admin** GUI with default settings.

domain|server
> Administer *domain* or *server* upon startup. This is equivalent to
> starting **Remote Access Admin** and using the **Server-Select Domain** or
> **Server** menu item.

/l   Set low-speed mode, disabling browsing of domains and usernames.
> This is useful when using **Remote Access Admin** to administer a
> remote domain or server on the other side of a low-speed connec-
> tion. This option has the same effect as selecting the **Options-Slow
> Speed Connection** menu item.

/h   Set high-speed mode (the default), enabling browsing of domains
> and usernames. This option has the same effect as deselecting the
> **Options-Slow Speed Connection** menu item.

Examples

Administer the remote RAS server *NTSERVER1* using a low-speed connection:

```
rasadmin \\NTSERVER1 /l
```

Reset *rasadmin* back to high-speed mode:

```
rasadmin /h
```

→

Notes

The *rasadmin* command, like other administration tools, remembers the low-speed settings from the last time it was used. It must be changed manually using the **Options-Slow Speed Connection** menu item or from the command line using */l* or */h*.

You may see references to setting the *focus*. The focus is the domain or computer you are administering.

See Also

<winnt root>\SYSTEM32\RAS\RASPHONE.HLP

GUI Equivalents

Remote Access Admin

Requires

NT Workstation or Server
Remote Access Service (RAS)

---

rasautou   rasautou [options]

The *rasautou* command can be used to debug problems with RAS autodialing. RAS can be configured to autodial certain sites when they are referenced from an application (such as a web browser). If RAS autodials when you do not want it to, or does not dial when it should, *rasautou* can be used to display all the sites that are configured for autodialing.

Options

- s   List addresses and names remembered by RAS Autodial.

Examples

List all autodial locations:

```
rasautou -s
Checking netcard bindings...
NetworkConnected: network (\Device\NetBT_E1001, 0) is up

Enumerating AutoDial addresses...
There are 2 Autodial addresses:

ftp.ora.com

204.139.200.1
```

This output indicates that autodialing will take place whenever the two sites are referenced.

NT Workstation or Server
Remote Access Service (RAS)

---

rasdial

The *rasdial* command can initiate or disconnect a RAS session from the command line. The RAS session can be either a conventional PPP/SLIP session or a PPTP session on top of an existing connection.

Options

`none`   List any active RAS sessions.

`session-name`
    Name of phonebook entry to dial.

`username` Username to be used to log on to remote system.

`password|*`
    Password for remote system. If * is specified, prompt user for password.

`/disconnect`
    Hangup session. If more than one session is active, specify a *session-name*. This can be shorted to */d*.

`/domain:domain`
    NT domain name of remote RAS server onto which you are logging.

`/phone:number`
    Phone number of remote system. When using PPTP, this is the IP address of the remote system.

`/callback:number`
    Callback number to be used by remote system to call your modem.

`/phonebook:file`
    Name of alternate phonebook file to be used to lookup *session-name*. The default phonebook file is *<winnt root>\SYSTEM32\RAS \RASPHONE.PBK*.

`/prefixsuffix`
    If you have a prefix or suffix configured for this site in the GUI Dial-Up Networking application, the */prefixsuffix* option will use these when dialing *session-name* with *rasdial*.

Examples

Connect to remote system *ORA* and specify a different phone number than the one in the phonebook file:

```
rasdial ora /phone:18005551212
Connecting to ORA...
Verifying username and password...
Registering your computer on the network...
Successfully connected to ORA.
Command completed successfully.
```

$\rightarrow$

rasdial

←

Connect to a PPTP server and specify a different IP address than the one in the phonebook file:

```
rasdial oravpn /phone:208.26.94.3
```

Check which systems are currently connected:

```
rasdial
Connected to
ora
```

Disconnect from remote system *ORA*:

```
rasdial /d
Command completed successfully.
```

Notes

If you have configured the GUI version of Dial-Up Networking to prompt you for the username and password via the Connect To dialog box, you must supply the username and password on the command line with *rasdial*.

If you get the following error when initiating a PPTP session:

```
Remote Access error 678 - There is no answer.
```

the PPTP server at the IP address may be unreachable or not running RAS with PPTP ports enabled.

GUI Equivalents
Dial-Up Networking

Requires
NT Workstation or Server
Remote Access Service (RAS)
Point to Point Tunneling protocol (for PPTP capability)

---

rasphone   rasphone [options]

The *rasphone* command can edit the contents of RAS phonebook files and start, stop, and display status of RAS sessions.

Options

none	Start Dial-Up Networking dialog box.
entry	Name of entry to perform operation on.
-a	Bring up dialog for adding a new entry.
-e	Edit an existing entry.
-c	Clone an existing entry.
-f pathname	

Use phonebook file stored in *pathname* instead of the default phonebook.

-v	Prevent entry from being renamed with *-a* or *-e* option This "greys out" the entry name in the dialog box.
-d	Dial entry.
-h	Hang up entry.
-r	Remove entry.
-s	Status of entry.

-1x *shortcut*

Execute command *x* on *shortcut* file. Command is any of the following: *a, e, v, c, d, b,* or *r.*

Examples

Dial entry *work* stored in phonebook file *temp**mybook.pbk:*

```
rasphone -f \temp\mybook.pbk -d work
```

Dial entry named by shortcut file *winnt**profiles**eap**desktop**ora.rnk:*

```
rasphone -1d \winnt\profiles\eap\desktop\ora.rnk
```

See Also
rasdial

GUI Equivalents
Dial-Up Networking

Requires
NT Workstation or Server
Remote Access Service (RAS)

Miscellaneous Commands

This section describes commands that do not fit into the previous categories.

convlog

convlog *[options]*

The *convlog* command processes logfiles generated by the Microsoft Internet Information Server (IIS), FTP server, and Gopher server. It can produce log files in either NCSA or EMWAC formats.

Options

-s[f|g|w]

Process specific log entries for specific services. The services are FTP (*f*), Gopher (*g*), and WWW (*w*).

-t[emwac|ncsa[:GMT offset]|none]

Produce output files in either EMWAC or NCSA formats, with an optional GMT time offset.

-o *outputdir*

Write output to *outputdir.* Output filenames are generated automatically and are prefixed by *HS* for EMWAC format and *NCSA* for NCSA format.

→

-f *inputdir*
　　　　Read logfiles from *inputdir.*
-n[m:[cachesize]|i]
　　　　When producing EMWAC files, set size of cache used for processing
　　　　and toggle conversion of IP addresses to hostnames on or off. The
　　　　default cache size is 5000 and IP conversion is on by default.
-d[m:cachesize]]
　　　　When producing NCSA files, set size of cache used for processing.
-h　　　　Print help screen.

Examples

Convert WWW logfiles in the current directory into NCSA format and store
them in the *D:\wwwlog* directory:

```
convlog -sw -t ncsa -o d:\wwwlog in*.log

Opening file in970417.log for processing
        Writing file d:\wwwlog\NCSA970417.log.
            file d:\wwwlog\NCSA970417.log already exists, adding data to it.
in970417.log completed, 32 lines processed.
32 Web lines written

Totals:
======

Total Lines Processed:        32
Total Web Lines Written:      32
```

Notes

The *convlog* command is in the *<winnt root>\SYSTEM32\INETSRV* directory,
which is not normally in the command path. You can add it using the **Environment** tab of the **System** control panel.

Requires

NT Workstation (Peer Web Services)
NT Server (Internet Information Server)

---

ipxroute   ipxroute [options]

The *ipxroute* command administers routes for the IPX protocol. It can also list IPX
parameters that are useful for debugging connectivity problems. Some of the
options are useful only for token-ring networks.

Options

none　　　Display current route settings for Default Node, Broadcast, and Mul-
　　　　ticast address types (either SINGLE ROUTE or ALL ROUTES).

```
servers [/type=SAP-type]
```
> Display a list of Novell servers and their Service Access Points (SAP). This is similar to the NetWare *slist* command. The display can be limited to a specific SAP number with the *type* option.

```
stats [/show][/clear]
```
> Display statistics for IPX routing. The */clear* option resets the statistics to zero.

```
table
```
Display IPX routing table.

```
board=n
```
Display routes for specific *board* (network interface).

```
clear
```
Clear source routing table for *board.*

```
def
```
Set Default Node addresses to ALL ROUTES (default is SINGLE ROUTE).

```
gbr
```
Set Broadcast addresses to ALL ROUTES (default is SINGLE ROUTE).

```
mbr
```
Set Multicast addresses to ALL ROUTES (default is SINGLE ROUTE).

```
remove=mac-address
```
> Remove *mac-address* from routing table.

```
config
```
Display IPX bindings for each interface.

Examples

List all NetWare servers:

```
ipxroute servers

NWLink IPX Routing and Source Routing Control Program v2.00


IPX Address               Server Type    Server Name
-------------------------------------------------------
00000001.00aa00a584ef     1600           ICA
00000001.00aa00a584ef     4              ICA_FPNW
32970f67.000000000001     4              NWSRV312
```

Each service being offered by a server is advertised with a SAP number. You can look for specific services by specifying the SAP type.

List just NetWare file servers (SAP type 4):

```
ipxroute servers /type=4

NWLink IPX Routing and Source Routing Control Program v2.00


IPX Address               Server Name
-----------------------------------------
00000001.00aa00a584ef     ICA_FPNW
32970f67.000000000001     NWSRV312
```

List network number, frame type, and network adapter for each IPX network:

```
ipxroute config

NWLink IPX Routing and Source Routing Control Program v2.00

IPX internal network number 12345678
net 1: network number 00000002, frame type 802.3, device AMDPCN1 (080009c76e6a)
net 2: network number 00000004, frame type ethernet ii, device AMDPCN1 (080009c76e6a)
net 3: network number 00000001, frame type 802.3, device SMCISA3 (0000c024588a)
```

→

This computer has two network adapters that use the IPX protocol, *AMDPCN1* and *SMCISA3*. The first adapter is using two different frame types, 802.3 and ETHERNET_II.

List route table:

```
ipxroute table

NWLink IPX Routing and Source Routing Control Program v2.00

Net Number        Ticks      Hops    Interface Net Number    Interface ID
---------------------------------------------------------------------------
00000001            1          1        00000001                  3
00000002            1          1        00000002                  1
00000004            1          1        00000004                  2
12345678            1          1        00000000                  0
```

Notes

IPX internal network numbers and external network numbers have to be unique on the network. Each frame type also has to have a network number. Most IPX services have an auto-detect capability, but this is sometimes unreliable. When you are setting up a new computer that is going to use the IPX protocol, you can use *ipxroute* to find out what network numbers and frame types are currently in use on the network. This way, you can specify new network numbers that do not conflict with existing ones and know what frame types to expect.

If you have access to a NetWare server that you are trying to reach, you can run the *config* command on the console or examine the *AUTOEXEC.NCF* file for frame types and internal and external network numbers.

Example *config* output:

```
IPX internal network number: 32870F67

AMD PCNTNW
   Frame type: ETHERNET_802.3
   LAN Protocol: IPX network 00000099
```

Example *AUTOEXEC.NCF*:

```
ipx internal net 32970F67
load C:PCNTNW port=ffe0 int=9 frame=ETHERNET_802.3
bind IPX to PCNTNW net=99
```

Cisco provides a useful list of NetWare SAP types on the Web at the URL *http://www.cisco.com/warp/public/111/9.html*.

Requires

IPX Protocol

RIP for NwLink IPX/SPX service (for routing)

The *jetpack* command compacts WINS databases. The WINS database can over time take up a significant amount of disk space. This is largely unimportant under NT 4.0, as the database is compacted automatically by the system. In NT 3.51 and earlier versions of NT, the database required manual compaction. The *jetpack* command is still included in NT 4.0 and can be run from the command line. It copies the WINS database to a temporary file, deletes the original file, and renames the temporary file back to the original filename. If you are doing this manually, stop the WINS service while running *jetpack*.

Options

database-name
> Name of WINS database file.

temp-database
> Name of temporary file used during compaction.

-351db   Use NT 3.51 WINS database format (default is 4.0 format).

Examples
Compact the WINS database manually:

```
net stop wins    stop WINS service
The Windows Internet Name Service service is stopping.
The Windows Internet Name Service service was stopped successfully.


jetpack wins.mdb tmp.mdb
Compacted database wins.mdb in 0.741 seconds.
moving tmp.mdb => wins.mdb
jetpack completed successfully.


net start wins    restart WINS service
The Windows Internet Name Service service is starting.
The Windows Internet Name Service service was started successfully.
```

Notes
If you are getting the following error:

```
jetpack failed with error = -106
```

you may be using a 3.51 WINS database on a 4.0 system. The WINS database changed between NT 3.51 and 4.0. Normally, an existing WINS database is converted to the 4.0 format as part of the upgrade process. If you are working a 3.51 format WINS database on a 4.0 system, use the *-351db* option with *jetpack*:

```
jetpack -351db wins.mdb tmp.mdb
```

Requires
NT Server
Windows Internet Name Service (WINS)
TCP/IP protocol

netmon

The *netmon* command starts the **Network Monitor** tool, which listens on network interfaces, captures network packets, and displays the packets in a raw form. It also provides network performance reports and can identify heavy network users. Several options can be specified on the command line to force **Network Monitor** to start capturing data.

Options

none   Start GUI version of **Network Monitor** normally.

/autostart
            Start capturing data immediately.

/autostop
            Stop capturing when capture buffer is full.

/buffersize:*size*
            Set size of capture buffer.

/capturefilter:*path*
            Start *netmon* with specified capture filter.

/displayfilter:*path*
            Start *netmon* with specified display filter.

/net:*number*
            Capture data from network specified by number.

/quickfilter:*path*
            Start immediately capturing using filter.

/remote:*name*
            Connect to remote **Network Monitor Agent**.

Examples

Start capturing and automatically stop when the capture buffer is full:

    netmon /autostart /autostop

Connect to the **Network Monitor Agent** running on the remote computer *ICA* and capture traffic from its network adaptor:

    netmon /autostart /remote:ica

GUI Equivalents

Network Monitor

Requires

NT Server
Network Monitor Agent and Tools service

---

pax

The *pax* command reads and writes file archives in several different formats. *pax* is part of the POSIX specification and is meant to allow archives to be moved between different operating systems (such as UNIX and Windows NT). It preserves file permissions and modification times within the archive. *pax* has a fairly complex mechanism for selecting files and changing their names based on a *regular expression* syntax borrowed from UNIX. *pax* is a real "kitchen-sink" command with lots of potentially confusing options. The Windows NT implementation is limited to reading and writing files to disk. This means that you cannot perform the operations directly to tapes or other media.

pax has four basic modes of operation:

List mode
> Display a list of files contained within an archive. This is analogous the to the -*v* option to *pkunzip* or -*t* to *tar* or *cpio*.

Read mode
> Extract files from an archive.

Write mode
> Write files to an archive.

Copy mode
> Act as a simple copy program, copying files or directories from one location to another.

All four modes allow you to change the filenames as the files are processed by *pax*. Filename conventions vary between systems, so this feature can be quite useful.

pax requires that pathnames must be specified in the POSIX syntax. For NT users, this means that *C:\WINNT\SYSTEM32* becomes *//C/WINNT/SYSTEM32*.

Options

pathname Either a source directory for the copy operation or a file containing a list of files to be copied.

directory
> Destination directory for copy operation.

pattern A *regular expression* that selects files by their pathnames for the selected operation.

-a   Append files to an existing archive.

-b blocking-factor
> Set blocking factor. This is the number of bytes written in a write operation to an archive. There are optional suffix characters that act as multipliers for the blocking factor: a trailing *k* indicates the blocking factor is expressed in kilobytes, and an *m* indicates megabytes. The -*b* option is most useful when working with tape devices, which you cannot access with this implementation.

-c   Reverse meaning of *pattern* or any files listed on the command line. Instead of using these files, use every file *except* these.

-d   Do not recursively copy, archive, or extract directories if a directory name is encountered during a *pax* operation.

-f archive-name
> Use *archive-name* for reading or writing instead of standard input or standard output (the default).

$\rightarrow$

-i   Turn on interactive file renaming. Prompt the user for the new filename as each file is processed. Entering an empty line leaves the file unchanged.

-l   Link files instead of copying them (if possible).

-m   Do not preserve file modification times.

-o   Preserve file ownership and permissions.

-p   Preserve file access times.

-r   Read an archive and extract those files that match *pattern*.

-rw   Use copy mode. Copy files and directories from *pathname* to *directory*. If the *-s* flag is specified, alter the pathnames of the files being copied according to *expression*.

-s *expression*

Use *regular-expression syntax* to alter filenames as they are copied. The expression has the following syntax:

      -s/*old*/*new*/[gp]

The *-s* option is followed by a delimiter character, such as a forward slash, then the *old* string being replaced, another delimiter, and then the *new* replacement string, another delimiter, and, optionally, the *g* or *p* characters. The *p* character *prints* a count of how many substitutions were made as a result of the *-s* command. The *g* character makes the replacement *global*, replacing every occurrence of the *old* string with the *new* string. You can use almost any character as the delimiter instead of a slash, as long as the character does not appear within the *old* or *new* string.

-t *device*

Use *device* for read or write operation instead of standard input or standard output.

-u   When copying a file with the same name as an existing file, do this only if the existing file is older than the file being copied.

-w   Write files and directories to an archive.

-v   Print a list of filenames as files are processed.

-x *format*

Set the archive format when writing. *pax* auto-detects the format when reading.

-y   Confirm filename modification. The user is prompted for each rename operation.

Examples

Copy contents of directory *one* to directory *two:*

```
pax -rw one two
```

Create an archive of the *stuff* directory in the *pax, tar,* and *cpio* formats:

```
pax -w -f stuff.pax stuff
pax -w -f stuff.tar -x ustar stuff
pax -w -f stuff.cpi -x cpio stuff
```

Extract the archives on a UNIX system using the *pax, tar,* and *cpio* commands:

```
% pax -r -f stuff.pax -v
% tar xvf stuff.tar
% cpio -i -d -I stuff.cpi
```

Notes

The UNIX heritage of *pax* may cause some grief among NT users by its use of UNIX regular expressions and filename conventions.

Requires

NT Workstation or Server

CHAPTER 7

Uncommon Sense

The following section describes various procedures that may not be intuitive to the new or casual user of NT. It also gives some examples of how to use the available tools in roles for which they were never intended or designed.

Installing and Maintaining Software

If you are the type of administrator who likes to run the latest software version, you are going to be installing or reinstalling software frequently. There are some procedures you can use to speed up the process and make sure you are always up to date.

Installing Software

Most people install NT in several stages. The first stage is usually getting the base OS onto the computer and configuring it to the point where you can logon. The second stage involves making the system useful, which includes creating user accounts, shares, and printers, and installing optional software to connect to remote computers over the network. You can greatly speed up the second stage by first copying the contents of the distribution CD-ROM onto your local hard drive. For Intel-based PCs, this means copying the entire \I386 directory to the hard disk. An easy way to do this would be to use **Windows NT Explorer** to drag the \I386 from the CD-ROM and drop it on the drive letter of your first disk. Once you have a local copy made, you no longer need the CD-ROM for most administrative tasks. When you need to install software, just use the hard disk path instead of the CD-ROM. The first time you do this, it will prompt you for the path (say *C:\I386*), but it will remember it for subsequent installs. When you need a printer driver or a network service, you can quickly install it off your local hard drive.

Service Packs

Microsoft distributes patches and fixes for NT in the *bussys/winnt/winnt-pub-lic/fixes* directory on *ftp.microsoft.com*. When a large enough group of patches is required, they are bundled in a service pack. In most cases, you will always want to install the latest service pack version. The service pack version is displayed during the boot process and is available online in the **Version** tab of **Windows NT Diagnostics** or the Help-About window of most tools. There have been problems with service packs, so it is probably wise to wait a week after a service pack release and check newsgroups and mailing lists for feedback.

Note the following points about service packs:

- The service packs released so far can be applied to either Workstation or Server.

- Service packs are cumulative, which means you only have to install the latest version.

- Service packs modify only the software that is currently installed. If you install optional software off the CD-ROM after a service pack has been applied, you must reapply the service pack.

As with the NT distribution, you may save time by keeping a local copy of the service pack on the system. This way, you can easily reapply the service pack after installing additional software over the life of the system.

Troubleshooting NT

When something is going wrong with your system, it can be hard to find out what is causing the problem. In most cases, this will be software, but it could also be hardware or the network connected to your computer.

Event Viewer

When something goes wrong, the first place you should look is **Event Viewer**. It displays informational and error messages generated by the operating system, applications, and security-related *events*. The messages recorded in **Event Viewer** are sometimes cryptic or misleading, but you can usually figure out what is going on by using a combination of **Event Viewer** and other tools.

One really annoying feature of **Event Viewer** is that events are not displayed in real time. If you want to see events as they occur, you have to manually refresh the event display by repeatedly hitting the F5 key.

If you look at the security log and there are no recorded events, it is likely that you have not enabled the auditing of security events. Go to the **Policies-Audit** menu of **User Manager** and enable the events you want audited. From this point on, every time one of the selected events occurs, an entry will appear in the security log.

The first time you look at **Event Viewer**, it will likely be filled with events that you are not interested in. You can limit the event display to certain criteria using the **View-Filter Events** menu. Try turning off the display of information events first. If you are trying to locate a specific event that may be related to the problem you are having, you can match the *Time* field with the time frame during which you experienced the problem. By default, the order of the events is from the most to least recent events. You can spot machine reboots by looking for the informational events with the *Source* field set to *Eventlog* and the contents "The Event Log service was started." This is always the first event after a reboot, as no events can be recorded until the **Eventlog** service is started.

GUI Versus Commands

In general, if an application fails or hangs in the GUI, see if there is a command version available. For example, if you are trying to browse the network via **Network Neighborhood**, and all you get is an hourglass symbol, try using the *net view* command in the DOS shell. The shell commands may still hang for a while, but they generally give you more information about the problem than the GUI.

Task Manager

If the entire computer becomes unresponsive or just slow, **Task Manager** may help in determining the cause. Hit CONTROL-ALT-DELETE and select **Task Manager** or right-click on the Task Bar. Look in the **Status** field of the **Applications** tab for a task that is not responding. The **End Task** button will kill off the selected task. The **Processes** tab may display a process that is taking up much more *CPU Time* or *Mem Usage* than others. This may be the process that is running wild and slowing down the machine. The **End Process** button will kill off the selected process.

Performance Monitor

Performance Monitor can also indicate which subsystem is causing the problem, but it is very GUI-intensive, and may be too difficult to get running on a machine that is just crawling along. **Performance Monitor** is very useful for performance tuning and analysis of subtle system or network problems.

Pmon

The **Pmon** utility gives a real-time display of processes and what resources they are using, similar to **Task Manager**. It is in the directory *SUPPORT\DEBUG\I386* on the Windows NT CD-ROM.

QuickSlice

The **QuickSlice** utility included with the Resource Kit is handy for spotting processes or services that are grabbing all your resources. It uses a bar graph to display resource usage, allowing you to spot a process that is getting more attention than others.

Stopping Services

You may also be able to use the *net stop* or *net pause* commands to stop or pause services to see what effect this has on performance. If the system is too sluggish to run the **Services** control panel, try running *net start* from the command line to get a list of currently running services.

Rebooting

If you just give up and reboot, you lose the opportunity to find out what is causing the problem and fix it. You also risk the wrath of everyone who is depending on the NT machine, if it is providing a critical function such as web serving, routing, or Internet connectivity.

Account Creation

The standard way to administer users and groups with an NT system or domain is with the **User Manager** application in the **Administrative Tools** menu.

Selection Methods

Since using a GUI interface can be mouse- and keyboard-intensive, **User Manager** has several methods of *selecting* multiple accounts (or groups) that will save time and effort when compared with administering accounts individually. Once a list of accounts is selected, options in the **User** menu take effect on all selection list members.

SHIFT-Click and CONTROL-Click
You can manually add accounts to the selection list by using the SHIFT and CONTROL keys while clicking the mouse.

To select a contiguous list of accounts, select the first account, and then hold down the SHIFT key while selecting the last account with the mouse. All accounts between the first and last will be selected.

To select a non-contiguous list of accounts, select the first, and then hold down the CONTROL key while clicking on any other accounts. The currently selected accounts will remain selected as you add more accounts to the selection list.

Groups
The **User-Select Users** menu option can be used to select users by group membership. If you are thinking ahead while adding new accounts, you can put them in groups that will aid the selection process later. For example, if you know a user is going to be working in a certain department, you can create a departmental group and put the user in it. When you need to perform some operation on all the department accounts, you will have a ready-made method of selecting all department members.

Account Templates

If you created several accounts with common attributes, such as group membership, password policies, and other account-specific information, you can speed up this process by using a *template account*, following these steps:

1. Create a template account with a username such as **Template User** and set all of the attributes that are common to the series of accounts that you are about to create.

2. Check the **Account Disabled** box so no one could actually use the template account to gain access to the system.

3. Put the template user in the appropriate groups.

4. Close the Add User window and select the template account you just created.

5. Select the **User-Copy** menu item. A new Add-User window appears with the title **Copy of Template User.**

6. Change just the fields that are specific to the first real user that you want to create, such as **Username, Full Name,** and **Description.**

7. Click **Add** and a new copy of the template appears. You can create as many accounts as you wish with the same attributes by using this method.

A template for each group of accounts can greatly speed up account administration. For example, if a new person joins the marketing department, it is a lot easier to create the account by copying the existing marketing user template than trying to remember what groups they should be in. You will still have to individually enter user-specific information such as **Username, Full Name,** and **Description** for each user.

Using the Command Line

If you really need to mass-produce accounts, you will probably want to use the command line to bypass the GUI. A neat way to do this is to put *net* commands in a batch file. For example, you can create a batch file containing any number of *net* commands:

```
net user larryc /add /comment:"PC Admin" /expires:never /fullname:"Larry Chapman"
net user larryc /homedir:"c:\users\larryc" /homedirreq:yes /passwordreq:yes
net localgroup "Print Operators" /add larryc
net user stevec /add /comment:"Mac Admin" /expires:never /fullname:"Steve Clark"
net user stevec /homedir:"c:\users\stevec" /homedirreq:yes /passwordreq:yes
net localgroup "Print Operators" /add stevec
```

This batch file creates two users, *larryc* and *stevec*, puts them in groups, and sets various account attributes. Just give the batch file a *.BAT* extension and execute it in a DOS window:

```
newuser.bat
net user larryc /add /comment:"PC Admin" /expires:never /fullname:"Larry Chapman"
The command completed successfully.
net user larryc /homedir:"c:\users\larryc" /homedirreq:yes /passwordreq:yes
The command completed successfully.
net localgroup "Print Operators" /add larryc
The command completed successfully.
net user stevec /add /comment:"Mac Admin" /expires:never /fullname:"Steve Clark"
The command completed successfully.
net user stevec /homedir:"c:\users\stevec" /homedirreq:yes /passwordreq:yes
The command completed successfully.
net localgroup "Print Operators" /add stevec
The command completed successfully.
```

Scripting

Scripting languages such as Perl offer a sophisticated approach to mass-producing accounts. A Perl program could generate *net* commands as output, which could be used within a batch file. Some versions of NT Perl contain functions to add users directly into the Registry, bypassing the GUI and command line entirely.

Debugging Network Problems

One of the challenges of solving network problems is figuring out where the problem is located. This is crucial, as you usually do not have access or control over the entire network you are using (especially in the case of the Internet). Once the location of the problem on the network has been determined, the next step is to contact the person responsible for that section of the network. In some cases, this will be your company network administrator or your ISP. This section describes some ways to isolate the problem.

ping

The *ping* command is the most basic test of network connectivity. It proves that you can communicate with another network device. It does not prove that any higher-level protocol, such as HTTP, is working.

A successful ping:

```
ping rs.internic.net

Pinging rs.internic.net [198.41.0.8] with 32 bytes of data:

Reply from 198.40.0.8: bytes=32 time=831ms TTL=244
Reply from 198.40.0.8: bytes=32 time=680ms TTL=244
Reply from 198.40.0.8: bytes=32 time=741ms TTL=244
Reply from 198.40.0.8: bytes=32 time=693ms TTL=244
```

A failed ping:

```
ping rs.internic.net

Pinging rs.internic.net [198.41.0.8] with 32 bytes of data:

Request timed out.
Request timed out.
Request timed out.
Request timed out.
```

An extremely slow or congested network may produce a mix of results:

```
ping rs.internic.net

Pinging rs.internic.net [198.41.0.8] with 32 bytes of data:

Request timed out.
Request timed out.
Reply from 198.40.0.8: bytes=32 time=991ms TTL=244
Request timed out.
```

Uncommon Sense

tracert

The *tracert* or Trace Route command is useful in identifying routing problems. Running *tracert* is the next logical step after a failed *ping*.

```
tracert nic.near.net

Tracing route to nic.near.net [192.52.71.4]
over a maximum of 30 hops:

  1    10 ms   <10 ms   <10 ms  router.foo.xo.com [208.89.78.253]
  2    40 ms    20 ms    30 ms  SanFrancisco01-Max1.POP.InterNex.Net [205.158.3.52]
  3   120 ms    30 ms    30 ms  SanFrancisco01-rtr.POP.InterNex.Net [205.158.3.49]
  4    30 ms    40 ms    30 ms  205.158.2.37
  5    30 ms    50 ms   431 ms  region-1A-rtr-fddi.InterNex.Net [205.158.0.4]
  6    60 ms    60 ms    60 ms  mae-west.SanFrancisco.mci.net [198.32.136.12]
  7   230 ms   291 ms   240 ms  core1-hssi3-0.SanFrancisco.mci.net [204.70.1.205]
  8   571 ms     *       121 ms  core2-hssi-3.Boston.mci.net [204.70.1.10]
  9   130 ms   261 ms   140 ms  core2-hssi-2.Boston.mci.net [204.70.1.2]
 10   130 ms   140 ms   131 ms  core.Boston.mci.net [204.70.4.137]
 11   120 ms   150 ms   141 ms  border1-fddi-0.Boston.mci.net [204.70.2.34]
 12   150 ms   151 ms   140 ms  nearnet.Boston.mci.net [204.70.20.6]
 13   320 ms   241 ms   160 ms  cambridge2-cr3.bbnplanet.net [192.233.33.10]
 14   311 ms   360 ms     *      cambridge2-cr2.bbnplanet.net [199.92.129.2]
 15    *       831 ms   711 ms  cambridge1-cr1.bbnplanet.net [192.233.149.201]
 16   430 ms     *       240 ms  cambridge1-cr5.bbnplanet.net [206.34.78.31]
 17    *       140 ms   161 ms  nic.near.net [192.52.71.4]

Trace complete.
```

A failed *tracert*:

```
tracert 10.0.0.1

Tracing route to 10.0.0.1 over a maximum of 30 hops

  1   <10 ms   <10 ms    10 ms  router.foo.xo.com [208.89.78.253]
  2    60 ms    20 ms    30 ms  SanFrancisco01-Max1.POP.InterNex.Net [205.158.3.52]
  3   210 ms    30 ms    30 ms  SanFrancisco01-rtr.POP.InterNex.Net [205.158.3.49]
  4    30 ms    30 ms    40 ms  205.158.2.37
  5   150 ms    40 ms    40 ms  region-1A-rtr-fddi.InterNex.Net [205.158.0.4]
  6   260 ms   350 ms   341 ms  agis-internex.santaclara.agis.net [206.62.13.17]
  7    *        *        *      Request timed out.
  8    *        *        *      Request timed out.
  9    *        *        *      Request timed out.
 10    *        *        *      Request timed out.
 11    *        *        *      Request timed out.
 12    *        *        *      Request timed out.
 13    *        *        *      Request timed out.
 14    *        *        *      Request timed out.
 15    *        *        *      Request timed out.
```

If the *tracert* never finishes or just endlessly prints * lines, there is probably a routing problem or failure. It is logical to try calling your ISP if the problem seems to be happening on a network outside of your organization. As the Internet is just a collection of different networks, there are frequent communication problems between different ISPs and carriers. Your ISP may blame someone else for them.

If you have multiple network paths available to reach a destination, the trace route can be used to prove which path traffic is using.

nbtstat

The *nbtstat* command displays the mappings of NetBIOS names to IP addresses. If you are having trouble reaching a remote computer, you can see if the remote computer name is in your name cache.

For example, try to view a computer:

```
net view \\goo
System error 53 has occurred.

The network path was not found.
```

Check the cache for the computer named *goo*:

```
nbtstat -c

Node IpAddress: [10.0.0.3] Scope Id: []

            NetBIOS Remote Cache Name Table

    Name              Type      Host Address    Life [sec]
    ---------------------------------------------------------
    FOO        <03>  UNIQUE     10.0.0.1          -1
    FOO        <00>  UNIQUE     10.0.0.1          -1
    FOO        <20>  UNIQUE     10.0.0.1          -1
    GOO        <03>  UNIQUE     10.0.0.2          256
    GOO        <00>  UNIQUE     10.0.0.2          256
    GOO        <20>  UNIQUE     10.0.0.2          256
```

The positive number in the *Life* column is a good clue that something is wrong. Normally, the *Life* should be −1. A possible cause of trouble is an incorrect or out-of-date *LMHOSTS* file. If the *Host Address* field is incorrect, edit the *LMHOSTS* file and try it again:

```
ping Host Address IP        make sure remote computer is reachable via its IP address
edit lmhosts               edit lmhosts file
nbtstat -R                 rebuild name cache
nbtstat -c                 display new cache
net view \goo              try to view remote computer
```

netstat

The *netstat* command can tell you what TCP connections are present between your computer and other computers. Unfortunately, it shows only TCP ports that are actively being used, not every one that is being offered. It does display which UDP ports your computer is listening on. This is useful if you want to know what UDP services your computer is offering to the Net. As UDP is not connection-oriented, *netstat* cannot show you who is using them.

```
netstat -a
Active Connections

      Proto  Local Address      Foreign Address      State
      TCP    eap:1117           mail.foo.com:pop3    ESTABLISHED
      TCP    eap:1028           localhost:1029       ESTABLISHED
      TCP    eap:1029           localhost:1028       ESTABLISHED
      TCP    eap:ftp            foo.com:32771        ESTABLISHED
      UDP    eap:1032           *:*
      UDP    eap:1040           *:*
      UDP    eap:name           *:*
      UDP    eap:domain         *:*
      UDP    eap:1149           *:*
      UDP    eap:135            *:*
      UDP    eap:domain         *:*
      UDP    eap:nbname         *:*
      UDP    eap:nbdatagram     *:*
      UDP    eap:nbname         *:*
      UDP    eap:nbdatagram     *:*
      UDP    eap:domain         *:*
      UDP    eap:domain         *:*
      UDP    eap:nbname         *:*
      UDP    eap:nbdatagram     *:*
```

From this output, you can tell there is an outgoing POP3 connection to the host *mail.foo.com,* and an incoming FTP connection from *foo.com.*

If the output of *netstat* seems to freeze for several seconds as it displays each line, there may be a problem with DNS. It tries to resolve each IP address to a hostname. You can turn off DNS resolution with the -n option.

Due to limitations with Microsoft's version of *netstat,* you have to do extra work to find out what TCP ports are available on your machine for others to connect to. You have to infer this from the services you are currently running and the ports that they use. You can consult the *<winnt root>\SYSTEM32\DRIVERS\ETC\SER-VICES* file for a list of ports. For example, if you are running the Microsoft DNS Server, the *services* file lists the ports used by DNS:

```
domain      53/tcp nameserver    # name-domain server
domain      53/udp nameserver
nameserver  53/tcp domain        # name-domain server
nameserver  53/udp domain
```

The DNS server will listen on TCP port 53 and UDP port 53.

nslookup

The *nslookup* command can be used to debug DNS problems or look up DNS information. Users frequently assume that the host they are trying to reach is down, while the problem may really lie with DNS. It is important to think of DNS as a database before anything else. It really has nothing to do with the ability to connect network devices. It simply provides a mapping between hostnames and IP addresses and vice versa. Due to the distributed nature of the Internet, your ability to use DNS depends on computers all over the world. The DNS lookup occurs before you make any connection, unless you use IP addresses.

Forward lookups

The *forward* lookup is one that translates a hostname into an IP address. If some application gives an error such as "Host unknown" or "This server does not have a DNS entry," try using *nslookup* to see if the problem is with DNS.

If you have a problem connecting to the web site *www.adtran.com*, you can see if DNS is working correctly:

```
nslookup www.adtran.com
Server: SanFrancisco01.POP.InterNex.Net
Address: 205.158.3.50


Name: adtrn-gw.adtran.com
Address:  204.199.143.42        DNS returns IP address ok...
Aliases: www.adtran.com


ping 204.199.143.42             now try to ping it...

Pinging 204.199.143.42 with 32 bytes of data:

Reply from 204.199.143.42: bytes=32 time=370ms TTL=244
Reply from 204.199.143.42: bytes=32 time=370ms TTL=244
Reply from 204.199.143.42: bytes=32 time=370ms TTL=244
Reply from 204.199.143.42: bytes=32 time=370ms TTL=244
```

This procedure proves that the problem lies somewhere else, since DNS is functioning and you can physically reach the host.

A DNS failure can look like this:

```
*** SanFrancisco01.POP.InterNex.Net: can't find www.goo.com: Non-existent domain
```

or:

```
DNS request timed out.
    timeout was 2 seconds.
DNS request timed out.
    timeout was 4 seconds.
DNS request timed out.
    timeout was 8 seconds.

*** Request to SanFransisco01.POP.InterNex.Net timed-out
```

or possibly:

```
ping www.goo.com
Bad IP address www.goo.com
```

This last message is an especially unhelpful one, as it sounds like something other than a DNS problem.

Reverse lookups

Most people do not pay much attention to DNS's role of converting IP addresses to hostnames, but computers do this all the time. Whenever your browser connects to a web server, your IP address is available to the remote web server, but not your hostname. The web server on the remote machine tries to "resolve" your IP address back to your hostname, so it can see where you are coming from and log it, or do something with the information. When you telnet or ftp to a remote machine, the telnet or ftp server tries to verify your hostname by looking up your IP address. If something is wrong with this process, the connection may seem to hang while the remote machine tries in vain to get your hostname. Some sites may not allow you to connect at all if a reverse lookup fails on your IP address.

To try a reverse lookup, reverse the order of the octets in the IP address and append the *IN-ADDR.ARPA* domain. You will also be looking up the *PTR* (pointer) record type instead of the default *A* (address) type.

For example, to lookup the hostname for 205.158.3.50:

```
nslookup
Server: SanFrancisco01.POP.InterNex.Net
Address: 205.158.3.50
> set q=ptr                      change query type to pointer
> 50.3.158.205.in-addr.arpa      type in reversed IP address

50.3.158.205.in-addr.arpa name = SanFrancisco01.POP.InterNex.Net
```

Other types of DNS lookups

You can gather various types of information about a site from DNS information. To see if the host has another host handle mail delivery for it, look up the *MX* or mail exchanger record:

```
> set q=mx
> whitehouse.gov
whitehouse.gov   MX preference = 100, mail exchanger = storm.eop.gov
```

If you need to contact a person responsible for a domain, you can try sending email to the address listed in the *SOA* (start of authority) record:

```
> set q=soa
> whitehouse.gov

whitehouse.gov
        responsible mail addr = postmaster.gatekeeper.eop.gov
```

The at (@) sign has a special meaning with DNS files, so a period (.) is used instead. Thus, *postmaster.gatekeeper.eop.gov* translates to the email address of *postmaster@gatekeeper.eop.gov.*

route

The *route* command displays the routing table for the local computer. If you get error messages such as "Host Unreachable," "Network Unreachable," or even "Request timed out," run *route print* to see if there is a problem with the routes on your computer:

```
route print

Active Routes:
   Network Address          Netmask  Gateway Address     Interface  Metric
          0.0.0.0          0.0.0.0   206.67.77.253   206.67.77.254  1
         10.0.0.0    255.255.255.0        10.0.0.2        10.0.0.2  1
         10.0.0.2  255.255.255.255       127.0.0.1       127.0.0.1  1
        127.0.0.0        255.0.0.0       127.0.0.1       127.0.0.1  1
    206.67.77.252  255.255.255.252   206.67.77.254   206.67.77.254  1
    206.67.77.254  255.255.255.255       127.0.0.1       127.0.0.1  1
    206.67.77.255  255.255.255.255   206.67.77.254   206.67.77.254  1
        224.0.0.0        224.0.0.0        10.0.0.2        10.0.0.2  1
        224.0.0.0        224.0.0.0   206.67.77.254   206.67.77.254  1
  255.255.255.255  255.255.255.255   206.67.77.254   206.67.77.254  1
```

The fields are as follows:

Network Address

Any network matched by this address should use this route. The default route is all zeros and is used if no other route is found.

Netmask

The mask to be applied to the network address. If all ones (255.255.255.255), the route is a host route and refers to a single machine, not a network.

Gateway Address

The IP address of the gateway for the route. The gateway will know what to do with traffic for the specified network address.

Interface

The IP address of the network interface that the route is going to use when leaving the local computer.

Metric

The hop count or number of gateways between the local computer and the destination network.

For example, this machine has two network interfaces, 206.67.77.254 and 10.0.0.2:

```
   Network Address          Netmask  Gateway Address      Interface  Metric
          0.0.0.0          0.0.0.0   206.67.77.253    206.67.77.254  1   ❶
         10.0.0.0    255.255.255.0        10.0.0.2         10.0.0.2  1   ❷
         10.0.0.2  255.255.255.255       127.0.0.1        127.0.0.1  1   ❸
        127.0.0.0        255.0.0.0       127.0.0.1        127.0.0.1  1   ❹
    206.67.77.252  255.255.255.252   206.67.77.254    206.67.77.254  1   ❺
    206.67.77.254  255.255.255.255       127.0.0.1        127.0.0.1  1   ❻
    206.67.77.255  255.255.255.255   206.67.77.254    206.67.77.254  1
        224.0.0.0        224.0.0.0        10.0.0.2         10.0.0.2  1   ❼
        224.0.0.0        224.0.0.0   206.67.77.254    206.67.77.254  1   ❽
  255.255.255.255  255.255.255.255   206.67.77.254    206.67.77.254  1
```

❶ Default route

❷ Route for 10.0.0.0 network

3 Loopback for network interface

4 Loopback route

5 Route for 206.67.77.252 network

6 Loopback for network interface

7 Multicast route for network interface

8 Multicast route for network interface

WHOIS Information

The InterNIC organization maintains a listing of domains and the person responsible for them. If you are having problems reaching a site or someone is complaining about not being able to reach your site, you may be able to contact the people listed in the InterNIC database.

UNIX users have always had the *whois* command available for querying the database, but NT does not supply an equivalent. You can use the **Telnet** program as a crude method of making queries:

1. Telnet to the *whois* port on *rs.internic.net*.

2. Turn on logging with **Terminal-Start Logging**.

3. Type in domain name (*ora.com* for example) and hit ENTER.

4. Quit **Telnet** session.

5. Turn off logging.

6. Examine log file:

```
type telnet.log
O'Reilly & Associates (ORA-DOM1)
    101 Morris Street
    Sebastopol, CA 95472

Domain Name: ORA.COM

Administrative Contact, Technical Contact, Zone Contact:
    Pearce, Eric  (EP86)  eap@ORA.COM
    707-829-0515 x221
Billing Contact:
    Johnston, Rick  (RJ724)  rick@ORA.COM
    707-829-0515 x331

Record last updated on 28-Jan-97.
Record created on 14-Jun-89.

Domain servers in listed order:

NS.ORA.COM                  207.25.97.8
NS.SONGLINE.COM             204.148.41.1
```

The InterNIC Registration Services Host contains ONLY Internet Information
(Networks, ASNs, Domains, and POCs).
Please use the whois server at nic.ddn.mil for MILNET Information.

NetBIOS over TCP/IP (NBT)

If you are going to establish communications between LANs separated by routers
or the Internet, you are going to want to use TCP/IP as your network protocol.
You can still use the NetBEUI protocol within a LAN, but you will need to map
the NetBIOS functions (file and print sharing, name service, etc.) onto TCP/IP for
them to work over a routed network. This process is called NetBIOS over TCP/IP
or NBT. Once you have this set up, you can browse the network, share files and
printers, and do anything you would normally do over the NetBEUI protocol. You
can remove NetBEUI entirely if you do not need it, but you must first configure
NBT to be able to resolve computer names.

As NetBEUI or TCP/IP broadcasts usually do not leave the local subnet, you need
to tell the local computers how to reach the computers on other side of a router.
You can do this by using *LMHOSTS* or a WINS server. *LMHOSTS* is simply a text
file that contains a mapping of computer names to IP addresses. When your computer wants to connect to another computer, it scans the *LMHOSTS* file for the
name of the remote computer, and, if it finds it, it connects to the remote computer by using NBT to the specified IP address.

The WINS server maintains a mapping of computer names to IP addresses. When
your computer wants to connect to a remote computer, it asks the WINS server for
the remote computer's IP address. If the WINS server has this information, a connection is made using NBT to the specified IP address.

The *LMHOSTS* mechanism is static and the WINS server is dynamic. Any time an IP
address changes, you have to edit the *LMHOSTS* file manually to reflect the
change. Some of *LMHOSTS* file maintenance can be centralized by using the repli-
cator service to copy a "master" *LMHOSTS* to other machines, but this still requires
manual administration. In addition, hosts that get their IP addresses via DHCP
should not be in *LMHOSTS*, as their IP addresses can change frequently. The WINS
server always has the most current name-to-IP address mapping and maintains it
for you.

Tips

When setting up the WINS server, put the IP address of the computer as its own
primary WINS server. The secondary WINS address should be another WINS
server on the same subnet. If you want to talk to a WINS server on another subnet, set up the remote WINS server as a replication partner.

Be aware that Windows NT 3.x servers that run the WINS service require you to
put the IP address of the computer as both the primary and secondary WINS
server address in the TCP/IP WINS configuration.

Uncommon Sense

Browsing

Some of the most frequently encountered problems with NT networks have to do with *browsing*. Browsing refers to the act of searching the network for lists of available resources. For most users, browsing means they do not have to know the name of a network resource in order to use it. They can click their way through a list of available domains or workgroups, then a list of servers, and then a specific resource such as a shared directory or printer. If there is a useful description in the comment field, you may be able to find the printer or shared directory that you are looking for without having to ask someone for help.

For Windows NT 4.0 and Windows 95 users, browsing means clicking on the **Network Neighborhood** icon and waiting for a list of servers, domains, and workgroups to appear. For Windows NT 3.x users, the **Disk-Connect Network Drive** menu in **File Manager** displays a list of disk shares. You can also browse from the command line with the *net view* command.

There is a common confusion among most end-users of Windows PCs about browsing. They tend to associate the ability to browse with connectivity. Connectivity means that you have a physical network path between your local computer and a remote computer. Browsing is the ability to search a local or remote network for resources. You can have no ability to browse, but still have connectivity. The most common problems with browsing have to do with network topology and security. In order for browsing to work in complex environments, someone has to take specific steps to enable it.

Most of the Microsoft networking features are designed to broadcast on the LAN to discover resources, essentially asking "Who and what is out there on the wire?" This gives you plug-and-play networking, where you can set up a new computer, give it a name, and it can immediately see the other computers on the network and be seen by them. This works fine on small networks or networks that use bridges to connect to each other. The bridges will transmit broadcasts and everybody still sees everybody else.

For the simplest case, assume a single LAN with several PCs on it and no NT domains. All you should have to do to enable browsing is to put every computer in the same workgroup and turn on file and print sharing. At this point, the computers should be able to browse each other's resources. The browsing mechanism is relatively self-administering when your computers are all on the same physical LAN and everybody trusts each other. Most companies will find themselves with multiple LANs, and security and network performance concerns.

Once you start implementing domain security, your ability to browse other computers will be dependent on how the security is configured. This is different than connectivity issues. You still have the physical ability to reach other computers, but whether they allow you to browse their resources is a security issue. For example, try to browse a remote computer with no security via the command line:

```
net view \\computer1

Share name    Type         Used as        Comment
------------------------------------------------------------------
NETLOGON      Disk                        Logon server share
TEMP          Disk
```

Then try one with security:

```
net view \\computer2
System error 5 has occurred.

Access is denied.
```

This means that your computer was able to reach *computer2* via the network, but was rejected for security reasons.

An example of a possible connectivity problem would be:

```
net view \\computer3
System error 53 has occurred.

The network path was not found.
```

This means that your computer was unable to find any computer called *computer3*. If you are able to *ping* the remote computer via its IP address, you are probably having a problem with *name resolution*, which is the process of translating a computer name to a network address. Name resolution is a function of *LMHOSTS* and *HOSTS* files, and WINS and DNS servers. If you are unable to *ping* a remote computer, you are most likely having a connectivity problem.

You are going to have problems browsing a LAN that is separated from your LAN by a router or, possibly, the Internet. In this situation, you are going to be dealing with several issues. You can no longer rely on broadcasting as a way of reaching remote computers. Broadcasts usually do not leave the local network. It is possible to configure some routers to forward certain types of broadcasts, but it will probably be less trouble to fully embrace the idea of routing and not rely on this. The plug-and-play features of Microsoft networking break down at this point. The first problem you may face is your LAN protocol. If you are using NetBEUI as your only network protocol, you need to switch to TCP/IP, as NetBEUI is non-routable. It is possible to do a lot of Microsoft networking with IPX, but it is not supported on the Internet. You can tunnel IPX over TCP/IP and do other tricks with routers, but it is probably less trouble to just join the rest of the Internet and run TCP/IP.

You will need to list the IP addresses and names of all of the PDCs (for domains that you want to browse) in the *LMHOSTS* file. This enables the PDCs to communicate browse list information regardless of their location on the network.

You cannot browse a workgroup on the other side of a router. Even if you are using the same workgroup name on both sides of the router, computers on opposite sides of the router will not be able to see each other in browse lists. You must implement an NT domain to enable cross-router browsing.

Note that computers do not have to be explicitly added to a domain for them to show up in a browse list for a domain. All you have to do is change their workgroup name to an existing domain name and they will be made available for browsing across routers. In this situation, you are exploiting a feature of domains to enable browsing, but not participating in domain security.

The WINS service only runs on NT Server. You must have an NT Server on each network that you want to be visible via WINS. Or you can set up an NT Workstation or Server as a WINS Proxy that forwards WINS requests from its subnet to a

WINS server on another subnet. You have to edit the Registry manually to do this under NT 4.0. Change the value of the key:

```
HKEY_LOCAL_MACHINE\SYSTEM\CurrentControlSet\Services\NetBT\Parameters\EnableProxy
```

from 0 to 1 and reboot. You should do this only if you are unable to install a WINS sever on the subnet in question.

Tips

In small, non-routed networks, browsing should work "out of the box." For anything larger, you can improve the performance of browsing by taking steps to specify which machines should maintain the browse list. Typically, you will want the PDC for a domain to be the browse master. You should also visit every other computer and configure them so they can never become the browse master. Windows 3.11 and Windows 95 machines should be prevented from trying to become browse masters when there are NT computers available.

On a Windows NT computer, the Registry values in the key:

```
\SYSTEM\CurrentControlSet\Services\Browser\Parameters
```

determine the browsing role. For the NT computer that is going to be the browse master (usually a PDC), set the following:

```
IsDomainMaster:    "TRUE"
```

For NT computers that can act up as backups to the browse master (usually the BDCs):

```
MaintainServerList:    "Yes"
```

For all other NT computers, set the following:

```
MaintainServerList:    "No"
```

For Windows 95 machines, go to the **Network** control panel, select **File and Print Sharing** and **Properties**. Change **Browse Master** from **Auto** to **Disabled**.

For Windows for Workgroups computers, edit *SYSTEM.INI* file and add the following line to the [Network] section:

```
MaintainServerList=no
```

If the entry already exists, and is set to *yes* or *auto*, change it to *no*.

For more information on browsing, check the following resources:

- MS Knowledge Base, Article ID: Q102878

- *Networking Guide* volume of the NT Server Resource Kit; Chapter 3, "Windows NT Browser Service"

- *Networking Guide* volume of the NT Server Resource Kit; Chapter 8, "Managing Microsoft WINS Servers"

Installing Hardware

NT can made to run on almost any recent PC. The Microsoft hardware compatibility list (HCL) is a good starting point, but because something does not appear on the HCL does not mean it cannot run NT. Do your homework on the Internet first.

Selecting Hardware for NT

When building a computer for use with NT, think of the Internet as the ultimate guide to hardware. If you can't find a web site for a hardware vendor with downloadable NT drivers, don't buy the product. Any vendor who offers only a BBS is out of date and you should really question their commitment to the technology. Building a modern PC is literally the act of visiting the web site for each vendor for every device in the PC and downloading the latest drivers.

Windows NT Diagnostics

The **Resources** tab in the **Windows NT Diagnostics** administrative tool displays IRQ, I/O Port, DMA, and Memory resources used by installed hardware. The **Resources-Devices** button displays a list of known hardware. You can also print an inventory of all the resources in use on your computer.

Plug and Play

As NT does not yet support plug-and-play as well as Windows 95 does, you might find that Windows 95 is useful as a diagnostic tool for Windows NT. If you have your own copy of the media and a fast CD-ROM drive, installing Windows 95 or Windows NT is fairly quick.

For example, on a dual-boot PC running both Windows NT and Windows 95:

1. Install new hardware under Windows 95.

2. Check the **Device Manager** menu of the **System** control panel for the new hardware.

3. Print out all the resource settings.

4. Reboot the machine under Windows NT.

5. Configure the hardware using the settings obtained from Windows 95.

Be aware that this could wreak havoc if you add hardware under Windows 95 that reshuffles existing IRQ and DMA settings, making the previous NT configuration invalid.

NTHQ

The **NTHQ** utility comes on the NT CD-ROM and tries to detect all the hardware and settings on your computer. It boots off a DOS floppy, interrogates your computer, and writes a logfile of everything it finds, producing output similar to Windows NT Diagnostics and Windows 95 Device Manager. Run *MAKEDISK.BAT* in the *SUPPORT/HQTOOL* subdirectory of the NT CDROM to generate the **NTHQ** boot floppy.

SCSITOOL

The **SCSITOOL** utility that comes on the NT CD-ROM can interrogate Adaptec and BusLogic SCSI controllers to see what SCSI devices are present. Run *SUP-PORT\SCSITOOL\MAKEDISK* to create a bootable floppy. Boot your computer from this floppy to run the utility.

Using NT as a System Administration Tool

Some network managers used to keep an old dumb terminal around the office for setting up UNIX machines, routers, terminal servers, and other devices controlled by RS232 serial ports. Now they carry around a laptop with NT Server on it. The combination of **Hyperterminal**, **Telnet**, and **Network Monitor** gives you almost everything you need to install and maintain computers and network equipment.

HyperTerminal

In addition to calling another computer using a modem, **HyperTerminal** can also be used as a terminal when directly connected to RS232 devices.

Using HyperTerminal as a terminal

For example, Ascend makes a popular ISDN Bridge/Router called the Pipeline 50 (P50). The P50 can be configured either using a VT100 terminal connected to the serial interface or through a telnet session to the Ethernet interface.* As it does not have an IP address when it comes from the factory, you cannot use the telnet program to connect to it. Instead, you can directly connect one of your COM ports to the P50 serial port and use **HyperTerminal** to configure it. In this particular example, the COM1 port on the laptop was connected to the P50 using a "straight-through" DB9 cable. **HyperTerminal** is configured with the following settings:

- **File-Properties-Connect using** is set to *COM1*

- **File-Properties-Configure-Bits per second** is *9600*

- **File-Properties-Configure-Data bits** is *8*

- **File-Properties-Configure-Parity** is *None*

- **File-Properties-Configure-Stop bits** is *1*

- **File-Properties-Configure-Flow control** is *Hardware*

As P50 uses VT100-specific graphic characters to draw boxes around the text in the configuration screens, you can change the **HyperTerminal** font to one that includes the graphic characters. Under the **View-Font** menu, change the font to *Terminal*. In order to resize the **HyperTerminal** window to fit the P50 session, right-click on the session window and then select **View-Snap** and the session window will automatically resize.

---

*Ascend has since released a web browser–based configuration tool that greatly improves on this process.

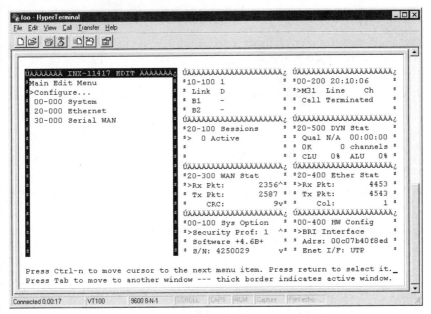

Figure 7-1: Hyperterminal session before changes

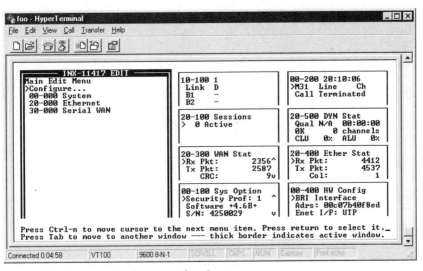

Figure 7-2: Hyperterminal session after changes

Save the session configuration using **File-Save As** so that you can start the next session by double-clicking on the session icon.

Using HyperTerminal for File Transfer

The file transfer features of **HyperTerminal** can also be used when configuring equipment. For example, the Ascend P50 firmware can be upgraded using the XMODEM protocol by following these steps:

1. Obtain the new firmware from the Ascend web site and ftp it to your hard drive.

2. Connect to the P50 using the **HyperTerminal** session you created previously.

3. Type the magic sequence of characters to force the P50 to go into the upgrade mode.

4. When the P50 is expecting the XMODEM protocol, it will start printing *CK* characters.

5. From **HyperTerminal**, Select **Transfer-Send File**. Type in the name of the new firmware file and specify the XMODEM protocol.

6. The new firmware is then uploaded to the P50.

This is a vendor-specific example, but it illustrates the kind of administration tasks that can be accomplished with **HyperTerminal**.

Telnet

The *telnet* command can also serve as a diagnostic tool. In addition to telneting to other computers, many network devices understand the telnet protocol. For example, you could use *telnet* to configure a HP JetDirect card:

```
telnet printer

== JetDirect Telnet Configuration==

    Configured Parameters
      IP Address     : 205.23.40.5
      MAC Address    : 08:00:09:a4:51:de

   ...more output...

 Type "?" for HELP Or "quit" to save-and-exit
 Or type "exit" to exit without saving configuration parameter entries
 >
```

You can also *telnet* to other ports than the normal telnet port (23). You can verify that various Internet services are functioning correctly if you know enough of their internal languages.

For example, to connect to the SMTP mail server on host *storm.eop.gov* and expand the *postmaster* alias, type in **storm.eop.gov** for *Host Name* and **smtp** for *Port*:

```
telnet storm.eop.gov smtp

220 Storm.EOP.GOV -- Server ESMTP (PMDF V5.0-7 #6879)
expn postmaster
```

```
250-<fox_J@EOP.GOV>
250-<postmaster@Whitehouse.GOV>
250 <mailadmin@a1.eop.gov>
quit
221 Bye received. Goodbye.
```

To check to see that the web server is operating correctly on the local machine, type in **localhost** for *Host Name* and **80** for *Port*:

```
telnet localhost 80

GET /
<!doctype html public "-//IETF//DTD HTML//EN">
<HTML>

<HEAD>

<BODY BACKGROUND="/samples/images/backgrnd.gif">

<TITLE>Microsoft Internet Information Server</TITLE>

</HEAD>

<BODY BGCOLOR="FFFFFF">
<CENTER>
<IMG SRC="/samples/images/h_logo.gif" ALIGN="BOTTOM" ALT="Microsoft Internet
Information Server">
```

Using this technique, you can verify that a service is working correctly even though you may not have the client for the service handy.

Network Monitor

Network Monitor is a protocol analyzer that understands common protocols (TCP/IP, NetBEUI, AppleTalk, IPX/SPX, and so forth) and can decode them, showing you the contents of the packets. Normally, your computer's network interface examines only traffic that is specifically addressed to it or traffic that is sent to every address (broadcast traffic). **Network Monitor** puts the network interface into *promiscuous* mode, which allows the interface to examine all traffic on the network segment, regardless of its addressee. This can be very helpful when debugging anything that uses the network, including operating systems other than NT. Anyone using this feature will also realize why encryption is important, as anyone running a promiscuous interface can see and read the contents of everything on the network, including email, passwords, and so on.

NT 4.0 Server comes with a cut-down version of the **Network Monitor** program. It does not put the network interface into promiscuous mode, so it can see only traffic going to and from the computer it is running on and broadcast traffic. This is actually a good thing, as you probably do not want every NT Server administrator to be able to capture all your network traffic. The "real" version of **Network Monitor** comes with the Systems Management Server (SMS) BackOffice package. It can be used by itself without any other part of SMS. The purchase price of SMS will keep most casual NT users from buying the promiscuous-enabled **Network Monitor**, but it be may be worth the cost for the system or network administrator.

See Chapter 5, *RAS and DUN*, for an example of how to use **Network Monitor** for debugging PPP sessions.

Registry

When reading Microsoft documentation or Knowledge Base articles, you will frequently encounter solutions that require editing the Registry. The instructions are always preceded by a scary warning about how dangerous it is to enter the realm of the Registry. In reality, you will make Registry changes frequently, and you should be able do so without fear of blowing up your system.

Most of the Registry tweaks are one-time only. Others are things that you may want to enable or disable repeatedly over time. You can use the *import* and *export* features of the **Regedit** program to automate and simplify the task of Registry editing.

For example, assume that you are debugging RAS scripts and want to turn on logging of the RAS session. The prescribed way to do this is:

1. Start **Regedit**.

2. Find the *SYSTEM\CurrentControlSet\Services\RasMan\Parameters* key.

3. Change the *Logging* value from 0 to 1.

4. Exit **Regedit**.

5. Start **DUN**.

To turn off logging, follow the same procedure but change the value of **Logging** from 1 to 0.

The **Regedit** program is able to export the entire Registry or any subkey of the Registry to a text file. It can also import Registry data from text files in the Registry format. Since most of what the GUI and command-line tools do is change values within the Registry, the next logical step is to start bypassing the GUI and command-line tools and write settings directly to the Registry using the import feature. When reading the Registry data file, **Regedit** will replace any existing keys or values with those from the datafile and add any keys or values that do not match an existing Registry entry. If your goal is to edit an existing key or value, the datafile entry must match the current Registry exactly, or else the new entries will simply be appended and ignored. The easiest way to ensure that the datafile is in the correct format is to use **Regedit** export current settings.

For the RAS logging example, use the following steps to create Registry data files:

1. Start **Regedit**.

2. Find the *SYSTEM\CurrentControlSet\Services\RasMan* key.

3. Select **Parameters**.

4. Select **Registry-Export Registry File**.

5. Choose a meaningful file name, such as *RASLOGOF.REG*, for RAS Logging Off.

6. Change the value for **Parameters-Logging** from 0 to 1.

7. Select **Registry-Export Registry File**.

8. Choose another file name, such as *RASLOGON.REG*, for RAS Logging On.

Contents of *RASLOGON.REG*:

```
REGEDIT4

[HKEY_LOCAL_MACHINE\SYSTEM\CurrentControlSet\Services\RasMan\Parameters]
"Logging"=dword:00000001
"Medias"=hex(7):72,61,73,74,61,70,69,00,00
```

Contents of *RASLOGOF.REG*:

```
REGEDIT4

[HKEY_LOCAL_MACHINE\SYSTEM\CurrentControlSet\Services\RasMan\Parameters]
"Logging"=dword:00000000
"Medias"=hex(7):72,61,73,74,61,70,69,00,00
```

The difference between the two files is the value of **Logging** (1 and 0). If you are unsure of what the differences were, the *fc* command can be used to do a "diff" of the files:

```
fc /l /n RASLOGON.REG RASLOGOF.REG
Comparing files RASLOGON.REG and RASLOGOF.REG
***** RASLOGON.REG
    3:  [HKEY_LOCAL_MACHINE\SYSTEM\CurrentControlSet\Services\RasMan\Parameters]
    4:  "Logging"=dword:00000001
    5:  "Medias"=hex(7):72,61,73,74,61,70,69,00,00
***** RASLOGOF.REG
    3:  [HKEY_LOCAL_MACHINE\SYSTEM\CurrentControlSet\Services\RasMan\Parameters]
    4:  "Logging"=dword:00000000
    5:  "Medias"=hex(7):72,61,73,74,61,70,69,00,00
*****
```

The *fc* command output is less than ideal, but you should be able to at least locate the line where the differences occur.

Now you have two Registry files that can be safely imported to turn logging on or off. You will never have to manually search the Registry for the right key or worry about making typing mistakes.

You can now toggle logging from the command line using *Regedit*.

To turn logging on:

```
regedit /s raslogon.reg
```

To turn logging off:

```
regedit /s raslogof.reg
```

The */s* option suppresses the "Information in *filename* has been successfully entered into the Registry" popup message.

An easier way to do this is to use **Explorer** to browse the directory where the .*REG* files are stored and double-click on the files. This will automatically run **Regedit** on any .*REG* file (be careful!).

You can even import the same .*REG* file multiple times without having to worry about damage, as just the single value is being overwritten, and nothing else.

You can watch the Registry changes take place in real time by starting the GUI version of **Regedt32**, selecting the keys you wish to observe, and then running the command-line **Regedit** in another window.

Using NT as a Multiprotocol Print Server

The ability of NT to speak multiple network protocols enables it to be used as a sort of protocol converter, where it accepts data using one protocol and sends the data out using another protocol.

Multiprotocol Printing

A good use of this feature is network printing. For example, a Windows 95 computer could print to an NT print queue using the NetBEUI protocol, and then the NT server could send the print job to an Apple LaserWriter using the AppleTalk protocol. The print job has been "converted" from NetBEUI to AppleTalk.

NT Server can accept print jobs via NetBEUI, TCP/IP (LPR/LPD), AppleTalk, and Novell IPX. It can print via NetBEUI, TCP/IP, AppleTalk, IPX, and DLC, in addition to hard-wired serial and parallel ports. NT Workstation can print to the same device as Server, but it can share only via the NetBEUI protocol.

For NT Workstation to print to a printer using IPX, you must install **Client Services for NetWare** (CSNW). NT Server can act as a gateway between NetWare printers and non-NetWare clients using **Gateway Services for NetWare** (GSNW). NT Server can act as a NetWare printer using **File and Print Services for NetWare** (FPNW), which does not come with NT Server, and must be purchased separately.

It also possible to print using TCP/IP via NBT (NetBIOS over TCP/IP), but this is quite different from using the native TCP/IP printing protocol, LPD.

Printing Versus Sharing

It is important to distinguish between the ability of an NT machine to offer a print queue to other machines on the network versus an NT machine printing to a networked printer (or other computer). When you add a *service*, such as **Services for the Macintosh**, you are adding the ability for another computer to print to your computer using the AppleTalk protocol. When you add a protocol, such as AppleTalk or DLC, you are adding the ability to print to a network device using that protocol.

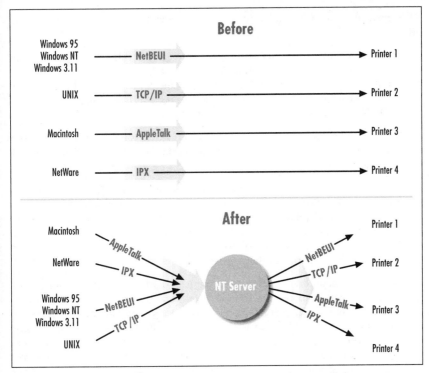

Figure 7-3: Decentralized network printing and centralized network printing and queuing

Printing via ports

Microsoft calls the network connection between your NT computer and a printer a *port*. A port can be a protocol and printer name combination, such as:

```
Port Name              Description:
--------------------------------------------------------------------------
\\PC248\HP4M           NetBIOS print queue HP4M on computer PC248
sales:sales            TCP/IP printer sales
ORA_MEDIA:color         AppleTalk printer color in Zone ORA_MEDIA
LPT1                   Parallel port
COM2                   Serial port
```

Sharing print queues

Microsoft's name for the ability to accept print jobs from remote computers is *sharing* a print queue. You will need a *monitor* for each protocol under which you want to share the print queue.

Installing Printing Protocols

The NT installation process tends to blur the distinction between offering a printing service for a protocol and the ability to print via that protocol. By default, adding one adds both. For example, adding **Services for the Macintosh** (SFM) adds the **Print Server for Macintosh**, which enables Macintosh computers to print to the

NT server, and the AppleTalk protocol, which enables printing to a AppleTalk printer.

The **Network** control panel display is very confusing in this regard. In order for NT Workstation to print via AppleTalk, you add the AppleTalk Protocol. AppleTalk then shows up in the **Protocols** tab of the **Network** control panel. Once AppleTalk is installed, you can create AppleTalk ports. NT Workstation has only a limited ability to act as a print server, and only for the NetBEUI protocol.

On NT Server, the AppleTalk protocol is installed when you install the **Services for the Macintosh** service, but it never shows up in the **Protocols** tab of the **Network** control panel!

To create a port to a networked printer using the **Add Printer Wizard**, choose **My Computer**, and **Add Port**. If you are adding an AppleTalk port, choose **AppleTalk Printing Devices**, and select an AppleTalk printer. If you have lots of printers to connect to, it may be quicker to just keep hitting the **Add Port** button to create all the printer ports at once. When you are setting up the next printer, you can then select from the list of ports you have created.

Installing a protocol under NT Server implies sharing all your existing print queues under that protocol, but you do have some control over what protocols are used for printer sharing. For example, if you do not want the printer queues to be shared under AppleTalk, but want to print via AppleTalk, you can simply stop the **Print Server for Macintosh** service from running, and none of your computer's print queues will be visible from AppleTalk. To stop or disable the service from running, use the **Startup** setting in the **Services** control panel. Set the **Startup Type** to **manual** or **disabled**, and the service will not start at the next reboot.

Centralized Queuing

One problem with having print jobs coming from multiple machines and multiple protocols is queue management and performance.

Centralized management

Using an NT server as a choke point for all print jobs allows the administrator to see every job being sent to a printer, regardless of where the print job originated (PC, Mac, UNIX, or NetWare). If you need to pause or stop a print queue in order to work on a printer, you can do so from a single location. If a print job goes haywire and starts printing out hundreds of pages of garbage, you can find the offending job, cancel it, and determine who sent it—all from the same machine.

For example, the NT server print queue in Figure 7-4 has four jobs being spooled. The first job was sent from a Macintosh, the second from a Sun (UNIX) computer, the third from a Windows 95 client, and the fourth from the local NT computer itself. All of these print jobs are being sent to the same network printer, but by sending them through the NT server first, the administrator has gained centralized queue control.

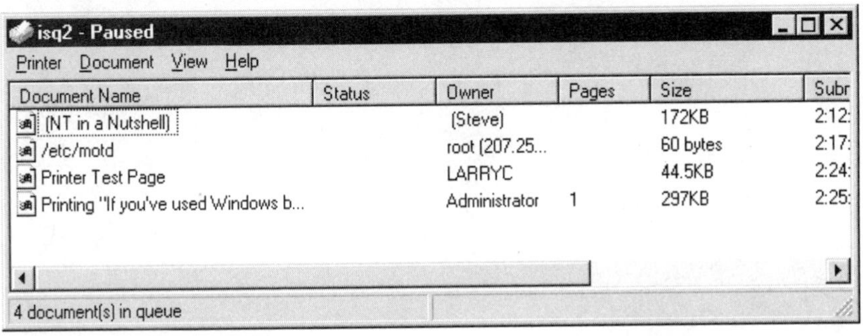

Figure 7-4: NT printer queue receiving jobs via multiple protocols

Performance

The performance of the computer sending the job is usually improved by spooling it to an NT server instead of directly to a printer. Most printers will occupy some resources on the computer while printing a large job, so sending to a server gets it off your machine quickly and lets you get back to work. Some network printers cannot handle being bombarded by multiple print jobs coming from different computers all at the same time. The NT server will feed jobs to the printer one at a time, keeping the printer happy.

APPENDIX A

NetBIOS

NetBIOS Tables

Many administrative GUI tools and commands display output about NetBIOS. This information is summarized here.

Node Type

Node types describe how NetBIOS name resolution takes place for a given computer. Client computers either broadcast on the local network when looking up a computer name, contact a specific name server, or do a combination of both. The node type is displayed in the output of the *ipconfig* command:

```
ipconfig/all
Windows NT IP Configuration
        ...
        Node Type . . . . . . . . . : Hybrid
        ...
```

This computer is a Hybrid (H-Node).

The node type can be changed via the Registry or supplied by DHCP.

The possible node types are:

B-node
    Uses only broadcasts for name resolution and registration.

P-node
    Uses only point-to-point communication with a NetBIOS name server (WINS) for name resolution and registration.

M-node

Name resolution uses broadcasts first, and then falls back to P-node behavior (point-to-point) if this fails. You can use M-node if the local network is connected to an expensive or slow WAN link. Broadcasts would be tried first, keeping unnecessary traffic off the WAN.

H-node

Uses point-to-point communication with a NetBIOS name server (WINS) for name resolution and registration. If this fails, it falls back to B-node behavior (broadcasts). WINS clients are normally configured as H-nodes. They will use the WINS server, but can fall back to broadcasting if it becomes unreachable.

NetBIOS Name Types

Microsoft Networking uses NetBIOS names to identify services running on individual computers or groups of computers. NetBIOS names are 16 characters in length, and the 16th character is used to identify what purpose the name is used for. The 16th character value is expressed as a hexadecimal number in output of several programs, including the *nbtstat* command:

```
nbtstat -n
Node IpAddress: [10.0.0.1] Scope Id: []
            NetBIOS Local Name Table

    Name              Type      Status
    -------------------------------------------
    ICA           <00>  UNIQUE    Registered
    ICA           <20>  UNIQUE    Registered
    HOME          <00>  GROUP     Registered
    HOME          <1C>  GROUP     Registered
    HOME          <1B>  UNIQUE    Registered
    ICA           <03>  UNIQUE    Registered
    FPNW SERVICE AC<03>  UNIQUE    Registered
    HOME          <1E>  GROUP     Registered
    INet~Services <1C>  GROUP     Registered
    IS~ICA........<00>  UNIQUE    Registered
    HOME          <1D>  UNIQUE    Registered
```

as well as the **WINS Manager, in Mappings-Show Database** (see Figure A-1).

The *nbtstat* command displays the hex values in angle brackets, as in <03>, and **WINS Manager** uses square brackets with an "h" appended to the hex number, as in [03h]. There are two types of names, *Unique* and *Group*. Unique names are services, such as **Workstation** or **Messenger**, and group names are domain names or groupings of computers. See Tables A-1 and A-2.

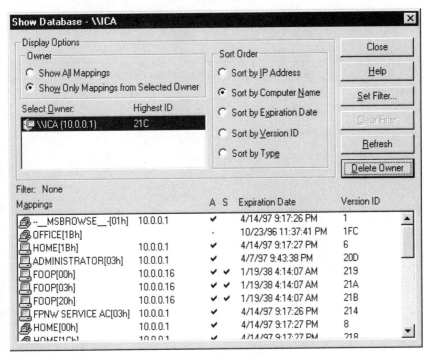

Figure A-1: NetBIOS names in WINS database

Table A-1: Unique Names

16th Byte	Description
00	Workstation service (usually the name of the computer)
03	Messenger service (used for sending messages to users or computers)
1B	Domain master browser
06	RAS server service
1F	NetDDE service
20	Server service
21	RAS client
BE	Network Monitor Agent
BF	Network Monitor Utility

Table A-2: Group Names

16th Byte	Description
1C	A domain group name (all members of the domain)
1D	Master browser name
1E	Normal group name (workgroup)
20	Special group name (Internet group)
MSBROWSE	Special case name for announcing the master browser to other computers

APPENDIX B

TCP/IP

TCP/IP Tables

The *LMHOSTS*, *HOSTS*, and *NETWORKS* files are used to provide a mapping between names and TCP/IP network addresses. All the files described here appear in the directory *<winnt root>\SYSTEM32\DRIVERS\ETC*.

LMHOSTS File

The basic form of the file is a listing of IP addresses and computer names:

```
IP-address   computer-name
```

Comments start with the hash character (#):

```
# this is a comment
```

There is a set of keywords that have been added to the file format since it was defined in Microsoft LAN Manager. In order to preserve backwards capability with LAN Manager, these new keywords are all prefixed with the comment character (the pound sign):

```
#PRE
#DOM:domain
#INCLUDE filename
#BEGIN_ALTERNATE
#END_ALTERNATE
```

The *#PRE* keyword preloads the computer name into the name cache. This means that the system will not have to look up the name in the *LMHOSTS* file, as it is already in the cache. If the *#PRE* keywork is used for commonly used names, this should improve name resolution performance. Entries in the *LMHOSTS* without the *#PRE* keyword will be ignored unless all other methods of name lookup fail (WINS, broadcast, and DNS).

```
208.25.98.100    PRINTSRV      #PRE
203.148.41.1     SALES         #PRE
198.102.209.5    FOO
207.35.97.2      MKTG
```

In this example, the names *PRINTSRV* and *SALES* will be loaded into the cache whenever the computer reboots or has the cache reloaded with the *nbtstat -r* command. You can display the contents of the cache with *nbtstat -c*.

The *#DOM:* keyword can be used to indicate what domain the computer is in. This is normally used to tell the local computer how to find a domain controller:

```
204.147.39.1     SALES1        #PRE    #DOM:SALES
```

If the local computer were a member of the domain *SALES*, this entry would enable it to find the domain controller *SALES1* on the other side of a router.

The *#INCLUDE* keyword is used to incorporate the contents of another *lmhosts* file into the current one. This makes it possible to centralize maintenance of the *lmhosts* file and share a single file from a server. The *#INCLUDE* keyword is followed by the UNC path of the file to be included. The computer name following the *#INCLUDE* keyword must be defined earlier in the *LMHOSTS* file in order for it to be preloaded:

```
208.25.98.100    SALES1        #PRE
#INCLUDE         \\sales1\public\lmhosts
```

The *#BEGIN_ALTERNATE* and *#END_ALTERNATE* keywords can be used to group multiple *#INCLUDE* keywords to create a fallback mechanism. The system tries to access each file named by an *#INCLUDE* keyword in the order they appear. The first file successfully read is used, and the rest are ignored. For example:

```
#BEGIN_ALTERNATE
#INCLUDE         \\sales1\public\lmhosts
#INCLUDE         \\sales2\public\lmhosts
#INCLUDE         \\sales3\public\lmhosts
#END_ALTERNATE
```

If *SALES1* is unavailable, and *SALES2* supplies the file, *SALES3* is never consulted.

Computer names that contain special nonprinting characters can be encoded in the *lmhosts* file with their hexadecimal value preceded by *\0x*. Some specialized applications use a nonprinting character as the 16th character of the computer name. For example, the DC4 character (ASCII value of 20 in decimal and 14 in hexadecimal) can be encoded as part of the computer name *ntsrv1*:

```
128.197.2.1 "ntsrv1          \0x14"
```

Make sure there is no filename extension on the *LMHOSTS* file. Some editors will silently append a *.txt* extension, causing the file to be ignored.

For more information, see the file *LMHOSTS.SAM*.

HOSTS File

The *HOSTS* file format consists of IP addresses followed by TCP/IP hostnames and aliases. It is customary to list the fully qualified domain name (FQDN) as the first hostname in the list of aliases. The hostname is fully qualified in that the complete domain name is appended to the hostname. The hash character (#) is used for comments:

```
# this is comment
#IP Address  FQDN          Aliases
#
127.0.0.1    localhost    loghost
204.138.45.3 nugget.eap.com      nugget ns
```

The *HOSTS* file distributed by Microsoft contains only the **localhost** entry. This can be used to test networking functions, as in the following command:

```
ping localhost
```

You can add your own entries to the *HOSTS* file, but you should do this only for information that is unlikely to change, such as routers, major servers, and so on. If you have a small network that does not need to support Internet access, the *HOSTS* file can suffice. DNS is much more preferable to a static *HOSTS* file once you have more than a few hosts, and makes administration easier doing anything using the Internet.

TCP/IP Addressing

The following tables may be useful if you are setting up a network or subnetting a network address:

Table B-1: Identifying Address Class by First Octet

Class	First Octet	Comment
A	001 to 126	
B	128 to 191	
C	192 to 223	
D	224 to 239	Multicast
E	240 to 247	Reserved for future use

Table B-2: Possible Network and Host Values by Address Class

Class	Network Values Range	Host Values Range	Netmask
A	001 to 126	0.0.1 to 255.255.254	255.0.0.0
B	128.0 to 191.255	0.1 to 255.254	255.255.0.0
C	192.0.0 to 223.255.255	1 to 254	255.255.255.0

Table B-3: Possible Networks and Hosts by Address Class

Class	Max Networks	Max Hosts per Network
A	126	16,777,214
B	16,384	65534
C	2,097,152	254

Table B-4: Subnetting by Address Class: Class A

Subnet Mask	Max Hosts per Subnet	Max Subnets
255.0.0.0	16,777,214	0
255.192.0.0	4,194,302	2
255.224.0.0	2,097,150	6
255.240.0.0	1,048,574	14
255.248.0.0	524,286	30
255.252.0.0	262,142	62
255.254.0.0	131,070	126
255.255.0.0	65,534	254

Table B-5: Subnetting by Address Class: Class B

Subnet Mask	Max Hosts per Subnet	Max Subnets
255.255.0.0	65,534	0
255.255.192.0	16,382	2
255.255.224.0	8,190	6
255.255.240.0	4,094	14
255.255.248.0	2,046	30
255.255.252.0	1,022	62
255.255.254.0	510	126
255.255.255.0	254	254

Table B-6: Subnetting by Address Class: Class C

Subnet Mask	Max Hosts per Subnet	Max Subnets
255.255.255.0	254	0
255.255.255.192	62	2
255.255.255.224	30	6
255.255.255.240	14	14
255.255.255.248	6	30
255.255.255.252	2	62

Some routers can be configured to permit "subnet 0" which has all zeros for the subnet address. For example, this can be enabled under Cisco IOS with the *ip sub-net-zero* command. This gives you another subnet that would normally be "wasted" as part of subnetting. This is not recommended unless you really understand all the implications of doing so.

APPENDIX C

Server Versus Workstation

There are differences between the services, protocols, and administrative tools available on each version of Windows NT.

Table C-1: Services

Service	Srv*	Wks*	Description
Client Service for NetWare		✓	Enable NT Workstation to use NetWare file and print services
Computer Browser	✓	✓	Maintain a list of computers on the network
DHCP Relay Agent	✓		Relay DHCP requests to a DHCP server
Gateway Service for NetWare	✓		Enable NT Server to use NetWare file and print services and redistribute them to Microsoft Networking clients
Microsoft DHCP Server	✓		Offers IP configuration informatic to TCP/IP clients which send DH▸
Microsoft DNS Server	✓		Provide Domain Name System fc
Microsoft IIS	✓		Microsoft Internet Web server
Microsoft Peer Web Services		✓	Cut-down version of IIS
Microsoft TCP/IP Printing	✓	✓	Print via LPD protocol
NetBIOS Interface	✓	✓	Use Microsoft Networking
Network Monitor Agent	✓	✓	Relay network capture traffic to ▸ Monitor
Network Monitor Agent and Tools	✓		Network Monitor application and▸ relay

Table C-1: Services (continued)

Service	Srv*	Wks*	Description
Network Monitor Agent and Tools	✓		Network Monitor application and traffic relay
Remote Access Service	✓	✓	Enable both client and server Dial-Up Networking
Remoteboot Service	✓		Boot diskless Windows clients
RIP for Internet Protocol	✓		Basic routing for TCP/IP networks
RIP for NwLink IPX/SPX	✓		Routing for IPX networks
RPC Configuration	✓	✓	Enable network-distributed applications
RPC support for Banyan	✓	✓	Banyan VINES support
SAP Agent	✓	✓	Advertise Microsoft Networking resources
Server	✓	✓	Server side of Microsoft Networking
Services for Macintosh	✓		File and print sharing for Macintosh clients
Simple TCP/IP Services	✓	✓	TCP/IP services for debugging.
SNMP Service	✓	✓	Send traps and alerts to SNMP console
Windows Internet Name Service	✓		Map NetBIOS computer names to IP addresses
Workstation	✓	✓	Client side of Microsoft Networking

* Srv = Server; Wks = Workstation.

Table C-2: Protocols

Protocol	Srv	Wks	Communicate with
AppleTalk Protocol	✓*	✓	Macintosh clients
DLC Protocol	✓	✓	IBM mainframe and HP printers
NetBEUI Protocol	✓	✓	Microsoft Networking
NWLink IPX/SPX Compatible Transport	✓	✓	NetWare
Point-to-Point Tunneling Protocol	✓	✓	Encrypted networks
Streams Environment	✓	✓	Port UNIX apps
TCP/IP	✓	✓	Internet and UNIX

* AppleTalk is installed as part of **Services for the Macintosh** (SFM), but it does not appear in the Protocols display on NT Server.

Table C-3: Administrative Tools

Administrative Tool	Srv	Wks	Purpose
Administrative Wizards	✓		Make initial setup easier
Backup	✓	✓	Backup and restore data
DHCP Manager	✓		Manage TCP/IP configurations
Disk Administrator	✓	✓	Partition and format disks
DNS Manager	✓		Manage domain name server
Event Viewer	✓	✓	Manage logging and auditing
File Manager	✓*	✓*	Browse files and directories
Internet Service Manager	✓	✓	Manage WWW, FTP, and Gopher services
License Manager	✓		Manage licenses for entire domain
Migration Tools for NetWare	✓		Move NetWare files and users to NT
Network Client Administrator	✓		Create install disks
Network Monitor	✓		Capture and analyze network traffic
Performance Monitor	✓	✓	Monitor system performance
Rdisk	✓*	✓*	Make emergency repair disks
Regedit	✓*	✓*	Edit Registry
Regedt32	✓*	✓*	Edit Registry
Remoteboot Manager	✓		Administer diskless clients
Remote Access Admin	✓	✓	Administer RAS server
Server Manager	✓		Administer remote NT computers
System Policy Editor	✓		Administer polices for clients
Task Manager	✓	✓	Show processes and resource usage
User Manager	✓	✓	Manage users and groups
Windows NT Diagnostics	✓	✓	Get current hardware and software configuration
Windows NT Explorer	✓	✓	Browse files, directories, computers, and network
WINS Manager	✓		Manage WINS service

* These tools do not appear in the menu system unless you manually add them.

APPENDIX D

NT Resources

There are many good resources available both in print and online. Web sites and newsgroups are highly transient, so please do not be surprised if some of the names have changed since this book was published.

Internet

WWW and FTP Sites

Microsoft Knowledge Base
http://www.microsoft.com/kb

NT Service Packs
ftp://ftp.microsoft.com/bussys/winnt/winnt-public/fixes/<country>/<version>

NT HCL
ftp://ftp.microsoft.com/bussys/winnt/winnt-docs/hcl

Mailing Lists

nt-list@netspot.city.unisa.edu.au
win95netbugs@lists.stanford.edu
ntsecurity-digest@iss.net

Newsgroups

comp.os.ms-windows.nt.*

Available from *msnews.microsoft.com*:
microsoft.public.windowsnt.*

Books and Online Magazines

Microsoft Windows NT Server Resource Kit
Microsoft Press, ISBN 1-57231-344-7

Microsoft Windows NT Workstation Resource Kit
Microsoft Press, ISBN 1-57231-343-9

DNS & BIND, Second Edition
O'Reilly & Associates, ISBN 1-56592-236-0

Microsoft TechNet CD
http://www.microsoft.com/technet

Windows NT Magazine
http://www.winntmag.com

BackOffice Magazine
http://www.backoffice.com

Windows NT Systems Magazine
http://www.ntsystems.com

ENT Magazine
http://www.entmag.com

Glossary

ACL (Access Control List)
Contains all permissions information for a file, directory. This is similar to the **DACL** that controls access to registry keys.

adapter
Usually, the network adapter card that connects a computer to a LAN. A display adapter is a video card that drives the computer monitor.

answer file
Read by programs in place of keyboard input. They are most commonly used to configure the operating system during unattended installation.

AppleTalk
Native network protocol of Apple Macintoshes.

ARP (Address Resolution Protocol)
Allows a computer running TCP/IP to find the MAC-level address for a given IP address.

auditing
Process of recording security-related events such as file access and user logons. System administrators can use audit information to track resource usage, discover break-in attempts, and debug security problems.

authentication
Process of verifying that a computer or user actually is who they are claiming to be.

BDC (Backup Domain Controller)
Provides some fault tolerance and load distribution for the NT domain system. It can reduce the load on a PDC or take over from a failed PDC.

binary value

A base-2 number, which is either a 0 or 1.

bindings

Association of a network protocol and service with a specific network interface.

BIOS (Basic Input/Output System)

Very low-level program that interacts directly with the PC hardware. You may have to change BIOS settings to enable slots on the motherboard, cache memory and so on.

bridge

Connects two networks at the MAC-level, forwarding traffic from one to the other. It works with any network protocol, as it does not examine the packets at the protocol level. Most bridges are smart enough to know which computers are each side of the bridge and only transmit traffic if it needs to go from one side of the bridge to the other. Broadcasts are propagated by bridges.

buffer

Unit of memory storage. Number or size of the buffers determines the amount of available storage.

bus

Shared communications path. For example: SCSI bus, PCI bus, and ISA bus.

cache

Unit of memory dedicated to holding recently used information in the hope that it will be used again, therefore increasing performance as opposed to reading or writing to disk.

callback

In RAS, the ability of a remote user to call a RAS server and have the RAS server hang up and call them back. This can be used to reverse call charges or enhance security.

capture

To read the network traffic from an interface using a tool such as **Network Monitor**.

CHAP (Challenge Handshake Authentication Protocol)

One of the authentication protocols used by PPP to authenticate a connection. It encrypts the password before sending it over the connection, preventing it from being intercepted in clear text.

client

Program or computer making a request of a server. It is one of the most over-used words in computing and has to be evaluated in the context that it is used.

DACL (Discretionary Access Control List)

Allows a selected list of users and groups to perform some action. For example, registry keys in the Windows NT Registry can be assigned DACLs, enabling some users to edit them and blocking others.

databits

Number of bits that represent actual data, as opposed to signaling bits, such as stop, start, and parity bits. Usually used when talking about asynchronous serial communications, such as RS232.

DDE (Dynamic Data Exchange)

Microsoft Windows applications use DDE to exchange data. DDE enables data to be linked and simultaneously changed in all applications.

default gateway

Router where all traffic to unknown networks is sent.

default router

See *default gateway*.

DHCP (Dynamic Host Configuration Protocol)

Protocol used to make TCP/IP plug-and-play. A computer that wishes to use TCP/IP broadcasts for a DHCP server. The DHCP server responds with a TCP/IP configuration for the client.

DLC (Data Link Control)

Protocol used by NT to communicate with IBM mainframes and HP printers.

domain, NT security

Group of computers that share a common security scheme. All usernames, group names, and computer names are unique within the domain.

domain, TCP/IP

Defines an organization within the Domain Name System (DNS). For example, *oreilly.com*.

DSN (Data Source Name)

Describes an ODBC database. Database clients wishing to interact with the database address the database by its DSN.

DUN (Dial-Up Networking)

Client side of RAS. It enables a Windows NT Workstation or Server to dial out to another computer or the Internet.

DWORD

Data type used within Win32 programming. It also appears as a data type within the Registry. It is displayed as four bytes of hexadecimal data.

enterprise server

NT Server that manages a resource (such as licensing) for an entire enterprise.

ERD (Emergency Repair Disk)

Floppy disk that contains enough information to recover an NT system if critical system files are damaged.

FAT (File Allocation Table)

Original DOS filesystem.

file lock

Mechanism to prevent simultaneous writes occurring on the same file. The file is "locked", preventing anyone except the first person who opens it from writing to it.

FPNW (File and Print Services for NetWare

Enables an NT Server to act like a Novell NetWare file server and offer NetWare file and print services to NetWare clients.

frame

Single network packet. The term *frame* is usually used to describe a low-level packet type, such as Ethernet and PPP.

FTP (File Transfer Protocol)

Protocol used by the program of the same name to transfer files over TCP/IP.

globbing

Wildcard mechanism for matching filenames. For example, "?" matches any single character within a filename and "*" matches zero or more characters.

Gopher

Predecessor of HTTP. It provided a menu-driven interface to text and graphic information.

GSNW (Gateway Service for NetWare)

Allows an NT Server to connect to a Novell NetWare server and redistribute NetWare file and print resources to Microsoft Networking clients.

GUI (Graphical User Interface)

Windowing system front end to an operating system, such as Windows NT and Windows95. Also called a "shell" in some cases.

hive

Tree of registry data stored in separate disk file.

HTTP (Hyper-Text Transfer Protocol)

Protocol used by the World-Wide-Web.

ICMP (Internet Control Message Protocol)

Maintenance protocol in the TCP/IP protocol suite. Used by the commands *ping* and *tracert* to find and isolate network problems.

IDE (Integrated Drive Electronics)

Very common and inexpensive disk and CD-ROM interface.

IP (Internet Protocol)

Native protocol of the Internet, and part of the TCP/IP protocol suite.

IPX/SPX (Internet Packet Exchange/Sequenced Packet Exchange)
Used by Novell NetWare to provide datagram and stream-oriented network services (analogous to UDP and TCP in TCP/IP).

ISDN (Integrated Service Digital Network)
Digital phone line that offers a data rate of 128 Kbps in its most common form.

LAN (Local Area Network)
Group of network devices communicating using Ethernet, token-ring, or FDDI within a small area, such as a building or campus.

LCP (Link Control Protocol)
Subprotocol of PPP used to negotiate PPP options between the PPP client and server.

LPD (Line Printer Daemon)
Protocol and UNIX service for transferring print jobs between TCP/IP computers (or networked printers).

MAC (Media Access Control)
The MAC layer of networking is the Ethernet or token-ring level, and deals with low-level issues such as access and collision detection. A MAC-level address is usually an Ethernet address. Bridges function at the MAC layer and do not decode frames farther than the MAC layer.

migration
Process of moving from one operating system to another or from one version of an operating system to another.

mirroring
RAID feature that copies all I/O for one disk drive to another, essentially keeping an online backup.

MS-CHAP (Microsoft CHAP)
Microsoft-specific version of the Challenge Handshake Authentication Protocol (CHAP), which is used to authenticate RAS PPP sessions.

multihomed
A multihomed computer has either multiple IP addresses for a single network interface or multiple network interfaces. Web servers are frequently multihomed, which allows the web server to serve different web content depending on which interface or IP address a client connects to.

nameserver, DNS
Server that accesses the Domain Name system of networked databases that converts hostnames to IP addresses and IP addresses to hostnames.

nameserver, NetBIOS
Usually a WINS server; translates NetBIOS computer names to IP addresses, allowing Microsoft Networking to take place over TCP/IP networks.

NetBEUI (NetBIOS Extended User Interface)
> Non-routable protocol used on small LANs. It is the default networking protocol of Windows for Workgroups and Windows 95.

NetBIOS (Network Basic Input/Output System)
> API for Microsoft Networking applications.

NNTP (Network News Transfer Protocol)
> Internet standard for transferring Usenet news articles between computers.

node type
> Indicates the NetBIOS name resolution mechanism in use (broadcast only, point-to-point only, broadcast first, point-to-point second, or point-to-point first, broadcast second)

NTFS
> Windows NT filesystem.

NVRAM (Non-volatile RAM)
> RAM used to store BIOS settings, even with the power off.

ODBC (Open Database Connectivity)
> Microsoft database interoperability standard that allows ODBC-compliant applications to connect to ODBC-compliant databases.

PAD (Packet Assembler/Disassembler)
> Communications device that connects a computer to a packet network, such as X.25.

PAP (Password Authentication Protocol)
> PPP authentication protocol. It is a simple exchange of username and passwords between client and server.

parity
> Extra bit (or bits) added to data in serial communications as a form of error detection.

PC Card
> New name for the PCMCIA interface. Originally intended for memory expansion, the interface is now most commonly used for modem and network cards.

PCL (Printer Control Language)
> Hewlett-Packard's printer language.

PCMCIA (Personal Computer Memory Card International Association)
> Old name for the PC Card interface.

PDC (Primary Domain Controller)
> NT server that controls the security relationship for an NT domain.

port number
> Identifies a specific endpoint of a TCP or UDP connection, which is usually a service running on a network device.

POSIX (Portable Operating System Interface)
> Set of standards for APIs that are intended to make porting UNIX applications easier.

PPP (Point-to-Point Protocol)
> Standard protocol for creating a network connection across a serial line.

PPTP (Point-to-Point Tunneling Protocol)
> Protocol used to create tunnels across intermediate networks, which can be encrypted and carry non-native protocols.

Profile, hardware
> Set of device driver and service settings that are associated with the presence of specific hardware. A laptop can use a hardware profile to disable the network when no network is available.

Profile, Remoteboot
> Combination of operating system type and network adaptor type used to boot a computer using the **Remoteboot service**.

Profile, user
> Collection of personal GUI preferences and settings that is stored on a server. This enables a user to log on from different computers and always download the same customization settings.

propagation
> Process of transmitting data received from one source to another.

protocol
> Set of standards for network communication.

proxy
> One computer acting on another computer's behalf. A WINS proxy receives WINS requests and forwards them to a WINS server.

push/pull partner
> In **WINS**, servers that can exchange computer names and addresses.

RAID (Redundant Array of Inexpensive Disks)
> Technologies for combining multiple disk drives into a larger virtual drive to improve performance or enable fault tolerance.

RAS (Remote Access Service)
> Windows NT facility for creating dialup network connections to other computers or the Internet.

registers
> Small amounts of NVRAM that store configuration settings on modems.

Registry
> Hierarchical database for NT system information.

registry key
> Analogous to a directory in a filesystem. Keys contain subkeys and values.

replication
> Process of copying data to different machines, usually with the requirement that it is to be kept consistent everywhere.

RFC (Request For Comments)
> Technical document that describes a protocol or standard used on the Internet.

RIP (Routing Information Protocol)
> Most common TCP/IP routing protocol used on small to medium networks.

roaming profile
> Profile that follows a user around, allowing him or her to log on from different computers and always get the same settings.

router
> Routes packets based on destination address. It typically does not propagate broadcasts.

RTS/CTS (Request To Send/Clear To Send)
> Form of hardware flow control used in serial communications. It is typically used on high-speed devices that support the necessary signaling leads.

SAP (Service Advertising Protocol)
> Microsoft Networking uses SAP to advertise the availability of shared resources, such as files and printers.

scavenging
> Checking the consistency of a database.

scope, DHCP
> Typically a subnet (defined by a subnet mask) of IP addresses that are to be handed out to DHCP clients.

scope, NetBIOS
> Means of grouping computers on the network. Only computers with the same scope ID can communicate.

SCSI (Small Computer System Interface)
> Interface standard for disks, tapes, and CD-ROMs. It is usually more expensive than IDE, but offers more devices and higher performance.

server
> Program or computer answering the requests of a client.

service
> Program running on NT that provides some service to the operating system, user, or remote computer. Services typically start at boot time and run until the computer is shut down.

service pack

    Microsoft releases a `service pack` for Windows NT when enough bug fixes and features have accumulated after a major release of the operating system.

SLIP (Serial Line IP)

    Older method of creating a network across a serial line. It has been largely supplanted by PPP.

SMB (Server Message Block)

    Protocol used for file sharing in Microsoft Networking.

SMTP (Simple Mail Transport Protocol)

    Defacto standard for exchanging electronic mail on the Internet.

SMS (System Management Server)

    Part of the Microsoft BackOffice suite. It is intended to make management of large numbers of computers easier. It includes the full-featured version of the **Network Monitor** tool.

SNMP (Simple Network Management Protocol)

    Protocol used by network devices to inform a network management console about the status of the network.

SPAP (Shiva Password Authentication Protocol)

    Modified version of the PAP authentication protocol that improves on regular PAP by encrypting the password before sending it over the PPP connection.

standard error
standard in
standard out

    The terms *standard error*, *standard in*, and *standard out* come from the C programming language and refer to sources or destinations of input or output from the program. *Standard in* is normally the user typing in commands; *standard out* and *standard error* are normally the screen that displays program output and error messages.

stop bits

    In async serial communication, indicate the end of data.

striped

    A *striped* set or striped disk is a form of RAID. Disk I/O is evenly spread over several disks, improving performance over using a single disk. A striped set is a group of disks being treated as a single unit for striping.

subkey

    Child of a higher-level registry key, much in the same manner as the filesystem, where a subdirectory is a child of a parent directory.

subnet mask

    Tells computers which part of an IP address is the network number and which is the host number. This is essential for routing the packet to the right destination.

TCP (Transmission Control Protocol)

Connection-oriented protocol in the TCP/IP suite. It is used where reliable, bidirectional communication is required.

TFTP (Trivial File Transfer Protocol)

Primitive file transfer protocol primarily used for downloading boot images. It is implemented in UDP and is unsuited for anything other than simple, LAN-based tasks.

transport

Network protocol.

trigger

Some event that is being waited for. The **Performance Monitor** and **Network Monitor** tools both have the ability to perform some action if a certain condition is met. For example, **Network Monitor** could be set to page the administrator if it sees a certain type of network traffic.

trigger action

What should be done when the trigger event occurs.

trust relationship

Mechanism for allowing resources to be used by users from another domain who do not have accounts in the local domain.

UDP (User Datagram Protocol)

Connectionless protocol that runs on top of the IP protocol. It is used for name service, route advertisements and other services that do not need or want to avoid the overhead of a connection-oriented protocol such as TCP. It is part of the TCP/IP protocol suite.

UNC (Universal Naming Convention)

Composed of two backslashes, followed by a computer name, a single backslash and a share name, all of which uniquely describe a resource on the network. A UNC path may also contain directory name(s) and a file name. For example:

```
\\NTSRV1\PUBLIC          the PUBLIC directory on NTSRV1
\\PRINTSRV\HP4MP         the HP4MP printer on PRINTSRV
```

volume

Typically a disk or a subdirectory of a disk being shared on the network to other computers.

VPN (Virtual Private Network)

Constructed out of a shared or public network, such as the Internet. It looks like a dedicated or private connection to the computers using it, even though it may be traversing multiple other networks. VPNs can save money compared with leased private lines and offer security through encryption.

WAN (Wide Area Network)

Usually a point-to-point network link, such as a PPP session over an analog phone or ISDN line, or a dedicated connection using a 56k DDS, T1 or fractional T1.

WINS (Windows Internet Name Server)

Translates NetBIOS computer names to IP addresses, allowing Microsoft Networking to function over TCP/IP networks.

X.25

Protocol used on some packet-switched WANs.

XON/XOFF

Form of software flow control. The XOFF character suspends communication and the XON character resumes it. This is normally used when hardware flow control is not available.

Task Index

Task	Control Panel	Admin Tool	Command Line
Accounts		User Manager	*net accounts* *net group* *net localgroup* *net user*
Apple Macintosh	MacFile Network	Server Manager File Manager	
Backup/ restore	Tape Devices	Backup Disk Administrator	*ntbackup* *backup* *restore*
Browsing	Network	Windows NT Explorer File Manager	*net view*
Database	ODBC		
Devices	Devices		
Disk	SCSI Adaptors	Disk Administrator	*convert* *chkdsk*
Display	Display	Windows NT Diagnostics	
DHCP		DHCP Manager	*ipconfig*
DLC	Network		
DNS	Network	DNS Manager	*nslookup* *ipconfig* *ping* *tracert*
Domain		Server Manager	*net computer*
Environment	System	Windows NT Diagnostics	

Task	Control Panel	Admin Tool	Command Line
FTP		Internet Service Manager	*ftp*
Groups		User Manager	*net group* *net localgroup* *net user* *net accounts*
Hardware	Devices Display Modems Multimedia Network PC Card Ports SCSI Adapers Tape Devices	Windows NT Diagnostics	
Hardware profiles		Devices Services System	
Licensing	Licensing	License Manager	
Logging	Printers	Event Viewer File Manager User Manager	*regedt32*
Messages	Server	Server Manager	*net send* *net name*
Modems	Modems Telephony		
NetWare	CSNW FPNW	Server Manager File Manager Netware User Manager	*ipxroute* *net view*
Network	Monitoring Agent	Network Monitor Performance Monitor Windows NT Diagnostics	
Performance	System Network	Performance Monitor	*net statistics server* *diskperf*
Permissions		Windows NT Explorer File Manager	*cacls* *attrib*
Policies		System Policy Editor	
PPP	Network	Remote Access Admin	
PPTP	Network	Remote Access Admin	
Printers	Printers Ports Network	Server Manager	*net print* *lpr* *lpq* *net view*

Task	Control Panel	Admin Tool	Command Line
			net use
			net share
Protocols	Network	Remote Access Admin	
RAS	Dial-Up Monitor	Dial-Up Networking	*rasdial*
	Ports	Remote Access Admin	*rasadmin*
	Modems	User Manager	*rasautou*
	Network		*rasphone*
	Telephony		
Replication	Server	Server Manager	
Security	Printers	User Manager	*cacls*
		File Manager	*attrib*
		Windows NT Explorer	
		Server Manager	
		Remote Access Admin	
Services	Network	Server Manager	*net continue*
	Services	Windows NT	*net pause*
		Diagnostics	*net start*
			net stop
Sharing	Server	Windows NT Explorer	*net share*
		File Manager	*net use*
		Server Manager	*net file*
		Disk Administrator	*net session*
SLIP	Dial-Up	Remote Access Admin	
	Networking		
SNMP	Network		
Software	Add/Remove	Windows NT	*winnt*
	Programs	Diagnostics	
	Network	Network Client	*winnt32*
		Administrator	
Sound	Multimedia		
TCP/IP	Network	DHCP Manager	*finger*
		WINS Manager	*ftp*
		Remote Access Admin	*hostname*
			ipconfig
			lpq
			lpr
			nbtstat
			netstat
			nslookup
			ping
			rcp
			rexec
			rsh
			telnet
			tftp
			tracert
Time/Date	Date/Time		*net time*

Task	Control Panel	Admin Tool	Command Line
UPS	UPS		
User Profiles	System	User Manager	
Users		User Manager	*net user* *net localgroup* *net group* *net accounts*
WINS		WINS Manager	*jetpack*
WWW	Internet	Internet Service Manager	*convlog*

Index

users (cont'd)
  licenses for (see licenses)
  locking out, 123, 125
  logging on as, 51
  managing with net user command, 204
  messages to, 84, 196
  moving accounts with Migration Tool, 87
  multiple, 4
  names for, 122
  NetWare, 14
  passwords for (see passwords)
  profiles, 55
  querying with finger command, 210
  RAS permissions, 105
  remote, permissions and, 2
  remote, permissions for, 80
  security (see security)
  User Manager tool, 120, 277
UUCP (UNIX-to-UNIX Copy), 154

V

variables
  environment, 127
  SCP scripts, 166
  system, 54
vendor information, 99
verifying
  backups, 59
  connections (pinging), 230, 279
  drive file integrity, 69
  file system integrity, 250
versions, 127
  WINS server records, 136
video cards, managing, 21
virtual
  memory, 54
  partitions, 66

Virtual Private Networks (VPNs), 34, 152
volume sets, 66
  extending, 68
VPNs (Virtual Private Networks), 34, 152

W

Wallpaper option, 12
WHOIS information, 286
windows, command-line sessions as, 7
Windows Internet Name Service (see WINS)
Windows NT
  informational resources on, 315
  installing, 259-261
  selecting hardware for, 291
  troubleshooting, 275
Windows NT Diagnostics tool, 125, 291
Windows NT Explorer browser, 27, 129
Windows NT Setup option, 6
winnt command, 259
WINS (Windows Internet Name Service), 32, 36
  compacting databases, 269
  DNS and, 74
  Manager tool for, 133
  NBT and, 287
workgroups, managing, 112
Workstation service, 32, 185
workstations
  generic, 4
  saving passwords, 19
  server versus, 2
  servers versus, 312-314
wrapping, event log, 76

Z

zones, 70

About the Author

Eric Pearce has been a system and network administrator for O'Reilly & Associates for five years. Previous to working for O'Reilly, he was a systems programmer for Boston University's Information Technology. He is also the co-author of the *X Window System Administrator's Guide* and has written for several O'Reilly publications. Eric specializes in networking, as it provides a challenging mix of protocols, platforms, and vendors.

Colophon

The animal featured on the cover of *Windows NT in a Nutshell* is a short-toed eagle. Actually, that description is inadequate, because most eagles are short-toed. Eagles fall into the category of bird known as "raptors," a category that also includes falcons and hawks. There are two types of raptor: grasping killers, with beaks shaped for tearing and cutting and short toes with curved claws designed for killing; and grasping holders, with beaks shaped for tearing and biting, and longer toes designed for holding. Eagles are grasping killers. Sea eagles have special adaptations to their toes that enable them to grasp smooth prey such as fish. Their excellent vision enables all eagles to spot prey from the air or a high perch. The eagle then swoops down, grabs its prey, and takes off in flight again, in one graceful movement. Eagles often eat their victims while still flying, breaking them apart and discarding the nonedible parts to lighten their load. Eagles, like most raptors, often dine on sick or wounded animals.

There are more than 50 species of eagle spread throughout the world, with the exception of New Zealand and Antarctica. All species of eagles build nests, or aeries, high above the ground, in trees or on rocky ledges. A pair of eagles will use the same nest year after year, lining it with green leaves and grass, fur, turf, or soft materials. The eagle will add to its nest each year. The largest eagle nest ever found was 20 feet deep and 10 feet across.

Hunting, increased use of pesticides, and the diminishment of their natural environment, with the attendant reduction in food sources, have endangered many species of eagle.

Edie Freedman designed the cover of this book, using a 19th-century engraving from the Dover Pictorial Archive. The cover layout was produced with Quark XPress 3.32 using the ITC Garamond font. The inside layout was designed by Nancy Priest and implemented in troff by Lenny Muellner. The text and heading fonts are ITC Garamond Light and Garamond Book. The illustrations that appear in the book were created in Macromedia Freehand 5.0 by Chris Reilley. This colophon was written by Clairemarie Fisher O'Leary. Whenever possible, our books use RepKover™, a durable and flexible lay-flat binding. If the page count exceeds RepKover's limit, perfect binding is used.

More Titles from O'Reilly

Windows NT System Administration

Windows NT in a Nutshell

By Eric Pearce
1st Edition June 1997
364 pages, ISBN 1-56592-251-4

Anyone who installs Windows NT, creates a user, or adds a printer is an NT system administrator (whether they realize it or not). This book features a new tagged callout approach to documenting the 4.0 GUI as well as real-life examples of command usage and strategies for problem solving, with an emphasis on networking. *Windows NT in a Nutshell* will be as useful to the single-system home user as it will be to the administrator of a 1,000-node corporate network.

Windows NT User Administration

By Ashley J. Meggitt &
Timothy D. Ritchey
1st Edition November 1997
218 pages, ISBN 1-56592-301-4

Many Windows NT books introduce you to a range of topics, but seldom do they give you enough information to master any one thing. This book (like other O'Reilly animal books) is different. *Windows NT User Administration* makes you an expert at creating users efficiently, controlling what they can do, limiting the damage they can cause, and monitoring their activities on your system. Don't simply react to problems; use the techniques in this book to anticipate and prevent them.

Windows NT SNMP

By James D. Murray
1st Edition January 1998
464 pages, Includes CD-ROM
ISBN 1-56592-338-3

This book describes the implementation of SNMP (the Simple Network Management Protocol) on Windows NT 3.51 and 4.0 (with a look ahead to NT 5.0) and Windows 95 systems. It covers SNMP and network basics and detailed information on developing SNMP management applications and extension agents. The book comes with a CD-ROM containing a wealth of additional information: standards documents, sample code from the book, and many third-party, SNMP-related software tools, libraries, and demos.

Essential Windows NT System Administration

By Æleen Frisch
1st Edition February 1998
486 pages, ISBN 1-56592-274-3

This book combines practical experience with technical expertise to help you manage Windows NT systems as productively as possible. It covers the standard utilities offered with the Windows NT operating system and from the Resource Kit, as well as important commercial and free third-party tools. By the author of O'Reilly's bestselling book, *Essential System Administration*.

Windows NT System Administration

Windows NT Backup & Restore

By Jody Leber
1st Edition May 1998 (est.)
250 pages (est.), ISBN 1-56592-272-7

Beginning with the need for a workable recovery policy and ways to translate that policy into requirements, *Windows NT Backup & Restore* presents the reader with practical guidelines for setting up an effective backup system in both small and large environments. It covers the native NT utilities as well as major third-party hardware and software.

Windows NT Server 4.0 for NetWare Administrators

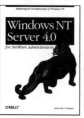

By Robert Bruce Thompson
1st Edition November 1997
756 pages, ISBN 1-56592-280-8

This book provides a fast-track means for experienced NetWare administrators to build on their knowledge and master the fundamentals of using the Microsoft Windows NT Server. The broad coverage of many aspects of Windows NT Server is balanced by a tightly focused approach of comparison, contrast, and differentiation between NetWare and NT features and methodologies.

Windows NT Desktop Reference

By Æleen Frisch
1st Edition January 1998
64 pages, ISBN 1-56592-437-1

A hip-pocket quick reference to Windows N commands, as well as the most useful commands from the Resource Kits. Commands are arranged ingroups related to their purpose and function. Covers Windows NT 4.0.

MCSE: The Core Exams in a Nutshell

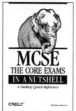

By Michael Moncu
1st Edition May 1998 (est.)
300 pages (est.), ISBN 1-56592-376-6

MCSE: The Core Exams in a Nutshell is detailed quick reference for administrators with Windows NT experience or experience administering a different platform, such as UNIX, who want to learn what is necessary to pass the MCSE required exam portion of the MCSE certification. While no book is a substitute for real-world experience, this book will help you codify your knowledge and prepare for the exams.

How to stay in touch with O'Reilly

Visit Our Award-Winning Site

http://www.oreilly.com/

★ "Top 100 Sites on the Web" —*PC Magazine*
★ "Top 5% Web sites" —*Point Communications*
★ "3-Star site" —*The McKinley Group*

Our web site contains a library of comprehensive product information (including book excerpts and tables of contents), downloadable software, background articles, interviews with technology leaders, links to relevant sites, book cover art, and more. File us in your Bookmarks or Hotlist!

Join Our Email Mailing Lists

New Product Releases

To receive automatic email with brief descriptions of all new O'Reilly products as they are released, send email to:
listproc@online.oreilly.com
Put the following information in the first line of your message (*not* in the Subject field):
subscribe oreilly-news

O'Reilly Events

If you'd also like us to send information about trade show events, special promotions, and other O'Reilly events, send email to:
listproc@online.oreilly.com
Put the following information in the first line of your message (*not* in the Subject field):
subscribe oreilly-events

Get Examples from Our Books via FTP

There are two ways to access an archive of example files from our books:

Regular FTP

- ftp to:
  ftp.oreilly.com
  (login: anonymous
  password: your email address)
- Point your web browser to:
  ftp://ftp.oreilly.com/

FTPMAIL

- Send an email message to:
  ftpmail@online.oreilly.com
  (Write "help" in the message body)

4. Contact Us via Email

order@oreilly.com
To place a book or software order online. Good for North American and international customers.

subscriptions@oreilly.com
To place an order for any of our newsletters or periodicals.

books@oreilly.com
General questions about any of our books.

software@oreilly.com
For general questions and product information about our software. Check out O'Reilly Software Online at **http://software.oreilly.com/** for software and technical support information. Registered O'Reilly software users send your questions to:
website-support@oreilly.com

cs@oreilly.com
For answers to problems regarding your order or our products.

booktech@oreilly.com
For book content technical questions or corrections.

proposals@oreilly.com
To submit new book or software proposals to our editors and product managers.

international@oreilly.com
For information about our international distributors or translation queries. For a list of our distributors outside of North America check out:
http://www.oreilly.com/www/order/country.html

O'Reilly & Associates, Inc.
101 Morris Street, Sebastopol, CA 95472 USA
TEL   707-829-0515 or 800-998-9938
          (6am to 5pm PST)
FAX   707-829-0104

International Distributors

UK, EUROPE, MIDDLE EAST AND NORTHERN AFRICA (except France, Germany, Switzerland, & Austria)

INQUIRIES
International Thomson Publishing Europe
Berkshire House
168-173 High Holborn
London WC1V 7AA, UK
Telephone: 44-171-497-1422
Fax: 44-171-497-1426
Email: itpint@itps.co.uk

ORDERS
International Thomson Publishing
Services, Ltd.
Cheriton House, North Way
Andover, Hampshire SP10 5BE,
United Kingdom
Telephone: 44-264-342-832 (UK)
Telephone: 44-264-342-806 (outside UK)
Fax: 44-264-364418 (UK)
Fax: 44-264-342761 (outside UK)
UK & Eire orders: itpuk@itps.co.uk
International orders: itpint@itps.co.uk

FRANCE

Editions Eyrolles
61 bd Saint-Germain
75240 Paris Cedex 05
France
Fax: 33-01-44-41-11-44

FRENCH LANGUAGE BOOKS
All countries except Canada
Telephone: 33-01-44-41-46-16
Email: geodif@eyrolles.com

ENGLISH LANGUAGE BOOKS
Telephone: 33-01-44-41-11-87
Email: distribution@eyrolles.com

GERMANY, SWITZERLAND, AND AUSTRIA

INQUIRIES
O'Reilly Verlag
Balthasarstr. 81
D-50670 Köln
Germany
Telephone: 49-221-97-31-60-0
Fax: 49-221-97-31-60-8
Email: anfragen@oreilly.de

ORDERS
International Thomson Publishing
Königswinterer Straße 418
53227 Bonn, Germany
Telephone: 49-228-97024 0
Fax: 49-228-441342
Email: order@oreilly.de

JAPAN

O'Reilly Japan, Inc.
Kiyoshige Building 2F
12-Banchi, Sanei-cho
Shinjuku-ku
Tokyo 160 Japan
Tel: 81-3-3356-5227
Fax: 81-3-3356-5261
Email: kenji@oreilly.com

INDIA

Computer Bookshop (India) PVT. Ltd.
190 Dr. D.N. Road, Fort
Bombay 400 001 India
Tel: 91-22-207-0989
Fax: 91-22-262-3551
Email: cbsbom@giasbm01.vsnl.net.in

HONG KONG

City Discount Subscription Service Ltd.
Unit D, 3rd Floor, Yan's Tower
27 Wong Chuk Hang Road
Aberdeen, Hong Kong
Telephone: 852-2580-3539
Fax: 852-2580-6463
Email: citydis@ppn.com.hk

KOREA

Hanbit Publishing, Inc.
Sonyoung Bldg. 202
Yeksam-dong 736-36
Kangnam-ku
Seoul, Korea
Telephone: 822-554-9610
Fax: 822-556-0363
Email: hant93@chollian.dacom.co.kr

TAIWAN

ImageArt Publishing, Inc.
4/fl. No. 65 Shinyi Road Sec. 4
Taipei, Taiwan, R.O.C.
Telephone: 886-2708-5770
Fax: 886-2705-6690
Email: marie@ms1.hinet.net

SINGAPORE, MALAYSIA, AND THAILAND

Longman Singapore
25 First Lok Yan Road
Singapore 2262
Telephone: 65-268-2666
Fax: 65-268-7023
Email: db@longman.com.sg

PHILIPPINES

Mutual Books, Inc.
429-D Shaw Boulevard
Mandaluyong City, Metro
Manila, Philippines
Telephone: 632-725-7538
Fax: 632-721-3056
Email: mbikikog@mnl.sequel.net

CHINA

Ron's DataCom Co., Ltd.
79 Dongwu Avenue
Dongxihu District
Wuhan 430040
China
Telephone: 86-27-3892568
Fax: 86-27-3222108
Email: hongfeng@public.wh.hb.cn

AUSTRALIA

WoodsLane Pty. Ltd.
7/5 Vuko Place, Warriewood NSW 2102
P.O. Box 935,
Mona Vale NSW 2103
Australia
Telephone: 61-2-9970-5111
Fax: 61-2-9970-5002
Email: info@woodslane.com.au

ALL OTHER ASIA COUNTRIES

O'Reilly & Associates, Inc.
101 Morris Street
Sebastopol, CA 95472 USA
Telephone: 707-829-0515
Fax: 707-829-0104
Email: order@oreilly.com

THE AMERICAS

McGraw-Hill Interamericana Editores,
S.A. de C.V.
Cedro No. 512
Col. Atlampa 06450
Mexico, D.F.
Telephone: 52-5-541-3155
Fax: 52-5-541-4913
Email: mcgraw-hill@infosel.net.mx

SOUTHERN AFRICA

International Thomson Publishing
Southern Africa
Building 18, Constantia Park
138 Sixteenth Road
P.O. Box 2459
Halfway House, 1685 South Africa
Tel: 27-11-805-4819
Fax: 27-11-805-3648

O'REILLY™

TO ORDER: **800-998-9938** • order@oreilly.com • http://www.oreilly.com/
OUR PRODUCTS ARE AVAILABLE AT A BOOKSTORE OR SOFTWARE STORE NEAR YOU.
FOR INFORMATION: **800-998-9938** • **707-829-0515** • info@oreilly.com

O'REILLY™

O'Reilly & Associates, Inc.
101 Morris Street
Sebastopol, CA 95472-9902
1-800-998-9938

Visit us online at:
http://www.ora.com/
orders@ora.com

O'REILLY WOULD LIKE TO HEAR FROM YOU

Which book did this card come from?

_____

Where did you buy this book?
- ❏ Bookstore
- ❏ Direct from O'Reilly
- ❏ Bundled with hardware/software
- ❏ Other _____
- ❏ Computer Store
- ❏ Class/seminar

What operating system do you use?
- ❏ UNIX
- ❏ Windows NT
- ❏ Other _____
- ❏ Macintosh
- ❏ PC(Windows/DOS)

What is your job description?
- ❏ System Administrator
- ❏ Network Administrator
- ❏ Web Developer
- ❏ Other _____
- ❏ Programmer
- ❏ Educator/Teacher

❏ Please send me O'Reilly's catalog, containing a complete listing of O'Reilly books and software.

Name _____ Company/Organization _____

Address _____

City _____ State _____ Zip/Postal Code _____ Country _____

Telephone _____ Internet or other email address (specify network) _____

Nineteenth century wood engraving
of a bear from the O'Reilly &
Associates Nutshell Handbook®
Using & Managing UUCP.

POST CARD

BUSINESS REPLY MAIL

FIRST CLASS MAIL   PERMIT NO. 80   SEBASTOPOL, CA

Postage will be paid by addressee

O'Reilly & Associates, Inc.
101 Morris Street
Sebastopol, CA 95472-9902